Strategies for College Readers

ELAINE GARCIA KRIEG

Houston Community College

PEARSON
Longman

New York San Francisco Boston
London Toronto Sydney Tokyo Singapore Madrid
Mexico City Munich Paris Cape Town Hong Kong Montreal

This text is dedicated to my parents,
Alice and Albert

Acquisitions Editor: Kate Edwards
Director of Development: Mary Ellen Curley
Development Editor: Gillian Cook
Marketing Manager: Tom De Marco
Senior Supplements Editor: Donna Campion
Production Manager: Ellen MacElree
Project Coordination, Text Design, and Electronic Page Makeup: Nesbitt Graphics, Inc.
Cover Designer/Manager: Wendy Ann Fredericks
Cover Photo: © R. J. Muna/Images.Com
Photo Researcher: Jody Potter
Senior Manufacturing Buyer: Alfred C. Dorsey
Printer and Binder: Courier/Kendallville
Cover Printer: Phoenix Color Corp.

For permission to use copyrighted material, grateful acknowledgment is made to the copyright holders on pp. 547-549, which are hereby made part of this copyright page.

Library of Congress Cataloging-in-Publication Data is on file at the Library of Congress

Please visit our website at www.ablongman.com

ISBN 13: 978-0-321-20275-8 (Student edition)
ISBN 10:   0-321-20275-9 (Student edition)

3 4 5 6 7 8 9 10—CKV—11

8/05

ISBN 13 978-0-205-53648-1 (Instructor's Edition)
ISBN 10   0-205-53648-4 (Instructor's Edition)

Brief Contents

Detailed Contents

* To download this online appendix, please go to
  http://www.pearsonhighered.com/samplechapter/0321202759_app.pdf

Preface to the Instructor

Strategies for College Readers is designed to improve students' confidence in their ability to apply the reading skills essential to academic and personal success. The unique strategies contained in the text provide students with practical tools they can use in a variety of reading situations. In addition, the text includes effective study strategies for note-taking and test preparation. The text is written in an interactive format which combines concise skill instruction with holistic concepts to help students to think critically about what they are reading and gain ownership and control over what they are learning.

PURPOSE

Developmental reading students are often proficient at reading short text messages or emails, but struggle to maintain concentration when presented with reading selections. Some of my students have difficulty finding the next line of text in the return sweep. They have become "word callers" who can read the words of a sentence aloud but are not able to connect the words in order to explain the meaning of the sentence. When reading is associated with such frustration, it is no wonder that it is avoided. Unfortunately, when reading is avoided, the problems associated with it remain.

Over the last fifteen years, I have developed several successful strategies designed to provide easy access to essential reading skills and concepts to a diverse student population who present a wide range of competencies, including students with learning differences. I wrote this text to share these strategies.

Lack of motivation is common among developmental reading students. I link essential reading skills to personal as well as academic goals. Students are constantly encouraged as they accomplish each step leading to mastery of a skill or concept relevant to their success.

Suggestions for presenting activities are contained in the Instructor's Manual. The instructor's manual also includes a test bank, additional exercises, and other ancillary materials, such as access to Longman's MyReadingLab. Longman is pleased to offer a variety of additional support materials. Please visit us at pearsonhighered.com.

STRATEGIES

This text emphasizes the use of thirteen easy strategies that students can use to gain confidence while they achieve mastery of essential reading skills. Here is an overview of each strategy.

1. **Go for the Goal** is a step by step process for achieving a desired goal. It identifies the meta-cognitive self-talk which accompanies effective goal setting.

2. **The Reading Workout: A Three-Step Strategy for Developing Stronger Reading Skills** encourages students to find reading material that interests them, to read for 20–30 minutes a day, and to engage in a dialogue with an author as they read.

3. **Word Wise: A Strategy for Decoding Unfamiliar Words** helps students understand how word part meanings can be used in order to break the code of a word.

4. **Words in Mind** is a strategy for using contextual elements within a sentence to derive the meaning of new words.

5. **Make Your Own Main Idea** is a strategy for creating a main idea sentence for a paragraph or passage. It provides an effective questioning method for identifying both stated and implied main ideas.

6. **The Main Idea Test: A Strategy for Confirming the Main Idea** provides a simple method for verifying the main idea of a paragraph or passage. Students learn to recognize the question-answer relationship between the main idea and the major supporting details.

7. **Picture Perfect: A Strategy for Improving the Visual Experience of Reading** emphasizes the importance of recognizing the relationship between major and minor supporting details in a paragraph or passage in order to improve comprehension.

8. **The RODEO Attention Plan for Note Taking and Test Preparation** provides simple guidelines for identifying the most important information presented during a lecture or in a reading so that students can create effective study guides and prepare for exams.

9. **Recall to Mind** is a strategy for creating "recall words" (acronyms) and "recall sentences" for learning outlines that contain important study information.

10. **List, Label, and Repeat,** used in conjunction with the *Recall to Mind* strategy, helps students to associate minor details, such as examples and definitions, with the major details that support the topic in an outline, so they can learn information and prepare for exams.

11. **The SQUARE Textbook Study Method** provides a step-by-step means for identifying, organizing, and learning the information authors and instructors consider the most important.

12. **The Eight-Day Action Plan** is a comprehensive study strategy for test preparation that includes methods for understanding and dealing with test anxiety.

13. **The Sherlock Method: A Strategy for Making Reasonable Inferences** helps students identify the evidence that supports a conclusion or inference in order to ascertain whether or not it is correct.

CONTENT OVERVIEW

The book is organized into five parts:

Part 1: Foundation for Success contains strategies for improving reading stamina and the vocabulary acquisition skills necessary to handle college-level coursework. The chapters in Part 1 help students relate what they are learning to a specific purpose or set of goals they hope to achieve and emphasizes the importance of developing reading and vocabulary skills in order to achieve both personal and academic success.

Part 2: Structure and Organization provides practical strategies for identifying the structural elements of a paragraph or passage. The chapters in Part 2 help students to improve their reading comprehension and speed by understanding the relationships among these elements.

Part 3: Study Skills for Effective Reading contains practical strategies for taking lecture and text notes for test preparation. The chapters in Part 3 help students improve the listening and attention skills necessary for effective reading and emphasizes the importance of identifying and recording key details of information presented in a lecture or in text material in order to perform successfully in college courses.

Part 4: Critical Thinking and Effective Comprehension provides students with specific strategies for evaluating written material. The chapters in Part 4 build on each other to help students develop their critical thinking skills, so they can evaluate arguments, distinguish between fact and opinion, identify bias and errors in reasoning, recognize an author's purpose and tone, and make inferences.

Part 5: Additional Practice Readings contains twelve selections, each of which corresponds to the topic of instruction provided in a chapter of the text. These additional reading selections can be used to provide students with further practice in applying specific chapter skills. They also allow instructors flexibility when considering assignments to accommodate individual classroom competencies.

Chapter Format

Each chapter follows the same basic format:

Preview and Predict: What do you know so far? Preview and predict questions at the beginning of each chapter and before each reading selection ask students to predict what will be discussed about the topic of each chapter to help activate their background knowledge prior to reading. These questions encourage thoughtful discussion and help students, through example, to form the habit of asking these kinds of questions prior to reading.

Memory Check: How much do you remember? Sets of Memory Check questions are included throughout each chapter to reinforce each step in the mastery of new skills or concepts. These questions help students develop the ability to monitor their comprehension as they recall important details from each section of reading in order to answer the Memory Check questions.

Chapter Activities: Each chapter contains numerous activities that provide students with opportunities to apply new skills or concepts. They are preceded by thorough explanations and examples to build confidence as well as mastery of each skill component so students can easily combine them for use in a variety of reading situations.

Test-Yourself Review Quiz: A comprehensive quiz at the end of each chapter allows students to review their understanding of key concepts.

Summarization Activity: This activity provides an opportunity for students to practice summary skills by having them outline the information they found most helpful in each chapter.

Skills in Practice: Reading Selections: Two selections at the end of each chapter provide students with an opportunity to apply chapter concepts to longer reading material. These selections include a variety of engaging essays, articles, stories, and textbook excerpts, that become progressively more difficult in reading level allowing instructors flexibility in making assignments. Each selection is preceded by the following activities: Preview and Predict, Questions for Discussion, Word Search and Discovery (vocabulary practice), and Text Notes in Practice (an activity starting in Chapter 8 that encourages students to use study strategies). Each selection is followed by The Write Assignment (that asks students to note the three most important things they have learned from the selection), Comprehension Check (comprehension questions), and Vocabulary Check (an activity that connects to Word Search and Discovery).

Acknowledgments

I wish to express my gratitude to the following instructors for their close reading, thoughtful comments, and insightful suggestions for how to improve this book through the course of its development: Dr. David-Michael Allen, Donnelly College; Dr. Joel L. Bailey, Mountain Empire Community College; Helen Carr, San Antonio College; Jessica Carroll, Miami Dade College; Allison DeVaney, El Camino College; David Elias, Eastern Kentucky University; Raymond J. Eliot, St. Philip's College; Ana Fillingim, Salt Lake Community College; Yvonne Frye, Community College of Denver; Dr. Nancy G. Kennedy, Community College of Beaver County; Lisa A. Kirby, North Carolina Wesleyan College; Julie Odell, Community College of Philadelphia; Betty J. Perkinson, Tidewater Community College; Robin Redmond Wright, Stephen F. Austin State University; Kathryn Ryder, Broome Community College.

I would like to thank Kate Edwards, Acquisitions Editor, for her unwavering clarity of vision and for providing the kind of support that promotes a highly productive team. I would also like to thank Gill Cook, Development Editor, for her extraordinary expertise, dedication, and brilliant sense of humor; words cannot sufficiently express my gratitude for her help. I am deeply grateful to Ellen McElree,

Joan Dixon, Jody Potter, and the editorial staff of Longman Publishers for their exceptional teamwork, to Harry Druding and the staff of Nesbitt Graphics for creating such a beautiful design, and to Kathy Smith for her thoroughness, thoughtfulness, and accuracy.

In addition, I could not have completed this project without the invaluable advice, support, and contributions of the following colleagues and reviewers: Yolanda Yzquierdo; Dr. Lee Mountain, University of Houston; Eberle Knight, School of the Woods; John Krieg; Diana O'Niell; Dr. Anna Harris, Houston Community College; Mike Lee, Houston Community College; James A. Stewart, Albuquerque Public School System; Richard V. Stewart; Marion Bechdel; Sara Vargas, Houston Community College.

Preface to the Student

Welcome to college! You have begun an exciting journey that will lead to a more successful future. Are you ready? Do you know what it takes to be successful in college courses? First, you need a goal or reason for going to college. What do you hope to accomplish? How important is your goal? College requires hard work. Yet, if you really want something, you'll do whatever it takes, no matter how difficult it may seem. You will be motivated to do the work, even when you don't feel like it. If you are willing to do the work, you will better your life in more ways than you can imagine.

Second, you need to realize that being in college is like having a job. The grades you earn as well your ability to get a job are based upon your record of dependability. You may have the skill, but what will happen if you don't do the work on time or if you don't come to work (class)? Employers and customers do not care about your reasons. They will just hire someone else. A mature, responsible attitude toward doing the work is essential to success in college as well as on the job. Now is the time to develop your dependability as well as your skills.

This text will help you become a more efficient reader: It is designed to teach you the skills and strategies you need for success in college level courses. It is a workbook with fill-in-the-blank questions that you can answer as you read. As you answer the questions, you will develop the ability to have a conversation with the author (me) who is talking to you on the page. Don't just skip to the exercises and activities contained in each chapter. Take the time to get the most out of the text. Work with it. Give yourself a chance to develop reading strategies for success in life. I want to give you what you need to be successful in college as well as in your personal life. So, talk to me. I will help you. In no time, you will see the difference in your reading speed and comprehension. You'll be on your way to success!

Best Wishes for a Successful Semester!

Elaine Garcia Krieg

1 Motivation and Success

" If you know where you are going, you will get there faster. "

– Anonymous

In this chapter you will learn how to:

Plan for Success

Set Goals

Manage Your Time

Develop Stronger Reading Skills

Consider, Analyze, and Ask Questions about What You Read (Metacognition)

Keep a Reading Journal

You will learn these strategies:

♟ Go for the Goal

♟ The Reading Workout

▲ A goal is a dream that you can make real by creating a strong mental image of what you want to achieve and having the motivation to make it happen.

Preview and Predict ► What do you know so far?

How many of the following questions can you answer before you read this chapter?

• Do you think it is important to have a specific goal or reason for attending college? Why or why not?

_____

- Why do people avoid reading? What can happen as a result?

  _____

- What is your best strategy for maintaining interest while you read?

  _____

- What do you expect to learn about motivation and success in reading?

  _____

- Think of one way in which the picture relates to this chapter's objectives.

  _____

Now, as you read the chapter, look for the answers to see if you were right.

Information About the Preview and Predict Feature

Preview and Predict is a feature you will find at the beginning of each chapter. It will help you develop the habit of considering what you already know about a subject before you read. Then, you will be able to make predictions as to what you expect the author to discuss about the subject. Doing this will help to improve your concentration as you read.

PLANNING TO SUCCEED

You may be wondering why you are in a reading class. After all, you can read, right? So why do you need a reading course?

In the past, attending college was very different from the way it is today. If you paid your money, you could take whatever courses you wanted: history, government, psychology, or physics. If you were able to pass them, fine. If not, you lost your money.

You may think that it was much better to be able to take any course you wanted without having to take reading classes. Yet, back then, many students dropped out of college before the end of their second semester. There were two main reasons why they failed. Can you guess one reason why so many students dropped out?

_____

The first reason so many students dropped out had to do with the *amount* of reading required in each college course. These students may have been smart, but they did not like to read. In other words, reading was not the first thing they did when they had spare time.

It takes reading strength to see beyond the words to form a continuous picture in your mind from the images the words create. These first-year college students were out of shape. Yet, because they were able to graduate from high school, they assumed that the workload in college would not be that difficult. They often enrolled in four or five courses in their first semester. They didn't realize that college courses can require between fifty and one hundred pages of reading per week, and that's just for one class! Many students dropped out, *not* because they weren't smart, or because they couldn't read. They dropped out because they did not have the *skills* to handle the *amount* of reading required in college courses.

On the other hand, some students could easily read four hundred pages per week, and yet, they also dropped out. They were missing something very important. Here is the second reason so many students dropped out before the end of their second semester: They didn't have the *discipline* to attend class regularly and do the required work every day on time, but they still thought they should be passed along to the next level. They didn't realize that being in college is like having a job. If you don't do the work, then you won't get paid. These students were not yet emotionally prepared or mature enough to handle their responsibilities, and they created excuses for avoiding the work.

It is because so many students were dropping out and wasting their time and money that numerous states decided to develop proficiency tests for measuring basic skills. This made colleges more responsible to their students. Colleges can no longer take your money and say, "Good luck." Today, most colleges are required to give placement tests to make certain that you do not take a class that you are not yet prepared to handle.

What is the purpose of a developmental reading course? It is an opportunity for you to develop the *reading skills* and the *discipline* that you need to take college-level courses so you will be more prepared to succeed.

The Student Contract: Your Commitment to Succeed

MyReadingLab

MyReadingLab:
Reading Skills
Diagnostic Pre-Test

The Student Contract below is an agreement that you can make with *yourself* as a commitment to succeed. It contains statements that represent the kind of commitment you will need to make if you want to develop the necessary reading skills and discipline for success in college.

As you read the statements in the contract, think about the requirements that your instructor has outlined for the completion of the course. Then, think of any additions you could make that will help you to maintain the commitment you need for college success. Finally, you can confirm your commitment by signing the contract.

CONTRACT

_____

Print your name

1. I understand that I am responsible for the grade that I earn.

2. I understand that I must attend class regularly and complete homework assignments on time if I want to earn a passing grade.

3. I understand that I am responsible for developing a professional attitude toward my college work.

4. I understand that if I do not read at least 2–3 hours per week and have specific study goals for this course, I may not be able to perform well on exams.

5. _____

6. _____

_____   _____ / _____ / _____
Sign name   *Today's Date*

FOCUS ON THE FUTURE

It is important to have a clear goal or reason for going to college. College courses can be very difficult, especially if you aren't used to the amount of reading required or the time it takes to complete assignments.

When you aren't exactly sure why you are taking college courses, you may make excuses to avoid the work required to succeed. You can easily talk yourself out of doing the assignments for your college courses if you don't see how the work applies to where you want to go in the future.

If, however, you have a goal that you really want to achieve, you won't let anything stand in your way. You'll do the work even when it is difficult or not very interesting. You will find ways to *make it* interesting because you are trying to achieve something that is really important to you. Having a meaningful goal will increase your motivation to improve the reading skills you need for success in college.

Information About the Memory Check Feature

Effective readers often stop to ask questions to see how much they have learned up to a certain point or how much they can remember about what they have just read. The Memory Check is a feature you will find in many sections of each chapter. It will help you form the habit of evaluating your comprehension as you read.

The Memory Check will also help you identify and remember important ideas presented in each section of a chapter. It can be fun to see how many questions you can answer without referring to what you just read and how many of the questions you can *predict* will be asked before each Memory Check. In time, you will find that you are able to do both very easily.

The Memory Check also helps you to build your motivation and increase your interest in the material because you will have confidence that you have understood what you have just read and can more easily apply what you have learned to new information as it is presented.

Memory Check 1 How much do you remember?

1. Many students dropped out of college because they did not have the reading _____ or the _____ that they needed to succeed.

2. One college course can require between _____ pages of reading per week.

3. What can happen if you aren't exactly sure why you are taking college courses?

   _____

4. What will increase your motivation to improve the skills you need for college success? _____

Go for the Goal: A Three-Step Strategy

Go for the Goal is a three-step strategy for achieving a particular goal. It also provides three goal phrases that are common among successful people who know how to motivate themselves to stay on track. Go for the Goal will help you to learn the thinking strategies that you need to succeed.

1. Think Ahead

"I'm going to . . ." Successful people are able to *think ahead*. They can see their goal so clearly that they are able to imagine themselves in the future having achieved what they wanted. They say "I'm going to" achieve a particular goal because they expect to succeed.

Do you have a particular goal in mind? Is it a career or an academic goal? For instance, do you want to earn a degree, make an A in your English class, or complete a particular assignment on time? Perhaps you have a personal goal, such as losing weight or going somewhere on vacation. When you say "I am going to" achieve a particular goal, you will be more likely to take the necessary steps to get what you want.

Activity 1.1 ▶ Think Ahead

Directions: *List your top three goals. They can refer to work, school, or your personal life.*

1. I want to _____.

2. I want to _____.

3. I want to _____.

Look at your goal statements. Now imagine how they would sound if you changed each statement to say "I am going to" instead of "I want to." Notice the difference between "I *want to* become a nurse" and "I am *going to* become a nurse." Which one is more likely to help you Go for the Goal? You may want to become a nurse, but, does wanting something mean that you will do whatever it takes to get what you want? There is no action implied when you just say "I want" something.

On the other hand, if you say that you are *going to* become a nurse, you are stating your goal as if you expect to achieve it in the future. Saying "I am going to" is a way of programming yourself to think about the actions that you will need to take to accomplish your goal.

From reading your list of goals, you can see that some of them are short term and involve just a few steps, whereas others are long term and involve a series of steps or short-term goals. When you have a long-term goal that you expect to achieve, you will begin to see the steps or actions that you need to take along the way.

2. Plan Ahead

"What will I need to do or have in order to achieve my goal?" Successful people *plan ahead*. Since their goal is clear, they are able to see the steps or short-term goals that they need to achieve in order to accomplish what they want. They are aware of the skills, materials, or assignments that are necessary in order to perform each step. Then, they plan a course of action for completing each step along the way.

By asking yourself, "What do I need to do or have in order to achieve my goal?" you will be able to see the obstacles that might get in your way. If you expect to achieve your goal, you will plan ahead to get what you need. You will be more motivated to think of ways to deal with an obstacle. You will find you are less likely to give up just because there is something you don't have or can't do immediately.

For instance, imagine that your goal is to go to Hawaii. You say to yourself, "I am *going to* Hawaii." You begin to plan ahead because you see yourself in Hawaii on the beach, or surfing, or looking at the ocean from your hotel balcony. You make a list of what you will need to achieve your goal. You start to plan ahead for the amount of money you will need for air fare, food, hotels, car rental, gas, and souvenirs. You might plan ahead for what you want to take with you on the trip.

What are some of the obstacles that might get in the way? You might not have enough money. In that case, you would plan ahead to do whatever it takes to raise the money, such as finding a temporary job or doing some overtime at work.

Activity 1.2 ▶ Plan Ahead

Directions: *Complete the goal statement below. Then, plan ahead. What will you need to have or be able to do before you can achieve your goal? For instance, you might say to yourself, "I will need to have . . . (completed assignments/projects, good test scores, etc.)." Or, "I will need to be able to . . . (improve reading and study skills, etc.)."*

Finally, are there any obstacles that might prevent you from attaining what you need in order to achieve your goal? Think of one action you can take to prevent each obstacle from getting in your way and decide when you will complete that action.

Goal Statement: I am going to earn a/an _____ in my _____ class.

1. I will need to _____ in order to earn that grade.

   Possible obstacle: _____

   Solution: I will _____ When? _____

2. I will need to _____ in order to earn that grade.

   Possible obstacle: _____

   Solution: I will _____ When? _____

♟ 3. Take Action

"What am I going to do now?" Successful people are able to *take action*. They are constantly thinking about what they are going to do to get one step closer to achieving their goal. They are always trying to see how many steps can be completed in the shortest amount of time or in the most effective way. They may say things like "I can finish this step in *x* amount of time" and often try to see if they beat that time. They may set up a restriction and reward system for completing steps that are less enjoyable. For instance, they may not allow themselves to watch TV, play video games, or participate in some activity that they enjoy until a particular step is completed to the best of their ability. Successful people feel rewarded with the completion of each step and know how to motivate themselves to take action.

In the case of going to Hawaii, you would plan ahead to see what you would need to get there and take action to get what you need. You could find out exactly how much money you would need by researching the airlines, hotels, and rental car companies for current prices. You could research the cost of any activities you have planned. You could apply for a temporary job or make an appointment to ask your employer for the overtime you would need to raise the money. Often, you will find that taking action to complete each little step along the way to your goal takes less time than you thought.

If you think about it, you already apply the thinking strategies contained in the Go for the Goal strategy every day. For instance, when you go to the store, you are probably using each of the Go for the Goal phrases in the process of getting what you want. You say to yourself, "I am going to the store to get groceries," because you can *think ahead* to see yourself getting what you want. Then, you begin to *plan ahead*. You say to yourself, "What do I need to have in order to get what I want at the store?" You make a mental list of the things you will need to do or have before you get there, such as money, car keys, gas, or a list of items to buy. Finally, you *take action*. You say to yourself, "What am I going to do now?" You find your car keys, buy gas, and get the money you'll need from the ATM machine so that you can get the items you want in the most efficient way possible. You see how every action you take relates to the completion of your goal.

At every step, evaluate your desire to achieve your goal. If you find that you are not motivated to take action or to complete the first steps required to eliminate an obstacle, then you may not truly want to achieve that particular goal. If, however, your goal is clear and it is something that you believe is important, then you will do whatever it takes to complete every step or eliminate every obstacle necessary to achieve what you want.

Activity 1.3 ▶ Take Action Grid

Directions: *Look at the grid in Figure 1.1 that Xavier created to plan ahead and take action for achieving an A in his reading class. Then, complete the grid in Figure 1.2 with your own plan for taking action.*

Figure 1.1 Xavier's Plan for Achieving an A in Reading Class

What am I going to do or achieve? I am going to make an A in my reading course.					
What will I need to do or have in order to achieve my goal?	**What is the first step, and when will I take it?**	**How long will it take?**	**Possible Obstacles**	**Possible Solutions**	**Did I take the first step?**
1. Complete all assignments on time	Complete next assignment Sunday at 4pm	1 hour	no time	Reduce TV time	Yes
2. Make an A on all exams	Study for next exam Thursday at 11pm	1 hour	I don't know what to study.	Take lecture and text notes every day	Yes
Do I still want to attain my goal? Yes No Why? Why not? Yes. I still want to make an A in my reading class because I am going to be a police officer and I must complete my reading requirements before I can take core classes in Criminal Justice.					

Figure 1.2 My Plan of Action

Name:					
What am I going to do or achieve?					
What will I need to do or have in order to achieve my goal?	**What is the first step, and when will I take it?**	**How long will it take?**	**Possible Obstacles**	**Possible Solutions**	**Did I take the first step?**
1.					
2.					
Do I still want to attain my goal? Yes No Why? Why not?					

Activity 1.4 ▶ Goal Setting: Where Are You Now and Where Are You Going?

Directions: *Write three paragraphs about a goal you want to achieve in college. The first paragraph should begin, "My goal is . . . ." The second paragraph should begin with the following sentence: "I know that I am going to make _____ in this class because I will do the following things . . . ." The third paragraph should begin with the following sentence: "By the end of the week, I will complete _____ to get one step closer to achieving my goal." Use the spaces below to write the first sentence of each paragraph.*

_____

_____

_____

_____

Memory Check 2 How much do you remember?

1. What are the three steps that will help you to Go for the Goal you want to achieve?

   a. _____

   b. _____

   c. _____

2. What are three goal-setting phrases that are commonly used by successful people?

   a. _____

   b. _____

   c. _____

TIME MANAGEMENT

Lack of time is one of the biggest obstacles to the achievement of any goal. All too often, we are unaware that there are periods of time in our daily lives that could be used more wisely. A weekly schedule and a "To Do" list are effective time management tools that are used by successful people who want to stay on track to achieve their goals.

A Weekly Schedule

A weekly schedule provides a grid for every hour of the day for one week. To complete the schedule, start by identifying the areas of time that you *cannot* change, such as your scheduled time in class or your hours at work. Then, add the activities that you *can* change, such as any time you spend on the Internet or watching television. If you complete a weekly schedule, you can see how you spend your time during a typical week. Then, you can make decisions about the areas of time that you can change in order to create more time to do what is necessary to achieve your goals.

Activity 1.5 ▸ Weekly Schedule 1

Directions: *Look at Xavier's Weekly Schedule in Figure 1.3 below. He wants to make an A in his reading class. Yet, he says that he doesn't have enough time to study or complete his assignments. Can you find areas of time that Xavier could use more wisely?*

Problem: No time to complete assignments or to study.

What are two specific things that you would suggest Xavier do, so that he will have more time to study and complete assignments?

1. _____

2. _____

Figure 1.3 Xavier's Weekly Schedule

	MON	TUES	WED	THURS	FRI	SAT	SUN
6–7 am	Take son to school	Take son to school	Take son to school	Take son to school McDonald's Dry Cleaners	Take son to school		
7–8 am	Work	School	Work	School	Work	Breakfast	Breakfast
8–9 am		READING		READING		Pick up shirts at dry cleaners	Work

Figure 1.3 Continued

9–10 am					Mom's	
10–11 am		ENGLISH		ENGLISH	Basketball with son at Mom's	
11–12 am		MATH		MATH		
12–1 pm					Lunch at Mom's	
1–2 pm		Lunch		Lunch		
2–3 pm					Work	
3–4 pm	Pick up son	Pick up son	Pick up son	Pick up son	Pick up son	
4–5 pm	Make dinner Clean house	Make dinner Clean house	Make dinner Clean house	Make dinner Clean house	Change — Pack clothes	Mom's — Laundry
5–6 pm	Dinner — then help son with homework	Dinner — then help son with homework	Dinner — then help son with homework	Dinner — then help son with homework	Take son to Mom's	Dinner
6–7 pm					Boy's night out	Pack — go home with son
7–8 pm	Prison Break	Cops	Forensic Files	Cops		
8–9 pm	Help son go to bed	Help son go to bed	Help son go to bed	Help son go to bed		Help son go to bed
9–10 pm	Internet	Law & Order: Suv	CSI: NY	Internet		CSI: NY
10–11 pm	Internet	Internet	Internet	Internet	Mom's	Internet
11 pm–12 am	Study for English	Internet	Internet	Study for Reading	Study for Math	Internet

Activity 1.6 ▶ Weekly Schedule 2

Directions: *Complete your own weekly schedule in Figure 1.4 to find available time to take the actions necessary to achieve your goals.*

What are two specific things that I can change in my schedule to create more time so that I can achieve my goals?

1. _____

_____

2. _____

_____

Figure 1.4 My Weekly Schedule

	MON	TUES	WED	THURS	FRI	SAT	SUN
6–7 am							
7–8 am							
8–9 am							
9–10 am							
10–11 am							
11–12 am							
12 am–1 pm							
1–2 pm							

Figure 1.4 Continued

2–3 pm							
3–4 pm							
4–5 pm							
5–6 pm							
6–7 pm							
7–8 pm							
8–9 pm							
9–10 pm							
10–11 pm							
11 pm–12 am							

A "To Do" List

A "To Do" list is another effective tool for managing your time. A "To Do" list is a record of all the things you need to accomplish during a particular day. By making a daily "To Do" list, you can focus on the actions that you want to complete each day. As you cross out or check-mark each completed item on the list, you will know you are one step closer to achieving your goal.

Activity 1.7 ▶ A "To Do" List

Directions: *Look at Xavier's "To Do" list for one week in Figure 1.5 and answer the questions that follow.*

1. What classes is Xavier taking this semester? _____

2. When did Xavier complete the assignment to review notes and exercises for his math exam? _____

3. When did Xavier read the essay and write a summary for his English class?

   _____

4. When did Xavier complete the Chapter 2 activity questions for his reading class? _____

5. When did Xavier learn page 1 of his study guide for the English exam?

   _____

Figure 1.5 Xavier's Daily "To Do" List for One Week

Mon 4/1	Tues 4/2	Wed 4/3	Thurs 4/4	Fri 4/5	Sat 4/6	Sun 4/7
Make dentist appt.	✓ Make dentist appt.					
✓ Read story Chp. 1 answer questions.	✓ Know all info on pg. 2 of study guide for English exam.	Review notes and exercises pp. 47–58 for Math exam.	✓ Review notes and exercises pp. 47–58 for Math exam.	Read essay and write a summary for English.	✓ Read essay and write a summary for English.	
✓ Know pg. 1 of study guide for English exam		✓ Complete pp. 1–10 for Reading Chp. 2.	✓ Read and complete pp. 11–20 for Reading Chp. 2	Complete Chp. 2 Reading activity questions.	Complete Chp. 2 Reading activity questions.	✓ Complete Chp. 2 Reading activity questions.
✓ Do exercise on pg. 58 Math.				Do exercises on pp. 68–70 Math.		

READING SKILLS: THE KEY TO SUCCESS

It is easy to see why effective reading skills are necessary in college. But, did you know that many companies today require prospective employees to pass a reading test as a condition for being hired? Employers want to make sure that you have the reading skills you will need to do the job, to benefit from additional on-the-job training, or to follow company policies that could prevent lawsuits. If you can't pass this kind of reading test, a company may not want to take a chance on you. Effective reading skills can increase your ability to find a good job.

Effective reading skills also allow you to learn more about the world and the ideas that are important to the society in which you live. When you listen to the way these ideas are expressed in written language, you can begin to form your own ideas. You can learn how to express your ideas more effectively. The desire to learn and use new information is the mark of an educated person. Reading is the best way to go beyond where you are now and to improve your circumstances in life.

The Biggest Obstacle to a Successful Future

There are many reasons why people avoid reading. For some, it's the memory of embarrassment or fear associated with reading in grade school. Perhaps they felt embarrassed reading in front of the class. Or, maybe it just seemed like they were the only one who didn't understand the material as easily as everyone else. Whatever the reason, avoiding reading is one of the biggest obstacles to a successful future. It can hold you back both personally and professionally.

Symptoms and Solutions

Effective reading requires that you have the ability to see beyond the words as you read to form a continuous picture in your mind from the images the words create. When you have effective reading skills, you are able to hold the meaning of one sentence in your mind so you can see how it relates to the meaning of the next sentence. You ask questions or have opinions about what you are reading. You compare what you are reading to what you already know so you can learn something new.

The ability to combine these skills so that they work together when you read is like developing a muscle. The more you read, the more you can strengthen the "muscle" that you need to read more effectively.

When you avoid reading, your muscles—the skills required to read or pay attention to the author—become weak or out of shape. It becomes more difficult to focus on the words or to hear anything except the sound of your own voice saying something negative like "I don't understand this," "I hate this," or "This is boring."

Here are some common problems or symptoms that you can develop when you avoid reading. Check any that apply to you.

_____ Poor concentration (forgetting what you read after a few sentences)

_____ Eye irritation (your eyes can become red or watery)

_____ Sleepiness

_____ Difficulty finding the next line of text

_____ Lights or "halos" appearing around the letters

_____ Anger, irritability, or depression

_____ Reading words one at a time without understanding what they mean within the context of the sentence

How many of these symptoms apply to you? _____

If you checked more than one of these symptoms, then you may have weak reading skills as a result of not reading enough. If you have some or all of these difficulties when you read, then it is no wonder that you avoid doing it. Unfortunately, if you avoid reading, the problems will not go away. In fact, the symptoms can get worse because the skills that you need to read or pay attention continue to weaken over time.

You might say, "But I have a reading or learning disability." If this is the case, you know that these symptoms are associated with more than just reading skill weakness. Yet, you can still increase your reading speed and comprehension with consistent reading practice.

Don't compare yourself with others. Remember, you have a goal that you want to achieve. You expect that you will achieve that goal no matter how long it takes. If you avoid reading, however, you cannot improve. So, what do you have to lose? Give yourself a chance to improve your reading skills and your life.

Memory Check **3** How much do you remember?

1. What is the biggest obstacle to the achievement of any goal? _____

2. What are two time management tools that can help you stay on track to achieve your goal? _____

3. What are two benefits of developing effective reading skills?

    a. _____

    b. _____

    _____

4. What is the best way to go beyond where you are now and to improve your circumstances in life? _____

5. What can hold you back personally as well as professionally? _____

6. What can happen if you avoid reading? _____

    _____

7. What is one symptom associated with the avoidance of reading? _____

    _____

8. What are two things that an effective reader is able to do? _____

    _____

The Reading Workout: A Three-Step Strategy for Developing Stronger Reading Skills

If you were an athlete who decided to watch TV for a year, do you think you would still be able to perform the same activities at the same level as when you were in shape? It would probably be extremely difficult. Any athlete will tell you that you have to maintain some form of exercise to stay in shape. Yet, getting your reading skills in shape can take only a few weeks if you apply the steps in the **Reading Workout.**

- *Step One:* **Find a book or magazine that interests you.**

- *Step Two:* **Read for at least 20–30 minutes every day.**

- *Step Three:* **Talk to the author as you read.**

Now, let's look more closely at each step.

1. Find a Book or Magazine That Interests You

You probably read email, chat room, or text messages every day. This type of material, however, tends to be brief and is very different from the type of reading you will be required to do in college.

To start your Reading Workout, find a book or magazine that will hold your interest for at least 20–30 minutes. You want to build the reading strength you need in order to handle the amount of reading required in college courses. Use your book or magazine to practice the ability to see and hold in your mind a picture of what you are reading for longer and longer periods of time. If English is not your first language, make sure that the material you select is written in English so that you can develop reading fluency for American college coursework.

The book or magazine you select is an important piece of equipment in your workout program. You may already have a favorite magazine or book in mind. There are many magazines that are devoted to particular interests, such as computers and computer games, nursing, fashion, hobbies, science fiction, mystery, business, travel, and romance as well as magazines about current events such as *Newsweek* and *Time*.

Activity 1.8 ▶ Internet Search: Finding a Magazine

Directions: *Here are two websites you can use to locate a magazine(s) about your favorite subject. As you look for your magazine(s), compare the websites by answering the questions below.*

www.giftsandmagazines.com/subscriptions/discount-index.htm

www.tradepub.com/

1. Which website contains more of the magazines that you find interesting?

   _____

   _____

2. List three topics that you are most interested in.

   a. _____

   b. _____

   c. _____

3. Write the titles of the three magazines you found that are the most interesting to you.

   a. _____

   b. _____

   c. _____

Appendix A, The Attitude and Interest Inventory located at the back of this textbook, is a questionnaire that can help you select a book about a topic you find interesting. At the end of the inventory, you will find a list of books and novels—divided by subject area—that are current favorites among students across the country. The Attitude and Interest Inventory can also help you and your instructor identify the types of problems you have experienced when you read.

Activity 1.9 ▶ Selecting a Book: The Attitude and Interest Inventory

Directions: *Complete the Attitude and Interest Inventory found in Appendix A at the back of this textbook.*

Memory Check 4 How much do you remember?

1. What are the three steps involved in the Reading Workout?

   a. _____

   b. _____

   c. _____

2. Why are books or magazine articles better than email or chat room material when selecting your Reading Workout equipment?

   _____

   _____

2. Read for at Least 20–30 Minutes Every Day

Consistent practice is the key to developing reading comprehension and speed. Remember that you are trying to strengthen your reading muscle or skills. Getting started can be the most difficult part of getting in shape, especially if you tend to avoid reading.

When you begin the workout process, you may find that you are only reading a few sentences at a time. This is normal if you have not been reading regularly. So, in the beginning, just read three or four sentences at one time. Then, stop. Make sure that you really understand what you read before you continue. You want to see and hold a picture in your mind of what the author has said. Then, read the next two or three sentences and do the same thing. You will soon find that you do not have to stop so often and that you can read a whole paragraph at a time without stopping.

If you read for 20–30 minutes every day, you will also find that it becomes much easier for you to see beyond the words on the page to form a picture of the author's meaning in your mind. Reading will become more like watching a movie and it will be the best movie you have ever seen because you are using your imagination and ideas to enhance the experience. As a result, you will find yourself becoming more interested in reading to find out what happens next or to learn something new.

Unfamiliar Words

When you see a word you don't know, underline it and try to pronounce it. Then, try to guess the meaning of the word by the way it is used in the sentence. If you cover the word and read the sentence again, the meaning of the word will often become clear to you. Finally, when you get to the end of the paragraph or selection, look up the word in a dictionary to see if you were right.

Additional Opportunities to Strengthen Reading Skills

"I don't have time" is the most common excuse people give for not reading. So, once you have selected a book or magazine, carry it with you at all times. Then, you will be ready to read, or work out, whenever an unexpected opportunity arises. Remember, it only takes 20–30 minutes of reading each day for approximately one week for you to see an improvement in your reading skills. Here are some examples of unexpected reading opportunities:

- when you find yourself waiting in a long line
- when you are a passenger in a car, bus, or subway
- during a break at work or in between classes
- after you have put your children to bed

If your reading class requires the completion of a program in a computer lab, then you will have an extra opportunity to get in shape. Think of your lab time as "gym time." If you also read your book or magazine when you are not in the lab, you will increase your skills more quickly.

Memory Check 5 How much do you remember?

1. How much should you try to read at one time when you begin to apply the Reading Workout strategy? _____

2. What should you do after you finish reading the first three or four sentences?

   _____

3. What should you try to see and hold in your mind as you read each new sentence? _____

4. When you see a word you don't know, you should:

   a. _____ and try to pronounce it.

   b. _____

   c. When you get to the end of the paragraph or selection, _____

   _____

5. What can you do to an unfamiliar word in a sentence to help you guess its meaning? _____

6. Why should you carry your workout book or magazine with you at all times? _____

7. What is one example of an unexpected opportunity to work out?

   _____

Activity 1.10 ▶ Planning Your Reading Workout

Directions: *Write a paragraph that includes each of the following statements.*

1. "I am going to improve my reading strength by reading . . . ." (*Write the title of the book or magazine that you have selected.*) Then, discuss why you selected that particular book or magazine.

2. "I will read for 20–30 minutes every day at . . . ." (*Write the time that you have scheduled for reading each day.*) Then, discuss how to increase your ability to hold in your mind the picture of the author's meaning for increasingly longer periods of time.

3. "I will be ready for any unexpected opportunities to read, such as . . . (*write an example of an unexpected opportunity*), because I am going to carry my reading material with me at all times."

4. "I will know that I am improving my reading skill when I can _____."

♟ 3. Talk to the Author

While you are reading, you want to have a conversation with the author who is talking to you through the words written on the page. Doing this helps you relate to what you are reading and will strengthen your comprehension in the process. You can use the same skills that you already use in face-to-face conversations.

For instance, when you are having a conversation with a friend, you listen in a way that allows you to form a picture in your mind of what he or she is telling you so that you can respond with a question, comment, or idea of your own. You can usually guess where the conversation is going because you are thinking about the topic that is being discussed. You can see how each sentence in the conversation relates to what you already know or what you expect will be discussed about the topic. These are the same skills you want to develop in order to have a conversation with the author.

Unfortunately, if you have developed a negative attitude toward reading, that attitude can interrupt your ability to think about what an author is saying. These attitudes are often developed in childhood. For instance, as a child, you may have felt helpless or frustrated if you experienced some difficulty when reading. You may not have known what to do or whom to ask for help. These feelings of helplessness and frustration may have taken the form of negative thoughts such as, "I'm lost," "I'm slow," or "I'm not as smart as the other kids in my class." You may not realize that you are still carrying these negative thoughts, nor how much they affect your attitude toward reading today as an adult. If you associate reading with negative feelings about yourself, it is understandable that you would want to avoid the experience. What are you thinking about when you are reading?

When you are having a conversation with a friend, are you thinking things like, "I'm a slow listener" or "I hate this"? No, because you feel confident in your ability to talk with a friend. You aren't thinking about yourself. You are thinking about what is being discussed so that you can add to the conversation. As you apply the Reading Workout, you will develop the same confidence when you are having a conversation with an author.

Memory Check **6** How much do you remember?

1. What is one way that you can apply your conversation skills as you read?

    _____

    _____

    _____

2. What can happen if you have developed a negative attitude toward reading?

    _____

METACOGNITION AND READING

Metacognition is a term that refers to the ability to analyze or think about what you are thinking, recognize what you do or don't know, and, when necessary, change how you learn. *Meta* means "change." *Cognition* means "thinking." Metacognition is important to reading well. When you are aware of what you are thinking while you read, you are able to think about how you are responding to the author's ideas in the same way that you do when you have a face-to-face conversation with someone. You can listen to the author speaking and hear yourself thinking about what is being said at the same time.

Metacognition also refers to the ability to change what you are thinking. Your actions are affected by what you think. So, if you can change what are thinking about yourself, then you can change or improve your actions.

How can you change any negative attitudes or thoughts that you may have about reading? If you keep a couple of questions in mind as you read, you will begin to form responses or opinions about what the author is saying instead of any negative things you might have said about yourself in the past. You will improve your concentration. Soon, you will find that you are able to maintain interest in the conversation you are having with an author as you read.

QUESTIONS FOR EFFECTIVE READING

Effective readers ask questions. They ask questions before, during, and after they read to maintain interest in learning something new about a particular subject. They ask questions about the title of a selection or textbook chapter *before they read.* They think about what they already know about the subject. Then, they ask questions that will help them to guess what will be presented about the subject. For instance, they may ask questions such as: "What or who is this going to be about?" "How is the author going to present the subject?"

Effective readers keep these questions in mind *as they read* to see if they were right about what they had predicted. They compare what they already know to what is being presented and form new questions along the way to help maintain interest and concentration as they read.

Finally, *after they read*, effective readers ask questions about what they have learned. For instance, they may ask, "What did I learn?" "Where can I apply what I learned?" or, "What did I like or dislike about the selection?" These questions assist readers in remembering what they have learned by helping them to summarize the information they feel is most important—using their own words.

When you ask a question, it means that you want to learn something new. The more questions you have when you read, the more you will learn. With practice, you will develop the ability to ask the questions that will help you to maintain the interest and concentration necessary to succeed with your educational goals.

Questions to Keep in Mind: Reading an Article or Textbook Chapter

Before Reading

Start by looking at the title and asking *who, what, when, where, how,* and *why* questions to preview what you already know about the topic and to predict what information you expect to be presented as you read.

- What do I already know about this subject? (For instance, have you or someone you know experienced what the author is going to talk about?)
- What do I expect to learn about the subject?

During Reading

- What is being said about the subject? (For instance, do you see a list of ways, types, steps, events, or reasons that support the topic?)
- Does the author have an opinion about the subject? Do I agree or disagree, and why?
- What does the author want me to learn or believe?
- What new words or terms are being used, and what do they mean?
- How can I use this information?

After Reading

- What did I learn? (What are the answers to the questions you asked before and during reading?)
- What information was particularly helpful?
- Where can I apply the information that I learned?

Questions to Keep in Mind: Reading a Novel or Short Story

Before Reading

- What do I already know about this topic? (For instance, have you or someone you know experienced what the author is going to talk about?)
- What do I expect to learn about the topic?

During Reading

- Who are the main characters, and how are they related?
- Where does the story take place?
- Which characters do I like or dislike, and why?
- What is the most important problem(s) the main characters are dealing with?
- How might the character(s) resolve the problem(s)?
- What was the last thing that happened?
- What do I think will happen next?

After Reading

- What was the story about?
- In what way did the story relate to my experience or to that of someone I know?
- What did I learn from the story that was interesting or that might be helpful to me or to someone I know?
- What did I think or feel about what I read? For instance, did I enjoy the article or short story? Why or why not?
- What did I like or dislike about the way the author wrote the story?

At first, you should just ask yourself one or two of these questions each time you read. Then, add more until you are used to asking all of them. The more questions you ask and answer, the more your reading comprehension will improve.

Memory Check 7   How much do you remember?

1. What is metacognition? _____

   _____

2. How can you maintain interest while you read?

   _____

3. Why do effective readers keep the questions they asked before reading in mind *as they read?* _____

4. What are two questions to keep in mind before reading an article or textbook?

   a. _____

   b. _____

5. What are two questions to keep in mind when reading a novel or story?

   a. _____

   b. _____

6. What are the three steps involved in the Reading Workout?

   a. _____

   b. _____

   c. _____

READING JOURNALS

Reading journals allow you to have a conversation with an author. In your journal, you can write the answers to your questions, as well as any opinions or responses you have about what you are reading.

Your reading journal can be a spiral notebook that is easy to carry along with your workout book or magazine. If you keep the reading journal with you, you can write important details in it about what you have read while the material is still fresh in your mind.

The reading journal should be large enough to divide into two sections: one for writing about textbook assignments or selections and the other for writing about short stories, magazine articles, or novels. You should include any new vocabulary words, along with definitions that you learned as you read.

Write in your journal after each reading workout or assignment. What should you write in your reading journal? You can start with writing the answers to each of the questions you asked yourself before, during, and after reading.

A reading journal is a valuable tool. It helps you maintain interest and concentration because you are thinking about what you will write in the journal while you are reading. You will find it easier to remember the important details and will improve your ability to maintain a conversation with the author.

Memory Check 8   How much do you remember?

1. Why should you carry a notebook or reading journal with your workout material?

   _____

   _____

   _____

2. What is one thing that you can write in your reading journal?

   _____

   _____

   _____

3. How will a reading journal help you to maintain interest while you read?

   _____

   _____

   _____

Activity 1.11 ▶ The Reading Journal

Directions: *Create a reading journal. Use one section for the workout book or magazine that you have selected. Use the other section for your textbook or reading assignments. Then, refer to the Questions to Keep in Mind on pp. 26–27 for guidelines about what you can write in your journal before, during, and after you read.*

Information About the Test Yourself Review Quiz Feature

On the next page you will find a Test Yourself Review Quiz. Effective readers evaluate what they have learned. The Test Yourself Review Quizzes at the end of each chapter contain the questions that were asked at the beginning of the chapter, as well as some of the questions included in the Memory Checks so you can evaluate how much you have learned.

Test Yourself Review Quiz

Chapter Review Questions

1. Before reading courses were made available, many students dropped out of college because they did not have the reading _____ and _____ required to succeed.

2. Why is it important to have a specific goal or reason for attending college?

   _____

   _____

3. What three steps are involved in the Go for the Goal Strategy?

   a. _____

   b. _____

   c. _____

4. What can happen if you avoid reading? _____

5. What are the three steps involved in the Reading Workout Strategy?

   a. _____

   b. _____

   c. _____

6. What can happen if you have developed negative attitudes toward reading?

   _____

7. What is one way to maintain interest while you read?

   _____

8. What are two questions that you can keep in mind *before* reading an article or textbook chapter?

   a. _____

   _____

   b. _____

9. What are two questions that you can keep in mind *before* reading a novel or short story?

    a. _____

    _____

    b. _____

10. How can a reading journal help you to maintain interest and concentration?

    _____

    _____

Information About the Summarization Activity Feature

College instructors often require you to summarize the most important information you learned from what you have read in the order that it was presented. A Summarization Activity is included at the end of each chapter to provide practice applying some of the basic steps necessary for writing a summary. In Chapter 4 you will learn specific steps for writing an accurate summary of an article, essay, or textbook chapter you have read.

For this activity, you begin by writing the major headings in a chapter. For instance, in this chapter, the major headings are "Planning to Succeed," "Focus on the Future," "Time Management," "Reading Skills: The Key to Success," and "Megacognition and Reading." First, review the topics presented between the first heading, "Planning to Succeed" on p. 2 and the next heading, "Focus on the Future." Then, write a few sentences about two or three things that are most important about the topics presented under the heading "Planning to Succeed." Now, repeat the process for the next heading. The first two sections have been completed for you and there are prompts under the headings to help you complete them accurately.

Summarization Activity

First Heading PLANNING TO SUCCEED

What information is most important? **Prompt:** There are two reasons why students dropped out of college before developmental reading classes were available. They didn't have the reading skills or the discipline to handle college-level work.

Second Heading *FOCUS ON THE FUTURE*

What information is most important? **Prompt:** It is important to have a clear goal or reason for attending college because *it motivates you to improve the reading skills you need for success in college.*

Prompt: There are three steps in the Goal for the Goal strategy. *First, Think Ahead. This means think about what you are going to do. Then, Plan Ahead. You should plan ahead for what you will need to do to achieve your goal. Finally, Take Action. Think about what you can do now.*

Third Heading *TIME MANAGEMENT*

What information is most important? **Prompt:** There are two effective time management tools. A weekly schedule _____

_____.

A "To Do" list _____.

Fourth Heading *READING SKILLS: THE KEY TO SUCCESS*

What information is most important? **Prompt:** There are two ways that good reading skills can lead to a successful future. _____

_____

Prompt: What can happen when reading is avoided? When reading is avoided, _____

_____.

Prompt What are the steps to apply The Reading Workout Strategy? _____

_____

_____

Fifth Heading *METACOGNITION AND READING*

What information is most important? **Prompt:** What is metacognition? _____

_____

_____

Prompt: Here are two examples of questions you should ask before, during, and after you read. Before reading you might ask yourself _____

_____

During reading, you can ask yourself _____

_____

After reading, you can ask yourself _____

_____

Prompt: To keep a reading journal, you should _____

_____.

Now, read the information you wrote in the summarization activity above. Think about the way it would appear as a short paragraph that summarizes the major skills or ideas presented in this chapter. For instance, your instructor may ask you to write a summary that combines what you have written above about the chapter. With practice, you will find that you can easily summarize information because you are thinking about what is important as you read.

Reflection Activity

How am I am going to apply what I have learned in this chapter?

Directions: *Write a paragraph discussing the two or three things you learned about improving your reading skills and motivation that were most helpful to you, and tell how you plan to use what you have learned.*

_____

_____

_____

_____

_____

_____

_____

_____

♟♟♟ **Skills In Practice** ▶ Reading Selection 1

A MOTHER'S ANSWER
Ben Carson with Gregg Lewis

Accessing Prior Knowledge

Questions for Discussion

1. Do you think that most parents have difficulty restricting the amount of time their children spend watching television and playing video games? Why or why not?

2. Did your parents think that reading was an important skill for you to develop? If so, what did they do in order to develop your reading skills?

3. Did you or someone you know pretend to be dumb in school because the "good students" were teased or bullied?

Preview and Predict

Directions: *Look at the title of the selection. Think about what you already know about the subject. Then, write a couple of predictions about what you are going to read. For instance, do you think the author will talk about his own mother or all mothers in general?*

1. _____

2. _____

Word Search and Discovery

Directions: *Skim through the selection to find the two words below. Underline both words in the selection. Then, use a dictionary to write their definitions in the spaces provided. As you read and encounter these words, see if the definitions you wrote fit the way each word is used in the selection.*

dilapidated (*adj*): _____

obsidian (*n*): _____

Also, underline at least one new word as you read the selection and write your guess as to its meaning in the right margin of the text.

A Mother's Answer
Ben Carson with Gregg Lewis

1   God gave her the wisdom—though my brother and I didn't think it was all that wise. It was to turn off the television. From that point on she would let us watch our choice of only two or three television programs during the week. With all that spare time, we were to read two books a week from the Detroit Public Library.

2   I was extraordinarily unhappy about this new arrangement. All my friends were outside, having a good time. I remember my mother's friends coming to her and saying, "You can't keep boys in the house reading. Boys are supposed to be outside playing and developing their muscles. When they grow up, they'll hate you. They will be sissies. You can't do that!"

3   Sometimes I would overhear this and I would say, "Listen to them, Mother." But she would never listen. We were going to have to read those books.

4   Sometimes, when I tell this story, people come up to me afterwards and ask, "How was your mother able to get you to read those books? I can't get my kids to read or even turn off the television or Nintendo."

5   I just have to chuckle and say, "Well, back in those days, the parents ran the house. They didn't have to get permission from the kids." That seems to be a novel concept to a lot of people these days.

6   At any rate, I started reading. The nice thing was my mother did not dictate what we had to read. I loved animals, so I read every animal book in the Detroit Public Library. And when I finished those, I went on to plants. When I finished those, I went on to rocks because we lived in a dilapidated section of the city near the railroad tracks. And what is there along railroad tracks, but rocks? I would collect little boxes of rocks and take them home and get out my geology book. I would study until I could name virtually every rock, tell how it was formed, and identify where it came from.

7   Months passed. I was still in fifth grade. Still the dummy in the class. Nobody knew about my reading project.

8   One day the fifth grade science teacher walked in and held up a big, shiny black rock. He asked, "Can anybody tell me what this is?"

9   Keep in mind that I never raised my hand. I never answered questions. So I waited for some of the smart kids to raise their hands. None of them did. So I waited for some of the dumb kids to raise their hands. When none of them did, I thought, *This is my big chance.* So I raised my hand . . . and everyone turned around to look. Some of my classmates were poking each other and whispering, "Look, look Carson's got his hand up. This is gonna be good!"

10   They couldn't wait to see what was going to happen. And the teacher was shocked. He said, "Benjamin?"

11   I said, "Mr. Jaeck, that's obsidian." And there was silence in the room because it sounded good, but no one knew whether it was right or wrong. So the other kids didn't know if they should laugh or be impressed.

12   Finally the teacher broke the silence and said, "That's right! This is obsidian."

13   I went on to explain, "Obsidian is formed after a volcanic eruption. Lava flows down and when it hits water there is a super-cooling process. The elements coalesce, air is forced out, the surface glazes over, and . . ."

14   I suddenly realized everyone was staring at me in amazement. They couldn't believe all this geological information spewing from the mouth of a dummy. But you know, I was perhaps the most amazed person in the room, because it dawned on me in that moment that I was no dummy.

15   I thought, *Carson, the reason you knew the answer is because you were reading those books. What if you read books about all your subjects—science, math, history, geography, social studies? Couldn't you then know more than all these students who tease you and call you a dummy?* I must admit the idea appealed to me—to the extent that no book was safe from my grasp. I read everything I could get my hands on. If I had five minutes, I had a book. If I was in the bathroom, I was reading a book. If I was waiting for the bus, I was reading a book.

16   Within a year and a half, I went from the bottom of the class to the top of the class—much to the consternation of all those students who used to tease me and call me Dummy. The same ones would come to me in seventh grade to ask, "Hey, Benny, how do you work this problem?" And I would say, "Sit at my feet, youngster, while I instruct you."

17   I was perhaps a little bit obnoxious. But after all those years it felt so good to say that to those who had tormented me.

18   The important point here is that I had the same brain when I was still at the bottom of the class as I had when I reached the top of the class.

19   The difference was this: In the fifth grade, I thought I was dumb so I acted like I was dumb, and I achieved like a dumb person. As a seventh grader I thought I was smart, so I acted and achieved accordingly. So what does that say about what a person thinks about his own abilities? What does this say about the importance of our self-image? What does it say about the incredible potential of the human brain our Creator has given us?

The Write Connection

Directions: *Write a paragraph about three things you learned or that you think are most important in the reading selection.*

_____

_____

_____

_____

_____

Information about the Comprehension Check and Critical Thinking Check Features

The questions that follow each reading selection often ask for information you can only understand by visualizing what the author has said from start to finish. So, *don't* read the questions that follow a selection before you read it. You will not develop the ability to maintain interest and concentration if you just read the questions and look for the answers in the text.

If you visualize what the author is saying, you will recall more easily the important details that you need to answer the questions that follow a reading selection. Then, when a question requires you to write a more complete response, you will know where to locate the information from within the selection very quickly.

After reading a selection, scan the Comprehension Check and Critical Thinking Check questions that follow to see how many you are able to answer without referring to the text. Then, review the selection to write complete answers. Here are the Comprehension Check questions for "A Mother's Answer."

Comprehension Check

1. In the beginning, what three subjects did the author enjoy reading about?

   _____

____ 2. In the fifth grade, the author amazed classmates who used to call him a dummy, when he

   a. showed them how to solve difficult problems.
   b. made a formal presentation to the class about the removal of obsidian.
   c. was the only one who could identify obsidian and explain its formation.
   d. informed the teacher that he had incorrectly identified the rock as obsidian.

_____ 3. What is the main point of paragraph 16?

    a. Reading more often helped the author move up to the top of his class.
    b. The author was able to confront classmates who had teased him in the past.
    c. Reading more often helped the author to become a seventh grade teacher.
    d. Reading more often helped the author choose better friends.

_____ 4. What is the meaning of the word *consternation* as it is used in paragraph 16?

    a. anger   b. impression   c. consistency   d. dismay

_____ 5. The author's mother can be described as person who was concerned about

    a. the opinions of others.   c. nature.
    b. her children's reading skills.   d. her children's athletic abilities.

Critical Thinking Check

_____ 1. Which of the following details is *least* supportive of the author's contention that his mother was wise?

    a. She required her sons to read two books a week from the Detroit Public Library.
    b. She made her sons turn off the TV except for two or three programs per week.
    c. She told her sons to keep reading in order to stop others from teasing them.
    d. She did not tell her sons what to read.

_____ 2. The author has written the selection for the purpose of

    a. persuading the reader to be more involved in the education of children.
    b. illustrating the negative effects of television on the reading skills of children.
    c. providing effective techniques for improving reading skills.
    d. illustrating the importance of reading in improving a child's self-confidence.

_____ 3. Which of the following conclusions can be drawn from the information provided in the selection?

    a. Some teachers are not impressed by the accomplishments of their students.
    b. It is important to listen to your parents' advice.
    c. Reading can improve your self-image.
    d. Parents today have more control over their children's activities.

Vocabulary Check

1

Directions: *See if any of the words you underlined in the selection are among the list of words below. If not, write your words in the spaces provided. Guess the meaning of the words from the way they were used in the selection. Then, look up the definition of each word in the dictionary to see if you were right.*

coalesce (*vb*): Your guess: _____

    Dictionary Definition: _____

glazes (*vb*): Your guess: _____

    Dictionary Definition: _____

obnoxious (*adj*): Your guess: _____

    Dictionary Definition: _____

Your word: _____ Your guess: _____

    Dictionary Definition: _____

Your word: _____ Your guess: _____

    Dictionary Definition: _____

HOW TO MARK A BOOK
Mortimer Adler

Accessing Prior Knowledge

Questions for Discussion

1. What kind of information do you usually mark when you are reading a book?

2. Do you know someone who marks everything as they read? Is this a good strategy? Why or why not?

Preview and Predict

Directions: *Look at the title of the selection. Think about what you already know about the subject. Then, write a couple of predictions about what you are going to read. For instance, what do you think the author will say about how to mark a book?*

1. _____

_____

2. _____

_____

Word Search and Discovery

Directions: *Skim through the selection to find the two words below. Underline both words in the selection. Then use a dictionary to write their definitions in the spaces provided. As you read and encounter these words, see if the definitions you wrote fit the way each word is used in the selection.*

mutilation (*n*): _____

receptacle (*n*): _____

Also, underline at least one new word as you read the selection and write your guess as to its meaning in the right margin of the text.

HOW TO MARK A BOOK

Mortimer Adler

1   You know you have to read "between the lines" to get the most out of any-thing. I want to persuade you to do something equally important in the course of your reading. I want to persuade you to "write between the lines." Unless you do, you are not likely to do the most efficient kind of reading.

2   I contend, quite bluntly, that marking up a book is not an act of mutilation but of love.

3   You shouldn't mark up a book which isn't yours. Librarians (or your friends) who lend you books expect you to keep them clean, and you should. If you decide that I am right about the usefulness of marking books, you will have to buy them. Most of the world's great books are available today in reprint editions.

4   Why is marking up a book indispensable to reading? First, it keeps you awake. (And I don't mean merely conscious; I mean wide awake.) In the second place, read-ing, if it is active, is thinking, and thinking tends to express itself in words, spoken or written. The marked book is usually the thought through book. Finally, writing helps you remember the thoughts you had, or the thoughts the author expressed. Let me develop these three points.

5   If, when you've finished reading a book, the pages are filled with your notes, you know that you read actively. The most famous active reader of great books. I know is President Hutchins, of the University of Chicago. He also has the hardest schedule of business activities of any man I know. He invariably reads with a pencil, and sometimes, when he picks up a book and pencil in the evening, he finds him-self, instead of making intelligent notes, drawing what he calls "caviar factories" on the margins. When that happens, he puts the book down. He knows he's too tired to read, and he's just wasting time.

6   But, you may ask, why is writing necessary? Well, the physical act of writing, with your own hand, brings words and sentences more sharply before your mind and preserves them better in your memory. To set down your reaction to important words and sentences you have read, and the questions they have raised in your mind, is to preserve those reactions and sharpen those questions.

7   And that is exactly what reading a book should be: a conversation between you and the author. Presumably, he knows more about the subject than you do; naturally, you'll have the proper humility as you approach him. But don't let anybody tell you that a reader is supposed to be solely on the receiving end. Understanding is a two-way operation; learning doesn't consist in being an empty receptacle. The reader has to question him or herself and question the teacher; even argue with the teacher, once he or she understands what the teacher is saying. And marking a book is literally an expression of your differences, or agreements of opinion, with the author.

8   There are all kinds of devices for marking a book intelligently and fruitfully. Here's the way I do it:

1. *Underlining:* of major points, of important or forceful statements.

2. *Vertical lines at the margin:* to emphasize a statement already underlined.

3. *Star, asterisk, or other doo-dad at the margin:* to be used sparingly, to emphasize the ten or twenty most important statements in the book. (You may want to fold the bottom corner of each page on which you use such marks. It won't hurt the sturdy paper on which most modern books are printed, and you will be able to take the book off the shelf at any time and, by opening it at the folded-corner page, refresh your recollection of the book.)

4. *Number in the margin:* to indicate the sequence of points the author makes in developing a single argument.

5. *Numbers of other pages in the margin:* to indicate where else in the book the author made points relevant to the point marked; to tie up the ideas in a book, which, though they may be separated by many pages, belong together.

6. *Circling of key words or phrases.*

7. *Writing in the margin, or at the top or bottom of the page, for the sake of:* recording questions (and perhaps answers) that a passage raised in your mind; reducing a complicated discussion to a simple statement; recording the sequence of major points right through the books. I use the end-papers at the back of the book to make a personal index of the author's points in the order of their appearance.

9   The front end-papers are, to me, the most important. Some people reserve them for a fancy bookplate. I reserve them for fancy thinking. After I have finished reading the book and making my personal index on the back end-papers, I turn to the front and try to outline the book, not page by page, or point by point (I've already done that at the back), but as an integrated structure, with a basic unity and an order of parts. This outline is, to me, the measure of my understanding of the work.

10   If you're a die-hard anti-book-marker, you may object that the margins, the space between the lines, and the end-papers don't give you room enough. All right. How about using a scratch pad slightly smaller than the page-size of the book—so that the edges of the sheets won't protrude? Make your index, outlines, and even your notes on the pad, and then insert these sheets permanently inside the front and back covers of the book.

11   Or, you may say that this business of marking books is going to slow up your reading. It probably will. That's one of the reasons for doing it. Most of us have been taken in by the notion that speed of reading is a measure of our intelligence. There is no such thing as the right speed for intelligent reading. Some things should be

read quickly and effortlessly, and some should be read slowly and even laboriously. The sign of intelligence in reading is the ability to read different things according to their worth. In the case of good books, the point is not to see how many of them you can get through, but rather how many can get through you—how many you can make your own. A few friends are better than a thousand acquaintances. If this be your aim, as it should be, you will not be impatient if it takes more time and effort to read a great book than it does a newspaper.

12   You may have one final objection to marking books. You can't lend them to your friends because nobody else can read them without being distracted by your notes. Furthermore, you won't want to lend them because a marked copy is a kind of intellectual diary, and lending it is almost like giving your mind away.

13   If your friend wishes to read your *Plutarch's Lives,* Shakespeare, or *The Federalist Papers,* tell him gently but firmly to buy a copy. You will lend him your car or your coat—but your books are as much a part of you as your head or your heart.

The Write Connection

Directions: *Write a paragraph about three things you learned or that you think are most important in the reading selection.*

_____

_____

_____

_____

_____

Comprehension Check

Directions: *See how many questions you can answer without referring to the selection. Then, review the selection to write more complete responses.*

_____   1. What is an act of love according to Mortimer Adler?

    a. mutilation
    b. reading between the lines
    c. getting the most out of your college course
    d. marking up a book

2. What are three reasons why marking up a book is indispensable?

a. _____

b. _____

c. _____

_____ 3. According to Mortimer Adler, you will know you have read actively if _____ after you have finished a book.

a. you feel as if you have wasted your time
b. you feel tired
c. the pages are filled with your notes
d. you are able to make caviar factories

4. Mr. Adler believes that writing book notes is necessary because the act of writing brings _____

_____.

5. The author believes that by setting down your reaction to the important words and sentences that you have read and the questions they have raised, you are

_____.

_____ 6. What is the meaning of the word *index* as it is used in paragraph 9?

a. a list of appropriate websites and particular reference addresses
b. an itemized list of information cited by page number
c. a central data log for compiling reference material for source information and graphic works
d. a list of authors who have contributed to a particular body of work

Critical Thinking Check

_____ 1. Which of the following statements *least* supports the author's contention that reading should be a conversation between you and the author?

a. Marking a book expresses the reader's differences or agreements with the author.
b. Understanding is a two-way operation.
c. The learner has to question himself and question the teacher.
d. The reader is supposed to be solely on the receiving end.

_____ 2. Which of the following statements *best* supports the author's opinion that the sign of intelligence is the ability to read different things according to their worth?

    a. There is no such thing as the right speed for intelligent reading.
    b. Reading speed is a sure measure of intelligence.
    c. A few friends are better than an acquaintance.
    d. It is important to see how many good books you can get through.

3. Which of the seven suggested devices listed for marking a book works best for you and why? _____

_____

_____

4. Which of the seven devices have you used before? Would you use them in the future? Why or why not? _____

_____

_____

Vocabulary Check

Directions: *See if any of the words you underlined in the selection are among the list of words below. If not, write your words in the spaces provided. Guess the meaning of the words from the way they were used in the selection. Then, look up the definition of each word in the dictionary to see if you were right.*

caviar (*n*): Your guess: _____

    Dictionary Definition: _____

_____

indispensable (adj): Your guess: _____

    Dictionary Definition: _____

Your word: _____ Your guess: _____

    Dictionary Definition: _____

Your word: _____ Your guess: _____

    Dictionary Definition: _____

2 Word Wise

"Your words create your world."

– E. F. Briley

In this chapter you will learn how to:

Use Basic Word Parts to Understand Words

Use a Dictionary and a Thesaurus

You will learn this strategy:

♟ The Word Wise Strategy

▲ **One word can have several meanings.**

Preview and Predict ▶ What do you know so far?

How many of the following questions can you answer before you read the chapter?

• In what areas of your life would it be helpful to have a good vocabulary?

_____

- What are the three basic word parts?

  _____

- What do you expect to learn in this chapter?

  _____

- Think of one way in which the picture relates to this chapter's objectives.

  _____

Now, as you read the chapter, look for the answers to see if you were right.

WHY YOU NEED A GOOD VOCABULARY

A good vocabulary is essential to success in college because you need to speak and write clearly about what you are learning. But, did you know that a good vocabulary will also help you to succeed in achieving your career goals? Companies today are concerned with the needs of the global market. In order to be successful, they must be able to communicate with businesses all over the world. There is a professional vocabulary that serves as a standard for business communication. A good vocabulary allows you to communicate in the business world where many opportunities are available.

Developing a better vocabulary does not mean you have to forget the language you use at home. It is very important to be proud of the language that represents your family, your upbringing, or your culture. By learning new ways to express an idea, however, you will have the flexibility to communicate with a wider audience. If you keep in mind that *better communication* is the main purpose for improving your vocabulary, you will develop the ability to speak the language your audience can understand.

BASIC WORD PARTS

Words can be divided into parts. Each part has its own meaning and purpose. If you know the meaning of common word parts, you can use them to figure out the meaning of unknown words and increase your vocabulary. There are three basic word parts:

Root: The root is the original source or *main part* of a word. Roots form the basic foundation of words.

> *Example:* **port**   *Meaning:* **to carry**
>
> **port**able   *Meaning:* able **to carry**

Prefix: A prefix is a word part that can be added *before* the root to change or add to the meaning of a word.

> *Example:* **ex**port   *Meaning:* to carry **out**

Suffix: A suffix is a word part that is added *after* the root to change the tense, action, or purpose of a word. A suffix can change a word into a noun, verb, adverb, or adjective.

> *Example:* export**ed** (verb)   *Meaning:* carri**ed** out
>
>   export**er** (noun)   *Meaning:* **a person who** carries out
>
>   export**able** (adjective)   *Meaning:* **able to** be carried out

Does every word have three word parts? No. For instance, the word *port* is a root that can stand by itself without a prefix or a suffix. Some words have only one part, whereas others have several parts. Yet, each part of a word has a meaning.

Memory Check 1   How much do you remember?

1. What are two areas in which a good vocabulary is essential to success?

   _____

2. What is the main purpose for improving your vocabulary? _____

3. What is a root? _____

4. Where would you find a prefix? _____

5. How does a suffix change the meaning of a word? _____

   _____

6. T/F _____ Every word has three parts.

Roots

The **root** is the *main part* of a word. Imagine the roots of a plant or a tree. The root of a plant or tree provides the main support needed to produce branches, leaves, and flowers. In the same way, the root of a word provides the main support on which words "grow" or produce meaning. The root of a word can originate from many languages: Greek, Latin, Germanic, Arabic, English, and numerous others. A good collegiate dictionary indicates the country or "land" from which the root of a word "grew" or originated.

Now, look at the way that roots support the meaning of words by filling in the spaces provided as you read.

For instance, here is a Latin root: *view*. What does the root *view* mean? It means to

_____. Can *view* be a word by itself? _____. So, does every word have three parts? _____.

Here is another root: *spect*. The Greek root *spect* or *spec* also means "to look,"
or "to see." For instance, what about the word in*spect*? What does *inspect* mean? It
means to *look* (spect) into. Think of another word that has the root *spect*.

_____ People wear *spect*acles to _____. *Spect*ators go to a stadium to _____

the game. The root *spect* means to _____.

Consider the root *port*. Port means "to carry." Think of a word that contains

the root *port*. _____ How about the word re*port*? Re*port* means to *carry*
(port) the information *back* or to repeat it *again*. Here is another example: Why is a

cell phone *port*able? It is able to be _____.

Activity 2.1 ▸ Root Wisdom

Directions: *Here is a list of common roots and their meanings. For each example, write
a definition in your own words, using the meaning of the root provided. Some answers
have been provided for you.*

Example	Root	Definition
anthropology	**anthrop:** *man*	1. the study or discussion of **man**
creditor	**cred:** *believe*	2. a person who _____ that you can pay on time
democracy	**dem:** *people*	3. democracy—government by the **people** for the **people**
contradict	**dict:** *say*	4. to _____ something in opposition
flexible	**flex:** *bend*	5. something you are able to _____
autograph	**graph:** *write*	6. to _____ or sign your name on a document
progress	**gress:** *go*	7. to _____ or move forward
criminology	**ology:** *study of*	8. the _____ crime
agoraphobia	**phob:** *fear*	9. the **fear** of open spaces
vocation	**voc:** *call*	10. something you are **called** to do in life

For an additional list of roots see Appendix B.

Memory Check 2   How much do you remember?

1. What are the three basic word parts? *Prefix, Suffix, Root*

2. What is a root? _____

3. The root *spect* means to *to See*

4. The root *port* means to *to carry*

5. When you have good *credit*, it means that businesses *believe* you will pay on time.

Prefixes

The prefix *pre-* means "before." **Prefixes** are word parts that are attached *before* the root to add or to change the meaning of a word.

Let's look at the prefix *re-*. *Re-* means "again" or "back." Look at the words *rewrite* and *replay*. What do these word meanings have in common? Both words have something to do with "again" or "back." To *rewrite* means to write *again*. To *replay* means to play something *back* or _____. What is the meaning of the word *review*? It means to view *again* or to look _____.

The prefix *de* means "down" or "away from." What does the word *depress* mean? It means to press _____. If you *degrade* some-one, you are putting them _____. If you are *depressed*, you are feeling _____. Write two words that begin with the prefix *de*. (1) *determine* (2) *depressed* What do these words have in common? They both have something to do with "down" or "away."

Activity 2.2 ▶ Prefix Wisdom

Directions: *On the next page is a list of common prefixes and their meanings. For each example, write a definition in your own words, using the meaning of the prefix provided. Some answers have been provided for you.*

Example	Prefix	Definition
<u>a</u>typical	**a:** *not*	1. **not** typical
<u>anti</u>freeze	**anti:** *against*	2. something you add to prevent **against** freezing
<u>auto</u>focus	**auto:** *self*	3. something you focus by your**self**
<u>bi</u>cycle	**bi:** *two*	4. a bike that has _____ wheels
<u>bio</u>logy	**bio:** *life*	5. the study of _____ or living things
<u>dis</u>agree	**dis:** *not*	6. to _____ agree
<u>il</u>legal	**il:** *not*	7. something that is _____ legal
<u>pro</u>mote	**pro:** *forward*	8. to move _____
<u>sub</u>marine	**sub:** *under*	9. something that is _____water
<u>tri</u>angle	**tri:** *three*	10. a figure with **three** sides

For an additional list of prefixes see Appendix B.

Memory Check 3 How much do you remember?

1. What is a prefix? _____

_____

2. The prefix *pre* means _____

3. The prefix *re* means _____ or _____.

4. The prefix *de* means _____ or _____.

5. A <u>bi</u>ped is an animal that has _____ feet.

Suffixes

Suffixes are word parts that are added *after* a root. When suffixes are added, they alter the tense, action, or purpose of a word. They can change a word into a noun, verb, adverb, or adjective.

For instance, the word *port,* by itself, is a *noun* because it names a place to which goods are carried. When the suffix *able* is added after the root *port,* the word port*able* is formed. What does port*able* mean? It means *able to* be carried. Now you have changed the word *port* into an **adjective** that *describes* the ability to be carried.

Consider the following words: teach**able**, lov**able,** and employ**able**. Each word means *able to* or *capable of* doing something. Teach**able** means *able to* be taught or *capable of* learning. Lov**able** means *capable of* _____. Employ**able** means *able to* be _____. The words, teach**able**, and employ**able** are _____ because they *describe* the ability to teach, love, or employ.

The suffixes *er* and *or* mean "person who." When you add the suffix *er* after the root *port*, the word port**er** is created. What does the word *porter* mean? It means a person who carries baggage. Look at the following words: teach**er**, instruct**or**, lov**er**, and employ**er**. Each word is a *noun* that names a person who teaches, instructs, loves, or employs.

Activity 2.3 ▶ Suffix Wisdom

Directions: *Here is a list of common suffixes and their meanings. For each example, write a definition in your own words, using the meaning of the suffix provided. Some answers have been provided for you.*

Example	Suffix	Definitions
medical	**al:** *relating to*	1. **relating to** medicine
employee	**ee:** *person who is*	2. a _____ employed
golden	**en:** *made of*	3. something that is _____ gold
audible	**ible:** *capable of*	4. **capable of** being heard
chemist	**ist:** *person who*	5. a _____ works with chemicals
sanity	**ity:** *quality of*	6. the **quality of** being sane
finalize	**ize:** *to make*	7. _____ final
helpless	**less:** *without*	8. someone who is _____ help
commitment	**ment:** *state of*	9. the **state of** committing
joyous	**ous:** *full of*	10. to be _____ joy

For an additional list of suffixes see Appendix B.

Memory Check ✓ **4** How much do you remember?

1. What is a suffix? _____

   _____

2. A violin*ist* is a _____ plays the violin.

3. A person who is help*less* is _____ help.

4. A fortuit*ous* event is one that is _____ fortune or luck.

5. See how many word part meanings below you can recall without looking at the text.

Prefix	**Root**	**Suffix**
a. *re* means:	d. *port* means: to	g. *er* and *or* mean:
_____	_____	_____
b. *de* means:	e. *spec/spect* means:	h. *ist* means:
_____	to _____	_____
c. *pre* means:	f. *cred* means: to	i. *able* means:
_____	_____	_____

 ## Word Wise: A Strategy For Decoding Unfamiliar Words

Each word part has a meaning. As you develop your vocabulary, you will begin to see that word parts are like codes that you can use to figure out the meaning of unfamiliar words as you read.

Word Wise is a strategy you can use to break the code of a new word. It involves making connections between word parts in a word you don't know and word parts in a word that you already know. The more word parts you know, the better you will be able to work out the meaning of new words that you encounter as you read. In addition, it will help you understand the way that words are constructed to form meaning.

To apply the Word Wise strategy:

- Read the meaning of each word part from *right to left*.
- Look for a root or prefix you recognize in an unfamiliar word and think of a word you know that contains a similar word part.

♟ 1. Read Each Word Part from *Right to Left*

You can understand the meaning of many words by reading their word parts from right to left. For instance, the word *respect* has two word parts: re and spect.

Reading from right to left, the root *spect* means to _____ and the prefix *re* means

_____. So, the word *respect* literally means to "*look* back" or to "*look* again." In what way do you think that looking back or again relates to the meaning of

the word *respect?* _____

Here are some examples:

flexible   *ible + flex*   *Meaning:* **able** to bend

portable   *able + port*   *Meaning:* **able** to carry

speaker   *er + speak*   *Meaning:* **a person who** speaks

export   *port + ex*   *Meaning:* **to carry** out

♟ 2. Look for a Root or Prefix You Recognize in an Unfamiliar Word and Think of a Word You Know that Contains a Similar Word Part

Roots and prefixes contain the most clues to the meanings of words. Look for a root or prefix you recognize within an unfamiliar word. Recall the meaning of the word part you recognize. Then, think of another word you already know that contains the same word part. If you think of the meaning of a word you know that has a similar word part, you can guess the meaning of an unfamiliar word. The more word parts you know, the more words you can figure out as you read.

Example 1

I think it would be important to **re**iterate the facts of the case for my jury

trial. Look at the word *reiterate*. You know that the prefix *re* means _____

or _____. Think of a word that contains the prefix *re*. _____

What does that word mean? _____ What do you think

*re*iterate might mean in Example 1? _____

Example 2

I'm afraid that the judge is going to look at my poor driving record and **re**voke my license

What do you think re*voke* might mean in Example 2? _____

Example 3

The detective was in**cred**ulous regarding the details of the suspect's story.

What does the root *cred* mean? _____ What do you think in**cred**ulous

might mean in Example 3? _____

Now, see if you were right by looking up the words, *reiterate, revoke,* and *incredulous* in the dictionary.

Word   **Dictionary meaning**

reiterate: _____

revoke: _____

incredulous: _____

Are the dictionary definitions similar to or different from your guesses about

the meanings of these words? _____

Were you able to correctly guess the meanings of these words? If so, your guesses were probably very similar to the dictionary definitions.

The Word Wise strategy helps you to work out the literal meaning of words by using word part meanings. As you increase your knowledge of word parts and apply the Word Wise strategy more often, you will soon find that you are able to break the code of many new words.

Memory Check 5 How much do you remember?

1. To apply the Word Wise strategy you should?

   a. _____

   b. _____

      _____

2. Identify the root in the word *respect?* _____

3. Identify the root in the word *report.* _____

4. Identify the root in the word *portable.* _____

5. Identify the root in the word *respectable.* _____

Table 2.1 Common Word Parts List

PREFIXES	ROOTS	SUFFIXES
con/com/col: with or together	**duc, duct:** to lead or make	**able:** able to or capable of
de: down or away	**gam:** marriage	**ion:** the act of, or state of
ex: out	**ject:** to throw	**or/er:** person who
mono: one	**miss, mit:** to send	**y:** having or full of
poly: many	**port:** to carry	
pre: before	**spect:** to look	
re: again or back	**tain:** to hold	
trans: across		

Activity 2.4 ▶ Word Wise 1: Roots and Prefixes

Directions: *Use the word parts list in Table 2.1 to fill in the answers below as you read. Begin by reading the word part meanings from right to left. The root of each word is in **bold**. Remember that you are using word parts to find the literal meanings of the words.*

Example: The United States will ex**port** food and medical supplies to Iraq. What are the word parts in the word *export*? *Ex* and *port*. Using The Word Wise strategy, *export* literally means to carry out.
                              (port)(ex)

1. Trans**port** means to _____ across. For instance, goods are *carried* across a
                    (port)   (trans)
   city, country, or ocean.

2. The root *miss* or *mit* means to _____. Trans**mit** means to send _____.
   (mit) (trans)

   For instance, radio and television signals as well as diseases are trans**mit**ted or

   sent _____ from one point to another.
   (mit)(trans)

3. The root *duc* or *duct* means to _____. For instance, a tear duct *leads* the water

   out of your eye. Con**duct** means to _____ others together. A person who
   (duct)   (con)

   conducts a meeting *leads* others _____.
   (con)

4. The root *ject* means to _____. For instance, when you re**ject** something, you

   _____ it *back*.
   (ject)   *(re)*

5. The root *tain* means to _____. For instance, when you re**tain** information,

   you are able to _____ it for use _____ at another time.
   (tain)   (re)

Mix and Match: Write the letter that best matches the meaning of each word below.

6. _____ conduct

7. _____ transmit

8. _____ reject

9. _____ retain

10. _____ transport

a. to **throw** back

b. to **carry** across from one point to another

c. to **hold again** for later use.

d. to **send** across

e. to lead **with** or **together**

Activity 2.5 ▶ Word Wise 2: More Roots and Prefixes

Directions: *Guess the meaning of the italicized word in each sentence below by using your knowledge of word parts. One word part in each word is in **bold** type. Then, select the dictionary definition that is most similar to your guess for the meaning of the word as it is used in the sentence.*

Example

You need to *com**port*** yourself appropriately in court.

What is the sentence about? _____ You

might say that the sentence is about what you need to do in court. The root *port* means to _____. Now think of a word or words that might replace *comport* in the example sentence. You might say, "You need to carry yourself appropriately in court."

Which dictionary definition below best fits the meaning of *comport* in the example sentence?

a. to lead into a particular action or cause
b. to work with others to achieve a specific result
c. to behave oneself
d. to speak in a reasonable manner

Choice (c) is the best replacement for the word *comport* in the example sentence. "To behave oneself" is the actual definition of the word *comport*. Can you see that your guess for the meaning of the word—using word parts—is very similar to the dictionary definition? By using your knowledge of word parts, you are better able to identify the meanings of new words.

See if you can apply your knowledge of word parts to figure out the meaning of the italicized words in each sentence below.

1. I had to attend a ***preliminary*** hearing to present my case.

    What is the sentence about? _____

    The prefix *pre* means _____. How would you define a preliminary hearing?

    _____

    _____ Which dictionary definition below best fits the meaning of the word *preliminary* in sentence 1?

    a. preceding an important event
    b. the period of time before dawn
    c. occurring now and then
    d. the interval between two events

2. When I was in the prison camp, I was ***deprived*** of food for three days.

    What is the sentence about? _____

    What does the prefix *de* mean? _____ or _____. If you are deprived of

    food for three days, it means that you are _____.

    _____ Which dictionary definition below best fits the meaning of the word *deprived* in sentence 2?

    a. to expel or force out
    b. to endure a situation for an extended period
    c. to indulge excessively, gluttony
    d. to take something away from

3. The boys were *detained* at the police station for further questioning.

   What is the sentence about? _____

   _____

   What does the root *tain* mean? _____ What does the prefix *de* mean? _____

   or _____ So, the boys were being _____ _____ at the police station.
   (tain)   (de)

   _____ Which dictionary definition below best fits the meaning of the word *detained*
      in sentence 3?

      a. to retire
      b. to pardon
      c. to delay
      d. to engage in conflict

Mix and Match: *Write the letter that best matches the meaning of each word below.*

   4. _____ preliminary   a. taken away from

   5. _____ detain   b. carry oneself

   6. _____ comport   c. happens beforehand

   7. _____ deprived   d. hold down

How many word parts meanings can you recall without looking at the text?

Prefixes

   8. *ex* means: _____

   9. *con* means: _____ or _____

   10. *trans* means: _____

   11. *pre* means: _____

   12. *re* means: _____ or _____

   13. *de* means: _____ or _____

Roots

   14. *miss/mit* means: to _____

   15. *duc/duct* means: to _____

   16. *port* means: to _____

   17. *tain* means: to _____

   18. *ject* means: to _____

   19. *spect* means: to _____

   20. *cred* means: to _____

Three-Part Words

Now let's see how to connect a suffix to the meaning of a word. The suffix *able* means
able to or *capable of.* Look at the word *transport.* It has two word parts, *trans* and *port.*

   trans   +   port
   (across)   (to carry)

From **right to left,** *transport* means to "carry across," right? So, what happens when we put the suffix, *able* at the end of the word, *transport*? What does transport*able* mean? Start on the right side of the word *transportable* below and the read the meaning of each word part from right to left.

trans   +   port   +   able
(across)   (to carry)   (able)

Transport*able* means *able to* carry (port) across (trans).

Look at the way that suffixes add meaning to a word by filling in the word part meanings in the examples below as you read. (You can refer to the Common Word Parts list on page 56).

Exportable means: *able* to carry _____.
(port) (ex)

De**port**able means: *able* _____ down or away.
(port)   (de)

Here is another three-part word: *monogamy*. *Monogamy* means that you have only *one* wife or husband. From **right to left,** the suffix *y* in the word, monogamy means "having" or "full of." The root *gam* in mono*gamy* means

_____. The prefix, *mono* in the word, monogamy means *one*. So, monogamy means: having marriage to _____ person. Now, change *monogamy*
(y)   (gam)   (mono)

to a word that means "having marriage to *many* people." _____

Another three-part word is *transmission*. The three word parts in *transmission* are: *trans, miss,* and *ion.* From right to left, the suffix, *ion* in transmiss*ion*

means _____. The word part to the left of *ion* is *miss*. The root *miss*

means to _____. The prefix *trans* means _____. So, *transmission* literally means *the act of sending across.*

Activity 2.6 ▶ Word Wise 3: Three-part Words

Directions: *Complete the meaning of the following words from* right to left *using your knowledge of word parts.*

1. Polygamy means having _____ to many people.
   (y)   (gam)   (poly)

2. An orchestra conductor is a person who _____ musicians _____ to play music.
   (or)   (duct)   (con)

3. An inspector is a _____ looks into something.
               (or)   (spect)(in)

4. Transportable means _____ to be carried _____ from one point to another.
          (able)   (port) (trans)

5. A commission is the act of sending money _____ the completion of a sale.
         (ion) (miss)   (con)

Memory Check **6** How much do you remember?

How many word part meanings can you recall without looking?

Prefixes	**Roots**	**Suffixes**
1. *re:* _____	9. *port:* to _____	17. *er, or:* _____
2. *pre:* _____	10. *spec/spect:* to _____	_____
3. *de:* _____	11. *duc/duct:* to _____	18. *able:* _____
_____	12. *miss/mit:* to _____	_____
4. *ex:* _____	13. *gam:* to _____	19. *ion:* _____
5. *trans:* _____	14. *tain:* to _____	20. *less:* _____
6. *con:* _____	15. *cred:* to _____	21. *y:* _____
_____	16. *ject:* to _____	
7. *mono:* _____		
8. *poly:* _____		

Activity 2.7 ▶ Word Wise 4: Combining Word Parts

Directions: *Select a root from Memory Check 6. Next, add a prefix or a suffix to the root you selected to create a word. Then, use the Word Wise Strategy to write your own definition for the word you created, using its word part meanings. Finally, write the dictionary definition of the word you created.*

Example

Root: <u>ject</u>   **Your Word:** <u>deject</u>

Your definition using word parts: <u>To throw (ject) down or away (de)</u>

Dictionary definition: *to cast down.* (The definitions are very similar.)

1. *Root:* _____ *Your Word:* _____

   Your definition using word parts: _____

   Dictionary definition: _____

2. *Root:* _____ *Your Word:* _____

   Your definition using word parts: _____

   Dictionary definition: _____

3. *Root:* _____ *Your Word:* _____

   Your definition using word parts: _____

   Dictionary definition: _____

4. *Root:* _____ *Your Word:* _____

   Your definition using word parts: _____

   Dictionary definition: _____

5. *Root:* _____ *Your Word:* _____

   Your definition using word parts: _____

   Dictionary definition: _____

6. *Your definition using word parts:* _____

   Dictionary definition: _____

WORD UPGRADE

MyReadingLab

Vocabulary: To practice
your skills go to:
>Reading Skills
>Vocabulary

You can upgrade your vocabulary by using two important resources: a dictionary and a thesaurus. Both contain information on hundreds of words and their meanings. If you develop the habit of using these resources regularly, you will find that you have a larger selection of words to choose from so that you can express yourself more clearly in a variety of situations.

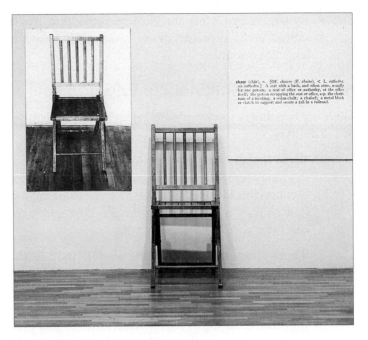

WHY YOU SHOULD USE A DICTIONARY

Although you should always carry a paperback dictionary with you for use at school, you should also invest in a larger collegiate dictionary to keep in your study area at home. Dictionaries such as *Webster's New Collegiate Dictionary* provide a more complete listing of word meanings, suffixes, and information about the etymology or origins of words. They also provide **synonyms** (words that have the **same** or nearly the same meaning as another word) and **antonyms** (words that have the **opposite** meaning of another word).

A good collegiate dictionary also includes additional information to help you understand word usage and rules for using the English language such as the following: examples of many words used in the context of a sentence; an appendix that contains rules for punctuation; a handbook for writing business letters; lists of signs and symbols used in various subjects; and lists of geographical and biographical names.

Here is a list of online dictionaries that you can use in addition to your larger collegiate dictionary.

- www.yourdictionary.com *The American Heritage® Dictionary of the English Language* provides a free online dictionary, thesaurus, audio pronunciations, word of the day, English Language resources, and vocabulary resources for learning many languages.

- www.dictionary.com This site provides a free online dictionary search, translator, word of the day, word games, and vocabulary resources for learning many languages.

- www.m-w.com Merriam-Webster provides a free online dictionary, the-saurus, audio pronunciations, word games, word of the day, and English language resources.

How to Use a Dictionary to Upgrade Your Vocabulary

There are two things you should do *before* you look up the meaning of a new word in a dictionary.

1. **Guess the meaning of a new word as you read.** Underline the word and try to pronounce it. As you continue reading, the meaning of the word will often become clear to you. When you look the word up in your dictionary, you can find the meaning that best fits the guess you had in mind. Often, you will discover that you are correct.

2. **Think about the way the new word is used in the sentence.** Dictionary meanings are listed according to the way a word is used as a part of speech, for example, as a noun, verb, adverb, or adjective. Therefore, it is important to know the part of speech of a new word so that you can find the most appropriate meaning in the dictionary. Remember that when a suffix is added after a word, it can change the word's part of speech.

Identifying Nouns (n)

A **noun** refers to a person, place, or thing. If the new word is a noun, it will answer a "What?" "Where?" or "Who?" question in the sentence. For instance, write a noun in each of the spaces provided to complete the sentence below:

Kelsey and _____ ran from the _____
             Who?   *What?*

Common Noun Suffixes			
er	*Example:* a teach**er**	*ion*	*Example:* an opin**ion**
or	*Example:* a communicat**or**	*ment*	*Example:* a commit**ment**
ic	*Example:* a fanat**ic**	*ism*	*Example:* commun**ism**
ist	*Example:* a dent**ist**	*ity*	*Example:* a commun**ity**

Consider the following sentence:

Jim is a food crit**ic**.

If you ask the question, "Who is Jim?" the answer would be, he is *a critic*. A critic is a *person who* evaluates something. In this sentence, the word *critic* is a noun (*n*) because it refers to a person, place, or thing. It tells you *who* Jim is.

Identifying Verbs (*vb*) or (*vt*)

A **verb** tells you the action of a person or thing in a sentence. If the new word is a verb, it will answer the question, "What did he/she/it *do*?" in the sentence. For instance, write a verb in the space provided to complete the sentence below:

Angela _____ to the mall.

What did Angela *do*?

Common Verb Tense Suffixes
ed   *Example:* Mary committ**ed** the crime.
ize   *Example:* Jerry will final**ize** the work. Jerry final**ized** the work.
ate   *Example:* Andy had to termin**ate** the project. Andy termin**ated** the project.

Consider the following sentence:

Michael *criticized* Joanna because she was late.

What did Michael *do*? He *criticized* Joanna. In this sentence the word *criticized* is a verb (*vb*) because it tells you the *action* of a person or thing.

Identifying Adjectives (*adj*)

An **adjective** describes a person, place, action, or thing. If the new word is an adjective, it will answer the question, "What *kind* of person, place, action, or thing?" in the sentence. For instance, write an adjective in the space provided to complete the sentence below.

Sharon ran from the _____ building.

What *kind* of building?

Common Adjective Suffixes	
able *Example:* a manage**able** assignment	*ous* *Example:* a fabul**ous** show
ible *Example:* an aud**ible** remark	*ful* *Example:* a help**ful** person
al *Example:* a medic**al** emergency	*en* *Example:* a gold**en** bowl
less *Example:* a help**less** child	

Consider the following sentence:

George makes *critical* remarks about everything I say.

If you ask the question, "What *kind* of remarks does George make?" the answer would be, he makes _____ remarks. In this sentence, the word *critical* is an adjective because it describes a *kind* of remark.

Identifying Adverbs (adv)

An **adverb** clarifies a verb, an adjective, or another adverb. If the new word is an adverb, it will answer the question, "*How* was the action completed?" For instance, write an adverb in the space provided to complete the sentence below.

Raymond _____ ran from the burning building.

How did he run?

Common Adverb Suffixes
-ily   *Example:* He sang merr**ily**.
-ly   *Example:* Theresa calm**ly** shut the door after he left.

Consider the following sentence:

Marissa thinks *critically* about her answers during an exam.

If you ask the question, "*How* does Marissa think?" the answer would be, she thinks

_____. The word *critically* is used as an adverb (*adv*) because it adds clarification to a verb as well as an adjective or other adverb.

Memory Check 7 How much do you remember?

1. What are two important resources that you can use to upgrade your

   vocabulary? _____

2. What is one reason you should invest in a good collegiate dictionary?

   _____

Mix and Match: Write the letter of the question on the right that matches each part of speech below.

3. _____ verb tense   a. What *kind* of person, place, or thing?

4. _____ adjective   b. What? Where? or Who?

5. _____ adverb   c. *How* was the action completed?

6. _____ noun   d. What did he/she/it *do*?

Mix and Match: Match the set of words on the right with each part of speech below.

7. _____ verb tense   a. insidious, comical, viable

8. _____ adjective   b. inevitably, momentarily, condescendingly

9. _____ adverb   c. propagate, romanticized, meandering

10. _____ noun   d. tenement, brevity, infatuation

11. Identify the part of speech of the underlined word in the following sentence.

There was so much levity in the room that it seemed as if everyone was on

laughing gas. Part of speech: _____

12. What are two things you should do before you look up a new word in a
dictionary?

a. _____

b. _____

How a Dictionary Works

If you know how a word is used in a sentence, you can find the most appropriate definition in a dictionary. For instance, look at the way the word *respect* is used in the following sentences:

Sentence 1: Josie wanted to respect the man by shaking his hand.

Sentence 2: She thought it was a sign of respect to shake the man's hand.

In Sentence 1, *respect* is used as a verb, because it means something Josie wanted

to *do*. In sentence 2, *respect* is used as a _____, because it names a *thing* or *idea*.

Figure 2.1 on p. 68 shows the word *respect* as it appears in a dictionary. There are two entries for the word *respect*. First, it can be used as a noun (*n*). There are *four* ways to use *respect* as a noun in a sentence. The word *respect* can also be used as a

verb. How many ways can you use the word *respect* as a verb? _____. As a verb,

respect can mean to esteem or to _____. If you wanted to look up the word *respect* as it is used in Sentence 1, you would look at the second entry for the verb definitions. Since Sentence 2 uses the word *respect* as a *noun,* you would look at the

_____ entry.

Figure 2.1 Dictionary Entries for the word, *respect*

Entry #1 ⟶	¹**re-spect** \ri'spekt\ *n.* [ME, fr, L *respectus,* act of looking back, fr. *re- + specere* to look—more at SPY] **1:** a relation to or concern with something usually specified: REFERENCE (with~to your last letter) **2:** an act of giving particular attention: CONSIDERATION **3a.** high or special regard: ESTEEM **b:** the quality or state of being esteemed **c.** pl: expressions of respect or deference (paid his ~ s) **4:** PARTICULAR DETAIL (a good plan in some ~s)
Entry #2 ⟶	²**re-spect** *vt.* **1a:** to consider worthy of high regard: ESTEEM **b:** to refine from interfering with **2:** to have reference to: CONCERN *syn* see REGARD *ant* abuse, misuse—re-spect-er *n.*

Source: By permission. From *Merriam-Webster's Collegiate ® Dictionary,* Eleventh Edition © 2008 by Merriam-Webster, Incorporated. (www.Merriam-Webster.com) http://www.merriam-webster.com.

Activity 2.8 ▶ Word Upgrade 1: Dictionary Search

Directions: *Guess the meaning of the underlined word in each sentence. Then, use a collegiate dictionary to find its definition based on the way the word was used as a part of speech.*

1. DeAndre needed to <u>obtain</u> a letter of recommendation from his employer.

   Your guess for the word *obtain:* _____

   How is *obtain* used as a part of speech? _____

   Write the dictionary definition that best fits your guess for the word *obtain.*

   _____

2. Mary tried to <u>conceal</u> the stolen necklace by putting it in her pocket.

   Your guess for the word *conceal:* _____

   How is *conceal* used as a part of speech? _____

   Write the dictionary definition that best fits your guess for the word *conceal.*

   _____

3. Harry was able to write a <u>concise</u> summary of the entire article in five sentences.

   Your guess for the word *concise:* _____

   How is *concise* used as a part of speech? _____

Write the dictionary definition that best fits your guess for the word *concise*.

_____

4. Teresa decided to <u>fabricate</u> a story about what happened so she wouldn't get in trouble.

   Your guess for the word *fabricate*: _____

   How is *fabricate* used as a part of speech? _____

   Write the dictionary definition that best fits your guess for the word *fabricate*.

   _____

5. Cameron <u>stubbornly</u> refused to turn off the television.

   Your guess for the word *stubbornly*: _____

   How is *stubbornly* used as a part of speech? _____

   Write the dictionary definition that best fits your guess for the word, *stubbornly*.

   _____

Were you able to find the word *stubbornly* in your dictionary? Many pocket collegiate dictionaries are too small to provide all of the suffixes that refer to the part of speech in which a word can be used. A larger collegiate dictionary will be a valuable asset to your education.

WHY YOU SHOULD USE A THESAURUS

A thesaurus, such as *The New Roget's Thesaurus in Dictionary Form,* is a reference book that provides several synonyms for each word. You can use these synonyms to improve your vocabulary and to express yourself more precisely. For instance, you could say, "He is worthy of our consideration (respect)." Or you could say "He is highly regarded (respected)."

Remember, better communication is the main purpose for improving your vocabulary. As you learn new words for expressing ideas, you will have the vocabulary you need in order to communicate with a wider audience.

How to Use a Thesaurus to Upgrade Your Vocabulary

There are two steps for using a thesaurus to upgrade your vocabulary.

1. **First, think of a word that you use every day.** For instance, you may use such words as *run, very, beautiful, ugly, good,* or *bad* every day. How many synonyms can you think of for each of these words?

2. **Then, make sure you know how the word is used in a sentence.** In a the-saurus, the synonyms for a particular word are grouped by part of speech. If you know how the word is used in a sentence, you can easily find the most appropriate synonyms in a thesaurus.

How a Thesaurus Works

Replace the word *run* in each sentence below.

Sentence 1: Manny had to <u>run</u> to catch the bus on time.

Manny had to _____ to catch the bus on time.

Sentence 2: Serena had a <u>run</u> of good luck last week.

Serena had a _____ of good luck last week.

In Sentence 1, *run* is used as a verb because it tells you what Manny had to *do*. How

is *run* used in Sentence 2? Run is used as a _____ because it refers to a thing.

Now look at the synonyms listed in the thesaurus for the word *run* in Figure 2.2 below.

Figure 2.2 Thesaurus Entries for the Word *Run*

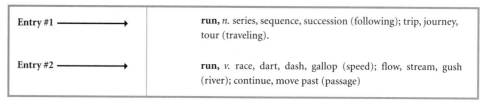

| Entry #1 ———————➤ | **run,** *n.* series, sequence, succession (following); trip, journey, tour (traveling). |
| Entry #2 ———————➤ | **run,** *v.* race, dart, dash, gallop (speed); flow, stream, gush (river); continue, move past (passage) |

There are two entries for the word, *run*. If you want to replace *run* as it is used in Sentence 1, you would look for a synonym among the list of verbs (*v*) in Entry

_____. For instance, you wouldn't say, "Manny had to *series* to catch the bus on time." Instead, you might say, "Manny had to *race* or to *dash* to catch the bus on time."

Choose a synonym from among the list of nouns (*n*) in Entry 1 to complete sentence 2 below:

Serena had a _____ of good luck last week.

The thesaurus also provides a group of synonyms for *phrases* that contain the word, *run* as in *run across, run down,* or *run on.* A thesaurus will often provide a list of antonyms at the end of a list of synonyms. For example, you will find the following antonyms for the word, *fear:* courage and protection.

If you see a word in the thesaurus that you don't know, look it up in a dictionary to further upgrade your vocabulary. Then, you can learn how its meaning compares to the other synonyms listed for that word.

Use new words as often as possible. The more you use a new word, the faster it will become part of your working vocabulary.

Memory Check 8 How much do you remember?

1. What is a thesaurus? _____

   _____

2. What are two steps for using a thesaurus to upgrade your vocabulary?

   a. _____

   b. _____

3. How can you upgrade your vocabulary further by using a thesaurus?

   _____

Activity 2.9 ▶ Word Upgrade 2: Thesaurus Search

Directions: *Think of a word that will replace the italicized word in each sentence. Indicate the part of speech for the word. Then, use your thesaurus to find a synonym to replace the italicized word.*

Example

The girl was *beautiful*. (Replace the underlined word in the sentence.)

Part of speech for the word *beautiful*: *adjective* (it *describes* the girl)

A thesaurus synonym for the word *beautiful*: *exquisite*

The girl was exquisite. (Use the new synonym to complete the sentence.)

1. Jonathan was *very* upset when he found the mistake in his order.

   Part of speech for the word *very*: _____

   A thesaurus synonym for the word *very*: _____

   Jonathan was _____ upset when he found the mistake in his order.

2. The book was easy to *understand.*

   Part of speech for the word *understand:* _____

   A thesaurus synonym for the word *understand:* _____

   The book was easy to _____

3. That dress is *ugly.*

   Part of speech for the word *ugly:* _____

   A thesaurus synonym for the word *ugly:* _____

   That dress is _____

4. The new mother was filled with *worry* when her son developed a fever.

   Part of speech for the word *worry:* _____

   A thesaurus synonym for the word *worry:* _____

   The new mother was filled with _____ when her son developed a fever.

5. His *fancy* jacket was studded with diamonds.

   Part of speech for the word *fancy:* _____

   A thesaurus synonym for the word *fancy:* _____

   His _____ jacket was studded with diamonds.

Activity 2.10 ▶ Word Upgrade 3: Thesaurus Search

Directions: *Using your thesaurus, find two synonyms for each of the underlined words in the sentences below. Then, choose one of the synonyms to fill in the space provided to complete the sentence.*

Example
Sonia was really <u>tired</u> after working at the store all day without a break.

Write two synonyms for the word *tired:* <u>exhausted, fatigued</u>

Sonia was really <u>exhausted</u> after working at the store all day without a break.

1. I plan to <u>study</u> the document.

   Write two synonyms for the word *study:* _____

   I plan to _____ the document.

2. Devon understood the <u>topic</u> immediately.

   Write two synonyms for the word *topic*: _____

   Devon understood the _____ immediately.

3. Janet tried to <u>hide</u> the money under her bed.

   Write two synonyms for the word *hide*: _____

   Janet tried to _____ the money under her bed.

4. It is a good idea to present a <u>brief</u> list of your accomplishments at an interview.

   Write two synonyms for the word *brief*: _____

   It is a good idea to present a _____ list of your accomplishments at an interview.

5. The detective knew that the criminal's story was a complete <u>lie</u>.

   Write two synonyms for the word *lie*: _____

   The detective knew that the criminal's story was a complete _____.

What is actually happening when you communicate? Usually, you have a picture in your mind. As you communicate, you are trying to send that picture to the mind of someone else, so they will see the same image. Vocabulary words are the colors you use to paint the picture you want to convey. The better your vocabulary, the more colors you will have to create a clear picture for the other person.

? Test Yourself Review Quiz

Chapter Review Questions

1. What is the main purpose for improving your vocabulary? _____

2. What are the three basic word parts?

   _____

3. To apply the Word Wise strategy you should:

   a. _____

   b. _____

   _____

4. What are two ways to use a dictionary to upgrade your vocabulary?

   a. _____

   b. _____

5. What are two steps for using a thesaurus to upgrade your vocabulary?

   a. _____

   b. _____

6. How many word part meanings can you recall without looking?

Prefixes	**Roots**	**Suffixes**
re: _____	*port: to* _____	*er, or:* _____
pre: _____	*spec/spect: to* ____	*able:* _____
de: _____	*duc/duct: to* ____	*ion:* _____
ex: _____	*miss/mit: to* ____	*y:* _____
trans: _____	*gam: to* _____	
con: _____	*tain: to* _____	
mono: _____		
poly: _____		

Application Questions

1. *Exportable* means _____ to _____ goods _____ to another location.
                  (able)   (port)   (ex)

2. *Retain* means to _____ _____ or to delay.
             (tain)   (re)

3. To *transmit* a virus means you have _____ it _____ to someone else.
                          (mit)   (trans)

4. To *contain* means to _____ _____ in one place.
             (tain) (con)

5. To *deduct* means to _____ _____.
            (duct) (de)

Identify the part of speech of the underlined word in each of the following sentences:

6. He was <u>extremely</u> upset to learn about the accident. *Part of speech:* _____

7. That is a hid**eous** pair of shoes. *Part of speech:* _____

8. Larry ran from the burning <u>building</u>. *Part of speech:* _____

9. You were <u>snoring</u> all night long. *Part of speech:* _____

10. Write a sentence that contains a noun, a verb, an adjective, and adverb. Then, identify each part of speech in your sentence.

    _____

    _____

Summarization Activity

Directions: *Complete the summary below, using the prompts provided. The first section has been completed for you.*

First Heading *WHY YOU NEED A GOOD VOCABULARY*

What information is most important?

There are two areas in which a good vocabulary is essential to success. A good vocabulary is

essential in college and in the business world. Better communication is the main purpose for

improving your vocabulary.

Second Heading *BASIC WORD PARTS*

What information is most important? **Prompt:** _____
form the basic parts of a word.

Third Heading *WORD WISE: A STRATEGY FOR DECODING*
UNFAMILIAR WORDS

What information is most important? **Prompt:** There are two steps to apply the Word

Wise Strategy. *First,* _____

_____.

Fourth Heading *WORD UPGRADE*

What information is most important? **Prompt:** There are two important _____
that you can use to upgrade your vocabulary. One is a dictionary and the other

resource is _____.

Fifth Heading _WHY YOU SHOULD USE A DICTIONARY_

What information is most important? **Prompt:** There are two things you should do before you look up a new word in a dictionary that will upgrade your vocabulary.

First, _____

_____

Sixth Heading _WHY YOU SHOULD USE A THESAURUS_

Prompt: There are two steps for using a thesaurus to upgrade your vocabulary. _First,_

_____

　　　Combine the information you wrote above into a paragraph to summarize what you have learned in this chapter.

Reflection Activity

How am I am going to apply what I have learned in this chapter?

Directions: _Write a paragraph about the two or three things you learned about improving your vocabulary that were most helpful to you and how you plan to use what you have learned._

_____

_____

_____

_____

_____

_____

_____

"BE SPECIFIC" FROM *WRITING DOWN THE BONES*
Natalie Goldberg

Accessing Prior Knowledge

Questions for Discussion

1. Are you offended when someone addresses you incorrectly or by the wrong name? Why? Or why not?

2. How would knowing the specific names of things improve the way you experience the world around you?

3. How would knowing the specific names of things improve your reading and writing skills?

Preview and Predict

Directions: *Look at the title of the selection. Think about what you already know about the subject. Then, write a couple of predictions about what you are going to read. For instance, what do you think the author will say about being specific?*

1. _____

2. _____

Word Search and Discovery

Directions: *Skim through the selection to find the two words below. Underline both words in the selection. Then, use a dictionary to write their definitions in the spaces provided. As you read and encounter these words, see if the definitions you wrote fit the way each word is used in the selection.*

blur (*vt*): _____

dignity (*n*): _____

Also, underline at least one new word as you read the selection and write your guess as to its meaning in the right margin of the text.

"BE SPECIFIC" FROM *WRITING DOWN THE BONES*
Natalie Goldberg

1   Be specific. Don't say "fruit." Tell what kind of fruit—"It is a pomegranate." Give things the dignity of their names. Just as with human beings, it is rude to say, "Hey, girl, get in line." That "girl" has a name. (As a matter of fact, if she's at least twenty years old, she's a woman, not a "girl" at all.) Things, too, have names. It is much better to say "the geranium in the window" than "the flower in the window." "Geranium"—that one word gives us a much more specific picture. It penetrates more deeply into the beingness of that flower. It immediately gives us the scene by the window—red petals, green circular leaves, all straining toward sunlight.

2   About ten years ago I decided I had to learn the names of plants and flowers in my environment. I bought a book on them and walked down the tree-lined streets of Boulder, examining leaf, bark, and seed, trying to match them up with their descriptions and names in the book. Maple, elm, oak, locust. I usually tried to cheat by asking people working in their yards the names of the flowers and trees growing there. I was amazed how few people had any idea of the names of the live beings inhabiting their little plot of land.

3   When we know the name of something, it brings us closer to the ground. It takes the blur out of our mind; it connects us to the earth. If I walk down the street and see "dogwood," "forsythia," I feel more friendly toward the environment. I am noticing what is around me and can name it. It makes me more awake.

4   If you read the poems of William Carlos Williams, you will see how specific he is about plants, trees, flowers—chicory, daisy, locust, poplar, quince, primrose, black-eyed Susan, lilacs—each has its own integrity. Williams says, "Write what's in front of your nose." It's good for us to know what is in front of our nose. Not just "daisy," but how the flower is in the season we are looking at it—"The dayseye hugging the earth/in August . . . brownedged,/green and pointed scales/armor his yellow." Continue to hone your awareness: to the name, to the month, to the day, and finally to the moment.

5   Williams also says: "No idea, but in things." Study what is "in front of your nose." By saying "geranium" instead of "flower," you are penetrating more deeply into the present and being there. The closer we can get to what's in front of our nose, the more *it* can teach us everything. "To see the World in a Grain of Sand, and a heaven in a Wild Flower . . ."

6   In writing groups and classes too, it is good to quickly learn the names of all the other group members. It helps to ground you in the group and make you more attentive to each other's work.

7   Learn the names of everything: birds, cheese, tractors, cars, buildings. A writer is all at once everything—an architect, French cook, farmer—and at the same time, a writer is none of these things.

The Write Connection

Directions: *Write a paragraph about three things you learned or that you think are most important in the reading selection.*

_____

_____

_____

_____

_____

Comprehension Check

Directions: *See how many questions you can answer without referring to the selection. Then, review the selection to write more complete responses.*

1. What did the author decide to learn?

   _____

   _____

   _____

2. What was surprising to the author about the people in her neighborhood?

   _____

   _____

   _____

3. According to the author, what happens when you know the name of something?

   _____

   _____

   _____

4. What example by poet William Carlos Williams is used to illustrate being specific?

   _____

   _____

   _____

5. What are the four specific qualities the author lists that she believes will sharpen your awareness of what is "in front of your nose"?

_____

_____

_____

6. Why does the author believe that you should study what is "in front of your nose"?

_____

_____

_____

_____ 7. According to the author, why is it a good idea to learn the names of other group members in your class?

    a. to find a partner for future study sessions in the course
    b. to improve your social life by learning personal information
    c. to ground you in the group and to build interest in the work of the other members
    d. to make a good impression on the instructor

Critical Thinking Check

1. What does the author mean when she says, "Give things the dignity of their names"?

_____

_____

_____

_____ 2. Which of the following conclusions can be drawn from the information contained in the selection?

    a. It is disrespectful to call a young girl by her name in a public setting.
    b. Many people are unaware of the names of the plants in their environment.
    c. You can improve your academic performance by knowing the names of other students in each class.
    d. William Carlos Williams is the author's favorite poet.

3. Do you agree with the author? Why or why not?

_____

_____

_____

Vocabulary Check

Directions: *See if any of the words you underlined in the selection are among the list of words below. If not, write your words in the spaces provided. Guess the meaning of the words from the way they were used in the selection. Then, look up the definition of each word in the dictionary to see if you were right.*

armor (*n*): Your guess: _____

    Dictionary Definition: _____

hone (*vb*): Your guess: _____

    Dictionary Definition: _____

Your word: _____ Your guess: _____

    Dictionary Definition: _____

Your word: _____ Your guess: _____

    Dictionary Definition: _____

"ENGLISH IS A CRAZY LANGUAGE," FROM *CRAZY ENGLISH: THE ULTIMATE JOY RIDE THROUGH OUR LANGUAGE*
Richard Lederer

Accessing Prior Knowledge

Questions for Discussion

1. What makes a joke funny to you?

2. Do you think that English is more difficult to learn than other languages? Why? Or why not?

3. Can you think of an example that illustrates how English is a crazy language?

Preview and Predict

Directions: *Look at the title of the selection. Think about what you already know about the subject. Then, write a couple of predictions about what you are going to read. For instance, why is English a crazy language?*

1. _____

2. _____

Word Search and Discovery

Directions: *Skim through the selection to find the two words below. Underline both words in the selection. Then, use a dictionary to write their definitions in the space provided. As you read and encounter these words, see if the definitions you wrote fit the way each word is used in the selection.*

paradox: _____

vagaries: _____

Also, underline at least one new word as you read the selection and write your guess as to its meaning in the right margin of the text.

ENGLISH IS A CRAZY LANGUAGE
Richard Lederer

1   English is the most widely spoken language in the history of our planet, used in some way by at least one out of every seven human beings around the globe. Half of the world's books are written in English, and the majority of international telephone calls are made in English. Sixty percent of the world's radio programs are beamed in English, and more than seventy percent of international mail is written and addressed in English. Eighty percent of all computer texts, including all web sites, are stored in English.

2   English has acquired the largest vocabulary of all the world's languages, perhaps as many as two million words, and has generated one of the noblest bodies of literature in the annals of the human race. Nonetheless, it is now time to face the fact that English is a crazy language—the most loopy and wiggy of all tongues.

3   In what other language do people drive in a parkway and park in a driveway?

4   In what other language do people play at a recital and recite at a play?

5   Why does night fall but never break and day break but never fall?

6   Why is it that when we transport something by car, it's called *a shipment,* but when we transport something by ship, it's called *cargo?*

7   Why do we pack suits in a garment bag and garments in a suitcase?

8   Why do privates eat in the general mess and generals eat in the private mess?

9   Why do we call it *newsprint* when it contains no printing but when we put print on it, we call it a *newspaper?*

10   Why does a man get a *her*nia and a woman a *hys*terectomy?

11   Why—in our crazy language—can your nose run and your feet smell?

12   Language is like the air we breathe. It's invisible, inescapable, indispensable, and we take it for granted. But, when we take the time to step back and listen to the sounds that escape from the holes in people's faces and to explore the paradoxes and vagaries of English, we find that hot dogs can be cold, darkrooms can be lit, homework can be done in school, nightmares can take place in broad daylight while morning sickness and day-dreaming can take place at night, tomboys are girls and midwives can be men, hours—especially happy hours and rush hours—often last longer than sixty minutes, quicksand works *very* slowly, boxing rings are square, silverware and glasses can be made of plastic and tablecloths of paper, most telephones are dialed by being punched (or pushed?), and most bathrooms don't have any baths in them. In fact, a dog can go to the bathroom under a tree—no bath, no room; it's still going to the bathroom. And doesn't it seem a little bizarre that we go to the bathroom in order to go to the bathroom?

13   English is crazy.

14   If adults commit adultery, do infants commit infantry? If olive oil is made from olives, what do they make baby oil from? If a vegetarian eats vegetables, what does a humanitarian consume? If *pro* and *con* are opposites, is *congress* the opposite of *progress*?

15   If the truth be told, all languages are a little crazy. As Walt Whitman might proclaim, they contradict themselves. That's because language is invented, not discovered, by boys and girls and men and women, not computers. As such, language reflects the creative and fearful asymmetry of the human race, which, of course isn't really a race at all.

16   That's why we wear a pair of pants but, except on very cold days, not a pair of shirts. That's why men wear a bathing suit and bathing trunks at the same time. That's why *brassiere* is singular but *panties* is plural. That's why there's a team in Toronto called the *Maple Leafs* and another in Minnesota called the *Timber-wolves*.

17   Still, you have to marvel at the unique lunacy of the English language, in which you can turn a light on and you can turn a light off and you can turn a light out, but you can't turn a light in; in which the sun comes up and goes down, but prices go up and come down—a gloriously wiggy tongue in which your house can simultaneously burn up and burn down and your car can slow up and slow down, in which you fill in a form by filling out a form, in which your alarm clock goes off by going on, in which you are inoculated for measles by being inoculated against measles, in which you add up a column of figures by adding them down, and in which you first chop a tree down—and then you chop it up.

The Write Connection

Directions: *Write a paragraph about three things you learned or that you think are most important in the reading selection.*

_____

_____

_____

_____

_____

_____

_____

Comprehension Check

Directions: *See how many questions you can answer without referring to the selection. Then, review the selection to write more complete responses.*

1. What is the most widely spoken language in the history of the planet? _____

2. How many of the world's books are written in English? _____

3. What percentage of all computer texts and web sites are stored in English?

   _____

_____ 4. What are the meanings of the words *loopy* and *wiggy* as they are used in paragraph 2?

   a. acceptable   b. common   c. crazy   d. disrespectful

5. What are two examples that the author gives to illustrate the most "loopy and wiggy of all tongues"? _____

   _____

_____ 6. What does Lederer say that we take for granted?

   a. the people in our lives   c. the air we breathe
   b. language   d. listening

7. What are two examples that Lederer gives to illustrate the "paradoxes and vagaries of the English language"? _____

   _____

8. What are two examples that Lederer gives to illustrate the "unique lunacy of the English language"? _____

   _____

Critical Thinking Check

_____ 1. Which of the following statements from the selection supports the author's contention that all languages are a little crazy?

   a. Half of the world's books are written in English.
   b. Language is invented . . . by boys and girls and men and women.
   c. People often take language for granted.
   d. English has acquired the largest vocabulary of all the world's languages.

_____ 2. The author has written the selection for the purpose of

    a. entertaining the reader with a humorous look at the various ways in which certain words and phrases can be interpreted differently in the English language.

    b. discussing the origins of words that are most commonly misunderstood.

    c. exploring the most common mistakes in the English language.

    d. persuading the reader to use context clues to find the meaning of confusing words and phrases in the English language.

_____ 3. Which of the following statements supports the author's contention that English is the most widely spoken language in the history of our planet?

    a. Language is like the air we breathe.

    b. People often take language for granted.

    c. Half of the world's books are written in English.

    d. English is the most loopy and wiggy of all tongues.

Vocabulary Check

Directions: *See if any of the words you underlined in the selection are among the list of words below. If not, write your words in the spaces provided. Guess the meaning of the words from the way they were used in the selection. Then, look up the definitions of each word in the dictionary to see if you were right.*

indispensable (*adj*): Your guess: _____

    Dictionary Definition: _____

infantry (*n*): Your guess: _____

    Dictionary Definition: _____

inoculate (*vb*): Your guess: _____

    Dictionary Definition: _____

    _____

Your word: _____ Your guess: _____

    Dictionary Definition: _____

Your word: _____ Your guess: _____

    Dictionary Definition: _____

3 Words in Context

By words the mind is winged

– Aristophanes

▲ **You can use words to paint an accurate picture of the message you want to convey.**

Preview and Predict ▶ What do you know so far?

How many of the following questions can you answer before you read the chapter?

• How do you figure out the meaning of a new word when you are reading?

_____

• What do you expect to learn about words in context?

_____

- How can playing word games increase your vocabulary?

_____

- Think of one way in which the picture relates to this chapter's objectives.

_____

Now, as you read the chapter, look for the answers to see if you were right.

CONTEXT CLUES

Some people skip over sentences that contain new words. Don't let new words get in the way of your understanding and your successful future. When you take the time to see what a sentence is about, you can often *guess* the meaning of a new word.

Context clues are the hints in a text that you can use to find the meaning of new words. There are five common types of context clues: definition, synonym, antonym, example/illustration, and description. Each type of context clue can be identified by signals. These signals can take the form of words, phrases, or punctuation. The signals for each type of context clue can show you where to find the meaning of a new word in written material. As you read about each type of context clue, look at the way that signals are used to help you figure out the meaning of new words.

Definition Clues

Definition clues are often used by textbook authors who want to provide a formal dictionary definition of a new word or an important term *immediately* after it is introduced in a sentence. Textbook authors also emphasize a new word or important term by using **boldfaced** or *italic* lettering either preceded or followed by a formal dictionary definition.

Common Signals	Example Definitions
refers to	**Xenophobia** *refers to* the fear of . . .
or	. . . because he was the **proprietor** *or* owner.
can be defined as	**Schizophrenia** *can be defined as* . . .
means	. . . involves **metacognition** which *means* to . . .
is	A **plutocracy** *is* a government controlled by the wealthy . . .

Definitions can also follow punctuation marks, such as a dash (–) or a comma.

Agoraphobia—the fear of crowded places—is a common symptom of paranoia.

What is agoraphobia? It is the _____.

The definition of agoraphobia is provided between the dashes (–) in the sentence.

Hydrocortisone, a steroid hormone, is used in the treatment of rheumatism.

What is hydrocortisone? It is _____.

The definition of hydrocortisone is found between the commas in the sentence.

Synonym Clues

Syn means "together," "similar," or "the same," and *onym* means "word" or "name." A **synonym** clue works by providing a word or phrase that has a meaning similar to that of the unfamiliar word in a sentence.

Common Signals	Example Synonyms
or	Darien saw the **apparition** *or* <u>ghost</u> of a young girl.
also called	The <u>share</u>, which is *also called* the **dividend** . . .
in other words	John's **compelling** arguments convinced everyone in the room. *In other words*, his arguments were very <u>forceful</u>.

Synonyms may also be found in a sentence that precedes or follows the sentence in which a new word appears.

By wearing a bit of make-up every day, Carrie was able to enhance her appearance. Her attitude also *improved*.

To enhance means to _____.

A synonym for the meaning of the word *enhance* is found in the next sentence. *Improved* is a synonym for the word *enhance*.

Antonym Clues

Antonym clues help you to figure out a new word by providing its *opposite* meaning. *Ant(i)* means "opposite" or "against," and *onym* means "word" or "name."

Common Signals	Example Antonyms
but or yet	Gary is an **atheist.** *Yet,* he talks to people who believe in God. (An atheist is a person who does *not* believe in God.)
while, whereas, or although	*While* Jim's ideas were easily understood, Kim's ideas were quite **obscure.** (Obscure ideas are *not* easily understood.)
however	Amber is outgoing. Jason, *however,* is an **introvert.** (An introvert is a person who is *not* outgoing.)
on the other hand	Kathy was **ravenous** because she had not eaten all day. Amy, *on the other hand,* was not very hungry and left the table. (A person who is ravenous *is* very hungry.)

Antonyms may be found in a sentence that precedes or follows the sentence in which a new word appears.

> Test scores were highest among students who attend schools in **affluent** neighborhoods. Students from schools located in poverty-stricken neighborhoods, *on the other hand,* scored in the lower percentiles.

An affluent neighborhood can be described as _____. The opposite meaning of *affluent* is found in the next sentence. *Poverty* is an antonym of the word *affluent. Affluent* means "rich" or "wealthy."

Example/Illustration Clues

Example/Illustration clues work by providing an *example* of a new word so you can understand its meaning. Some authors will use a list of examples that have something *in common* with the meaning of a new word.

Common Signals	Examples/Illustrations
such as	Lin gathered **empirical** evidence *such as* statistics and historical records to support her theory. (Statistics and historical records provide data which can be proven.)

for example (or *for instance*)	Arlen tried to **impugn** Audrey's reputation at work. *For example*, he sent an unfavorable letter to Audrey's boss and he complained to other managers about her "lousy" performance. (Unfavorable letters and comments to someone's boss or other managers might be used to *attack* a person's reputation.)
include (or *including*)	The use of **amphetamines**, which *include* caffeine and cocaine, became widespread among the overworked night crew.

Example 1

Sharon said that her boyfriend is very **frugal**. *For instance*, he offered to pick her up from the airport for a ten-dollar fee; he bought one hot dog at the basketball game and cut it in half for both of them to share; and whenever they went out to dinner, he insisted that she pay half. What does *frugal* mean? It

means _____. The meaning of *frugal* is found in the examples, which have one thing in common. They describe someone who is cheap or careful with money.

Example 2

Deleterious behaviors *such as* drinking, smoking, and unprotected sex can lead to an early death. What do these behaviors have in common? They are all

_____ behaviors. So, *deleterious* describes something that is harmful or has a very bad effect.

Description Clues

Description clues provide such a clear picture of a word that its meaning is obvious and no signal words or phrases are necessary. How do you find the meaning of a new word if there are no signals? If you can see what is being described in the sentence, you will understand the meaning of the new word. Here are some examples.

Example 1

Sue's _____ activities landed her in jail without parole.

What type of activities would land someone in jail without parole?

_____ Here is the rest of the sentence: Sue's **nefarious**

activities landed her in jail without parole. If you see what is being described in the sentence, you will know that *nefarious* refers to activities that are *criminal*. So, *nefarious* means "criminal."

Example 2

The _____ employee did absolutely nothing and was eventually fired. What kind of employee does absolutely nothing? A *lazy* employee. Here is the rest of the sentence: The **indolent** employee did absolutely nothing and was eventually fired. You can guess that the employee was fired

because he or she was *lazy*. So, *indolent* means _____.

Memory Check 1   How much do you remember?

1. What are context clues? _____

_____

_____ 2. Which *type* of context clue is used to help you find the meaning of the word *democracy* in the following sentence?

Democracy *means* government by the people.

a. description   c. example/illustration
b. antonym   d. definition

3. What is a synonym? _____

_____

4. How can an antonym clue help you to find the meaning of an unfamiliar

word? _____

5. List three signals that an author may use to indicate an example clue is being

provided. _____

6. What can you do to find the meaning of a word when there are no signals?

_____

Activity 3.1 ▶ Recognizing Context Clues

Directions: *Apply your knowledge of context clues by identifying the meanings of the new words in bold below. After you have completed the activity, look in a dictionary to see if you were right.*

1. **protocol** (pro tah call)

   Protocol, which means rules of behavior, can be important to the success of a politician.

   Protocol means: _____.

2. **inebriated** (in nee bree ated)

   From the minute Donny entered the room, I could tell that he was inebriated. For instance, he walked sideways, mumbled to himself, and smelled of alcohol.

   Inebriated means: _____.

3. **loquacious** (low kway shuss)

   My teacher is so loquacious that from the time class begins until it ends she never stops talking.

   Loquacious means: _____.

4. **fortuitous** (for two ah tuss)

   Sam always said it was a fortuitous or lucky decision to eat at the café that particular day because he met his future wife there.

   Fortuitous means: _____.

5. **ludicrous** (lew dah kris)

   Cary's ideas were so ludicrous that everyone in the meeting laughed in his face and walked out.

   Ludicrous means: _____.

6. **impudent** (im pew dent)

   Marcus tried to be polite and courteous to the police officer, but James continued to be impudent.

   Impudent means: _____.

7. **precocious** (pre koe shuss)

   Lakeisha's four-year-old son, Christian, is quite precocious. For example, he can already recite his ABC's, write his name, and read a first grade book all by himself.

   Precocious means: _____.

8. **etymology** (Et tim mall ogee)

   Etymology is the study of the structure and history of words.

   Etymology means: _____.

9. **enhance** (in hanse)

   Marie studied with a tutor three times a week in order to enhance or improve her performance in algebra.

   Enhance means: _____.

10. **tenacious** (tin nay shuss)

    Don't give up when faced with a problem. Instead, be tenacious and you will succeed.

    Tenacious means: _____.

Activity 3.2 ▶ Applying Context Clues

Directions: *Use context clues to fill in the blanks with the appropriate meaning of the underlined word in each sentence below. Don't use your dictionary.*

1. John was so <u>morose</u> after his wife died that he cried all day long.

   Morose means _____.

2. Some people believe that <u>fortuitous</u> events, such as winning the lottery and meeting that special someone by being in the right place at the right time, are the result of positive thinking.

   Fortuitous means _____.

3. From an early age, Leon was <u>precocious</u> and able to speak to adults with ease, but Sally was far behind in her verbal development.

   Precocious means _____.

4. Kelly is a very quiet person. Debra, on the other hand, is so <u>loquacious</u> that I wonder if she will ever stop talking.

   Loquacious means _____.

5. My roommate is very <u>indolent</u>. For example, she leaves dirty dishes in the sink, doesn't pick up her clothes, and never takes out the trash.

   Indolent means _____.

6. Etymology—the study of the structure and history of words—is included in Chapter Two.

   Etymology means _____.

7. Greg was a frugal man who took his girlfriend to a fast-food restaurant on her birthday to save money.

   Frugal means _____.

8. Nefarious activities, such as selling drugs, engaging in prostitution, and stealing cars can result in significant jail time.

   Nefarious means _____.

9. I was so ravenous today that I ate an entire roast chicken without stopping.

   Ravenous means _____.

10. Tuan was amenable, or agreeable, to the idea of going out to a club after the party.

    Amenable means _____.

Activity 3.3 ▸ Word Insert 1

Directions: *Use the words in the box to fill in the appropriate word in each sentence.*

> morose   fortuitous   amenable   ravenous   precocious   nefarious

1. The lost boys walked in the mountains for two days. When the boys were rescued, they were so _____ that they almost choked on their food.

2. It is often difficult to cope with the end of a relationship. Some people become very _____ or depressed for months after the break-up.

3. The homeless man found that few people were _____ to the idea of helping a stranger in need.

4. Teenagers who engage in _____ activities such as stealing are usually crying for the attention of an absent parent.

5. Making an unscheduled stop at the corner market proved to be very _____ for Dante. He bought a lottery ticket worth $2.5 million.

6. Studies show that parents who engage in reading and word play activities are more likely to develop a _____ child.

Activity 3.4 ▶ Word Insert 2

Directions: *Use the words in the box to fill in the appropriate word in each sentence.*

> ludicrous   frugal   loquacious   indolent   apparition   protocol

1. It is a good idea to know the rules of behavior or _____ when interviewing for a job.

2. If you save every penny and try to be _____, you can eliminate debt.

3. Your suggestion that I stole the money is just _____ and makes no sense.

4. Sandra was fired because she was _____, which forced other employees to complete her work.

5. Nicole decided to avoid calls from Kevin because he tended to be very _____ and she had a lot to do.

6. Demonica was afraid to clean the tables on the second floor of the restaurant where she had seen the _____ of the owner who had recently passed away.

Memory Check 2   How much do you remember?

Match the word on the left with the letter that represents its definition on the right.

1. _____ morose   a. agreeable

2. _____ frugal   b. evil, criminal

3. _____ fortuitous   c. very hungry

4. _____ amenable   d. smart, beyond average

5. _____ nefarious   e. the study of word structure and history

6. _____ precocious   f. talkative

7. _____ ravenous   g. sad

8. _____ etymology   h. proper rules

9. _____ protocol   i. ghost

10. _____ indolent   j. careful with money

11. _____ loquacious   k. lucky

12. _____ apparition   l. lazy

Words in Mind Strategy

Words in Mind is a strategy that will help you understand the meaning of a sentence so you can guess the definition of an unfamiliar word. It helps you use your knowledge of word parts and context clues to enhance your vocabulary and thinking skills.

To apply the Words in Mind Strategy you should follow these steps:

- Underline and write the new word in the right-side margin next to where it appears in the text and write your guess for the word meaning beside it.

- Break it apart and look for word parts that you already know.

- Play hide and seek by covering the new word and thinking of a replacement.

- Continue reading and keep the word in mind while you look for clues that signal its meaning.

After you learn each step in the strategy, you will be able to guess the meaning of new words very quickly as you read.

1. Underline and Write the New Word in the Right-Side Margin Next to Where It Appears in the Text

Leave a space in the margin for writing your guess as to the meaning of the word.

Example

	New Word: Your Guess
Santa Ana gave up any further effort to <u>dislodge</u> Taylor in order to meet a new and more serious American threat.	*dislodge:* _____

Doing this helps you to keep the new word in mind as you read and apply each step in the strategy. Then, when you are ready to write your guess for the meaning of the new word, it will be easier to find.

 ## 2. Break It Apart

Try to pronounce each part of the word. You can guess the meaning of a new word if it contains word parts you know. Look for prefixes or roots that provide the best clues as to its meaning. When you read the sentence again, ask yourself how the meaning of the prefix or root relates to the meaning of the sentence. What if you are still unable to guess the meaning of a new word?

3. Play Hide and Seek

First, *hide* the new word. Then, *seek* another word or synonym that will make sense in the place of the hidden word in the sentence. Asking questions about the sentence will help you figure out the meaning of the word you have hidden. For instance, what does the word *commissary* mean in the following sentence?

Max went to the *commissary* to buy groceries.

First, hide the new word.

Example

Max went to the _____ to buy groceries.

Now think of a word that will make sense in place of the hidden word in the sentence. You might ask yourself the question, "Where would Max go to buy groceries?" From this question you would probably guess that a commissary is a *store*.

	New Word: Your Guess
Max went to the **commissary** to buy groceries. He was only there for a few minutes when the alarm went off.	*commissary:* store

If you hide the new word, you will be able to fill in the most logical meaning for it by looking at the way it is used in the sentence. Play Hide and Seek to guess the meaning of the word *dislodge* in the following sentence.

Santa Ana gave up any further effort to <u>dislodge</u> Taylor in order to meet a new and more serious American threat	**New Word: Your Guess** *dislodge:* _____

 ## 4. Continue Reading

As soon as you form a good guess about the meaning of a new word, write it next to where it appears in the right margin and keep reading. Even when you are unable to form a guess right away, keep the word in mind. The meaning of the word will often become clear to you by the time you reach the end of the paragraph or passage. Then, when you have finished reading, you can look the word up in the dictionary to see if your guess was correct.

By using the Words in Mind strategy, you will learn new words by comparing your guesses to the definitions in a dictionary. Most of the time, you will find that your guesses are very similar. For instance, how does your guess for the word *dislodge* compare to the difinition found in the dictionary?

Memory Check 3   How much do you remember?

1. What are the four steps in the *Words in Mind* strategy?

   _____

   _____

   _____

   _____

2. What should you do after you hide the new word and reread the sentence?

   _____

3. What will help you to think of a synonym for the hidden word?

   _____

Activity 3.5 ▶ Applying the Words in Mind Strategy

Directions: *Write each underlined word in the margin next to where it appears in the passage and write your guess as to its meaning beside it.*

	New Word: Your Guess
Zachary Taylor, who sported the nickname Old Rough and Ready, crossed the Rio Grande into Mexico and finally met and defeated an army that Santa Ana was rushing northward, at the town of Buena Vista in February 1847. Santa Ana gave up any further effort to dislodge Taylor in order to meet a new and more serious American threat. An American army was moving by sea toward Vera Cruz, with the obvious intention of mounting an overland attack on the capital of Mexico. The Americans were commanded by General Winfield Scott—he was called Old Fuss and Feathers because he wore ornate uniforms and insisted on a strict discipline. After a siege, Scott forced Vera Cruz to surrender. Then he began a long and difficult campaign, moving across rough terrain toward Mexico City and meeting stiff and skilled resistance in battle after battle. Finally, in September 1847, he was at the fortress of Chapultapec, just south and west of the capital. The garrison consisted largely of the teenage cadets of the Mexican military academy. -From *The Pursuit of Liberty: A History of the American People.* 3rd ed. pp. 492–493. Allyn&Bacon.NY. © 1996	dislodge: _____

Dictionary Definitions: *Write the dictionary definition for each word below so you can compare it to your guess.*

overland: _____

ornate: _____

siege: _____

terrain: _____

garrison: _____

A WORD JOURNAL

MyReadingLab

Active reading
strategies:
To practice your
skills go to:
Study Plan
>Reading Skills
>Active Reading
Strategies

A word journal is an effective way to remember new words that you learn as you read. These new words can be included in a section of your reading journal, or you can keep a separate journal if you prefer. To create an effective word journal you should:

- Write the title of the selection or book that contains the new word.

- Write the sentence that contains the new word. This will help you to remember the context in which the word was used.

- Write the definition of the new word underneath the sentence.

By writing out the sentence and the definition of the word, you will store the information more easily in your long-term memory. Soon, you will find that you can more easily recall the meanings of words you have looked up when you read or hear them again.

WORD PLAY

There are many types of word games, including crossword puzzles, brain teasers, word matching games, word association games, word searches, or word scrambles, just to name a few. Word games can also include "plays" on words or puns. Many jokes are based on bloopers or mistakes. For example, here is a blooper found on a child's test paper:

> *Question:* What is the difference between unlawful and illegal?
> *Answer:* One is against the law and the other is a sick bird.

How Playing Word Games Can Increase Your Vocabulary

Playing word games is an effective way to increase your vocabulary because you are actively involved in looking for ways to use words to complete them. Word games provide a fun and easy way for you to learn and apply new words.

Although there are many places where you can find word games and activities, here are three main areas to investigate:

1. **The Internet.** Go online and type the following phrases: *word games, crossword puzzles, Scrabble®,* or *word play.* Your search engine will find numerous word game sites for you to explore. The Internet sites provided in this chapter contain a variety of word games and activities that can enhance your vocabulary.

2. **Newspapers and magazines.** Crossword puzzles can be found in almost every daily newspaper, and in many magazines including *TV Guide, People* magazine, and *The National Enquirer.*

3. **Toy stores and bookstores.** Scrabble® and Boggle® are excellent word play activities that can be played with family or friends. You will also find crossword and other word game magazines for every level of vocabulary at your local book store.

Memory Check 4 How much do you remember?

1. To create an effective word journal, you should:

    a. _____

    b. _____

       _____

    c. _____

2. Why should you write out the sentence and the definition of the word in your word journal? _____

_____

3. Why is word play an effective way to increase your vocabulary?

_____

_____

4. Where are three places that you can find word games or activities?

_____

_____

Activity 3.6 ▶ Evaluating Word Play Websites

Directions: *Explore each website below. Assign a first, second, or third prize to each site for being the most fun in terms of word games or activities. Explain your reasons for selecting the winners.*

1. http://www.english-zone.com *Best-Language Fun Pages:* Interactive: Includes grammar, punctuation, oxymorons, proverbs, and bloopers contained in advertisements, signs, insurance reports, excuses from parents and transcripts, quips, and limericks.

2. http://www.manythings.org Interesting things for ESL/EFL students: Word games, puzzles, quizzes, exercises, slang, proverbs, and much more.

3. http://www.englishclub.com English Club: Games and quizzes

First Prize: _English Zone_

Why?: _fun well organized_

Second Prize: _English Club_

Why?: _____

Third Prize: _Many things_

Why?: _Carfully and it's organized_

Here are some additional sites where you can find word play activities:

- http://owl.english.purdue.edu/ Owl Online Writing Lab: Writing résumés, research papers, and general English usage. ESL section includes vocabulary, quizzes, tests, idioms, and links to other interesting sites.

- http://www.msnbc.com/comics/default.asp?0bb=-e1 MSN Living Comics and Games. Includes political cartoons, and comics. Word games: crosswords, sports crosswords, word searches, cryptogram, hangman, and phrase invaders.
- http://signup.dictionary.com/wordoftheday Register to access the dictionary online and to learn a new word each day.
- http://www.alphadictionary.com Free online dictionary. Also contains games and articles.

Activity 3.7 ▶ Crossword Puzzle

Directions: *See how well you can apply what you have learned in this chapter by completing the following puzzle. Some of the words have been provided for you. You can also use a dictionary and a thesaurus.*

Across

3. A suffix that means "capable of."
4. A person who saves money is _____.
7. The earth can **spin** around its axis.
9. He felt he had to _____ her respect.
10. It literally means "to see again."
12. Poodle is a type of _____.
13. The prefix *con-* means "together" or "_____."
16. The prefix *mono-* means _____.
17. The meaning of the prefix *trans-*.
18. The root in the word *conductor* means "to _____."
20. America is the land of the ___; home of the brave.
22. He gave an **apple** to the teacher.
25. A synonym for *deleterious*.
28. A short word for *police officer*.
30. A synonym for *ravenous*.
31. The root in the word *portable* means "to _____."
32. A suffix that means "act of" or "state of being."
33. Dirt and water create_____.
35. If you are on a *mission*, you are in the state of being _____.

Down

1. The suffix *-y* means _____ or "full of."
2. Stealing is described as a _____ activity.
5. A synonym for "agreeable."
6. A **pretentious** person pretends to know everything.
7. The antonym of *happy*.
8. It refers to the rules of behavior.
11. The antonym of *fast*.
13. School desks are made of _____.
14. The antonym of *out*.
15. The root *spect* means "to _____ or see."
19. The root that means "to marry."
20. A synonym for *lucky*.
21. The prefix that means, "out" or "out of."
23. A very smart child is a _____ child.
24. A person who is indolent is _____.
26. The prefix in the word *polygamy* means_____.
27. The prefix *re* means _____ or "back"
29. The root of the word in 31 across.
34. The prefix that means "down" or "away."

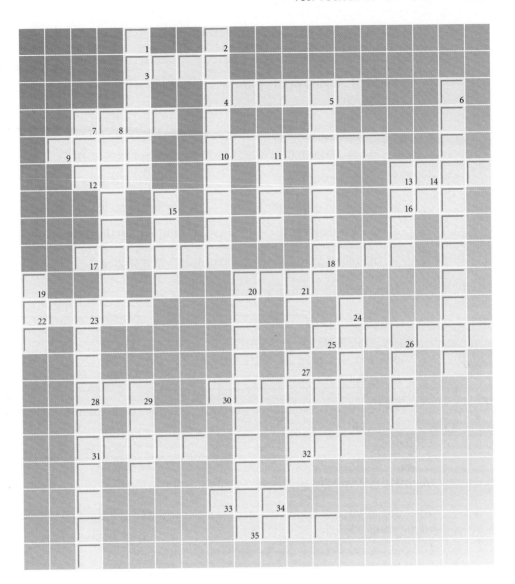

 Test Yourself Review Quiz

Chapter Review Questions

1. What is one of the best ways to increase your vocabulary?

_____

2. What are the five types of context clues?

_____

3. Match the signal word or phrase on the right with the appropriate context clue on the left.

1. _____ antonym

2. _____ synonym

3. _____ example

4. _____ description

5. _____ definition

a. no signal

b. means, refers to, or

c. comma or dashes

d. for instance, for example, such as

e. but, yet, on the other hand

4. What are the four steps of the Words in Mind strategy?

a. _____

_____

b. _____

c. _____

d. _____

5. What are two examples of word play activities that can improve your vocabulary?

_____

Application Questions

Apply the Words in Mind strategy to guess the meaning of four of the underlined words in the passage below.

	Word: Your guess
Trish had just celebrated her fortieth birthday and she looked good for her age. She was recently divorced and hadn't dated anyone since high school. So, when Frederick, who was a handsome man ten years younger than Trish, asked her to go with him to the Hip-Hop Fest downtown, she was ecstatic, at first. But, then she wondered if her age and inexperience would <u>foil</u> the relationship. Trish was nervous about her first date with Frederick.	ecstatic: _____ foil: _____

To impress Frederick, Trish decided that she would wear what she thought was appropriate hip-hop attire. She found some oversized black shorts that rode so low on her hips that they covered her knees and a long black muscle shirt.

attire: _____

When Frederick arrived, he seemed pleased and escorted her to his car, opening her door like a gentleman. Trish enjoyed learning about the artists that Frederick was excited to see at the Fest and she began to relax. She felt that they really had a good rapport, despite their age difference. Yet, Trish couldn't help but feel nervous. She couldn't keep from saying to herself, "Please don't mess up," "You can do it." "Just relax."

rapport: _____
_____

As they walked around the concession stands amid the crowd listening to the music, Trish wondered if anyone could tell that she was much older than Frederick. Everyone at the Fest seemed so young. "I look good for my age," she thought, but decided she had better check her make-up. She told Frederick that she needed to make a stop.

concession: _____
_____

"Sure," Frederick said, "but Code G is about to play." So they hurried to the rest area. Frederick sat on the bricks surrounding a fountain along with other men who were waiting for their girlfriends.

How Trish hated those repulsive portable restrooms. She held her breath and hurriedly checked her make-up in the process before she ran out of air. When she emerged, Trish noticed that some of the men who were sitting beside Frederick at the fountain were smiling and giggling at her. "See?" Trish said confidently to herself. "You still got it."

repulsive: _____
_____

That's when she looked down and noticed she had tucked the muscle shirt inside her waist-high underwear.

Use context clues to write the meaning of the italicized word in each sentence below.

1. Trish was *ecstatic* when Frederick asked her out on a date.

   If you are *ecstatic*, it means that you are: _____.

2. Trish was concerned that her age and inexperience would *foil* the relationship.

   To *foil* means to: _____.

3. Trish wanted to wear appropriate hip-hop *attire*.

   Another word for *attire* would be: _____.

4. Trish thought that she and Frederick had a good *rapport*.

   Another word for *rapport* would be: _____.

5. Trish hated the *repulsive* portable restrooms at the Festival.

   Another word for *repulsive* would be: _____.

Summarization Activity

Directions: *Complete the summary below, using the prompts provided. The first section has been completed for you.*

First Heading _CONTEXT CLUES_

What information is most important?

Prompt: There are five types of context clues. _They include synonym, definition,_

example/illustration, antonym, and description.

Second Heading _WORDS IN MIND STRATEGY_

What information is most important?

Prompt: There are four steps to apply the Words in Mind strategy. _____

_____

_____

Prompt: To create an effective word journal you should _____

_____

_____

Third Heading _WORD PLAY_

What information is most important?

Prompt: How can playing word games increase your vocabulary? _____

_____

_____

      Combine the information you wrote above into a paragraph to summarize what you have learned in this chapter.

Reflection Activity

How am I am going to apply what I have learned in this chapter?

Directions: *Write a paragraph discussing the two or three things you learned about words in context that were most helpful to you and how you plan to use what you have learned.*

_____

_____

_____

_____

_____

_____

_____

HOW TO BE A GOOD INVESTOR
Donald J. Trump

Accessing Prior Knowledge

Questions for Discussion

1. What personal quality do you think is most necessary in order to become wealthy?

2. Do you know anyone who invests in the stock market or in real estate? If so, is the person successful? Have you ever talked to him or her about the process? Why or why not?

Preview and Predict

Directions: *Look at the title of the selection. Think about what you already know about the subject. Then, write a couple of predictions about what you are going to read. For instance, what do you think you will learn from Donald Trump about being a good investor?*

1. _____

2. _____

Word Search and Discovery

Directions: *Skim through the selection to find the two words below. Underline both words in the selection. Then use a dictionary to write their definitions in the spaces provided. As you read and encounter these words, see if the definitions you wrote fit the way each word is used in the selection.*

holdings (*n*): _____

_____

misery (*n*): _____

_____

Also, underline at least one new word as you read the selection and write your guess as to its meaning in the right margin of the text.

MONEY: HOW TO BE A GOOD INVESTOR
Donald Trump

1   When you have a lot of money, it can cause misery. But I'd rather have that kind of misery than the misery without it.

2   Money may not grow from trees, but it does grow from talent, hard work, and brains. I have a talent for making money; some people don't. But part of my "talent" is my drive and my work ethic, so even if you don't have the genetic makeup to be a billionaire, you can still work hard and maybe, if you're lucky and smart, you can be a millionaire. Maybe you can even be a billionaire.

3   I won't deny that some people are luckier than others. That's a simple fact of life. But you can create luck. I remember one night, when I was billions of dollars in debt and the media that had at one point called me brilliant was now making me out to be a total dope, I had to be at a dinner party that I wanted to skip in the worst way. I just didn't feel up to it, but something inside me made me get up and go.

4   At the dinner that night, I ended up sitting next to one of many bankers. It *was* one of the luckiest nights of my life. He gave me some great advice and pointed me in a new direction. The rest is history. So when it comes to money, even if you're broke or in debt, your luck can change. You have to work hard to make that luck change, so keep reading to learn how to do just that.

5   Good investing requires financial intelligence. Billionaires are often blessed with a high financial IQ. Most of them could be considered financial geniuses. But your financial IQ is not a fixed number, and you can improve it each and every day. My financial IQ is constantly improving as I watch over my many businesses and my staff. I work hard to make sure that they remain assets, not liabilities, and you should look at your holdings in the same way.

6   Having a degree from Wharton and a lifetime of investing experience, I will explain a few things for those who haven't been blessed with such advantages. Finance and business are a complex mix of components that embrace a large spectrum of enterprises. I think of it the way an artist thinks about technique. You need to have a basic technique before you can apply it to different media such as drawing, or sculpture, or painting. As a builder, I use my financial technique as a basic blueprint for increasingly complex transactions. Over the years, those blueprints have become larger and more complicated—and also more profitable.

7   Good investors are good students. It's as simple as that I spend hours each day reading the financial media (*The Wall Street Journal, Forbes, Business Week, Fortune, The New York Times, Financial Times*). I also read a lot of books and other magazines; you never know where your next great idea is going to come from. You should be on top of all the news within your industry and, beyond that, all local, national,

and global news as well. Ignorance in current affairs can go a long way toward destroying your credibility—and your bank account.

8   People always ask what I like to watch on television. Typically, I only watch television that I know will improve my financial IQ. My one indulgence when it comes to television is sports. For news and financial advice, of course, I watch *The Apprentice*, but I also watch the CNBC business report, Larry King, Bill O'Reilly, the *Today* show, and Fox Cable. Whatever you watch or read, study something every day. It's essential that you keep your mind open and alert.

9   And if you're young, don't think you don't have the experience to come up with good investment ideas. I had some of my best ideas when I was twenty-two years old. When you're that young, you don't censor yourself as much, and ideas that you may have will not be clouded by your business experiences. Genius is the ability to assemble in new forms what already exists, and sometimes the youngest people are the greatest geniuses.

10   If you're still in school, pay attention. Education is a money machine. If you're long gone from school, consider enrolling in a financial education class. Some financial courses can be dry, but I always made them more interesting by applying the principles immediately to some project, either imaginary or real, that I could work through in my mind. That way, I was already getting real life experience while I was still in school.

The Write Connection

Directions: *Write a paragraph about three things you learned or that you think are most important in the reading selection.*

_____

_____

_____

_____

_____

Comprehension Check

Directions: *See how many questions you can answer without referring to the selection. Then, review the selection to write more complete responses.*

1. According to Donald Trump, money grows from _____

_____.

_____ 2. What is main point of paragraph 2?

    a. Luck and brains are not as essential as talent to becoming a millionaire or a billionaire.
    b. It is important to have a substantial inheritance for investments.
    c. Hard work is the most essential requirement for becoming a billionaire.
    d. Brains, luck, and hard work are essential to becoming a millionaire or a billionaire.

_____ 3. At one time, the media tried to make Donald Trump look like a "total dope," probably because he was

    a. the richest man in America.   c. at a political dinner party.
    b. brilliant.   d. billions of dollars in debt.

_____ 4. The dinner party was a fortuitous event for Mr. Trump because he was

    a. given a lifetime achievement award.   c. seated next to his future wife.
    b. given great advice by a banker.   d. called "brilliant" by the media.

5. According to Donald Trump, even if you are broke or in debt, you can change your luck by _____.

6. How does Mr. Trump improve his financial IQ as he watches over his staff and businesses? _____

7. Donald Trump compares the way he thinks about his approach to finance and business to the way that _____.

8. What can go a long way toward destroying your credibility and your bank account? _____

9. Why does Donald Trump suggest that you study something every day?

_____

10. What does Mr. Trump refer to as "a money machine"? _____

Critical Thinking Check

_____ 1. Which of the following conclusions can be drawn from the selection?

    a. You need to have money to make money.
    b. Political rallies provide opportunities to meet influential people.
    c. It is possible to achieve financial success after being billions of dollars in debt.
    d. Most millionaires and billionaires are experienced bankers.

_____ 2. Which of the following statements does NOT support the author's contention that education is a money machine?

    a. It is essential to keep your mind open and alert.
    b. Take a financial education class and apply the principles to some project.
    c. Good investors are good students.
    d. Censor yourself as much as possible.

3. Give an example of the kind of employee who would be a liability to a company owned by Donald Trump? _____

4. Think of another title for the selection. _____

_____

Vocabulary Check

Directions: *See if any of the words you underlined in the selection are among the list of words below. If not, write your words in the spaces provided. Guess the meaning of the words from the way they were used in the selection. Then, look up the definition of each word in the dictionary to see if you were right.*

blueprint (*n*): Your guess: _____

    Dictionary Definition: _____

censor (*vb*): Your guess: _____

    Dictionary Definition: _____

enterprise (*n*): Your guess: _____

    Dictionary Definition: _____

Your word: _____ Your guess: _____

    Dictionary Definition: _____

Your word: _____ Your guess: _____

    Dictionary Definition: _____

♟♟♟ Skills In Practice ▶ Reading Selection 2

THE MORALS OF THE PRINCE
Niccolo Machiavelli

Accessing Prior Knowledge

Questions for Discussion

1. How are some political leaders and CEOs able to convince so many people to believe the promises that they don't intend to keep?

2. Do political and business leaders need to be good liars in order to be successful? Why or why not?

Preview and Predict

Directions: *Look at the title of the selection. Think about what you already know about the subject. Then, write a couple of predictions about what you are going to read. For instance, what do you think the author will discuss about the morals of a prince?*

1. _____

2. _____

Word Search and Discovery

Directions: *Skim through the selection to find the two words below. Underline both words in the selection. Then, use a dictionary to write their definitions in the spaces provided. As you read and encounter these words, see if the definitions you wrote fit the way the word is used in the selection.*

breach (*n*): _____

centaur (*n*): _____

craftiness (*n*): _____

Also, underline at least one new word as you read the selection and write your guess as to its meaning in the right margin of the text.

THE MORALS OF THE PRINCE

Niccolo Machiavelli

1   How praiseworthy it is for a prince to keep his word and live with integrity rather than by craftiness, everyone understands; yet we see from recent experience that those princes have accomplished most who paid little heed to keeping their promises, but who knew how craftily to manipulate the minds of men. In the end, they won out over those who tried to act honestly.

2   You should consider then, that there are two ways of fighting, one with laws and the other with force. The first is properly a human method, the second belongs to beasts. But as the first method does not always suffice, you sometimes have to turn to the second. Thus a prince must know how to make good use of both the beast and the man. Ancient writers made subtle note of this fact when they wrote that Achilles and many other princes of antiquity were sent to be reared by Chiron* the centaur, who trained them in his discipline. Having a teacher who is half man and half beast can only mean that a prince must know how to use both these two natures, and that one without the other has no lasting effect.

3   Since a prince must know how to use the character of beasts, he should pick for imitation the fox and the lion. As the lion cannot protect himself from traps, and the fox cannot defend himself from wolves, you have to be a fox in order to be wary of traps, and a lion to overawe the wolves. Those who try to live by the lion alone are badly mistaken. Thus a prudent prince cannot and should not keep his word when to do so would go against his interest, or when the reason that made him pledge it no longer apply. Doubtless if all men were good, this rule would be bad; but since they are a sad lot, and keep no faith with you, you in your turn are under no obligation to keep it with them.

4   Besides, a prince will never lack for legitimate excuses to explain away his breaches of faith. Modern history will furnish innumerable examples of his behavior, showing how many treaties and promises have been made null and void by the faithlessness of princes, and how the man succeeded best who knew best how to play the fox. But it is a necessary part of his nature that you must conceal it carefully; you must be a great liar and hypocrite. Men are so simple of mind, and so much dominated by their immediate needs, that a deceitful man will always find plenty who are ready to be deceived. One of many recent examples calls for mention. Alexander VI never did anything else, never had another thought, except to deceive men, and he

---

*According to Greek Mythology, Chiron taught the arts of war and peace, such as hunting and medicine.

always found fresh material to work on. Never was there a man more convincing in his assertions, who sealed his promises with more solemn oaths, and who observed them less. Yet his deceptions were always successful, because he knew exactly how to manage this sort of business.

5   In actual fact, a prince may not have all the admirable qualities we listed, but it is very necessary that he should seem to have them. Indeed, I will venture to say that when you have them and exercise them all the time, they are harmful to you; when you just seem to have them, they are useful. It is good to appear merciful, truthful, humane, sincere, and religious; it is good to be so in reality. But you must keep your mind so disposed that, in case of need, you can turn to the exact contrary. This has to be understood: a prince, and especially a new prince, cannot possibly exercise all those virtues for which men are called "good." To preserve the state, he often has to do things against his word, against charity, against humanity, against religion. Thus he has to have a mind ready to shift as the winds of fortune and the varying circumstances of life may dictate. And as I said above, he should not depart from the good if he can hold to it, but he should be ready to enter on evil if he has to.

The Write Connection

Directions: *Write a paragraph about three things you learned or that you think are most important in the reading selection.*

_____

_____

_____

_____

_____

Comprehension Check

Directions: *See how many questions you can answer without referring to the selection. Then, review the selection to write more complete responses.*

_____   1. Select the best synonym for the word *suffice* as it is used in paragraph 2.

      a. chill   c. harm

      b. work   d. suffer

    2. According to Machiavelli, what are the two ways of fighting?

_____

3. According to Machiavelli, a prince must know how to use the methods of both man and _____.

_____ 4. Ancient writers note that Chiron trained many princes in what discipline?

    a. the language arts
    b. the arts of kindness and virtue
    c. the arts of myth and legend
    d. the arts of war and peace

_____ 5. According to Machiavelli, those who live by the lion are badly mistaken because

    a. the lion cannot defend himself from wolves.
    b. the lion needs the wolf for protection against traps.
    c. the lion cannot protect himself against traps.
    d. the lion cannot defend himself against foxes.

_____ 6. Select the best synonym for the word *prudent* as it is used in paragraph 3.

    a. careful
    b. truthful
    c. wealthy
    d. doubtful

7. According to Machiavelli, a prudent prince should not keep his word when doing so would _____

_____

8. Give one example from the selection which illustrates Machiavelli's opinion of men. _____

9. Who does Machiavelli cite as an example of a "great liar and hypocrite?"

_____

_____ 10. Select the best synonym for the word *disposed* as it is used in paragraph 5.

    a. removed
    b. willing
    c. distracted
    d. rejected

Critical Thinking Check

_____ 1. Which of the following can you infer about Machiavelli?

    a. He believes in the goodness of all human beings.
    b. He believes that human beings are easily fooled.
    c. He believes that a strong leader must create new laws for simple men.
    d. He believes that a prince should try to have the characteristics of a lion.

_____ 2. Which of the following statements best represents the main idea of the selection?

   a. A successful prince knows how to keep promises without making a fool of himself or his people.
   b. A thoughtful prince understands the importance of maintaining mercifulness, truthfulness, and sincerity while ruling the people with the strength of a lion.
   c. A careful prince knows when and how to protect his interests by using deceit to manipulate the minds of people.
   d. A wise prince is one who has gained the love and admiration of his people.

3. Do you agree or disagree with Machiavelli's suggestions for being a successful

   leader? Why or why not? _____

   _____

   _____

Vocabulary Check

Directions: _See if any of the words you underlined in the selection are among the list of words below. If not, write your words in the spaces provided. Guess the meaning of the words from the way they were used in the selection. Then, look up the definition of each word in the dictionary to see if you were right._

antiquity (_n_): Your guess: _____

   Dictionary Definition: _____

hypocrite (_n_): Your guess: _____

   Dictionary Definition: _____

Your word: _____ Your guess: _____

   Dictionary Definition: _____

Your word: _____ Your guess: _____

   Dictionary Definition: _____

PART 2

4 Main Idea and Paragraph Structure

> "Reading furnishes the mind only with material for knowledge; it is thinking [that] makes what we read ours."
>
> – John Locke

In this chapter you will learn how to:

Improve Your Reading Speed and Comprehension

Find the Main Idea

Write an Accurate Summary

You will learn the following strategies:

Make Your Own Main Idea

The Main Idea Test

▲ In a paragraph, the major details support the main idea sentence.

Preview and Predict ▶ What do you know so far?

How many of the following questions can you answer before you read the chapter?

• What are the five places in a paragraph where the main idea can be found?

_____

• What is an implied main idea?

_____

- What do you already know about paragraph structure?

_____

- Think of one way in which the picture relates to this chapter's objectives.

_____

Now, as you read the chapter, look for the answers to see if you were right.

IMPROVING READING SPEED AND COMPREHENSION

You probably know someone who is able to read whole paragraphs in a matter of seconds and still remember all of the details. You might believe that you will never be able to read that well. But, it's not true. If you can understand the basic structure of a paragraph, you will improve your reading speed and comprehension.

The Outline Structure of a Paragraph

An outline consists of two parts: a *topic* and a *list* of details about the topic. Look at the following outline.

Cars

Ford

BMW   **List of details about the topic, cars**

Toyota

In a paragraph, the topic is found in a sentence called the **main idea**. The list is contained in sentences called **major details**. *The main idea and the major details are the two parts that form the basic outline of a paragraph.* Here is the basic outline of a paragraph about cars:

Main Idea: There are three top-selling **cars** on the market today.

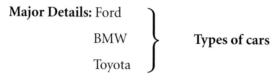

Major Details: Ford

BMW   **Types of cars**

Toyota

As soon as you see this outline, then you have understood the paragraph. It's that easy.

The main idea and the list of major details work together to provide the meaning of a paragraph. For instance, what do the major details, Ford, BMW, and Toyota have in common? They are all *types* of _____ The main idea makes the main point about the topic by telling you what the major details in a paragraph have *in common.*

The major details support the topic of the main idea by explaining it *in detail.* Major details may be a list of *types, reasons, ways, steps, causes, differences,* or *effects* that explain the topic. For instance, Ford, BMW, and Toyota support the topic of the main idea because they are "the three top-selling (types) of **cars** on the market today." When you summarize the list of major details in a paragraph, you will understand the main idea.

Almost everything written is organized in an outline. For instance, a textbook has a title, or topic, and a list of chapters that support the title. If you look at a chapter in a textbook, you will see the title or topic, and a list of major headings that support the title. This models the way our minds naturally organize information. All of the information you know is stored under a topic in your mind. So, when you think of a particular topic, your mind will *list* or recall everything you know about that topic.

Computers also copy the way our minds work. What happens when you select a topic presented on a computer application? A list about the topic appears on the screen. It's just like the list you make in your mind when you see a topic.

For instance, look at the following topic: **colors.** What happens when you see this word? As soon as you see the topic *colors,* your mind will recall or "list" every color you know. How long did it take to make a list of colors in your mind? Did you really have to think about it? No. It happened in seconds, automatically. As soon as you *see the topic* of a paragraph, your mind will make a list of everything you know about the topic. Consider how fast you can read when you find the same items you were expecting to see within a paragraph or passage.

Imagine that you are going to read a paragraph that begins with the following main idea sentence:

There are three primary *colors* in an artist's palette.

What is the topic? _____ How many colors will be listed in the major details of

the paragraph? _____ What major details (colors) do you expect to see in the

paragraph? _____ Perhaps you thought of the colors red, blue, and yellow. If so, you would easily find these words in the paragraph if you were looking for them, and you would read and understand the paragraph very quickly.

Now as you read the rest of the paragraph below, see if the major details include the colors that you expected.

There are three primary colors in an artist's palette. The first primary color is *red.* The types of red may vary from a light shade of purple to a dark shade of pink. *Blue* is also a primary color in an artist's palette. Artists have used midnight blue to depict the color of a stormy sky. Finally, *yellow* is a primary color. It appears in several shades that can range from orange to the palest sunlight.

Can you see the difference in the speed of your comprehension when you *see the topic* of a paragraph *before* you read it? You can quickly find the major details that support the topic. You understand what the paragraph is about.

Here is the outline structure of the paragraph:

Topic: colors

Main Idea: There are three primary **colors** in an artist's palette.

Major Details: red
         blue   }   **Three primary colors**
         yellow

What do the major details have in common? They are all primary (*types of*)

_____ in an artist's palette. *The main idea sentence tells you what the major details have in common about the topic.*

If you see the topic before you read, you will find that you are able to learn more as you read. You can compare what you expected to see about a topic to what is actually listed in the major details of a paragraph. For instance, you might be thinking, "See, I'm right. I knew the author would say that." Or, you might say, "Oh, I didn't think of that one. Now I know." You can learn something new.

Memory Check 1 How much do you remember?

1. What are the two parts that form the basic outline structure of a paragraph?

   _____

2. What happens in your mind when you can see the topic of a paragraph?

   _____

3. The main idea makes the main point about the topic by telling you _____

   _____.

Transition Words and Major Details

Writers often use **transition words** such as *first, next, also,* and *last* to highlight each major detail they are listing in the outline of a paragraph. What does the prefix *trans* mean? It means "across." *Transition* words help writers get their major details *across* to the reader. Will there be a transition word in every major detail sentence? No. But, when you see a transition word, you will know you have found a major detail. You can use transition words to search for what is listed in a paragraph. Then, you can see how the major details relate to the topic.

Activity 4.1 ▶ Finding the Outline of a Paragraph

Directions: *Underline each of the transition words in the paragraph below. Identify the outline of the paragraph before you read it by answering the following questions. Then, read the paragraph and complete the outline that follows it.*

The first sentence of the paragraph below tells you that it is going to discuss what

topic? _____

How many major details do you expect to see in the paragraph?

_____

What will the major details discuss about the topic?

_____

There are three stages of memory. The first stage is sensory memory. This is the information that we get from our senses. Sensory memory only retains information for a fraction of a second, unless you try to remember it. Working memory or short-term memory is the second stage of the memory process. It takes the information from sensory memory, such as a phone number that you just looked up, and holds the information temporarily. Long-term memory is the last stage. It takes the information from working memory and stores it for permanent use.

Major Detail: _____

Major Detail: working or short-term memory

Major Detail: _____

What do these major details have in common? (Topic): The three _____

_____.

Main Idea Sentence: There are _____

The three transition words used to highlight each major detail in the paragraph are:

First, _____ , and _____. Can you find a sentence in the paragraph that tells you what the major details have in common about the topic? Yes. The main idea can be found in the first sentence.

PLACES TO FIND THE MAIN IDEA

The outline structure of a paragraph is easy to find when the main idea is in the first sentence. All you have to do is find the topic and look for the major details that match the list you are making in your mind as you read. You can see right away if you were correct about what you expected to be listed in the paragraph. But, the main idea is *not* always found in the first sentence. There are five places where the main idea sentence may be found in a paragraph:

1. In the first sentence

2. In the last sentence

3. In the first and last sentences

4. In the middle (preceded by an introduction)

5. Implied. (The main idea is in the paragraph, but it is not directly stated.)

1. Main Idea in the First Sentence

Authors often place their main idea sentences at the beginning of paragraphs. Read the following paragraph in which the main idea sentence comes first. Then, underline the four major detail sentences in the paragraph which contain a transition word.

> Improving your performance on an exam can be easy if you follow these steps. *First,* attend class regularly and take good notes. If you attend class regularly, you will have all the information you need for the exam. *Second,* complete all assignments and take notes on information presented in your textbook. Instructors assign homework to reinforce important ideas or skills you will need in order to perform well on an exam. *Then,* review all lecture and text notes every day for a week before the exam. You can divide your review into sections and create questions to test yourself on the information. When you have learned the information in each new section of your notes, you can review previous sections. *Finally,* prepare your body. Get a good night's sleep before the exam. Eat something that contains protein such as eggs or bacon for breakfast to reduce fatigue and hunger.

The topic of this paragraph is *performance on an exam*. What is listed in the major details about performance on exams? Do you see a list of *ways*, *types*, or *steps* to follow to improve your performance on an exam? The major details list the four steps to improve your performance on an exam. The transition words used to highlight each step or major detail listed in the paragraph are: First, second, _____, and finally.

2. Main Idea in the Last Sentence

How would the same paragraph look if the main idea were located in the *last* sentence?

> The *first* step for improving your performance on an exam is to attend class regularly and take good notes. If you attend class regularly, you will have all the information you need for the exam. *Second*, complete all assignments and take notes on information presented in your textbook. Instructors assign homework to reinforce important ideas or skills you will need in order to perform well on an exam. *Then*, review all lecture and text notes every day for a week before the exam. You can divide your review into sections and create questions to test yourself on the information. When you have learned the information in each new section of your notes, you can review previous sections. *Finally*, prepare your body. Get a good night's sleep before the exam. Eat something that contains protein such as eggs or meat for breakfast to reduce fatigue and hunger. If you follow these steps, you can easily improve your performance on an exam.

Look at the way the author changes the wording of the main idea sentence to *summarize* the major details presented in the paragraph. In this paragraph, the first sentence is the first _____ detail or step for improving performance on exams.

3. Main Idea in the First and Last Sentences

Here is an example where the main idea is given in the first sentence of the paragraph and then restated at the end.

> Improving your performance on an exam can be easy if you follow these steps. *First*, attend class regularly and take good notes. If you attend class regularly, you will have all the information you need for the exam. *Second*, complete all assignments and take notes on information presented in your textbook. Instructors assign homework to reinforce important ideas or skills you will need in order to perform well on an exam. *Then*, review all lecture and text notes every day for a week before the exam. You can divide your review into sections and create questions to test yourself on the information. When you

have learned the information in each new section of your notes, you can review previous sections. *Finally,* prepare your body. Get a good night's sleep before the exam. Eat something that contains protein such as eggs or meat for breakfast to reduce fatigue and hunger. If you follow these steps, you can easily improve your performance on an exam.

You should *always* read the last sentence of a paragraph, because authors often restate their main idea there. For instance, which word, contained in both main idea sentences tells you what *kind* of information is listed in the major details

of the paragraph? _____ Both of the main idea sentences tell you that the paragraph is about the *steps* to improve your performance on an exam.

4. Main Idea in the Middle of a Paragraph

When the main idea is in the middle of a paragraph, it means the author has added an introduction. An **introduction** can be one or more sentences added to the *beginning* of a paragraph to get the reader interested in the topic. What is the meaning of the root *duct* in the word intro*duct*ion? It means to "lead." An introduction *leads* to the main idea sentence in a paragraph.

An introduction is *not* part of the basic outline structure of a paragraph. It is *not* a main idea or a major detail. An introduction is like whipped cream on top of a pie. It sounds good, but it is not what the paragraph is about. However, if you can see the outline of the paragraph, you can find the main idea sentence even when it appears after an introduction. For instance, here is the paragraph with an introduction.

Some students fail exams because they feel unprepared. Do you have trouble performing well on exams? Improving your performance on an exam can be easy if you follow these steps. *First,* attend class regularly and take good notes. If you attend class regularly, you will have all the information you need for the exam. *Second,* complete all assignments and take notes on information presented in your textbook. Instructors assign homework to reinforce important ideas or skills you will need in order to perform well on an exam. *Then,* review all lecture and text notes every day for a week before the exam. You can divide your review into sections and create questions to test yourself on the information. When you have learned the information in each new section of your notes, you can review previous sections. *Finally,* prepare your body. Get a good night's sleep before the exam. Eat something that contains protein such as eggs or meat for breakfast to reduce fatigue and hunger.

You can see the main idea is the third sentence. The first two sentences make up the introduction, which leads to the main idea. Many students are confused by introductions because they do not know how to find the basic outline of a paragraph.

How do you find the main idea when there is an introduction to a paragraph? One way is to look for the list of major details. What is listed in the major details of the sample paragraph? The _____ for improving performance on an exam are listed in the paragraph. Do you see the word *steps* in the first two sentences of the paragraph? No. These sentences do *not* mention the *steps* for improving performance on an exam. That is because these are introductory sentences that *lead to* the main idea. *The main idea is the only sentence that will tell you what is listed in the major details of a paragraph.*

Here is another way to find the main idea sentence when a paragraph contains an introduction. Look for the *first* major detail in the paragraph. For example, write the first step to improve your performance on an exam. _____

_____ Where is the main idea? Read the sentence located directly *before* the *first* major detail you wrote down. *The main idea sentence is usually found before the first major detail listed in a paragraph when it contains an introduction.*

5. Implied Main Idea

Every paragraph contains a main idea. An *implied* main idea is *not* directly stated in the paragraph. You *infer* it from the details in the paragraph. It is a sentence you create by asking yourself what the list of major details has in common about the topic. Here is the paragraph written so that the main idea is *implied*.

> The *first* step for improving your performance on an exam is to attend class regularly and take good notes. If you attend class regularly, you will have all the information you need for the exam. *Second,* complete all assignments and take notes on information presented in your textbook. Instructors assign homework to reinforce important ideas or skills you will need in order to perform well on an exam. *Then,* review all lecture and text notes every day for a week before the exam. You can divide your review into sections and create questions to test yourself on the information. When you learn the information in each new section of your notes, you can review previous sections. Finally, prepare your body. Get a good night's sleep before the exam. Eat something that contains protein such as eggs or meat for breakfast to reduce fatigue and hunger.

What do the major details have in common about the topic? They are all _____ to improve your performance on an exam. What main idea sentence could you create that tells you what the list of major details have in common about improving your performance on an exam?

There are four _____

Memory Check 2   How much do you remember?

1. Why do writers use transition words? _____
   _____
   _____

2. What are the five places where the main idea can be found in a paragraph?
   _____
   _____

3. When the main idea is implied, this means that _____
   _____

4. Where would you find an introduction? _____

5. How can you find the main idea sentence when it appears after an introduction? _____
   _____
   _____

6. The main idea is the only sentence that tells you _____
   _____
   _____

STRATEGIES FOR LOCATING THE MAIN IDEA

There are two qualities of a main idea sentence that make it easy to locate. First, the main idea is the *only* sentence that tells you what the list of major details in the paragraph have in common. Second, the main idea is the *only* sentence that can be turned into a question that is answered by the major details in the paragraph. The following strategies help you to use these qualities to find the main idea very quickly while you are reading.

Make Your Own Main Idea Strategy

Make Your Own Main Idea is a strategy that will help you to create a main idea sentence. There are two reasons why you should make your own main idea sentence as you read. First, the main idea sentence in the paragraph will be easier to find because you will be looking for a sentence that is similar to the one that you have created. Also, your ability to make your own main idea will be helpful for understanding the main point of a paragraph in which the main idea is implied (or not stated). By applying the Make Your Own Main Idea Strategy, you will be able to recognize the outline or basic meaning of a paragraph very easily.

There are Three Key Questions you can ask to help you make your own main idea sentence as you read.

Three Key Questions to Make Your Own Main Idea Sentence

1. What is the *topic* of the paragraph?

2. What is *listed* about the topic?

3. What do the major details have in *common*?

 ## 1. What Is the Topic?

It only takes a second to skim the paragraph and see certain words that you would associate with a particular topic. For instance, if you skim a paragraph and see the words *prefixes, roots, suffixes,* then you might guess that the topic of the paragraph is *word parts.*

2. What Is Listed About the Topic?

Look for what is listed in the major details about the topic. Do the details describe a list of types, ways, reasons, differences, effects, events, or perhaps steps? For instance, if you see the words *prefixes, roots,* and *suffixes,* then, what is being listed about the topic, word parts? *Prefixes, roots,* and *suffixes* are all *types* of word parts. These are the *major details* of a paragraph about word parts.

 ## 3. What Do the Major Details Have in Common?

For example, what do *prefixes, roots,* and *suffixes* have in common? They are all *types* (major details) of *word parts* (topic). So, you would look for a main idea sentence in the paragraph that contains the phrase "types of word parts" or "three word parts."

Asking the Three Key Questions will help you to form your own main idea sentence as you read. If you can make your own main idea sentence, you can look for a sentence in the paragraph that is similar to the one that you have created. The main idea will be easier to find. If the main idea of the paragraph is implied, you will still be able to understand the author's main point.

Activity 4.2 ▶ Make Your Own Main Idea Sentence I

Directions: *From the list of common words and phrases below write your own main idea sentences. Start by writing "There are . . ." and then add a word or phrase from each of lists 1, 2, and 3.*

List	1	2	3
There are:	many	ways to	What? (Topic
	several	reasons for/why	of your choice)
	some	types of	
	a few	differences between	
	a number	similarities among	
	(three, four, etc.)	causes of	
		effects of	
		Steps to	

Example

There are	many	ways to	cook chicken
There are	several	types of	drivers on the road
There are	_____	_____	_____
There are	_____	_____	_____
There are	_____	_____	_____

The Main Idea Test: A Strategy for Confirming the Main Idea

How can you be certain that you have found the main idea of the paragraph? The main idea is the only sentence that can be turned into a question that is answered by the major details of the paragraph. If a sentence passes the Main Idea Test, you will know you have found the main idea. When you find a sentence that you believe is the main idea you should:

- First, turn the sentence that you think is the main idea into a *question*.

- Next, think about the *answer* you expect to see as you skim the paragraph. If you see the answer to your question, then you have found the main idea.

♟ 1. Turn the Sentence into a *Question*

For example, here is the first sentence of a paragraph:

There are five types of context clues that can help you find the meaning of an unknown word.

Question: What are the five _____ of context clues that can help you find the meaning of an unknown word?

Often, the main idea sentence tells you *how many* major details to look for in the paragraph. Using the example above, how many major details would you expect to see in the paragraph? _____

♟ 2. Think About the *Answer* to Your Question

What are the five types of context clues? _____

_____

If you see the answer *antonym, synonym, example, definition,* and *description* listed in the major details of the paragraph, then you will know you have found the main idea. *The main idea is the only sentence that can be turned into a question that is answered by the major details in the paragraph.*

Activity 4.3 ▶ Applying The Main Idea Test Strategy

Directions: *Apply the Main Idea Test to predict what you expect would be presented in the major details of paragraphs that begin with the following sentences.*

Example

There are three stages of memory.

1. **Question:** What are the three stages of memory?

2. What three major details (answers) would you expect to see in the paragraph?

a. <u>sensory memory</u>

b. <u>working or short-term memory</u>

c. <u>long-term memory</u>

A. Paragraph 1: Here are two guidelines for losing weight.

1. **Question:** What are two _____

2. What two major details (answers) would you expect to see in the paragraph?

a. <u>avoid junk food</u>

b. _____

B. Paragraph 2: Smoking can lead to harmful results.

1. **Question:** What are the harmful results of _____

2. What two major details (answers) would you expect to see in the paragraph?

a. <u>respiratory problems</u>

b. _____

C. Paragraph 3: There are three ways to prepare potatoes.

1. **Question:** What are _____

2. What three major details (answers) would you expect to see in the paragraph?

a. <u>fried</u>

b. _____

c. _____

D. Paragraph 4: There are differences between high school and college students.

1. **Question:** What are the _____

2. What two major details (answers) would you expect to see in the paragraph?

a. _____

b. _____

E. Paragraph 5: The three top-rated cars on the market today are the most popular.

1. **Question:** What are the _____

2. What three major details (answers) would you expect to see in the paragraph?

a. _____

b. _____

c. _____

You can read much faster when you know what to look for in the paragraph. When you turn the main idea sentence into a *question*, you will be able to see the major details in the outline of a paragraph very quickly because you will be looking for a specific answer.

Applying Strategies for Locating the Main Idea

As you have learned, the main idea is not always found in the first sentence. By applying the Make Your Own Main Idea strategy, you can find the main idea wherever it appears in the paragraph.

Example

Imagine that you are reading a paragraph which contains the following major details:

Major Details: Roses

Lilies

Carnations

Orchids

Topic: What do the major details have in common? They are all <u>flowers</u>.

Main Idea: There are ____<u>several</u>____   _____   ____<u>flowers.</u>____

How many?   ways to? types of?   topic

three? several?   reasons for/why?

steps to?

The major details tell you that the paragraph is about the types of flowers. Now, look for a main idea sentence in the paragraph that is similar to the one you created.

> Roses are traditionally given on special occasions because of their beauty and fragrance. Florists report an average increase of 80 percent in the sale of roses on Valentine's Day. Lilies are commonly associated with the celebration of Easter. They can be found on altars of churches because they represent the resurrection of Christ. Carnations are often used to denote an important person at

a particular event. The carnation is usually pinned to the left side of their garment. Orchids are often given to women by their dates on special occasions, such as weddings or proms. There are several types of flowers that are used for specific occasions.

1. **Main Idea Test:** Turn your main idea into a question: What are several _____

   _____

   Do you see the answer to the question in the paragraph? Yes. Now, you understand the main idea of the paragraph.

2. Underline the main idea if it is stated in the paragraph.

   Is there a sentence in the paragraph which is similar to the one you created? Yes. It is located in the last sentence of the paragraph. Cover the last sentence of the paragraph. Now, the main idea is implied (or not stated). Even so, you can still understand the main idea of the paragraph because you know what the list of major details has in common.

Activity 4.4 ▶ Applying Strategies for Locating the Main Idea Sentence

Directions: *For each list of major details write a main idea sentence that summarizes what they have in common. Then answer the questions that follow.*

Paragraph 1

Major Details: Toyota

BMW

Honda

Topic: What do the major details have in common? They are all _____

Main idea: There are _____ _____ _____

How many?   ways to? types of?   Topic
three? several?   reasons for/why?
                  steps to?

Are you looking for a new car? There are three top-selling cars on the market today. The Toyota Corolla maintains its popularity because it is reliable and easy to drive. It has been one the top three best sellers for the last five years. All BMW models are top sellers because of their consistent safety rating. BMW has always represented status and success. Finally, the Honda Fit offers reliability at an affordable price. It has been on the top-seller's list since its arrival in 2006.

1. **Main Idea Test:** Turn your main idea into a question: What are the three

   _____

2. Underline the main idea if it is stated in the paragraph.

Paragraph 2

Major Details: Boil water

Add spaghetti

Stir

Wait nine–eleven minutes

Strain

Serve

Topic: What do the major details have in common? _____

Main Idea: There are _____ _____ _____
                                    How many?   ways to? types of?   Topic
                                    three? several? reasons for/why?
                                                     steps to?

   Spaghetti is one of the easiest meals to make because it involves only a few easy steps. First, boil water in a pot that is large enough to hold the amount of spaghetti you wish to make. Then, add the spaghetti. Stir the spaghetti as soon as you place it in the boiling water to separate the strands of pasta for even cooking. Wait nine to eleven minutes depending upon the thickness of the spaghetti. Strain the pasta when it begins to have a clearer appearance. Last, serve the spaghetti with sauce and parmesan cheese.

1. **Main Idea Test** Turn your main idea into a question: _____

   _____

2. Underline the main idea if it is stated in the paragraph.

Paragraph 3

Major Details: Pediatrician

Cardiologist

Anesthesiologist

Topic: What do the major details have in common? _____

Main Idea: There are _____ _____ _____

           How many?   ways to? types of?   Topic

           three? several?   reasons for/why?

                            steps to?

       Pediatricians are doctors who specialize in the health of children. They are among the busiest physicians in a hospital or clinic. Cardiologists are heart specialists. They often maintain a consistent clientele of patients who have specific heart-related problems. Anesthesiologists are doctors who administer anesthesia during surgery. Anesthesiologists make certain that pain medication is given appropriately according to the specific needs of the patient.

1. **Main Idea Test:** Turn your main idea into a question: _____

_____

2. Underline the main idea if it is stated in the paragraph.

Paragraph 4

Major Details: Because she ran a red light

                Because she was speeding

                Because she made an illegal turn

Topic: What do the major details have in common? _____

_____

Main Idea: There are _____ _____ _____

           How many?   ways to? types of?   Topic

           three? several?   reasons for/why?

                            steps to?

       Angie ran a red light at Elgin Street. She was speeding and didn't want to stop at the light. When she noticed a patrol car behind her, she panicked and made an illegal left turn at the next street. The policeman pulled her over and gave her a ticket.

1. **Main Idea Test:** Turn your main idea into a question: What are the reasons why

_____

2. Underline the main idea if it is stated in the paragraph.

Paragraph 5

Major Details: Learn the meanings of common word parts

Use context clues

Play word games

Use a thesaurus and a dictionary

Topic: What do the major details have in common? _____

Main Idea: There are _____ _____ _____

How many?	ways to? types of?	Topic
three? several?	reasons for/why?	
	steps to?	

There are several things you can do to improve your vocabulary. First, learn the meanings of common word parts. Each prefix, root, or suffix has a meaning that you use to learn new words. You can also use context clues. Context clues provide signals that can help you to determine the meaning of a new word by the way it is used in the sentence. Third, play word games. Word games, such as crossword puzzles or Scrabble®, provide an opportunity to learn new words while you are engaged in a fun activity. Finally, use a thesaurus and a dictionary. By using these two valuable resources, you will increase your knowledge of new word meanings.

1. **Main Idea Test:** Turn your main idea into a question: _____

   _____

2. Underline the main idea if it is stated in the paragraph.

Additional Hints for Locating the Main Idea

1. The main idea is often found in the sentence that is directly above the first major detail in the paragraph. Look for transition words, such as *first* or *one*, which indicate the first major detail. Then, you can turn the sentence directly above it into a question to confirm that it is the main idea.

2. The main idea may be restated at the end of a paragraph. Or, the main idea may only be found in the last sentence. By turning the last sentence into a question, you can make certain that you are not missing the main idea of a paragraph you are reading.

Memory Check 3   How much do you remember?

1. What are the two steps in the Main Idea Test Strategy?

   a. _____

   b. _____

2. What are the Three Key Questions you should ask to Make Your Own Main Idea?

   a. _____

   b. _____

   c. _____

3. What are the two qualities of the main idea?

   a. _____

   _____

   b. _____

   _____

4. Why should you create your own main idea while you read?

   _____

   _____

Activity 4.5 ▶ Applying Strategies for Locating the Main Idea: Textbook Application

Directions: *Identify the major details listed in each paragraph. Then, answer the questions that follow each paragraph.*

Paragraph 1

There are two major aims in studying biology. One aim is to become acquainted with scientific facts and with the ideas that are built on them. These ideas have shown us that we have a place in nature; we are not apart from it. They have made our lives today very different from those of our ancestors. The second aim in studying biology is even more important. It is to understand what science is—to feel its spirit, to appreciate its methods, and to recognize its limitations. We need this understanding to make intelligent decisions in our science-oriented word.

—From *Biological Science: An Ecological Approach*. Preface to the Student. Copyright © 1978 by BCBS. All rights reserved. Used with permission.

1. Topic: _____

2. What is listed in the major details about the topic? The two _____ in studying biology.

3. Make Your Own Main Idea: There are two _____

4. Main Idea Test: What are _____

5. Answer to the Main Idea Test question:

   a. Major Detail: _____

   _____

   b. Major Detail: _____

   _____

6. Underline the main idea sentence if it is stated in the paragraph.

Paragraph 2

There are four kinds of dynamic competition: lowering production cost, creating a new product category, improving existing products, and product differentiation. Lowering production costs is illustrated by everything from egg production to microchips. Creating new product categories is illustrated by the introduction of the automobile, personal computers, and word processing software. Improving existing products is illustrated by the tremendous improvements in cars, tires, software and personal computers. Finally, product differentiation is illustrated by the many types of word processing software, cars, trucks, planes, and computers.

—From *Principles of Economics*. 7th ed. by Roy J. Ruffin and Gregory, Paul R. p. 232.

1. Topic: _____

2. What is listed in the major details about the topic? Four types of _____

   _____

3. Make Your Own Main Idea: There are _____

4. Main Idea Test: What are the four _____

5. Answer to the Main Idea Test question:

   a. Major Detail: _____

   b. Major Detail: _____

   c. Major Detail: _____

   d. Major Detail: _____

6. Underline the main idea sentence if it is stated in the paragraph.

Paragraph 3

Does your mind wander when others are speaking? Understanding requires active listening. Active listening can be improved in four ways. First, determine how the information you are hearing is organized. You can listen for key points or details that support the goal of the person's message. Second, ask questions. For instance, you can ask yourself what you are supposed to be learning from the message or whether there is additional information that you would like to know. Third, silently paraphrase. When you can paraphrase what someone is saying in your own words as you listen, you know that you have really understood the information. Fourth, attend to non-verbal cues. Pay attention to what is not being said. The speaker's tone of voice, facial expressions, and gestures can give you valuable information about what is behind their message.

—Adapted from *The Challenge of Effective Speaking*, 14th edition by Verderber/
Verderber/sellnow. 2008. Reprinted with permission of Wadsworth, a division
of ThomsonLearning: www.thomsonrights.com
Fax 800-730-2215.

1. Topic: _____

2. What is listed in the major details about the topic? The four ways to _____

   _____

3. Make Your Own Main Idea: There are four _____

4. Main Idea Test: What are four _____

5. Answer to the Main Idea Test question:

    a. Major Detail: _____

    b. Major Detail: _____

    c. Major Detail: _____

    d. Major Detail: _____

6. Underline the main idea sentence if it is stated in the paragraph.

Paragraph 4

    Changes that alter the physical form of matter without changing its chemical identity are called physical changes. The melting of ice is a physical change, as is the freezing of liquid water. The substance is still water after it melts and after it refreezes. Dissolving sugar in water is another physical change. The sugar seems to disappear, but if you taste the water, you'll know the sugar is there. You can recover the dissolved sugar by evaporating the water, another physical change. A chemical change occurs when the chemical identity of a substance is destroyed and a new substance forms. A chemical change is also called a chemical reaction. As a group, all the chemical changes possible for a substance make up its chemical properties. One or more of our five physical senses can usually detect chemical changes. A change of color almost always indicates a chemical change, as when you caramelize sugar. You can feel the heat and see light given off as a match burns. You can smell and taste milk that becomes sour. Explosions usually give off sound.

—From *Introductory Chemistry: An Active Learning Approach.* 3rd ed. by Cracolice/Peters. 2007. Reprinted with permission of Brooks/Cole, a division of Thomson Learning: www.thomsonrights.com Fax 800-730-2215

1. Topic: _____

2. What is listed in the major details about the topic? Two types of _____

    _____

3. Make Your Own Main Idea: There are two _____

4. Main Idea Test: What are _____

5. Answer to the Main Idea Test question:

    a. Major Detail: _____

    b. Major Detail: _____

6. Underline the main idea sentence if it is stated in the paragraph.

Paragraph 5

The Texas revolution was the result of a number of things. One was racism, a deep conviction on the part of most Anglo-Americans that the Mexicans of Spanish and Spanish–Native American descent were inferior people not fit to govern. Another was a different kind of racism, which made the Texas rebels defend slavery against Mexican attempts to abolish it. A third was a demand for "liberty" from the rule of the man who in 1834 had made himself practically the dictator of Mexico, General Antonio López de Santa Ana. Santa Ana had abolished the federal system, threatening the states' rights convictions of many Mexicans and all the Anglo-American immigrants.

—From *The Pursuit of Liberty: A History of the American People.*
3rd ed. vol. I p. 488.

1. Topic: _____

2. What is listed in the major details about the topic? Three causes of _____

   _____

3. Make Your Own Main Idea: There were three _____

4. Main Idea Test: What were three _____

5. Answer to the Main Idea Test question:

   a. Major Detail: _____

   _____

   _____

   b. Major Detail: _____

   _____

   c. Major Detail: _____

   _____

6. Underline the main idea sentence if it is stated in the paragraph.

IMPLIED MAIN IDEAS

There is a main idea in every paragraph. But, as you have learned, when the main idea is **implied**, it means that it is *not* directly stated. However, it can be stated in a sentence you create by summarizing what the list of major details in the paragraph has in common. If you know how to create your own main idea as you read, it won't matter whether the main idea is implied or whether it is stated. You will know what the paragraph is about.

Implied main ideas can sometimes be found in **expository** material, such as textbook excerpts or technical manuals, which explain the *facts* about a particular topic. You can create a main idea sentence for an expository paragraph by asking yourself the Three Key Questions: "What is the *topic*?" "What is *listed* about the topic (such as types, ways, or steps)?" and "What do the major details have in *common*?"

For instance, the following expository paragraph has an implied main idea. Can you create a main idea sentence for the paragraph?

> If you want to develop your child's vocabulary, read to him or her at bed time. You can explain the meaning of a new word by relating it to a character or to an event in the story. You can also develop your child's vocabulary by setting a time each day for family meals. Doing this will provide opportunities to use vocabulary to describe or summarize daily events. Finally, you can play word games to develop your child's vocabulary. For instance, kindergarten-aged children can be asked to identify common objects at home that begin with a particular sound or letter. Older children can benefit from word games that involve the family, such as Scrabble® or Boggle®.

What is the topic? The topic of the paragraph is *developing your child's vocabulary*. What is listed about the topic? (ways? types? steps?) The paragraph is about the *ways* you can develop your child's vocabulary. Write a main idea sentence that summarizes what the major details have in *common* with the topic.

There are three _____

Implied main ideas are also found in **narratives** or stories. In each full paragraph of a story or narrative, the topic can be a character, place, thing, or event. The list of major details either describes the topic or tells you what is happening. To create a main idea for a narrative paragraph, you should ask yourself, "How would I describe the character, place, thing, or event?" And "What is the main event that happened in the paragraph?" By asking these questions, you can create a main idea sentence that summarizes each paragraph of a narrative or story.

For instance, the following narrative paragraph has an implied main idea. Can you make your own a main idea sentence for the paragraph?

> Josie stayed up until midnight reviewing what she would say during the interview scheduled for 8:30 AM. When Josie awoke at 7:30 AM, she was horrified. The alarm did not go off! Josie jumped out of bed and ran to the bathroom get ready. When she turned on the light, the bulb burned out. Josie grabbed a chair

and a new bulb from the kitchen. When Josie jumped on the chair and leaned over to unscrew the bulb, she lost her balance and fell off the chair. She rescheduled the interview from her hospital room.

How would you describe Josie? She was in a hurry. Is the paragraph about how Josie stayed up until midnight? No. Is it about how Josie overslept? No. Is it about the burned out light bulb in the bathroom? No. How would you summarize what happened to Josie? "Josie fell off of a chair when she was in a hurry and she tried to change a light bulb." This main idea sentence describes the character, Josie, and summarizes what happened to her.

To test the main idea that you have created, turn it into a question. For instance, your might say, "Why did Josie fall off a chair?" The answer would be: "She fell off the chair because she was in a hurry to change the light bulb." The major details support the main event of the paragraph.

Activity 4.6 ▶ Creating Implied Main Ideas Sentences

Directions: *Write a main idea sentence for each of the following paragraphs, and answer the questions that follow them.*

Example

He was about eight years old, hiding behind a dumpster, eating something that looked like a hamburger someone had thrown away. His face and hands were filthy and his ragged clothes barely covered his little body. He didn't see me. But, as I tried to approach him to offer assistance, he looked up at me with terror and fled down the street. I started to chase after him until I heard a woman shout, "Benny. Get over here!" The child jumped into the woman's old station wagon and they drove away.

1. Topic: (What or who is it about?) a little boy

2. How would you describe the boy? (topic) He appears to be homeless.

3. What main event happened to the boy? The boy ran away when the author tried to approach him.

4. Make Your Own Main Idea: A homeless boy ran away when he was approached by the author.

This sentence summarizes what happened to the boy.

Paragraph 1

Charlene sat nervously in the back of the classroom. *Where are they?* she wondered as class began. She had not completed her part of the homework for the group presentation. Terry and Bonnie had said they would do all of the speaking. Charlene was only supposed to write their data on the board. When the instructor asked the first group to give their presentation, Charlene could hardly breathe. *What am I going to do if they don't show up?* By the time the third group had finished, Charlene realized that Terry and Bonnie were not coming. The sound of the class clapping swirled in her head. "Charlene?" The instructor said. "I guess you're a one-woman group." Charlene could feel herself standing up and then falling down. When she awoke, Terry and Bonnie were standing over her saying, "Way to go, Charlene."

1. Topic (What or who is the paragraph about?): _Presntation in School_
2. How would you describe Charlene? _She 's Narvous_ _She fainted_
3. What is the main event that happened in the paragraph? _her fainting as mentioned_
4. Make Your Own Main Idea: Charlene fainted because she was nervous about _Presenting by herself_

This sentence summarizes what happened to the topic (Charlene) of the story.

Paragraph 2

If you want to reduce your fear of public speaking, the first step is to *be brief*. Make a list of three or four important points you want to present about the topic. You will feel more confident if you only have to remember a few major details. Next, *be accurate*. Check to make sure that the information that you are going to present is correct. You will feel more confident if you know what you are talking about. Last, *be prepared*. Practice talking about each point with a friend or in front of a mirror. Rehearsing your presentation will enhance your confidence because you will know you have practiced what you are going to say and how you are going to say it.

1. Topic (What or who is the paragraph about?): _Public Speaking_
2. What is listed in the major details about the topic? (ways? steps? events? types?) _Steps to be Confident While Speaking_
3. Make Your Own Main Idea: There are three steps _be Prepared_ _be accurate be brief_

Paragraph 3

After the Weight Wonders meeting, Wanda and Betty decided to go to the new restaurant, Chez Mirage, to celebrate losing five pounds by having an expensive salad. They were wearing the new smaller-sized dresses they had purchased earlier. "We'd like a table for two," Betty announced proudly to the girl at the reservation desk. But, the girl didn't say a word. She studied the bodies of the two oversized women and gestured with the menu as if to say, "Follow me." Although there were empty tables near the entrance, Wanda and Betty were led to the far back of the restaurant. The waiter walked past them several times without stopping to take their order. Wanda and Betty chatted about their success for twenty minutes until they realized that customers sitting nearby who had arrived later had already received their meals. So, they left.

1. Topic (What or who is the paragraph about?): _____

2. How would you describe Wanda and Betty? _____

3. What is the main event that happened in the paragraph? _____

   _____

   _____

4. Make Your Own Main Idea: _____

   _____

Paragraph 4

The first step you should take to reduce frustration at the airport, is to be familiar with federal guidelines regarding baggage and the list of currently restricted items before you pack. For instance, your checked luggage cannot be locked. So, valuable items should be placed in carry-on bags. *Next,* you can reduce frustration at the airport if you arrive at least two hours before your scheduled flight. You may need to wait 30 to 40 minutes in each check-in and screening line. *Last,* have your ticket and identification ready at all times to reduce problems at the airport. If you cannot find your documents, you may not be allowed to board the plane.

1. Topic (What or who is the paragraph about?): _____

2. What is listed in the major details about the topic? (ways? steps? events? types? reasons?) _____

3. Make Your Own Main Idea: _____

_____

Paragraph 5

If you want to get a good night's sleep, avoid anything that contains caffeine at least six hours before going to bed. Coffee, chocolate, and most soft drinks contain caffeine. *Also,* avoid eating a large meal three hours before bedtime. The body's process of digesting food can keep you awake. *Finally,* avoid late-night news programming. Studies show that negative images and stories presented at bedtime can interrupt one's ability to fall asleep.

1. Topic (What or who is the paragraph about?): _____

2. What is listed in the major details about the topic? (ways? steps? events? types? reasons?) _____

3. Make Your Own Main Idea: _____

WRITING AN ACCURATE SUMMARY

A **summary** is a restatement of an author's main points in the order in which they were presented. College instructors may ask you to write summaries of articles, essays, textbook chapters, or stories that you have read. A good summary provides a *brief* outline of the main points of a reading in paragraph form and is always shorter than the original work. Here are three basic steps for writing an accurate summary.

Three Steps for Writing an Effective Summary

Step 1. Read the material carefully before you begin your summary. A good summary focuses on the most important points and the details that support them. If you read the material carefully before you begin your summary, you can identify the author's most important points more easily.

Step 2. List only the most important ideas or events presented by the author, in the order in which they were presented. Divide the selection into three or four sections. Then, list the most important points that are presented in each section. Make a note of the page number(s) on which each important point was found.

- In textbooks and articles, the most important ideas directly support the topic or title.

- In novels, plays, and other fiction, the most important events directly support what happens to the main character.

- In a persuasive essay, the most important points directly support the author's argument about a particular issue.

Step 3. Rewrite the main points you have listed *using your own words*. For each point you have listed, you should ask yourself, "How would I tell someone who has not read this selection what this point means so that they will understand what the author is saying?" In other words, your summary should *not* copy the author's exact words in a sentence. Copying the exact words of the author and presenting them as if they were your own is called **plagiarism**. Plagiarism is an offense that can have serious consequences ranging from receiving zero credit on your work to expulsion from school. If you want to quote or cite an author's exact words in your summary, you must give the author credit. To do this, include the quoted material in quotation marks (" ") and include the page number(s) where you found the information in parentheses ( ) immediately after the quotation. For example:

According to Dr. Friedman, the results of the Crampton Study show that "before developmental courses were available, 50% of the students dropped out of college within two semesters of initial enrollment" (22).

MyReadingLab

Outlining and
Summarizing: To
practice your skills
go to: Study Plans
>Reading Skills
>Outlining and
Summarizing

In this example, the sentence appeared on page 22 of the selection. The quotation marks at the beginning and end of the section indicate that it is a direct quote or copy of the author's words.

? Test Yourself Review Quiz

Chapter Review Questions

1. What are the two parts of an outline that form the basic structure of a paragraph?

   _____

2. What are the five places where the main idea can be found in a paragraph?

   _____

   _____

3. When a main idea is implied it means _____

4. What are the two qualities of the main idea?

   a. _____

   _____

   b. _____

   _____

5. What Three Key Questions should you ask to Make Your Own Main Idea?

   a. _____

   b. _____

   c. _____

6. Why do authors use transition words?

   _____

   _____

7. How do you test a sentence to see if it is the main idea of a paragraph?

   _____

   _____

Application Questions

Make your own main idea sentence for each of the following paragraphs. Then, underline the main idea sentence if it is stated in the paragraph.

Paragraph 1

Subatomic Particles. Physicists have split the atom into more than a hundred types of subatomic particles. However, we need to consider only three. A proton is a subatomic particle with a single positive electrical change (+). An electron is a subatomic particle with a single negative electrical charge (2). A third type of subatomic particle, the neutron, is electrically neutral (has no electrical charge).

—From *Biology: Concepts and Connections.* 5th ed. Neil Campbell et al. p. 20.

1. Write a main idea sentence for Paragraph 1.

   _____

2. Underline the main idea only *if it is stated* in the paragraph.

Paragraph 2

One urban legend involves the story of a man who travels to Las Vegas on business. He meets a woman at the hotel bar and they share a couple of drinks. Later, he wakes up in a pool of blood in his hotel bathtub. His kidney has been removed. Another urban legend tells the story of woman who goes to a department store to shop for clothes. Her husband becomes concerned when she doesn't come home at the end of the day. Then, he gets a call from the hospital. His wife's finger was cut off to steal her diamond ring while she was in the fitting room. These are just two examples of urban legends.

—Adapted from *Urban Legends: A Modern Day Mythology*, by Corrina Underwood. *After Dark Newsletter, Aug 2004 pp. 8–10.*

3. Write a main idea sentence for Paragraph 2.

   _____

4. Underline the main idea only *if it is stated* in the paragraph.

Paragraph 3

Romantic love has been portrayed in a variety ofways in Western cultures for centuries. The love story of Isis and Osiris was recorded in Egypt more than 3000 years ago. Ovid composed poems to romantic love in the first century B.C. in ancient Rome. And the *Kama Sutra* (Hindu words for "love" and for "pleasure and sensual gratification," respectively), a Hindu treatise on the art of love, including explicit sexual instructions, was composed sometime between the first and fourth centuries A.D.

—From Schwartz, Scott, *Marriages and Families: Diversity and Change,* 4th edition, © 2003, p. 89. Reprinted by permission of Pearson Education, Inc. Upper Saddle River, NJ.

5. Write a main idea sentence for Paragraph 3.

   _____

6. Underline the main idea only *if it is stated* in the paragraph.

Paragraph 4

The most common type of situation comedy or "sitcom," according to Dr. Richard F. Taflinger, is the actcom. An *actcom* is a sitcom which emphasizes verbal or physical action of the characters. "Bewitched" and "Ghost Whisperer" are examples of an actcom. A domcom, or domestic comedy is usually centered around a family unit, particularly the children. The greatest emphasis in a *domcom* is on the growth and development of the characters as human beings. Unlike an actcom, a *domcom* tends to have a wider sense of seriousness. Examples of *domcom* include; "Roseanne," "The Fresh Prince of Bel-Air," "Girlfriends," and "The Cosby Show." Dramedy is the rarest and most serious type of sitcom. A *dramedy* emphasizes thought-provoking themes, such as war, crime, aging, racism, sexism, poverty, etc. While humor is used, it is not the main purpose of a *dramedy*. "M*A*S*H" and "South Park" are examples of *dramedy*.

—Adapted from *Sitcom: What It Is, How It Works*, by Richard F. Taflinger, PhD

7. Write a main idea sentence for Paragraph 4.

   _____

8. Underline the main idea only *if it is stated* in the paragraph.

Summarization Activity

Directions: *Write the major headings in this chapter. Under each heading, write a couple of sentences about the most important topics presented in the section of text that follows that heading.*

First Heading _____

What information is most important? _____

_____

_____

_____

Second Heading _____

What information is most important? _____

_____

_____

Third Heading _____

What information is most important? _____

_____

_____

_____

Fourth Heading _____

What information is most important? _____

_____

_____

_____

Combine the information you wrote in this outline into a paragraph to summarize what you have learned in this chapter.

Reflection Activity

How am I am going to apply what I have learned in this chapter?

Directions: *Write a paragraph discussing the two or three things you learned about paragraph structure that were most helpful to you and how you plan to use what you have learned.*

_____

_____

_____

_____

_____

_____

_____

♟♟♟ Skills In Practice ▶ Reading Selection 1

LIAR, LIAR—HOW CAN YOU TELL?
Tina Kells

Accessing Prior Knowledge

Questions for Discussion

1. Can you tell if someone is lying? If so, what behaviors do they exhibit?

2. Can you remember a particular incident in which you were surprised by the lie of someone you trusted? If so, what happened? How were they able to fool you?

Preview and Predict

Directions: *Look at the title of the selection. Think about what you already know about the subject. Then, write a couple of predictions about what you are going to read. For instance, what will the author discuss about lying?*

1. _____

2. _____

Word Search and Discovery

Directions: *Skim through the selection to find the two words below. Underline both words in the selection. Then, use a dictionary to write their definitions in the spaces provided. As you read and encounter these words, see if the definitions you wrote fit the way each word is used in the selection.*

combust (*vb*): _____

fidget (*vb*): _____

Also, underline at least one new word as you read the selection and write your guess as to its meaning in the right margin of the text.

LIAR, LIAR – HOW CAN YOU TELL?
Tina Kells

1   If only it were as simple as the "liar, liar, pants on fire" nursery rhyme to tell when a person is lying to you. Unfortunately liars rarely spontaneously combust and so we must find other ways to identify when somebody is being untruthful. You get a gut feeling that all is not right with the other person's words. This is your first and best sign that you are dealing with a liar. But there are some tell-tale body language cues that will add credence to your instincts. If you just have a feeling you're being deceived keep your guard up, but if you get that feeling AND observe any of the following six behaviors rest assured that all is not as it appears.

2   **1. Liars fidget.** They fidget a lot. They shift their feet, they sway while talking and they gesture awkwardly and inappropriately with their hands. Subconsciously, when we lie we feel on display and this makes some people feel uncomfortable. It is this discomfort that makes one act all fidgety.

3   **2. It's all in the eyes!** Liars don't like to look you in the eye for too long. Or, conversely if a liar is aware of this fact, they may look you in the eye much longer than social norms dictate. Liars also blink less frequently than the norm, as if they need to keep their eyes open and on you in order to assure themselves that you believe their tale. If a person makes eye contact too little, or too much, they may be lying. At the very least they are not comfortable with the subject of the conversation. Shifty eyes, looking away and looking back quickly and awkwardly is another sign that somebody may be lying. After all, we call being dishonest "being shifty" for a reason.

4   **3. Liars touch their face and mouth a lot.** This is something that most liars can't control even if they are aware they are doing it. It is a reflexive psychological response to being untruthful, a symbolic way of stopping the lies from coming out. This behavior is most often seen in liars who feel bad about being untruthful or who are being untruthful for so called noble reasons like sparing another hurt feelings or keeping a promise to another to hold a secret in strict confidence.

5   **4. More often than not, liars look down when telling a story.** It's as if they are thinking of what to say next. It is a well known and well studied reflexive psycho-social reaction that people who are truthfully recounting a real event look up when trying to recall the details. They are looking up and mentally picturing the events that they are talking about almost as if they are looking at their brain for answers. Liars look down because they are not remembering but creating a story and they need to look at a blank canvas,

like the ground, in order to spin their story and make it convincing. It's a way of concentrating on what is being said and making it work with what has already been said, in other words convincingly lying.

6   **5. Liars mix up fine details.** When a liar spins a lie they make a point of registering the core of what is being said for future use but they often forget the minor credibility building details they've incorporated into their lie. A truthful person is more likely to be consistent in recalling smaller details of an event than a liar because the truth-sayer has the mental picture to pull up and think of when asked a question. A liar lacks this mental picture and therefore has no fail-safe way to recall smaller details.

7   **6. People who lie tend to get defensive or they take a defensive posture with others when confronted about the lie, even if they are not actually being accused of lying.** When you second-guess a liar they are quick to react in anger in order to put YOU on the defensive and deflect attention from the lie at hand. Even if you ask an innocent question like, "Where did it happen again?" or, "Can you tell that story over again to Bob?" a liar may get defensive, angry or irritated. In very rare cases, a liar may act like they don't even know what you are talking about. Inconsistency and a defensive posture combined almost always signal a liar.

8   So next time you fear you're being lied to take a closer look at the body language of the liar. Non-verbal cues aren't burning pants but they are a pretty good indication of what is going on in a person's subconscious. Unless an individual suffers from a serious social disorder lying will, on some level, make them uneasy and this discomfort will come out in their body language. The reality is most people are uncomfortable with being untruthful and body language, unlike the spoken word, cannot tell a lie.

The Write Connection

Directions: *Write a paragraph about three things you learned or that you think are most important in the reading selection.*

_____

_____

_____

_____

_____

Comprehension Check

Directions: *See how many questions you can answer without referring to the selection. Then, review the selection to write more complete responses.*

1. What is the topic of the selection? _____

   _____

2. What do the six major details have in common about the topic? (*ways? steps?*

   reasons?) _____ to tell if someone is lying or the *types* of behaviors
   that can indicate when someone is lying.

3. Make your own main idea sentence for the selection.

   _____

   _____

4. Underline the sentence in paragraph 1 that best describes the main idea of the selection.

5. What is one reason why a liar fidgets? _____

   _____

   _____

6. What are two ways you can use eye movements to spot a liar?

   _____

   _____

_____ 7. What is meant by the term *reflexive psychological response*, as it is used in
   paragraph 4 of the selection?
   a. a response caused by mental illness
   b. a response indicative of muscle strain
   c. a response that is meant to hurt others
   d. an uncontrollable response to lying

8. Why is a person who is telling the truth more likely to look up when recalling

   details? _____

9. Why is a truthful person more likely to be consistent in recalling smaller details

   of an event than a liar? _____

   _____

_____ 10. Liars tend to react in anger when confronted about a lie, even when they are not actually being accused of lying because:
   a. they know they are right.
   b. they are upset you did not believe them and are worried about the consequences of lying.
   c. they want to put you on the defensive and distract you from the lie they told.
   d. they think looking angry will make it look as though they were telling the truth.

Critical Thinking Check

1. What is another way to spot a liar?

   _____

   _____

   _____

_____ 2. The author has written the selection for the purpose of
   a. persuading the reader to avoid lying.
   b. illustrating the behaviors that are common among people who are lying.
   c. entertaining the reader with humorous examples of people who are caught in a lie.
   d. explaining several ways to tell a convincing lie.

_____ 3. Which of the following conclusions can be drawn from the information contained in the selection?
   a. Most liars are unaware that they are lying.
   b. Liars often believe that they are telling the truth.
   c. If you suspect that someone is lying, you should never trust the person again.
   d. Liars often lack the ability to convince others that they are telling the truth.

4. Do you think it would be impossible to spot a liar who is aware of the six signs of lying? Why or why not? _____

   _____

   _____

   _____

Vocabulary Check

Directions: *See if any of the words you underlined in the selection are among the list of words below. If not, write your words in the spaces provided. Guess the meaning of the words from the way they were used in the selection (use context clues). Then, look up the definition of each word in the dictionary to see if you were right.*

dictate (*n*): Your guess: _____

    Dictionary Definition: _____

reflex (*n*): Your guess: _____

    Dictionary Definition: _____

psycho-social (*adj*): Your guess: _____

    Dictionary Definition: _____

Your word: _____ Your guess: _____

    Dictionary Definition: _____

Your word: _____ Your guess: _____

    Dictionary Definition: _____

♟♟♟ Skills in Practice ▶ Reading Selection 2

"POWER: VERBAL AND NONVERBAL BEHAVIORS," FROM *PRACTICAL APPLICATIONS OF PSYCHOLOGY*
Anthony Grasha

Accessing Prior Knowledge

Questions for Discussion

1. Do you know someone who changed in some way after being promoted? In what way did the person change?

2. How can you tell when a person has power or authority?

Preview and Predict

Directions: *Look at the title of the selection. Think about what you already know about the subject. Then, write a couple of predictions about what you are going to read. For instance, what will the author discuss about power?*

1. _____

2. _____

Word Search and Discovery

Directions: *Skim through the selection to find the two words below. Underline both words in the selection. Then, use a dictionary to write their definitions in the spaces provided. As you read and encounter these words, see if the definitions you wrote fit the way each word is used in the selection.*

subordinate (*adj*): _____

subtle (*adj*): _____

Also, underline at least one new word as you read the selection and write your guess as to its meaning in the right margin of the text.

THE USE OF POWER IS SEEN IN OUR VERBAL AND NONVERBAL BEHAVIORS

Anthony Grasha

1   Demanding that someone do something, shouting at a subordinate, or shaking your fist at someone are rather obvious expressions of power. Yet there are also a number of more subtle ways that power is expressed in our interactions with others: In a review of the literature, Nancy Henley (1977) reports several ways that this occurs.

2   **Posture.** People who perceive themselves as equal in power and status tend to assume postures when talking. If equal, both may sit in a relaxed position or stand together while casually discussing something. When there are power differences, the person with less power often has to stand, or if sitting, is in a much less relaxed posture.

3   **Height.** Judges, police desk sergeants, and the rabbi, priest, or minister all tell us what to do from several feet over our heads. In business organizations, the heads of the organization are typically on an upper floor while subordinates occupy the lower floors.

4   **Space.** Individuals with more power tend to occupy more space. Key managers in an organization have more office space than do their subordinates. The rich and powerful typically have bigger homes and yards than do the poor and less powerful. In most homes, adults tend to have larger territory claims than do children. Not only do more powerful people have more space, but they are generally freer to enter the space of those with less power. A guard can enter the cell of a prisoner anytime. A boss can typically enter the office of a subordinate unannounced, but the opposite is not generally true.

5   **Time.** The use of time reflects the amount of power people have. People with less power are often asked to wait to see those with more. Patients wait to see a doctor and subordinates must wait to see their boss. Poorer and less powerful individuals in fact spend more time waiting than do the more powerful. Their lives are filled with waiting in hospital emergency rooms and clinics, for unemployment or welfare benefits, for food stamps, in courts, and for other services. People with less power are often treated as if their time is unimportant. "They can afford to wait" is a comment sometimes heard. Yet people with more power treat their time as a precious commodity. They account for every minute and may even take time management seminars to see how to use it better. They may make those with less power feel guilty for taking some of it. Students, for example, are sometimes apologetic because they took some of a faculty member's time outside of class. I have noticed that the faculty members involved send verbal and nonverbal messages that suggest they are busy and do not have much time to be bothered. It is also not unusual for people with more power to sell their time as consultants. Expertise is an important source of influence, and people are willing to pay for it.

6   **Style of Speech.** People who are dominant and have more power are much more confident and precise when they speak. Individuals with less power tend to have more hesitancy and self-doubt in their expressions. They use many more qualifying phrases and tend to put themselves down somewhat. They might say, "I may not know anything about this and probably should not say anything, but I think the solution may be . . ."

7   **Interruptions.** Individuals with more power and status typically interrupt those with less power more often. Teachers interrupt students more often, and within an academic setting, instructors with a higher academic rank interrupt those with a lower academic rank. In male-female conversations, Henley argues that men tend to have more power. This gets reflected in the pattern of interruptions. Some studies have shown that as many as 96 percent of the interruptions and 100 percent of the overlaps in conversation were made by men.

8   **Touch.** People with more power and status tend to touch those with less more often. In conversations, bosses touch their subordinates more, physicians touch their patients, and men touch women more than they do other men.

The Write Connection

Directions: *Write a paragraph about three things you learned or that you think are most important in the reading selection.*

_____

_____

_____

_____

_____

Comprehension Check

Directions: *See how many questions you can answer without referring to the selection. Then, review the selection to write more complete responses.*

1. What is listed in the major details about the topic? (Are they *ways, types, steps, reasons, differences* or *similarities, effects,* or *events?*) _____

   _____

2. Make your own main idea sentence for the selection.

   There are _____

3. Underline the sentence that is most similar to the main idea sentence you created.

_____ 4. People who have more power tend to have postures that are
   a. stiff. b. expressive. c. formal. d. relaxed.

5. Give one example that illustrates the way height is used to express power.

   _____

_____ 6. People with power not only have more space, but also have
   a. more claims.
   b. more freedom to enter the space of those with less power.
   c. more freedom to enter the space of the rich and powerful.
   d. more exciting vehicles.

7. Give one example that illustrates the way in which time expresses power.

   _____

_____ 8. Powerful people often treat their time as a precious commodity by
   a. creating waiting rooms to make subordinates more comfortable.
   b. accounting for every minute.
   c. seeking the advice of a consultant.
   d. attending benefit seminars.

9. Individuals with less power tend to have more _____

_____

10. According to Nancy Henley, what have studies shown about interruptions and

overlaps in conversation? _____

_____

11. Give an example that illustrates the way in which touch expresses power.

_____

Critical Thinking Check

1. Do you think that being inconsiderate is necessary to be powerful? Why, or
   why not?

_____

_____

_____ 2. The author has written the selection for the purpose of
   a. informing the reader about the ways in which power can be expressed.
   b. relating the most effective ways to achieve power through verbal and non-
      verbal behaviors.
   c. engaging the reader by relating humorous examples of powerful people
      and how they behave.
   d. persuading the reader to be mindful of behaviors that can lead to miscom-
      munication.

_____ 3. Which of the following statements supports the author's contention that power
   can be expressed in subtle ways?
   a. Judges and police desk sergeants tell us what to do.
   b. People with power often hesitate when they speak.
   c. A guard can enter the cell of a prisoner at any time.
   d. Expertise is an important source of influence.

4. Who has the most power in your family? Based on what you learned from the selection, illustrate the ways that this person exhibits power. _____

_____

_____

Vocabulary Check

Directions: *See if any of the words you underlined in the selection are among the list of words below. If not, write your words in the spaces provided. Guess the meaning of the words from the way they were used in the selection. Then, look up the definition of each word in the dictionary to see if you were right.*

commodity (*n*): Your guess: _____

   Dictionary Definition: _____

overlaps (*n*): Your guess: _____

   Dictionary Definition: _____

Your word: _____ Your guess: _____

   Dictionary Definition: _____

Your word: _____ Your guess: _____

   Dictionary Definition: _____

5 Supporting Details and Transitions

"Knowledge is power."

– Sir Francis Bacon

In this chapter you will learn how to:

Use Transition Words to Locate Major Details

Recognize the Relationship Between Major and Minor Details

You will learn the following strategy:

♟ Picture Perfect

▲ Authors add transition words in order to introduce and emphasize major supporting details.

Preview and Predict ▶ What do you know so far?

How many of the following questions can you answer before you read the chapter?

• What are two types of supporting details?

_____

- How can transition words help you find the major details of a paragraph?

  _____

- Think of one way in which the picture relates to this chapter's objectives.

  _____

Now, as you read the chapter look for the answers to see if you were right.

MAJOR AND MINOR SUPPORTING DETAILS

There are two types of supporting details in a paragraph: major details and minor details. **Major details** are sentences that help to form the basic outline of a paragraph by directly discussing or supporting the main idea. For instance, when a main idea sentence is turned into a question, the answer will be found in the major details listed in the paragraph.

On the other hand, **minor details** are sentences that are added to further illustrate, explain, or support a major detail. Minor details may include additional facts, statistics, examples, or descriptions. For instance, a _major_ detail might be "First, take lecture notes." A _minor_ detail would be "By taking lecture notes, you will ensure that you have the information you need to study." _Minor details_ fill in the information that you need in order to create a more complete picture of an author's major ideas. Imagine reading a paragraph that contained only the following sentences:

> There are three primary colors in an artist's palette. The first major color is red. Blue is the second major color. Yellow is the third major color.

How boring! Think of a _type_ of color for each major detail in the outline below.

Main Idea: There are three primary colors in an artist's palette.

    Major Detail: _One_ primary color is red.

        For instance, _____ (Minor Detail)
            (Can you think of a type of red?)

    Major Detail: Blue is _also_ a primary color.

        For example, _____ (Minor Detail)
            (Can you think of a type of blue?)

Major Detail: *Finally*, yellow is a primary color.

For instance, _____ (Minor Detail)
(Can you think of a type of yellow?)

The answers you wrote above are called *minor details*. When minor detail sentences are added, you are able to see more information about each major detail (color) that is presented. Minor detail sentences sometimes begin with phrases such as *for instance, for example,* or *these include.* These phrases indicate that additional information related to the major detail is about to follow.

Recognizing the relationship between the major and minor details in a paragraph as you read helps you to improve your comprehension because you can see how the author's ideas relate to one another to provide meaning.

TRANSITION WORDS AND MAJOR DETAILS

Authors often use transition words to highlight the list of *major* details in a paragraph or passage. Here are some examples of commonly used transition words.

Commonly Used Transition Words		
first	then	as a result
one	next	consequently
also	last	in conclusion
second	but	therefore
another	however	in a like manner
third	in addition	on the other hand
finally	yet	similarly

Will you always see transition words in a paragraph? No. When transition words are included, however, you can see the outline structure of a paragraph very quickly.

Using Transition Words to Find the Organization of a Paragraph

You can read very quickly when you know in advance what type of information will be presented in a paragraph. Transition words can help you to see how the major details in a paragraph are organized to present certain types of information. For instance, *first, next, then, before, after,* and *last* are examples of transition words that are used to indicate steps, stages, events, or processes in a *sequence of events* that must be presented in a specific order.

How would you discuss the *steps* involved in making French toast? What transition words would you use to present each step in the process? Fill in the blanks below with transition words that would indicate the right order in which to prepare French toast:

_____ mix 2 eggs and 4 tablespoons of milk in a medium-sized bowl.

_____ dip 3 slices of white bread one at a time into the mixture until each one is well-coated.

_____ place each slice on a hot, lightly oiled skillet.

_____ each side of the slices of bread is browned to your liking, remove and place on a large plate.

_____ serve with syrup or powdered sugar.

You might have used the transition words *first, then, next, when,* and *last* to present each *step* to make French toast. These words tell you that the major details must appear in a specific order.

On the other hand, *one, also, another,* and *finally* are examples of transition words used to indicate major details that can be listed *in any order*. These types of transition words tell you that it doesn't matter which major detail appears first. For example, what transition words would you use to present each type of home or dwelling below?

_____ apartment

_____ condominium

_____ townhouse

You might have used the transition words *first, one, also, another,* or *finally* because the types of homes or dwellings can be listed *in any order*. It doesn't matter which major detail appears first. By recognizing the organization of major details, you will improve your comprehension because you will know what to expect in a paragraph as you read.

Memory Check 1 How much do you remember?

1. What are the two types of supporting details in a paragraph?

   _____

2. What are minor details?

   _____

   _____

_____ 3. Transition words are generally found in sentences that contain
   a. major details.   c. any order.
   b. an introduction.   d. specific order.

4. Write two examples of transition words that can be used for presenting steps, stages, or events *in a specific order.*

_____

5. Write two examples of transition words used for presenting major details *in any order.*

_____

Activity 5.1 ▶ Using Transition Words to Find the Organization of a Paragraph

Directions: *Write appropriate transition words next to each major detail in the outlines below. Then, decide if the major details in each outline are presented in a specific order or if they are presented in any order.*

Examples of transition words for major details include the following:

In any order: *one, another, also, finally*

Specific order: *first, second, next, then, third, before, after, last*

1. There are three **stages** in the memory process.

   _____ Sensory Memory

   _____ Working or Short-Term Memory

   _____ Long-Term Memory

   _____ The major details in the outline above are listed
   a. in any order.   b. in a specific order.

2. There are four **steps** in the home buying process.

   _____ Find a Realtor.

   _____ Investigate the neighborhood.

   _____ Hire a professional inspector.

   _____ Negotiate the final cost.

   _____ The major details in the outline above are listed
   a. in any order.   b. in a specific order.

3. There are three **ways** to cook potatoes.

    _____ fried

    _____ baked

    _____ mashed

    _____ The major details in the outline above are listed
    a. in any order.   b. in a specific order.

4. There are four **things** to remember if you want to reduce debt.

    _____ Use cash instead of credit cards.

    _____ Sell possessions you don't absolutely need or use.

    _____ Maintain a diary to keep track of spending.

    _____ Create a budget and stick to it.

    _____ The major details in the outline above are listed
    a. in any order.   b. in a specific order.

5. There are several college **courses** required for nursing majors.

    _____ Biology

    _____ Chemistry

    _____ Microbiology

    _____ Anatomy and Physiology

    _____ The major details in the outline above are listed
    a. in any order.   b. in a specific order.

Using Transition Words to Separate the Main Idea from an Introduction

Authors may include one or several sentences of introduction at the beginning of a paragraph to get you interested in the topic *before* they present the main idea. For instance, an introductory sentence might be "Everyone wants to save money." The main idea would be "There are several ways to save money." If you turn an introductory sentence into a question, however, you will *not* see the answers listed in the major details because an introduction is *not* part of the basic outline of a paragraph.

Transition words can help you to find the main idea sentence when there is an introduction at the beginning of a paragraph. Look for the *first* transition word in the paragraph. *The main idea sentence is usually found **directly before** the first major detail in a paragraph that contains an introduction.*

For instance, the paragraph below contains an introduction. Underline the transition words in the paragraph. Then, answer the questions that follow. Some of the answers have been provided for you.

Example

¹Does your mind wander when others are speaking? ²Do you miss important information during lectures? ³Understanding requires active listening. ⁴Active listening can be improved if you follow four procedures. ⁵First, determine the organization of the speaker's ideas. ⁶This will help you listen for key points or details that support the goal of the person's message. ⁷Second, ask questions. ⁸For instance, you can ask yourself what you are supposed to be learning from the message or whether there is additional information that you would like to know. ⁹Third, silently paraphrase. ¹⁰When you can summarize what someone is saying in your own words as you listen, you will know that you have really understood the information. ¹¹Fourth, attend to non-verbal cues. ¹²Pay attention to what is not being said. ¹³The speaker's tone of voice, facial expressions, and gestures can give you valuable information about what is behind the message.

—Adapted from *The Challenge of Effective Speaking.* 10th ed. by Rudolph Verderber. pp. 52–55.

1. How many major details are listed in the paragraph? _____

2. Write the first major detail in the example paragraph. First, __S_____

   _____

3. Write the sentence which appears *before* the *first* major detail: _____

   _____ This is the main idea sentence.

How can you be certain that sentence 4 is the main idea? *Turn it into a question.*

What are the four _____ to improve active listening? Do you see the four procedures listed in the major details found in the rest of the paragraph? Yes. Now you know you have found the main idea. In fact, the first procedure or *answer* is

found in sentence _____. The first answer to your question immediately follows the main idea sentence. The first three sentences in the example paragraph are

called the _____. Look at the *first* sentence. How do you know that this sentence is *not* the main idea? *Turn it into a question.* Is the paragraph about how your mind wanders when others are speaking? No. Now, turn sentence 2 into a question. Is the paragraph about missing important details during lectures?

_____ Turn the third sentence into a question. Do you see a list of major details that discuss how understanding requires active listening? No. Now turn sentence 4 into a question. Can you see the four procedures for improving active listening listed in the major details of the paragraph? Yes. The main idea is the *only* sentence in the paragraph that can be turned into a question that is answered by the major details in the paragraph.

Complete the following outline for the example paragraph. Some of the answers have been provided for you.

Main Idea: _____

Which are?

The answer will be listed in your responses below.

Transition Words	**Major Details**
First	_____
_____	ask questions
Third	_____
_____	attend to non-verbal cues

Activity 5.2 ▶ Using Transition Words to Find the Outline of a Paragraph

Directions: *Underline the transition words in each of the following paragraphs. Locate the main idea. Use the prompt, "Which are . . . ?" to turn the main idea into a question. Then, fill in the transition words and major details in the outline spaces that follow them. Some of the answers have been provided for you.*

Paragraph 1

Do you like to garden, but you're afraid of spiders? Here are a few facts about garden spiders. First, garden spiders can protect flowers and plants from harmful insects and bugs. You can reduce the amount of pesticides you use if you have garden spiders because their webs catch many undesirable garden intruders. The design of the garden spider web is <u>also</u> one of nature's most artful creations. The silk that the spider weaves as it spins around and around forms a perfect pattern that is as strong as it is beautiful. Finally, the garden spider is not interested in you. The garden spider is only concerned with finding dinner and is probably more afraid of you than you are of it.

Main Idea: _____ Which are?

    Transition Words   **Major Details**

    _____   garden spiders can protect flowers and plants from
                 harmful insects and bugs.

    also   _____

                      _____

    _____   _____

Paragraph 2

    Do you have many friends? If not, perhaps you need to ask yourself if you have what it takes to be a good friend. The rules of friendship are few but valuable for developing a long-lasting relationship. The first rule of friendship is trust. A good friend can be trusted to keep damaging or sensitive information from others who might use it to their advantage. You can trust a good friend to guard your back in times of trouble or weakness. The second rule of friendship is dependability. You can depend upon a good friend when you need help. A good friend will be there when you need one. The third rule of friendship is respect. A good friend will show respect even in times of disagreement. A good friend knows how to play fair. You can be sure that a good friend will see the best in you at times when you may not see the best in yourself.

Main Idea: _____

_____ Which are?

    Transition Words: **Major Details**

    _____   _____

    second   _____

    _____   _____

Paragraph 3

    Do you have too much stress in your life? Do you sometimes feel as if you are losing control? There are several ways to ease stress. First, you can prioritize your responsibilities. Make a list of the things you need to do each day so that you can see which obligations are most important. In this way you can make sure you accomplish the most important tasks each day rather than trying to do every task in one day. You can also delegate some of your required tasks. For instance, ask your spouse or children to help with certain household chores or errands that you need to do. Exercise is another way to ease stress. Just thirty minutes of walking three times a week can improve your body's ability to handle stress. Finally, learn to say no. Realize that you need time for rest and reflection in order to have a healthy life.

Main Idea: _____ Which are?

Transition Words	Major Details
_____	_____
also	_____
another	_____
_____	_____

Paragraph 4

How much rent do you pay per month? Have you ever thought about buying a house? There are several steps in the home buying process. First, find a Realtor. A Realtor will be able to find a house in the area you like and the price range you can afford. Next, when you find a house that you like, investigate the neighborhood. Drive around the area at night and on weekends to see if there is excessive noise. Look at the local police web sites for crime statistics on the neighborhood. Check the quality of the neighborhood schools your children would attend. Then, if you like the results of your investigation, hire a professional inspector. An inspector will look at everything from the appliances to the foundation and plumbing. If the house requires too many costly repairs, you may want to reconsider your purchase. Finally, negotiate the final cost based on your credit. Sometimes you can work with the owner to pay for closing costs before you buy the house.

Main Idea: _____ Which are?

Transition Words	Major Details
_____	_____
_____	When you find a house you like, investigate the neighborhood.
Then	_____
_____	Negotiate the final cost based on your credit.

Paragraph 5

Would you like to save money on gasoline? Here are some helpful tips to improve your fuel efficiency. First, make sure your tires are properly inflated. If they are low on air, the engine must work harder to move your car. Also, try to maintain an even speed of 55 mph. Your engine uses extra fuel when you drive faster than this. Finally, get regular tune-ups. An engine that is not regularly tuned uses extra gas.

Main Idea: _____ Which are?

Transition Words	**Major Details**
_____	_____
_____	Try to maintain an even speed of 55 mph.
_____	_____

Using Transition Words to Find or Make a Main Idea Sentence

Transition words can help you to create a main idea sentence because they emphasize the major details in a paragraph. Once you see the list of major details in a paragraph that you are reading, you can ask yourself what they have in common to make your own main idea sentence. Then it will be easier for you to find the main idea sentence when it is stated in a paragraph or when it is implied or not directly stated. For example, what is the main idea of the following paragraph?

One way to reduce debt is to use cash instead of credit cards. It is easy to overspend when you do not see how much cash is represented by a purchase. *Another* way to reduce debt is to sell possessions you don't absolutely need or use. The money you earn can be used to pay off credit cards or loans that include finance charges on the balance each month and can add late fees. *Third,* you can maintain a diary to keep track of your spending. Keeping a spending diary helps you recognize and eliminate bad habits such as spending more money when you are hungry or depressed. *Finally,* you should create a budget and stick to it. You can increase your likelihood of sticking to a budget if it is strict, but reasonable. Remembering these four things can help you to reduce debt.

How many major details are listed in the paragraph? _____ . What do the four major details have in common? They are all ways to _____

Create a main idea for the paragraph using the following format:

1. There are _____ ways to _____

_____ 2. The main idea is
   a. in the first sentence.   c. implied.
   b. in the middle of a paragraph.   d. in the last sentence.

See if you can create a main idea sentence for the paragraph by summarizing the major details about the topic.

> *First,* make the commitment to improve your health. Smoking is a leading cause of cancer as well as of heart and lung disease. *Then,* seek professional help. Your doctor can recommend a program designed to help smokers kick the habit. The program may include the use of nicotine patches or chewing gum that help to curb the craving for tobacco. *Next,* form a support group. Family and friends as well as people who have successfully quit smoking can be a source of encouragement during the withdrawal process. *In addition,* you should avoid activities or environments you associate with smoking. For instance, it is a good idea to avoid going to bars or casinos if you find it difficult to drink or gamble unless you are smoking. *Finally,* replace smoking with exercise. Walking or biking for thirty minutes every day will seem difficult at first, but you will soon feel the benefits in your improved emotional and physical well-being.

How many major details are listed in the paragraph? _____ . What do the major details have in common? _____

Create a main idea for the paragraph using the following format:

1. There are _____ ways to _____ .

_____ 2. The main idea is
   a. in the first sentence.   c. implied.
   b. in the middle of the paragraph. d. in the last sentence.

When you see transition words, you know you have found the major details in a paragraph. Remember, however, that *you will not always have transition words to help you find every major detail.* You need to be able to *see* what is being listed in the major details of a paragraph to find or make the main idea sentence.

Memory Check 2 How much do you remember?

1. What is one reason some people are easily confused by an introduction?

   _____

   _____

2. When there is an introduction, you can usually find the main idea sentence directly _____ the *first* major detail in the paragraph.

3. The main idea is the *only* sentence that can be turned into a _____ that is answered by the major details in the rest of the paragraph.

4. You can use transition words to find the list of major details in a paragraph so that you can make _____.

5. You can create a main idea for a paragraph by asking yourself what the major details have _____.

6. You can also use transition words to create a sentence that summarizes what the paragraph is about when the main idea is *not* stated, or _____.

RECOGNIZING THE RELATIONSHIP BETWEEN MAJOR AND MINOR DETAILS

Reading is a visual experience. The more involved you are in the process of reading, the more you can see in terms of the pictures you are able to create in your mind as you read. Then, reading will become more like watching a movie as the words go by.

Picture Perfect: A Strategy for Improving the Visual Experience of Reading

Picture Perfect is a strategy that helps you to recognize the relationship between the major and minor details in a paragraph. It involves asking questions that help you visualize the picture created by each new major detail as you read.

To apply the Picture Perfect strategy, you should follow these steps.

1. Find the First Major Detail Sentence in the Paragraph

Look for transition words like *first* or *one* as a way to locate it.

2. Stop and Imagine

Stop and imagine what is happening in the major detail sentence. A major detail presents a picture for you to see. You want to relate the image you have created to the topic being discussed in the paragraph.

3. Question the Next Sentence

The sentence that follows the first major detail could be a new major detail or it could be a minor detail. When you can recognize the difference between major and minor details, you will improve the visual experience of reading.

There are two questions that you should ask as you read the sentence following the first major detail sentence:

1. **Do I still see the same picture in my mind?** Minor details support or illustrate what is happening in a major detail sentence. Each sentence that *still* supports or describes the scene created in your mind by the first major detail sentence is a *minor detail sentence.*

2. **Did the picture change?** Each major detail sentence creates a new scene for you to picture in your mind. So, every time the scene *changes*, you have found

a new *major detail*. When you find a new major detail, stop and imagine what is happening in the sentence. Then, question the next sentence to see how it relates to the picture created by the major detail. If you take the time to stop and imagine each major detail, then it will be easy for you to recognize a minor detail or a new major detail when it appears in the next sentence.

Now, apply the Picture Perfect strategy to see the relationship between the major and minor details in the familiar paragraph below. Then, answer the questions that follow.

Example

¹There are three primary colors in an artist's palette. ²The *first* primary color is red. ³The types of red may vary from a light shade of purple to a dark shade of pink. ⁴Blue is *also* a primary color in an artist's palette. ⁵An artist could use midnight blue to depict the color of a stormy sky. ⁶*Finally,* yellow is a primary color. ⁷It appears in several shades that can range from hues of orange to the palest sunlight.

The *first* major detail involves what color in sentence #2? _____ A major detail creates a scene or picture in your mind. Do you still see the color red in sentence #3? Yes. It is describing the shades or types of red. This is a minor detail because it is *still* talking about the color red. Are you still looking at the color red in

sentence #4? _____ The scene has changed! Now you are looking at the color _____.

Every time the scene changes, you have found a *major detail*. Sentence #4 is a major detail about the color blue. If you can see the picture, you will be able to tell whether the next sentence is still talking about what you see or whether the scene or picture has changed to a new major detail or picture. Are you *still* looking at the color

blue in sentence #5? _____ You still see the color blue. So, sentence #5 is a *minor*

detail. Are you still looking at the color blue in sentence #6? _____ The scene

has changed in sentence #6. This means that sentence #6 is a _____ detail about

the color _____. Sentence #7 is a _____ detail. Why? _____

_____

Sentence Identification: You can identify each sentence in the example paragraph as follows:

| #1 Main Idea | #2 Major Detail | #3 Minor Detail | #4 Major Detail |
| #5 Minor Detail | #6 Major Detail | #7 Minor Detail | |

Memory Check 3   How much do you remember?

1. What are the three steps to apply when you use the Picture Perfect strategy?

   a. _____

   b. _____

   c. _____

2. What are the two questions you should ask in order to see the difference between a major detail and a minor detail in a paragraph as you read?

   a. _____

   b. _____

Activity 5.3 ▶ Sentence Identification I

Directions: *Identify each of the sentences in the following paragraphs as an introduction (Intro), main idea (Main), major detail (Major), or a minor detail (Minor). Then, answer the questions that follow each paragraph. Some of the answers have been provided for you.*

Paragraph 1

¹Do you want to buy a new car? ²It's not easy to buy a car you like that is also affordable. ³You can find the right car for you if you follow these steps. ⁴First, you should study Internet sites for the specific features that you want. ⁵For instance, choose the size and model that you can afford. ⁶Check for special options that you definitely want to include as well as those that can be eliminated in order to get a better price. ⁷Then, visit several dealerships to compare prices. ⁸Some dealerships may offer better incentives for end-of-season sales. ⁹Finally, don't buy a car at any dealership until you have investigated the service department. ¹⁰You can do this by calling the Better Business Bureau to make certain that there are no complaints. ¹¹You can find the right car for you if you follow these steps.

Sentence Identification:

1. #1 <u>Intro</u>   #2 <u>Intro</u>   #3 _____   #4 _____   #5 _____   #6 _____

   #7 _____   #8 _____   #9 _____   #10 _____   #11 <u>Main</u>

_____ 2. The major details are organized in

   a. any order.   b. a specific order.

Paragraph 2

¹The meat department of the modern grocery store contains a wide selection of beef, pork, and chicken. ²Some grocery stores may even offer selections of buffalo and ostrich meat. ³In the dairy department, you can find milk, eggs, and yogurt. ⁴You may also find a wide selection of cheeses from all over the world. ⁵Finally, in the produce department, you can find a wide variety of fruits and vegetables. ⁶Everything from apples to zucchini can be found in most produce departments. ⁷You can find a lot of variety in the three most common departments of the modern grocery store.

Sentence Identification:

1. #1 <u>Major</u>   #2 _____   #3 <u>Major</u>   #4 _____   #5 _____   #6 _____
   #7 _____

_____ 2. The major details are organized in
   a. any order.   b. a specific order.

Paragraph 3

¹If you want to find a main idea sentence within a paragraph, or to create one for a passage, you should ask, "What is the topic?" ²As you skim the paragraph, you will see words or phrases that will tell you what it is about. ³Second, you should ask, "What is listed about the topic?" ⁴Do you see a list of ways, steps, or types? ⁵These are the major details. ⁶Third, ask, "What do the major details have in common?" ⁷The main idea summarizes what is listed about the topic in the major details of the paragraph.

Sentence Identification:

1. #1 <u>Major</u>   #2 _____   #3 _____   #4 _____   #5 _____   #6 _____
   #7 _____

_____ 2. The major details in are organized in
   a. any order.   b. a specific order.

Paragraph 4

¹Camping in the wilderness is fun. ²You can sleep under the stars and enjoy the sweet smell of fresh air. ³Unfortunately, many campers are injured each year in the wilderness. ⁴There are some guidelines to follow if you want to avoid injury. ⁵First, stay away from high cliffs. ⁶It is easy to lose your balance if you

are afraid of heights. ⁷Railings are not often found at the edge of a cliff that is located in the wilderness where loose rocks can give way. ⁸It is also important to stay away from wildlife. ⁹Wild animals can cause serious injury. ¹⁰Never try to feed or pet an animal no matter how cute or harmless it may appear. ¹¹You should avoid swift flowing rivers. ¹²Many people have drowned in swift flowing rivers that contain sudden deep areas or strong undercurrents.

Sentence Identification:

1. #1 _____   #2 _____   #3 Intro   #4 _____   #5 _____   #6 _____

   #7 _____   #8 Major   #9 _____   #10 _____   #11 _____   #12 Minor

_____ 2. The major details are organized in

   a. any order.   b. a specific order.

Paragraph 5

¹If you are a new employee, you can make a good impression by arriving on time each day. ²If you are late more than once, you will give the impression that you don't care about the job or other employees who may depend on your timely arrival. ³You can also make a good impression as a new employee by demonstrating an interest in doing the work. ⁴If you waste time, take too many breaks, or make personal phone calls while on duty, you will give the impression that you are lazy or uninterested. ⁵Finally, as a new employee, you can make a good impression by limiting your absences. ⁶If you are absent more than twice during the first three months, you will give the impression that you would prefer to be unemployed.

Sentence Identification:

1. #1 Major   #2 _____   #3 _____   #4 _____   #5 _____   #6 _____

_____ 2. The major details in Paragraph 5 are organized in

   a. any order.   b. a specific order.

Activity 5.4 ▶ Sentence Identification II: Textbook Application

Directions: *Identify each of the sentences in the following paragraphs as an introduction (Intro), main idea (Main), major detail (Major), or minor detail (Minor). Then, answer the questions that follow each paragraph. Some of the answers have been provided for you.*

Paragraph 1

[1]Each day you use products containing substances that were developed and prepared by chemists. [2]When you shower in the morning, chemicals in soaps and shampoos combine with oils on your skin and scalp and are removed by rinsing with water. [3]When you brush your teeth, the chemicals in toothpaste clean your teeth and prevent plaque and tooth decay. [4]Toothpaste contains chemicals such as abrasives, antibacterial agents, enamel strengtheners, colorings, and flavorings. [5]In cosmetics and lotions, chemicals are used to moisturize, prevent deterioration of the product, fight bacteria, and thicken the product. [6]Your clothes may be made of natural fibers such as cotton or synthetics such as nylon or polyester. [7]Perhaps you wear a ring or watch made of gold, silver, or platinum. [8]Your breakfast cereal is probably fortified with iron, calcium, and phosphorus, while the milk you drink is enriched with vitamins A and D. [9]Antioxidants are chemicals added to your cereal to prevent it from spoiling.

—From *Basic Chemistry*, 2nd ed. © Karen C Timberlake and William Timberlake. pp. 3–4.

Sentence Identification:

1. #1 <u>Main</u>   #2 _____   #3 _____   #4 _____   #5 _____   #6 _____

    #7 <u>Major</u>   #8 _____   #9 _____

_____ 2. The major details in Paragraph 1 are organized in

   a. any order.   b. a specific order.

Paragraph 2

[1]During the past one and a half centuries, as nations and their citizens have made economic choices, they have been influenced by one of two competing philosophies. [2]The philosophy of *capitalism* maintains that private ownership and private decision making provide the best framework for creating growth and prosperity; that is, if people are simply left alone to pursue self-interests, good things will happen. [3]The competing philosophy of *socialism* teaches that private ownership and self-interest lead to bad economic results—inequality, poverty, and depressions. [4]Socialism argues that the state can better look after the interests of society at large through state ownership and central planning.

—From *Principles of Economics*, 7th Ed. by Roy J. Ruffin and Paul R. Gregory. p. 5.

Sentence Identification:

1. #1 _____   #2 <u>Major</u>   #3 _____   #4 _____

_____ 2. The major details in are organized in

    a. any order.   b. a specific order.

Paragraph 3

[1]"Chemistry plays an integral part in all aspects of medical legal death investigation," says Charles L. Cecil, forensic anthropologist and medical legal death investigator, San Francisco Medical Examiner's office. [2]"Crime-scene analysis of blood droplets determines whether they are human or nonhuman, while the analysis of toxicological samples of blood and/or other fluids helps determine the cause and time of death. [3]Specialists in forensic anthropology can analyze trace-element ratios in bones to identify the number of individuals in mixed human bone situations. [4]These conditions are quite often found during investigations of massive human-rights violations, such as the site of El Mozote in El Salvador."

—From *Basic Chemistry*, 2nd ed. © Karen C Timberlake and
William Timberlake. p. 1.

Sentence Identification:

1. #1 <u>Main</u>   #2 _____   #3 _____   #4 _____

_____ 2. The major details in are organized in

    a. any order.   b. a specific order.

Paragraph 4

[1]Toward the end of 1834 the pace of events quickened. [2]In November eighty-three members of the removal faction met at the comfortable home of John Ridge and organized themselves into a "Treaty party." [3]Early in 1835 two rival delegations arrived almost simultaneously in Washington: one was headed by John Ross, the other by John Ridge. [4]The "National party," as Ross's antitreaty forces were now known, was received politely enough by Jackson. [5]But it was with Ridge's Treaty party men that the administration negotiated. [6]By March a provisional treaty was drawn up. [7]It provided 13 million acres of land across the Mississippi in the Indian Territory (modern-day Oklahoma), along with $4.5 million in cash and various additional benefits—in exchange for the entire Cherokee Nation.

—From *The Pursuit of Liberty: A History of the American People*. 3rd ed. vol. I
by R. Jackson Wilson [et al.] p. 310.

Sentence Identification:

1. #1 <u>Main</u>   #2 _____   #3 _____   #4 _____   #5 <u>Minor</u>

   #6 _____   #7 _____

_____ 2. The major details in are organized in

    a. any order.   b. a specific order.

Paragraph 5

[1]Reasons are supported by factual statements and expert opinion. [2]The best support for reasons are verifiable factual statements. [3]Thus, suppose you support the speech goal "People should donate money to Alzheimer's research" with the reason "Alzheimer's disease is a major killer." [4]The statement "According to statistics presented in a recent article in *Time* magazine, Alzheimer's disease is the fourth leading cause of death among adults" provides factual support for that reason. [5]Statements from people reputed to be knowledgeable on the subject represent expert opinions. [6]Thus, expert-opinion support for the reason "Alzheimer's disease is a major killer" might be the statement "According to the U.S. surgeon general, 'By 2050 Alzheimer's disease may afflict 14 million people a year.'"

—From *The Challenge of Effective Speaking.* 10th ed. by
Rudolph Verderber. p. 359.

Sentence Identification:

1. #1 _____   #2 _____   #3 _____   #4 _____   #5 <u>Major</u>   #6 _____

_____ 2. The major details in are organized in
    a. any order.   b. a specific order.

Have you ever wondered why some people say that reading the book was better than watching the movie based on the book? When you can see the difference between major and minor details, you will automatically improve your visual experience of reading. Reading will be like watching a movie. Yet, it will be the best movie that you ever saw because it comes from your imagination.

Test Yourself Review Quiz

Chapter Review Questions

1. What are the two parts that form the basic outline structure of a paragraph?

   _____

_____ 2. *One, another,* and *also* are examples of transition words used for listing major details which can appear in

   a. any order.   b. a specific order.

_____ 3. *First, then,* and *last* are examples of transition words used for listing major details that must appear in

   a. any order.   b. a specific order.

4. When there is an introduction, you can usually find the main idea sentence

   directly _____ the *first* major detail in the paragraph.

5. The main idea is the *only* sentence that can be turned into a _____ that is answered by the major details in the rest of the paragraph.

6. What is a minor detail? _____

   _____

7. What are the three steps in the Picture Perfect strategy?

   a. _____

   b. _____

   c. _____

Application Questions

Read the paragraphs below. Then, answer the questions that follow.

Paragraph 1

[1]Do you want to achieve a particular goal? [2]Would you like to know how to achieve it? [3]There are three steps you can take in order to achieve any goal. [4]First, state your goal in terms of what you are "going to do." [5]If you say that

you are going to lose weight, you will automatically begin the programming process that will lead to success. [6]Next, ask yourself what you will need to do in order to achieve your goal. [7]If you think about what you will need in advance, you can prepare a plan of necessary actions to get what you want and avoid obstacles. [8]Last, ask yourself what can you do now. [9]If you ask what you can do now, you will begin to see what you can most easily accomplish in order to be one step closer to achieving your goal.

_____ 1. The major details in Paragraph 1 are listed in

    a. any order.   b. a specific order.

2. Complete the following outline for Paragraph 1.

   Main Idea: There are _three steps you can take in order to achieve any goal._

Transition Words	Major Details
_____	_____
_____	_____
	_____
_____	_____

3. **Sentence Identification:** Identify each sentence in Paragraph 1 as an introduction (_Intro_), a main idea (_Main_), a major detail (_Major_), or a minor detail (_Minor_).

   #1 _____   #2 _____   #3 _____   #4 _____   #5 _____

   #6 _____   #7 _____   #8 _____   #9 _____

Paragraph 2

[1]How many times have you heard of a woman who is repeatedly beaten by her partner and wondered, "Why doesn't she just leave him?" [2]There are many reasons why some women find it difficult to break their ties with their abusers. [3]Many women, particularly those with small children, are financially dependent on their partners. [4]Others fear retaliation against themselves or their children. [5]Some hope the situation will change with time (it rarely does), and others stay because cultural or religious beliefs forbid divorce. [6]Finally, some women still love the abusive partner and are concerned about what will happen to him if they leave.

—From _Access to Health_, 10th ed. by Rebecca J. Donatelle. p. 116.

_____ 4. The major details of Paragraph 2 are listed in

    a. any order.   b. a specific order.

5. List the major details of the paragraph.

    a. Major Detail: _____

    b. Major Detail: _____

    c. Major Detail: _____

                 _____

    d. Major Detail: _____

                 _____

6. **Main Idea:** There are many _____

    _____

7. **Sentence Identification:** Identify each sentence in Paragraph 2 as an introduction (*Intro*), a main idea (*Main*), a major detail (*Major*), or a minor detail (*Minor*).

    #1 _____   #2 _____   #3 _____   #4 _____   #5 _____

    #6 _____

Paragraph 3

[1]In 1799, ten years after taking his first oath as president, George Washington died. [2]It was the middle of December, cold and wet, but he was back home at Mount Vernon. [3]For eight years he had served as first president of the new republic, and then had come a brief and final period of retirement. [4]Washington's health had been good almost to the end, and he died gently. [5]"I am just going," he said to a friend. [6]"Have me decently buried and do not let my body be put into a vault in less than two days after I am dead. [7]Do you understand me?" [8]"Yes, sir," answered the friend. [9]"Tis well," said Washington, and soon he was dead. [10]His body had to be measured for a coffin, and the doctor recorded that he was "in length, six feet, three-and-one-half inches, exact."

—From *The Pursuit of Liberty: A History of the American People.* 3rd ed. vol. I
by R. Jackson Wilson [et al.] p. 232.

_____ 8. The transition words in Paragraph 3 indicate that the major details are listed in

   a. any order.   b. a specific order.

9. **Sentence Identification:** Identify each sentence in Paragraph 3 as an introduction (*Intro*), a main idea (*Main*), a major detail (*Major*), or a minor detail (*Minor*).

#1 _____   #2 _____   #3 _____   #4 _____   #5 _____   #6 _____

#7 _____   #8 _____   #9 _____   #10 _____

Summarization Activity

MyReadingLab

Supporting Details: St Louis Arch, Missouri
To practice your skills go to
>Study plan
>Reading skills
>Supporting details

Directions: *Write the major headings in this chapter. Under each heading, write a couple of sentences about the most important topics presented in the section of text that follows that heading.*

First heading _____

What information is most important? _____

_____

_____

Second heading _____

What information is most important? _____

_____

_____

Third heading _____

What information is most important? _____

_____

_____

Combine the information you wrote in this outline into a paragraph to summarize what you have learned in this chapter.

Reflection Activity

How am I am going to apply what I have learned in this chapter?

Directions: *Write a paragraph about the two or three things you learned about supporting details and transitions that were most helpful to you and how you plan to use what you have learned.*

_____

_____

_____

_____

_____

_____

_____

"The Successful Job Interview," from *Human Relations: Career and Personal Success*
Andrew J. DuBrin

Accessing Prior Knowledge

Questions for Discussion

1. Recall your worst interview. What mistakes do you think you made?

2. What is one reason (not mentioned in the article) why you think someone may not be hired?

Preview and Predict

Directions: *Look at the title of the selection. Think about what you already know about the subject. Then, write a couple of predictions about what you are going to read. For instance, will the author discuss the ways or the steps you should take in order to have a successful job interview?*

1. _____

2. _____

Word Search and Discovery

Directions: *Skim through the selection to find the two words below. Underline both words in the selection. Then, use a dictionary to write their definitions in the spaces provided. As you read and encounter the words see if the definitions you wrote fit the way each word is used in the selection.*

compensation (*n*): _____

evasive (*adj*): _____

Also, underline at least one new word as you read the selection and write your guess as to its meaning in the right margin of the text.

The Successful Job Interview
Andrew J. DuBrin

1   A general guide for performing well in the job interview is to present a positive but accurate picture of yourself. Your chances of performing well in a job increase if you are suited for the job. Tricking a prospective employer into hiring you when you are not qualified is therefore self-defeating in terms of your career. Following is a list of some key points to keep in mind when being interviewed for a job you want:

2   1. *Prepare in advance.* Be familiar with pertinent details about your background, including your employment history. Bring to the interview your social security number, driver's license, résumé, and the names of references. Prepare a statement in your mind of your uniqueness—what differentiates you from other job candidates. Sometimes the uniqueness is not strictly job related, such as being a champion figure skater.

3   As described previously, it is important to know some significant facts about your prospective employer. Annual reports, company brochures, and newspaper and magazine articles should provide valuable information. Search the Internet, including www.hoover.com (for business firms), for quick access to information about the employer. A brief conversation with one or two current employees might provide some basic knowledge about the firm.

4   2. *Dress appropriately.* So much emphasis is placed on dressing well for job interviews that some people overdress. Instead of looking businesslike, they appear to be dressed for a wedding or a funeral. The safest tactic is to wear moderately conservative business attire when applying for most positions. Another important principle is to gear your dress somewhat to the type of prospective employer. If you have a job interview with an employer where sports attire is worn to the office regularly, dress more casually. Dress standards are slowly moving back toward the more formal attire of years ago, yet do not turn down an invitation to dress casually for the interview. But be very cautious about wearing athletic shoes to a job interview.

5   3. *Focus on important job factors.* Inexperienced job candidates often ask questions about noncontroversial topics, such as paid holidays, benefits, and company-sponsored social activities. All these topics may be important to you, but explore them after the basic issue—the nature of the job—has been discussed. In this way, you will project a more professional image.

6   4. *Be prepared for a frank discussion of your strengths and areas for improvement.* Almost every human resources interviewer and many hiring managers will ask you to discuss your strengths and developmental needs (or weaknesses). Everyone has room for improvement in some areas. To deny them is to appear uninsightful or defensive. However, you may not want to reveal problem areas unrelated to the job, such as recurring nightmares or fear of spiders. A mildly evasive approach is to

emphasize areas for improvement that could be interpreted as strengths. An example: "I get too impatient with people who do sloppy work."

7   5. *Do not knock former employers.* To justify looking for a new position or having left a position in the past, job candidates often make negative statements about former employers. Employer bashing makes you appear unprofessional. Furthermore, it may suggest that you are likely to find fault with any employer. Take a positive approach by briefly explaining what went wrong, such as a change in your job that left you without the opportunity to use the skills you were hired for.

8   6. *Ask a few good questions.* An intelligent interviewee asks a few good questions. An employment specialist for managers said, "The best way to impress somebody on an interview is to ask intelligent questions." Here are two questions worth considering:

If hired, what kind of work would I actually be doing?

What would I have to accomplish on this job to be considered an
    outstanding performer?

9   7. *Let the interviewer introduce the topic of compensation.* Often the interviewer will specify the starting salary and benefits, allowing little room for questioning. If asked what starting salary you anticipate, mention a realistic salary range—one that makes you appear neither desperate nor greedy. Careful research, such as compensation data found on the Internet (e.g., www.salary.com) or checking with the placement office, will help you identify a realistic salary range. If the interviewer does not mention salary, toward the end of the interview ask a question such as, "By the way, what is the starting salary for this position?"

10   8. *Smile and exhibit a positive attitude.* People who smile during job interviews are more likely to receive a job offer. It is also important to express a positive attitude in other ways, such as agreeing with the interviewer and being impressed with facts about the company. If you want the job, toward the conclusion of the interview explain why you see a good fit between your qualifications and those demanded by the job. For example, "The way I see it, this job calls for somebody who is really devoted to improving customer service. That's me. I love to take good care of customers." Smiling also helps you appear relaxed.

11   9. *Emphasize how your skills can benefit the employer.* An effective job-getting tactic is to explain to a prospective employer what you think you can do to help the company. . . . If you were applying for a billing specialist position in a company that you knew was having trouble billing customers correctly, you might make this skill-benefit statement: "Here is how I would apply my skill and experience in setting up billing systems to help develop a billing system with as few bugs as possible: _____."

12   Another way to show how your skills can benefit the employer is to relate the employer problem to one you successfully resolved in the past. In the billing system example, you might state that your previous employer had a billing problem and then explain how you helped solve the problem.

13   10. *Avoid appearing desperate.* A prolonged job search—particularly one lasting more than six months—makes many job seekers appear desperate. A problem with projecting desperation is that it creates a negative impression that is likely to result in being rejected once again. An executive search firm notes five signs of a desperate job seeker:

- You have considered accepting a position earning significantly less (e.g., 50 percent) than your previous job. (Or you are willing to accept a starting salary much below what other people in your field are receiving.)

- You have applied for jobs that you know will make you miserable, but you think you can cope because the pay is adequate.

- You have been asked what your job preferences are, and you responded with "I'm open."

- You have called an employment agency or placement office daily even though you have been asked to call back in two weeks.

14   If you recognize these signs in yourself, work hard at appearing upbeat. Role-play with a friend to learn if he or she thinks you are making a positive pitch.

15   11. *Ask for the job and follow through.* If you want the job in question, be assertive. Make a statement such as, "I'm really interested. What is the next step in the process?" "Is there any other information I could submit that would help you complete your evaluation of me?" Part of asking for the job is to follow through. Mail a follow-up letter or send an e-mail message within three working days after the interview. Mention that you would like to send a follow-up note in another 10 days. Even if you decide not to take the job, a brief thank-you letter is advisable. You may conceivably have contact with that firm in the future.

> —From DuBrin, Andrew J., *Human Relations for Career and Personal Success,* 7th edition, © 2005, pp. 335–338. Reprinted by permission of Pearson Education, Inc., Upper Saddle River, NJ.

The Write Connection

Directions: *Write a paragraph about three things you learned or that you think are most important in the reading selection.*

_____

_____

_____

_____

_____

Comprehension Check

Directions: *See how many questions you can answer without referring to the selection. Then, review the selection to write more complete responses.*

1. Underline the thesis or main idea of the selection.

2. According to the author, what is a general guide for performing well in a job interview? _____

_____ 3. A statement of your uniqueness can tell an employer
   a. how much you need the job.
   b. that you care about the job.
   c. what makes you different.
   d. key details about your resume.

_____ 4. According to the author, you will project a professional image during the interview if you discuss _____ first.
   a. how much vacation you will receive
   b. company-sponsored social activities
   c. the nature of the job
   d. company benefits

_____ 5. Making negative statements about a former employer may suggest that
   a. you have high standards.
   b. you were mistreated in some way.
   c. you are likely to be a good judge of character.
   d. you are likely to find fault with any employer.

_____ 6. According to an employment specialist in the selection, what is the best way to impress an interviewer?
   a. Ask about benefit options.
   b. Ask intelligent questions.
   c. Discuss how you want to be treated.
   d. Explain why you need the money.

_____ 7. Which of the following is *not* recommended for a successful job interview?
   a. letting the interviewer introduce the topic of conversation
   b. smiling and demonstrating a positive attitude
   c. calling the employer or employment agency daily
   d. emphasizing how your skills can benefit the employer

8. After you have shown interest in the job, you should send a _____

_____ within three days after the interview.

Critical Thinking Check

_____ 1. Which of the following conclusions can be drawn from the information contained in the selection?
   a. Sending a follow-up letter after a job interview can make you appear desperate.
   b. Dressing appropriately is the best way to impress a prospective employer.
   c. You should avoid mentioning former employers.
   d. Preparation and a positive attitude are essential to a successful job interview.

2. Imagine that you are preparing for an interview and you want to describe what makes you unique. What are some things you would say about yourself

   that might impress the interviewer? _____

   _____

3. Do you agree with the author's suggestion that you should mention your

   weaknesses as well as your strengths? Why or why not? _____

   _____

Vocabulary Check

Directions: *See if any of the words you underlined in the selection are among the list of words below. If not, write your words in the spaces provided. Guess the meaning of the words from the way they were used in the selection. Then, look up the definition of each word in the dictionary to see if you were right.*

attire (*n*): Your guess: _____

   Dictionary Definition: _____

controversial (*adj*): Your guess: _____

   Dictionary Definition: _____

Your word: _____ Your guess: _____

   Dictionary Definition: _____

Your word: _____ Your guess: _____

   Dictionary Definition: _____

THE STORY OF AN HOUR
Kate Chopin

Accessing Prior Knowledge

Questions for Discussion

1. How do you think people handled being in a bad marriage before divorce was acceptable?

2. Why are some people unable to be happy when they are in a committed relationship?

Preview and Predict

Directions: *Look at the title of the selection. Think about what you already know about the subject. Then, write a couple of predictions about what you are going to read. For instance, what does the author mean by "The Story of an Hour"?*

1. _____

2. _____

Word Search and Discovery

Directions: *Skim through the selection to find the two words below. Underline both words in the selection. Then, use a dictionary to write their definitions in the spaces provided. As you read and encounter these words, see if the definitions you wrote fit the way each word is used in the selection.*

afflicted (*vb*): _____

veiled (*adj*): _____

Also, underline two new words as you read the selection and write your guesses as to their meanings in the right margin of the text.

THE STORY OF AN HOUR
Kate Chopin

1   Knowing that Mrs. Mallard was afflicted with a heart trouble, great care was taken to break to her as gently as possible the news of her husband's death.

2   It was her sister Josephine who told her, in broken sentences; veiled hints that revealed in half concealing. Her husband's friend Richards was there, too, near her. It was he who had been in the newspaper office when intelligence of the railroad disaster was received, with Brently Mallard's name leading the list of "killed." He had only taken the time to assure himself of its truth by a second telegram, and had hastened to forestall any less careful, less tender friend in bearing the sad message.

3   She did not hear the story as many women have heard the same, with a paralyzed inability to accept its significance. She wept at once, with sudden, wild abandonment, in her sister's arms. When the storm of grief had spent itself she went away to her room alone. She would have no one follow her.

4   There stood, facing the open window, a comfortable, roomy armchair. Into this she sank, pressed down by a physical exhaustion that haunted her body and seemed to reach into her soul.

5   She could see in the open square before her house the tops of trees that were all aquiver with the new spring life. The delicious breath of rain was in the air. In the street below a peddler was crying his wares. The notes of a distant song which someone was singing reached her faintly, and countless sparrows were twittering in the eaves.

6   There were patches of blue sky showing here and there through the clouds that had met and piled one above the other in the west facing her window.

7   She sat with her head thrown back upon the cushion of the chair, quite motionless, except when a sob came up into her throat and shook her, as a child who has cried itself to sleep continues to sob in its dreams.

8   She was young, with a fair, calm face, whose lines bespoke repression and even a certain strength. But now there was a dull stare in her eyes, whose gaze was fixed away off yonder on one of those patches of blue sky. It was not a glance of reflection, but rather indicated a suspension of intelligent thought.

9   There was something coming to her and she was waiting for it, fearfully. What was it? She did not know; it was too subtle and elusive to name. But she felt it, creeping out of the sky, reaching toward her through the sounds, the scents, the color that filled the air.

10   Now her bosom rose and fell tumultuously. She was beginning to recognize this thing that was approaching to possess her, and she was striving to beat it back with her will—as powerless as her two white slender hands would have been.

11   When she abandoned herself a little whispered word escaped her slightly parted lips. She said it over and over under her breath: "free, free, free!" The vacant stare and the look of terror that had followed it went from her eyes. They stayed keen and bright. Her pulses beat fast, and the coursing blood warmed and relaxed every inch of her body.

12   She did not stop to ask if it were or were not a monstrous joy that held her. A clear and exalted perception enabled her to dismiss the suggestion as trivial.

13   She knew that she would weep again when she saw the kind, tender hands folded in death; the face that had never looked save with love upon her, fixed and gray and dead. But she saw beyond that bitter moment a long procession of years to come that would belong to her absolutely. And she opened and spread her arms out to them in welcome.

14   There would be no one to live for her during those coming years; she would live for herself. There would be no powerful will bending hers in that blind persistence with which men and women believe they have a right to impose a private will upon a fellow-creature. A kind intention or a cruel intention made the act seem no less a crime as she looked upon it in that brief moment of illumination.

15   And yet she had loved him—sometimes. Often she had not. What did it matter! What could love, the unsolved mystery, count for in face of this possession of self-assertion which she suddenly recognized as the strongest impulse of her being!

16   "Free! Body and soul free!" she kept whispering.

17   Josephine was kneeling before the closed door with her lips to the keyhole, imploring for admission. "Louise, open the door! I beg; open the door—you will make yourself ill. What are you doing, Louise? For heaven's sake open the door."

18   "Go away, I am not making myself ill." No; she was drinking in a very elixir of life through that open window.

19   Her fancy was running riot along those days ahead of her. Spring days, and summer days, and all sorts of days that would be her own. She breathed a quick prayer that life might be long. It was only yesterday she had thought with a shudder that life might be long.

20   She arose at length and opened the door to her sister's importunities. There was a feverish triumph in her eyes, and she carried herself unwittingly like a goddess of Victory. She clasped her sister's waist, and together they descended the stairs. Richards stood waiting for them at the bottom.

21   Some one was opening the front door with a latchkey. It was Brently Mallard who entered, a little travel-stained, composedly carrying his grip-sack and umbrella. He had been far from the scene of the accident, and did not even know there had been one. He stood amazed at Josephine's piercing cry; at Richards' quick motion to screen him from the view of his wife.

22   But Richards was too late.

23   When the doctors came they said she had died of heart disease—of joy that kills.

The Write Connection

Directions: *Write a paragraph about three things you learned or that you think are most important in the reading selection.*

_____

_____

_____

_____

_____

Comprehension Check

Directions: *See how many questions you can answer without referring to the selection. Then, review the selection to write more complete responses.*

1. Why was Josephine concerned about her sister's reaction to the news of her husband's death? _____

   _____

_____ 2. Richards learned that Mr. Mallard had been "killed" in a
   a. disastrous fire.   c. railroad disaster.
   b. traffic accident.   d. newspaper office.

3. How did Mrs. Mallard react to the news of her husband's death? _____

   _____

_____ 4. What is the meaning of the word *bearing*, as it is used in paragraph 2?
   a. carrying   c. holding
   b. exposing   d. feeling

_____ 5. When she looked out of the open window, Mrs. Mallard noticed many things that made her feel
   a. depressed.   c. disgusted.
   b. annoyed.   d. hopeful.

6. Mrs. Mallard's sadness was replaced by the realization that she was _____

   _____

_____ 7. Mr. Mallard is described as a man who was
    a. loving and kind.
    b. unfaithful.
    c. cruel and abusive.
    d. careless.

8. Which paragraph in the selection describes Mrs. Mallard's view of marriage in general? _____

9. As Mrs. Mallard and her sister descended the stairs, Mrs. Mallard carried herself like a *goddess of Victory* because _____

_____

10. Why did Josephine scream? _____

_____

Critical Thinking Check

1. The last line of the story says, "When the doctors came they said she had died of heart disease—of joy that kills." Why do think Mrs. Mallard died? Explain your answer. _____

_____

_____

_____ 2. Which of the following conclusions can be drawn from the selection?
    a. The effects of grief after a loved one has died are harmful and in some cases deadly.
    b. We should try to be more honest about the way we feel about others.
    c. The way that people who are in a relationship really feel about each other is not always apparent to others.
    d. Losing a loved one is a deeply personal experience.

_____ 3. Which of the following can be inferred from the information contained in the selection?
    a. Mr. Mallard was the love of Mrs. Mallard's life.
    b. Mrs. Mallard was unhappy in her marriage.
    c. Mrs. Mallard was a woman who was difficult to please.
    d. Mrs. Mallard was elderly and had numerous health issues.

Vocabulary Check

aquiver (*adj*): Your guess: _____

    Dictionary Definition: _____

bitter (*adj*): Your guess: _____

    Dictionary Definition: _____

tumultuous (*adj*): Your guess: _____

    Dictionary Definition: _____

Your word: _____ Your guess: _____

    Dictionary Definition: _____

Your word: _____ Your guess: _____

    Dictionary Definition: _____

6 Patterns of Organization

I think, therefore I am.

– Rene Descartes

In this chapter you will learn how to:

Recognize Patterns of Organization

Definition and Example

Classification

Sequence of Events/Process

Comparison and Contrast

Cause and Effect

Listing or Enumeration

▲ A pattern of organization refers to the way an author presents the major details that support the topic.

Preview and Predict ▶ What do you know so far?

How many of the following questions can you answer before reading the chapter?

• What would be different about the way you would tell someone how to make spaghetti and the way you would tell someone about several kinds of spaghetti?

- What is a pattern of organization?

  _____

- Why is it important to recognize an author's pattern of organization?

  _____

- Think of one way in which the picture relates to this chapter's objectives.

  _____

Now, as you read the chapter, look for the answers to see if you were right.

SIX COMMON PATTERNS OF ORGANIZATION

A **pattern of organization** refers to the way an author organizes the major details that support a topic. Patterns of organization may also be called *thinking patterns* or *rhetorical modes.* For instance, imagine you are about to read a paragraph about the topic *candy.* How will the author organize the major details in the paragraph? Will the author present a *definition* of candy, the different *types* or *classes* of candy, the *steps* for making candy, the *differences or similarities* between two brands of candy, the *effects* of eating too much candy, or a list of the different *ways* that candy can be made?

Six common patterns of organization are:

Definition and Example

Classification

Sequence of Events/Process

Comparison and Contrast

Cause and Effect

Listing or Enumeration

Recognizing an author's pattern of organization will help you succeed in college courses in several ways:

- **You will improve your reading comprehension and speed** if you can predict the type of information an author is going to present.

- **You will improve your writing skills** if you know how to organize your ideas. For instance, in a literature class, you may need to compare and/or contrast one author's point of view with that of another author. In a history course, you might be asked to explain the causes and/or effects of a major historical event such as a war. In a biology course, you might be asked to describe the steps in a lab experiment you performed.

- **You will be more prepared for standardized reading tests** that ask you to identify authors' patterns of organization.

Definition and Example

Each academic discipline has its own set of vocabulary or key terms. There are certain definitions that you need to know in order to discuss what you have learned using the language of the course. When textbook authors write a paragraph or passage that provides *examples of an important definition* or of a key term, they are using a **definition and example** pattern of organization.

Imagine that you have been asked to write about the meaning of the word *responsibility*. You might begin with the formal dictionary definition of the word. Then, you might provide one or two examples to help the reader understand the meaning of the term *responsibility*. Notice how the major details support the main idea in the following example.

Definition: *Responsibility* is the quality of being able to fulfill one's obligations.

Example: the ability to find a way to pay for rent and utilities

Example: the ability to fulfill a promise to complete a particular job

---

Authors usually highlight the definition or key term they are going to discuss by using **bold letters** or *italics*. They may also provide signal words or phrases that tell the reader the type of organizational pattern being used. Here are some examples of signal words and phrases found in a definition and example pattern of organization. (A more complete list can be found in Table 6.1 on page 226.)

Signal Words and Phrases: Definition and Example Pattern

A pattern of organization *refers to* . . .

Applied psychology *is* . . .

For example, applied psychologists . . .

Manic-depression, *also called* . . .

Integrity is a word that *means* . . .

Responsibility *can be defined as* . . .

Look at the way the author of the following paragraph uses definition and example signal words and phrases to discuss applied psychology. Then, see if you can answer the questions that follow.

> **Applied Psychology** *is* the branch of psychology that uses psychological principles to help solve practical problems of everyday life—whether those problems come up on the job, at school, or on the playing field. *For example,* applied psychologists examine how the basics of behavior, such as learning and memory, affect athletic activities. They consider how coaches can motivate athletes to perform their best by using common psychological concepts to help them visualize possibilities, overcome obstacles, and achieve fulfillment.

> —From Lefton, Lester A. & Linda Brannon, *Psychology* 8e. Published by Allyn and Bacon, Boston, MA. Copyright © 2002 by Pearson Education. Reprinted by permission of the publisher.

_____   1. The author has written the paragraph in order to
  a. present the steps for becoming a better athlete.
  b. define the term *psychological effects* and provide possible solutions.
  c. explain the effects of behavior on applied activities.
  d. define the term *applied psychology* and provide an example.

_____   2. The main idea of the paragraph is
  a. implied.
  b. found in the first sentence.
  c. there are several ways that learning and memory affect athletic activities.
  d. found in the last sentence.

Activity 6.1 ▶ Applying Patterns of Organization: Definition and Example

Directions: *Use a dictionary to write a definition of each term below. Then, provide an example that illustrates or explains the term.*

Term 1: **Dependable** _____

_____.

For example, _____

_____

_____

Term 2: **Friendship** _____

_____

For example, _____

_____

_____

Classification

Many academic courses deal with subjects that can be divided and grouped into major types, categories, parts, or classes that have common characteristics. For instance, in biology, the *types* of plant cells are *organized* into three major tissue systems. In chemistry, elements are distinguished by the number of protons in the nucleus and *organized* on the periodic table according to common chemical and physical *characteristics*. When textbook authors want to discuss how *groups* or *types* of information relate to one another, they are using a **classification** pattern of organization.

Imagine that you have been asked to write about *types* of popular music. You might begin by dividing the topic into smaller categories such as rock, pop, and hip-hop. Then, you would discuss the common characteristics that identify each type or *class* of popular music.

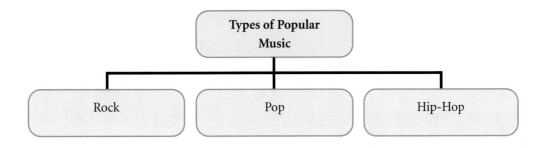

Here are some examples of signal words and phrases found in the classification pattern of organization. (A more complete list can be found in Table 6.1 on page 226.)

Signal Words and Phrases: Classification Pattern
Sociologists *divide groups into* . . .
Organisms *can be classified by* . . .
One type of music is . . .
Another kind of element is . . .
A cell is *composed of* . . .
There are *several categories* of . . .
It is much longer than the other *types* . . .

Look at the way the author of the following paragraph uses classification signal words and phrases to discuss groups within society. Then, see if you can answer the questions that follow.

> Sociologists *divide* groups into primary groups, secondary groups, in-groups, reference groups, and networks. The cooperative, intimate, long-term, face-to-face relationships provided by **primary groups** are fundamental to our sense of self. **Secondary groups** are *larger*, relatively temporary, and *more* anonymous, formal, and impersonal *than* primary groups. **In-groups** provide members with a strong sense of identity and belonging. **Out-groups** also foster identity by showing in-group members what they are now. **Reference groups** are groups whose standards we mentally refer to as we evaluate ourselves. **Social networks** consist of social ties that link people together. The new technology has given birth to a new type of group, the **electronic community**.

> —From Henslin, James M. *Sociology: A Down-to-Earth Approach, Core Concepts*, 1e. Published by Allyn and Bacon, Boston, MA. Copyright © 2006 by Pearson Education. Reprinted by permission of the publisher.

_____ 1. The author has written the paragraph in order to
   a. explain the difference between primary and secondary groups.
   b. define the term *group* and provide leadership styles.
   c. discuss the characteristics of each type of group.
   d. discuss the similarities between reference groups and in-groups.

_____ 2. The main idea of the paragraph is
   a. implied.
   b. found in the first sentence.
   c. there are several steps for developing an effective group.
   d. found in the last sentence.

Answers to the questions about applied psychology on page 208: 1. d, 2. b.

Activity 6.2 ▶ Applying Patterns of Organization: Classification

Directions: *Think of three types of music and three types of movies. Then, describe each type in the spaces provided.*

1. There are three types of popular music.

    One type of popular music is _____

    You can identify this type of music by listening for such things as _____

    _____ .

    Another type of popular music is _____ .

    You can identify this type of music by listening for such things as _____

    _____ .

    Finally, there is _____ .

    You can identify this type of music by listening for such things as _____

    _____ .

2. There are three types of movies.

    One type of movie is _____ .

    You can identify this type of movie by looking for such things as _____

    _____ .

    Another type of movie is _____ .

    You can identify this type of movie by looking for such things as _____

    _____ .

    Finally, there is _____ .

    You can identify this type of movie by looking for such things as _____

    _____ .

Sequence of Events/Process

When authors want to present events, stages, or a process, step by step in a specific order, they are using a **sequence of events/process** pattern of organization. For instance, a psychology text might discuss the *stages* of childhood development. A biology text might present the *steps* in the process of cell division. A history text might present a timeline of the major *events* that occurred during an important historical period.

Imagine that you have been asked to write about the steps for making your favorite recipe. You might begin by discussing the necessary ingredients. Then, you would present each step *in a specific order* so that the reader can add or combine each ingredient to make your recipe. Notice how the major details are organized in the following example.

Steps for Making Spaghetti

> **Step 1:** Gather the ingredients
>
> **Step 2:** Boil water
>
> **Step 3:** Add spaghetti
>
> **Step 4:** Strain and serve

Here are some examples of signal words and phrases found in a sequence of events/process pattern of organization. (A more complete list can be found in Table 6.1 on page 226.)

Signal Words and Phrases: Sequence of Events Pattern/Process

There are three simple *steps* . . .

Next, gather the ingredients such as . . .

Then, on March 21, 1607 . . .

Before he became president, Abraham Lincoln . . .

The *final stage* in the memory *process* is . . .

After she made the remark, she . . .

Look at the way the author of the paragraph below uses sequence of events pattern/process signal words and phrases to discuss the first colony of Jamestown. Then, see if you can answer the questions that follow.

> *In 1607*, three ships, the *Susan Constant, Discovery,* and *Godspeed,* reached the North American coast. Captain Christopher Newport was in sole command of the original 104 settlers. *After a few weeks* of scouting, the reconnaissance party decided on a marshy island in the lower Chesapeake Bay on which to establish their settlement. *It was not long before* Newport returned to England for supplies, and Captain John Smith emerged as the unofficial leader of the group.
>
> —From *American Dreams and Reality: A Retelling of the American Way.*
> Vol I, 5th ed. by Louise A. Mayo et al. p. 46.

Answers to the example questions about groups within society on page 210 : 1. c, 2. b.

_____ 1. The author has written the paragraph in order to
   a. explain the difference between Captain Newton and John Smith.
   b. define the term _reconnaissance_ and provide examples.
   c. discuss the events occurring after settlers arrived in 1607.
   d. discuss the three ships that carried settlers to the North American coast.

_____ 2. The main idea of the paragraph is
   a. implied.
   b. found in the first sentence.
   c. there are several steps for developing a reconnaissance party.
   d. found in the last sentence.

Activity 6.3 ▶ Applying Patterns of Organization: Sequence of Events/Process

Directions: _Write your own sequence of events/process paragraph by completing the sentences below._

1. Making my favorite recipe is easy if you follow these simple steps.

   First, gather the ingredients. You will need _____

   _____

   _____.

   Then, _____

   _____.

   (Next) (After) (Before) _____

   _____.

   Last, _____

   _____

   _____.

2. This is what I do each day before I leave the house.

   First, _____

   _____.

   Then, _____

   _____.

(Next) (After) (Before), _____

_____ .

Last, _____

_____ .

Answers to the example questions about Jamestown on pages 212–213: 1. c, 2. a.

Comparison and Contrast

Comparison

A **comparison** pattern of organization discusses the *similarities* between or among people, places, ideas, or events. For instance, a history text might include a discussion about the similarities between the Civil War and the war in Iraq. If you were asked to *compare* two friends, you might discuss interests, appearance, or other *similar* qualities they share, as in the example below.

Comparing Two Friends
Similarities between Joseph and Kim
Dependable
Enjoy horror movies
Like Kim, Joseph is dependable.
Both Kim and Joseph like to watch horror movies.

Here are some examples of signal words and phrases to look for in a comparison pattern of organization. (A more complete list can be found in Table 6.1 on page 226.)

Signal Words and Phrases: Comparison
There are *similarities among* . . .
Both high school and college students . . .
Like coffee, tea also contains large amounts of . . .
Hip-hop artists *as well as* rap artists . . .

Look at the way the author of the next paragraph uses comparison signal words and phrases to discuss high school and college students. Then, see if you can answer the questions that follow.

Similarities Between High School and College Students

There are several *similarities* between high school and college students. They must *both* attend school regularly in order to benefit from their courses. Students who are consistently absent find that they have difficulty succeeding in subsequent subject-related courses, such as mathematics or English. High school students *as well as* college students must also devote adequate time to study in order to benefit from their courses. Students who learn the importance of regular reading and review of instructional materials tend to be most successful. Finally, *both* high school and college students must learn to deal with stress. Students who develop healthy ways to deal with stress, such as exercising, are able to maintain the energy needed to accomplish more work in less time.

_____ 1. The author has written the paragraph in order to
   a. explain the steps for improving academic performance.
   b. define the term *similarities* and provide examples.
   c. discuss the differences between high school and college students.
   d. discuss the similarities between high school and college students.

_____ 2. The main idea of the paragraph is
   a. implied.
   b. found in the first sentence.
   c. There are several classes or types of students.
   d. found in the last sentence.

Contrast

On the other hand, a **contrast** pattern of organization emphasizes the *differences* between or among people, places, ideas, or events. For instance, an anthropology text might discuss the differences between humans and primates. If you were asked to *contrast* two of your favorite beverages, you might discuss the *differences* between the appearance, taste, or appeal of each one.

Contrasting Two Beverages
Differences between Suave and Crunk
Alcohol
Flavor
Unlike Crunk, Suave contains alcohol.
Crunk has a strawberry flavor, *while* Suave tastes like lime.

Here are some examples of signal words and phrases to look for in a contrast pattern of organization. (A more complete list can be found in Table 6.1 on page 226.)

Signal Words and Phrases: Contrast

There are some important *differences* between . . .

On the other hand, college students . . .

Primates *differ* from humans in . . .

In contrast, media . . .

Unlike Justin Timberlake, Eminem . . .

While most psychologists agree that . . .

Human language progresses at a faster rate *than* . . .

As you read the contrast paragraph below, notice how the transition words differ from the previous example, which *compared* high school and college students. Then, answer the questions which follow.

Differences Between High School and College Students

There are some important *differences* between high school and college students. Students in high school have a limited selection of courses they can take. Most of the time, their schedules are chosen for them. High school students do not have to pay for the classes they take. Most high school students do not have to worry about adult responsibilities. They have more time to be involved in recreational activities. *On the other hand,* college students have *more* flexibility in the courses they can select. They are responsible for paying for their education. College students often deal with adult responsibilities such as child care and work-related issues and tend to exhibit *more* maturity regarding the pursuit of an education. *In contrast* to high school, recreational time is limited because college courses tend to require *more* reading and study outside of class.

_____ 1. The author has written the paragraph in order to
   a. explain the difference between productive and nonproductive behaviors.
   b. discuss the causes of stress among high school and college students.
   c. present the differences between high school and college students.
   d. discuss the similarities between high school and college students.

Answers to the example questions about the similarities between high school and college students on page 215: 1. c 2. b.

_____ 2. The main idea of the paragraph is
  a. implied.
  b. found in the first sentence.
  c. there are several steps for developing an effective group.
  d. found in the last sentence.

Using Both Comparison and Contrast

Finally, a **comparison and contrast** pattern of organization presents *both* similarities and differences between or among people, places, ideas, or events. If you were asked to compare and contrast two rooms in your house, you might list the similarities and differences in the function, décor, or appeal of both rooms using either the *point-by-point method* or the *subject-by-subject method*.

When you compare and contrast using the **point-by-point method**, you list the points you want to discuss, such as the function and appearance of both rooms. Then, you discus the similarities and differences of both rooms point by point. Here is an example of the topic using the point by point method.

Comparing and Contrasting Two Rooms of a House	
Point-by-Point Method	
Living Room and Bedroom	
Similarities	**Differences**
Point 1: Activity	
I like to relax in *both* rooms.	I sleep in the bedroom, *but* watch TV in the living room.
Point 2: Appearance	
Pictures of loved ones are found in the living room *as well as* in the bedroom.	*Unlike* the bedroom, my living room has a sofa.

If you use the **subject-by-subject** method of comparison and contrast, you present what you know about one subject, and then present what you know about the other subject. The example on page 218 shows you how to discuss the same topic using the subject-by-subject method.

Comparing and Contrasting Two Rooms of a House

Subject-by-Subject Method

Living Room and Bedroom

Bedroom

I like to relax in the bedroom.

I have pictures of loved ones in the bedroom.

I sleep in the bedroom.

Living Room

Just as in the bedroom, I like to relax in the living room.

Pictures of loved ones are found in the living room *as well as* in the bedroom.

Unlike the bedroom, I watch TV in the living room.

My living room has a sofa.

Notice how the author in the following example presents the similarities as well as the differences between high school and college students. Then, answer the questions that follow.

Comparing and Contrasting High School and College Students

High school and college students are *not as different* as one might expect. Students in high school may be *more* limited *than* their college counterparts in the selection of courses they can take. Yet, *both* must commit to regular class attendance in order to be successful. *Unlike* college students, high school students do not have to pay for the classes they take. Motivation, *however,* is essential for success regardless of the cost. *While* high school students do not have to worry about adult responsibilities, their level of stress is often *similar* to that of their college counterparts.

_____ 1. The author has written the paragraph in order to
   a. explain the effects of certain behaviors on academic success among high school and college students.
   b. discuss the various types of courses commonly taken by high school as well as college students.
   c. emphasize the similarities between high school and college students.
   d. present the similarities and differences between high school and college students.

Answers to the example questions about the differences between high school and college students on pages 216–217. 1. d, 2. b.

_____ 2. The main idea of the paragraph is
    a. implied.
    b. found in the first sentence.
    c. there are several effects of behavior on academic success.
    d. found in the last sentence.

Activity 6.4 ▶ Applying Patterns of Organization: Comparison/Contrast

Directions: _Write your own comparison/contrast paragraph by completing the sentences below._

1. I have two friends who are very similar.

    Like my friend, _____ my other friend, _____

    enjoys _____.

    For instance, _____.

    Both are _____

    _____.

2. There are differences between the two beverages I drink most often.

    My favorite drink, _____ has a taste I would describe as

    _____. But I

    enjoy my other favorite drink, _____, even though it has

    a different flavor, which I describe as _____.

    Unlike _____, my other favorite beverage, _____,

    differs in appearance. For instance, _____.

    _____

Cause and Effect

A **cause and effect** pattern is used to explain the causes (events or actions) that led to a particular effect (or result). It can also be used to explain the effects (or results) of a particular cause (action or event).

When causes are emphasized in a paragraph, they answer the question, "Why did it happen?" For instance, a history text might discuss the events leading up to the American Revolution. However, although the events are presented in a time sequence, the author's main reason for writing is to explain the *causes* of the American Revolution: to tell you *why it happened.*

Imagine that you have been asked to write about *why* you decided to take college courses. You will be presenting the *causes* or reasons that *led to* your decision. You might present such reasons as the following: losing a job, being turned down for a job you wanted, or an experience or experiences that inspired you to pursue a particular skill or career. You might present the events in order of importance or in the order in which each one occurred.

Cause and Effect

Why I decided to take college courses.

Cause 1: *Due to* the fact that I lost my job . . .

Cause 2: *Since* the children are grown . . .

Cause 3: *Because* I fell in love with nursing when I volunteered at the hospital . . .

Effect: I decided to take college courses

On the other hand, when effects are emphasized in a paragraph, they answer the questions "What happened *as a result* of this event?" or "What can happen?" For instance, a psychology text might discuss the *effects* of stress on test performance. In this case, the author's main reason for writing is to explain *what can happen* to test performance *as a result* of stress. If you were asked to write about *what can happen* to college students who regularly drink too much, you might discuss poor academic performance, health problems, or relationship conflicts. You would present the *effects* of regular excessive drinking among college students.

Notice how the effects are emphasized in the following example.

Answers to the example questions about the similarities and differences between high school and college students on pages 218–219: 1. d, 2. b.

Cause and Effect

What can happen to college students who regularly drink to excess?

Cause: Regular excessive drinking

Effect 1: It can *lead to* poor academic performance.

Effect 2: Health problems may also develop *as a result* of regular excessive drinking.

Effect 3: Relationship conflicts can be *caused by* regular excessive drinking.

Finally, authors may discuss both causes and effects. For instance, a psychology text might discuss the *effects* of stimulants as well as the reasons (*causes*) for moderate use. A history text might discuss the *events* (causes) that *led to* the war in Iraq (effect) and its *effects* upon the Iraqi people.

Here are some examples of signal words and phrases to look for in a cause and effect pattern of organization. (A more complete list can be found in Table 6.1 on page 226.)

Signal Words and Phrases: Cause and Effect

. . . *as a result* of the attack . . .

Therefore, we can conclude that . . .

. . . *due to* the actions . . .

Consequently, the decision was . . .

Several events *led to* the . . .

Because of the . . .

. . . which *caused* the Supreme Court to make these decisions.

Notice how the author in the paragraph below uses cause and effect signal words and phrases to discuss the September 11, 2001 attack. Then, see if you can answer the questions that follow.

On September 11, 2001, nineteen terrorists were able to hijack four separate American passenger flights. Two of the planes crashed into the World Trade Center in New York City. The third aircraft crashed into the Pentagon in Washington, D.C. The fourth aircraft crashed onto a field in Pennsylvania. American airports were closed until September 13. *As a result*, Continental, American, United, and Northwest Airlines cut their flight schedules. By the end of the week, both Continental and United Airlines announced massive layoffs *due to* the loss of revenue after the attacks. On September 20, President Bush announced the creation of the Department of Homeland Security. The Transportation Security Agency (TSA), a component of the Department of Homeland Security, was formed on November 19. The TSA is responsible for overseeing and implementing security measures at airports and other transportation facilities. The events *since* the September 11, 2001 attacks have *led to* the creation of government agencies designed to ensure the safety of Americans.

_____ 1. The author has written the paragraph in order to
   a. discuss the events that led to the September 11 attack.
   b. discuss the types of aircraft that hit the World Trade Center and their effect upon the safety of Americans.
   c. present differences in air travel before and after the September 11 attack.
   d. discuss the events that led to the creation of government agencies as a result of the September 11 attack.

_____ 2. The main idea of the paragraph is
   a. implied.
   b. found in the first sentence.
   c. there are several causes for the September 11, 2001 attack.
   d. found in the last sentence.

Activity 6.5 ▶ Applying Patterns of Organization: Cause and Effect

Directions: *Write your own cause and effect paragraph by filling in the spaces provided below.*

1. There are two events that *led to* my decision to take college courses.

   The first thing that happened was _____

   _____

   _____.

   Then, _____

   _____.

   Consequently, I decided to take college courses.

2. There are two main effects of excessive sleep deprivation among college students.

An excessive lack of sleep can lead to _____

_____ .

Students who lose sleep are also more likely to _____

_____ as a result of excessive sleep deprivation.

Listing or Enumeration

The root *numer* in the word **enumeration** means *to number*. You may have seen feature articles on the Internet such as "Three Ways You Can Tell If Your Mate is Cheating," "Ten Things to Remember When You Take a Cruise," or, "Easy Decoration Tips for Small Spaces." The details in these lists do not have to be listed in any particular order.

In academic reading, the listing pattern might be used in a history text discussion of the presidents who served during an important time period. A psychology text might enumerate the various ways in which people avoid conflict. A literature text might list the criteria you should use to evaluate a particular story. When authors want to present a *number* of details or items in *any order*, they use an **enumeration or listing** pattern of organization.

Imagine you have been asked to enumerate the benefits of regular reading. You might list such things as increased vocabulary, expanded knowledge about the world, and improved chances of getting a good job. Or, if you were asked to discuss the three things you like about a particular song, you might list the singing style of the artist, the lyrics, and the rhythm.

Listing or Enumeration		
Three Benefits of Regular Reading		
Item 1	**Item 2**	**Item 3**
One benefit of regular reading is increased vocabulary.	Knowledge about the world is *also* a benefit of regular reading.	*Finally*, regular reading can improve one's chances of getting a good job.

Authors may use bullets (•), letters (a, b, c), or numbers (1, 2, 3) to list their ideas in an enumeration pattern. Here are some examples of additional signal words and phrases to look for in a listing or enumeration pattern of organization. (A more complete list can be found in Table 6.1 on page 226.)

Signal Words and Phrases: Listing or Enumeration

There are several *ways* to . . .

The second *guideline* . . .

Another benefit of . . .

One reason why I like . . .

There are three *things* that you can do to . . .

Notice how the author discusses the topic of energy costs in the paragraph below. Then, answer the questions that follow.

> Would you like to reduce the amount of your monthly electricity bill? Here are three ways to cut your energy costs. First, central air conditioning and heating units use the most energy in a typical household. Use ceiling fans instead of the air conditioner as much as possible during hot weather. Turn the thermostat to 68 degrees during winter months and 78 degrees in the summer. Second, water heaters also add to your energy costs because they keep water heated 24 hours a day even when you are not using it. You can save on energy costs by turning the water heater thermostat down to 120 degrees. Finally, an electric range top can use as much as 2000 watts of electricity. To reduce energy costs, use the microwave or an electric skillet whenever possible.

> —*Source:* http://www.leeric.lsu.edu/bgbb/7/ecep/home/b/b.htm

_____ 1. The author has written the paragraph in order to
   a. explain the three steps for reducing energy costs.
   b. discuss the types of appliances commonly used by consumers.
   c. present three ways to reduce energy costs.
   d. discuss the difference between central air and heating units and ceiling fans.

Answers to the example questions about cause and effect, 9/11, on page 222: 1. d, 2. d.

_____ 2. The main idea of the paragraph is
   a. implied.
   b. found in the first sentence.
   c. three ways to reduce energy costs.
   d. found in the last sentence.

Activity 6.6 ▶ Applying Patterns of Organization: Listing or Enumeration

Directions: _Write your own listing or enumeration paragraph by completing the sentences below._

1. There are three things that I like about my favorite song, titled _____

   _____ , by _____

   First, I like the _____

   _____.

   In addition, I like the _____

   _____.

   The last thing I like about the song is _____

   _____.

2. There are three ways to enjoy a vacation.

   One way to enjoy a vacation is to _____

   _____.

   Another way to enjoy a vacation is to _____

   _____.

   Finally, _____

   _____.

Table 6.1   Common Patterns of Organization: Signal Words and Phrases

Organizational Pattern	Information Presented in the Major Details	Typical Signal Words and Phrases
Listing or Enumeration	ways, things, items	*one, also, another, first, second, finally, last, in addition, additionally, moreover, list, furthermore, first of all, last of all*
Sequence of Events/Process	steps, events, phases, stages	*first, second, next, then, after, at this point, now, presently, subsequently, before, previously, preceding, following, earlier, later, when, last*
Comparison and/or Contrast	similarities	*comparatively, similar, similarly, both, as well as, like, likewise, as, just as, in comparison, alike, equally, comparable, in a like manner*
	differences	*yet, in contrast, unlike, though, despite, but, than, more, less, larger, smaller, however, instead, although, on the other hand, instead, on the contrary, nevertheless, rather than*
Cause and/or Effect	causes, effects, reasons, motives, results	*leads to, consequently, as a result, results in, therefore, due to, thus, therefore, thereby, since, so, because of, because, if . . . then*
Definition and Example	meaning, examples	*means, is, refers to, is referred to as, can mean, or, is defined as, means to*
Classification	types, kinds, groups, categories, classes, ranks	*one kind of, another type of, also classified as, divided into, more, than, less, larger, smaller, grouped by, several characteristics, traits*

Answers to the example listing questions about reducing electricity costs on pages 224–225: 1. c, 2. c.

Memory Check 1   How much do you remember?

1. Match the following patterns of organization with the signal words and phrases most commonly associated with them.

_____ 1. classification   a. *next, then, last*

_____ 2. definition and example   b. *means, refers to, is*

_____ 3. sequence of events/process   c. *similarly, on the other hand*

_____ 4. comparison and contrast   d. *as a result, consequently*

_____ 5. cause and effect   e. *grouped by, divided into*

2. What kind of information is presented in a comparison and contrast pattern?

_____

3. What kind of information is presented in a classification pattern?

_____

4. What is one signal word or phrase associated with a sequence of events/ process pattern? _____

5. What is one signal word or phrase associated with an enumeration pattern?

_____

6. What question is answered by a cause and effect pattern in which the *causes* are emphasized? _____

7. What questions are answered by a cause and effect pattern in which the *effects* are emphasized? _____

8. What is one signal word or phrase associated with a cause and effect pattern?

_____

9. What is one signal word or phrase associated with a definition and example pattern? _____

10. What are three ways you will benefit by recognizing an author's pattern of organization?

   a. _____

   b. _____

   c. _____

Activity 6.7 ▶ Recognizing Patterns of Organization I

Directions: *Write the pattern of organization indicated by the signal words or phrases found in each of the main idea sentences below.*

1. Jean and Joe are twins, but they are *different* in many ways.

   Pattern of Organization: _____

   _____

2. The abuse of alcohol can *lead to* poor health, financial difficulties, and the breakdown of relationships.

   Pattern of Organization: _____

   _____

3. There are three *stages* in the memory process.

   Pattern of Organization: _____

   _____

4. Here is a *list* of questions you can use to prepare for an interview.

   Pattern of Organization: _____

   _____

5. The *types* of mood disorder include major depression, dysthymia, and bipolar disorder.

   Pattern of Organization: _____

   _____

6. An inference *is* a reasonable conclusion based on evidence that has a common reference point.

   Pattern of Organization: _____

   _____

COMBINED PATTERNS: HOW TO RECOGNIZE THE DOMINANT PATTERN OF ORGANIZATION

Authors often combine patterns of organization to get their ideas across, but they usually emphasize one dominant or stronger pattern of organization. Here are some examples:

- A **definition and example** pattern of organization may also include the similarities and differences between the definition and a related term. In this case, you may see such signal words and phrases as *unlike* or *similarly*, but the author's main reason for writing is to provide examples that will help you learn the meaning of a particular *definition* or *definitions*.

- A **cause and effect** pattern of organization may contain examples in order to explain the reasons why something happened. In this case you may find sequence of events/process signal words and phrases such as *then* or *next*, but the author's main reason for writing is to emphasize the *causes* of an event.

- A **classification** pattern of organization may enumerate a list of ways to identify characteristics among groups or types of things. While you may see signal words and phrases such as *one* or *also,* the author's main reason for writing is to *classify* a particular *group* or *type*.

There are three questions you can ask to help identify the dominant pattern of organization of the material you are reading:

- What is the topic?

- What kind of information does the author most want me to learn about the topic?

- What does the main idea say about what kind of information the author wants to emphasize about the topic?

If you know what the author wants to present, you will not be confused by signal words and phrases associated with another pattern of organization that may be included in a paragraph or passage.

Notice how a cause and effect pattern is combined with a comparison and contrast pattern of organization in the paragraph below. Then, answer the questions that follow to find the more dominant pattern of organization. Some parts of the answers have been provided for you.

> Many children who become violent and antisocial have suffered neurological impairments, a result not of genetics, but of physical battering and subsequent brain injury (Milner & McCanne, 1991; Moffit, 1993). Consider the chilling results of a study that compared two groups of delinquents: violent boys who had been arrested for repeated incidents of vicious assault, rape, or murder; and boys whose violence was limited to fistfights. Nearly all of the extremely violent boys (98.6 percent) had at least one neurological abnormality, and many had more than one, compared with 66.7 percent of the less violent boys. More than three-fourths of the violent boys had suffered head injuries as children, had had serious medical problems, or had been beaten savagely by their parents, compared with "only" one-third of the others (Lewis, 1981).

> —From *The Longman Textbook Reader,* p. 25.

1. What is the topic? _____

2. What kind of information does the author want the reader to learn most

    about the topic? _____ why many children become violent and antisocial

3. What does the main idea say about the kind of information the author wants

    to emphasize about the topic? the _____ of battering and subsequent brain injury among many children who become violent or antisocial

4. What is the dominant pattern of organization? While the author uses comparison to show the reason for violent or antisocial behavior among children, the paragraph illustrates a more dominant _____ pattern of organization.

Memory Check 2   How much do you remember?

1. Authors may combine two patterns of organization to get their point across. Give one example. _____

_____

_____

2. What are the three questions you can ask to help identify the stronger or dominant pattern of organization of a paragraph or passage?

a. _____

b. _____

_____

c. _____

_____

Select the pattern of organization indicated for each of the main idea sentences below.

_____ 1. There are several outcomes resulting from the War of 1812.
   a. enumeration   c. sequence of events/process
   b. classification   d. cause and effect

_____ 2. The presidents can be ranked according to the following characteristics.
   a. contrast   c. sequence of events/process
   b. classification   d. cause and effect

_____ 3. Emergency room activity differs from the way it is portrayed on TV.
   a. contrast   c. sequence of events/process
   b. classification   d. cause and effect

Activity 6.8 ▶ Recognizing Patterns of Organization II: Textbook Applications

Directions: *Identify the dominant pattern of organization in each of the paragraphs below.*

Paragraph 1

Sociologists have compared how working-class and middle-class parents rear their children. Melvin Kohn (1959, 1963, 1976, 1977; Kohn et al. 1986) found that working-class parents are mainly concerned that their children stay out of trouble. They also tend to use physical punishment. Middle-class parents, in contrast, focus more on developing their children's curiosity, self-expression, and self-control. They are more likely to reason with their children than to use physical punishment.

—From Henslin, James M. *Sociology: A Down-to-Earth Approach, Core Concepts*, 1e. Published by Allyn and Bacon, Boston, MA. Copyright © 2006 by Pearson Education. Reprinted by permission of the publisher.

1. What is the topic? _____

2. Which of the following kinds of information does the author want the reader to learn about the topic? (types of? ways to? steps to? events in? differences between? similarities among? effects of? causes for?) _____

   _____

3. Write a main idea sentence for Paragraph 1.

   There are _____

   _____

_____ 4. The dominant pattern of organization for Paragraph 1 is
   a. comparison and contrast.   c. sequence of events/process.
   b. cause and effect.   d. classification.

Paragraph 2

The first step in problem solving is to define, or understand the problem. This involves being able to see what the problem entails. You need to separate facts from emotional responses to clarify the various components of the problem.

To define a problem means to look at the situation clearly and to set boundaries against a background of information. The second step is to gather facts and then generate alternative solutions, evaluating both the positive and negative elements of each solution. Finally, you need to select the best solution based on the problem-solving process.

—From "Critical Thinking." *College Study Strategies: Thinking and Learning* by Laskey and Gibson, p. 35.

1. What is the topic? _____

2. Which of the following kinds of information does the author want the reader to learn about the topic? (types of? ways to? steps to? events in? differences between? similarities among? effects of? causes for?) the _____

   _____

3. Write a main idea sentence for Paragraph 2.

   There are three _____

_____ 4. The dominant pattern of organization for Paragraph 2 is
   a. definition and example.   c. cause and effect.
   b. sequence of events/process.   d. classification.

Paragraph 3

Each year there are over 35,000 reported suicides in the United States. Experts estimate that there may actually be closer to 100,000, due to the difficulty in determining the causes of many suspicious deaths. More lives are lost to suicide than to any other single cause except cardiovascular disease and cancer. Suicide often results from poor coping skills, lack of social support, lack of self-esteem, and the inability to see one's way out of a bad situation. Factors contributing to suicide are common risks in many regions of the world. . . . Risk factors for suicide include a family history of suicide, previous suicide attempts, excessive drug and alcohol use, prolonged depression, financial difficulties, serious illness in the suicide contemplator or in his or her loved ones, and loss of a loved one through death or rejection. Societal pressures often serve as a catalyst.

—From *Access to Health*, 10th ed. by Rebecca J. Donatelle, p. 65.

1. What is the topic? _____

2. Which of the following kinds of information does the author want the reader to learn about the topic? (types of? characteristics or parts of ? ways to? steps to? events in? differences between? similarities among? effects of? causes for?)

   _____

3. Write the main idea of Paragraph 3.

   _____.

_____ 4. The dominant pattern of organization for Paragraph 3 is
   a. definition and example.   c. cause and effect.
   b. comparison.   d. contrast.

Paragraph 4

You may be surprised to realize that you use the scientific method in your everyday life. Let's suppose that you visit a friend in her home. Soon after you arrive, your eyes start to itch and you begin to sneeze. Then you observe that your friend has a new cat. Perhaps you ask yourself why you are sneezing and form the hypothesis that you are allergic to cats. To test your hypothesis, you leave your friend's home. If the sneezing stops, perhaps your hypothesis is correct. You test your hypothesis further by visiting another friend who also has a cat. If you start to sneeze again, your experimental results indicate that you are allergic to cats. However, if you continue sneezing after you leave your friend's home, your hypothesis is not supported. Now you need to form a new hypothesis, which could be that you have a cold.

—From *Basic Chemistry*, 2nd ed. © Karen C. Timberlake and William Timberlake, p. 6.

1. What is the topic? _____

2. Which of the following kinds of information does the author want the reader to learn about the topic? (types of? characteristics or parts of? ways to? steps to? events in? differences between? similarities among? effects of? causes for?)

   the _____

3. Write a main idea sentence for Paragraph 4.

   _____

_____ 4. The dominant pattern of organization for Paragraph 4 is
   a. definition and example.   c. comparison and contrast.
   b. sequence of events.   d. classification.

Paragraph 5

Influencing the content of shows and motion pictures can happen in at least two ways. The first is product placement, where advertisers pay to have their product displayed in a movie or show with the brand name highly visible to the audience. Second, advertisers or marketers sometimes work directly with media organizations to sponsor specific programs on television or special sections in newspapers. A brand of beer or soft drink sponsoring a concert tour that is televised on MTV is an example of this.

—From *Converging Media: An Introduction to Mass Communication* by John Pavlick and Shawn McIntosh, p. 51. Copyright © 2004. Allyn and Bacon.

1. What is the topic? _____

2. Which of the following kinds of information does the author want the reader to learn about the topic? (types of? ways to? steps to? events in? differences between? similarities among? effects of? causes for?) _____

   _____

3. Write a main idea sentence for Paragraph 5.

   _____

   _____

_____ 4. The dominant pattern of organization for Paragraph 5 is
   a. listing or enumeration.   c. comparison.
   b. contrast.   d. definition and example.

? Test Yourself Review Quiz

Chapter Review Questions

1. Match the following patterns of organization with the kinds of information most commonly associated with them.

   _____ 1. sequence of events/process   a. types, groups, classes, kinds

   _____ 2. cause and effect   b. ways, items, things

   _____ 3. classification   c. steps, stages, phases, events

   _____ 4. comparison and contrast   d. similarities and differences

   _____ 5. listing or enumeration   e. reasons or results

2. Provide two signal words or phrases commonly associated with a cause and effect pattern of organization. _____

_____

3. Provide two signal words or phrases commonly associated with a definition and example pattern of organization. _____

_____

4. Provide two signal words or phrases commonly associated with a classification pattern of organization. _____

_____

Application Questions

Directions: *Identify the pattern of organization for each paragraph. Then, provide at least one reason, such as a signal or clue, that led to your response.*

Paragraph 1

In the early 1910s and 1920s the most powerful movie mogul of all did not live in Hollywood. Marcus Loew, a financier, theater chain owner, and owner of Metro movie studio, lived 3000 miles east in New York City. In 1924 he merged his studio with Louis B. Mayer Productions and the Samuel Goldwyn Company to form Metro-Goldwyn-Mayer, or MGM. In a move typical of movie moguls of the day, Loew ousted Goldwyn from the team but kept his name in the company, because M & M: was already taken by another company.

—From *Converging Media: An Introduction to Mass Communication* by John Pavlick and Shawn McIntosh, p. 123. New York, NY: Allyn & Becan, 2004.

_____ 1. What is the dominant pattern of organization of Paragraph 1?
   a. definition and example   c. contrast
   b. sequence of events   d. cause and effect

2. How do you know? _____

_____

Paragraph 2

In the United States, there are about 20 million business enterprises. The overwhelming majority of these are proprietorships (70 percent); the rest are corporations (20 percent) and partnerships (10 percent). Although proprietorships dominate in number, their share of total business revenues is relatively small, accounting for only 6 percent. Corporations, on the other hand, account for 90 percent of business revenues. Proprietorships are concentrated in the trade and services industries, where small family businesses are common. Corporations are prevalent in manufacturing and trade. Partnerships are active in trade, finance, and services industries.

—From *Principles of Economics*, 7th ed. by Roy J. Ruffin and Paul R. Gregory, p. 150.

_____ 3. What is the dominant pattern of organization of Paragraph 2?
   a. definition and example   c. contrast
   b. sequence of events   d. cause and effect

4. How do you know? _____

_____

Paragraph 3

Reference groups are the groups we use as standards to evaluate ourselves. Your reference groups may include your family, neighbors, teachers, classmates, co-workers, and the Scouts or the members of a church, synagogue, or mosque. Even a group you don't belong to can be a reference group. For example, if you are thinking about going to graduate school, graduate students or members of the profession you want to join may form a reference group. You would consider their standards as you evaluate your grades or writing skills.

—From Henslin, James M. *Sociology: A Down-to-Earth Approach, Core Concepts*, 1e. Published by Allyn and Bacon, Boston, MA. Copyright © 2006 by Pearson Education. Reprinted by permission of the publisher.

———— 5. What is the dominant pattern of organization of Paragraph 3?
     a. definition and example   c. contrast
     b. sequence of events   d. classification

6. How do you know? _____

_____

Summarization Activity

Directions: *Write the major headings in this chapter. Under each heading, write a couple of sentences about the most important topics presented in the section of text that follows that heading.*

First Heading _____

What information is most important? _____

_____

_____

Second Heading _____

What information is most important? _____

_____

_____

Third Heading _____

What information is most important? _____

_____

_____

Fourth Heading _____

What information is most important? _____

_____

_____

Fifth Heading _____

What information is most important? _____

_____

_____

Sixth Heading _____

What information is most important? _____

_____

_____

Seventh Heading _____

What information is most important? _____

_____

_____

     Combine the information you wrote in this outline into a paragraph to summarize what you have learned in this chapter.

Reflection Activity

How am I am going to apply what I have learned in this chapter?

Directions: *Write a paragraph discussing the two or three things you learned about patterns of organization that were most helpful to you and how you plan to use what you have learned.*

_____

_____

_____

_____

_____

_____

_____

_____

HOW BODY MOTIONS ARE USED
Rudolph F. Verderber

Accessing Prior Knowledge

Questions for Discussion

1. What are some ways that people show, without speaking, that they are bothered by someone sitting next to them?

2. How do you use body movements to let someone know you are ready to end a conversation?

Preview and Predict

Directions: *Look at the title of the selection. Think about what you already know about the subject. Then, write a couple of predictions about what you are going to read. For instance, what will the author discuss about body motions?*

1. _____

2. _____

Word Search and Discovery

Directions: *Skim through the selection to find the two words below. Underline both words in the selection. Then, use a dictionary to write their definitions in the spaces provided. As you read and encounter these words, see if the definitions you wrote fit the way each word is used in the selection.*

continuum (*n*): _____

_____

shrugging (*vb*): _____

_____

Also, underline two new words as you read the selection and write your guesses as to their meanings in the right margin of the text.

How Body Motions Are Used
Rudolph F. Verderber

1   Body motions in general and gestures in particular help us considerably in conveying meaning (Ekman and Friesen 1969).

2   **1. Body motions may be used to take the place of a word or phrase.** We could make a considerable list of the **emblems** (nonverbal symbols that take the place of words) that we use frequently. For instance, thumbs up means "everything is go"; first and second fingers held in a V shape means "peace" or "victory"; shaking the head from side to side means "no" and up and down means "yes"; shrugging the shoulders means "maybe," "I don't care," or "I don't know."

3   In many contexts, emblems are used as a complete language. **Sign language** refers to systems of body motions that include sign languages of the deaf and alternate sign languages used by Trappist monks in Europe and the women of Australia (Leathers 1992, p. 75).

4   **2. Body motions may be used to illustrate what a speaker is saying.** We use gestures to illustrate in at least five ways:

- To *emphasize* speech. A man may pound the table in front of him as he says, "Don't bug me."

- To show the *path* or *direction* of thought. A professor may move her hands on an imaginary continuum when she says, "The papers ranged from very good to very bad."

- To show *position*. A waiter may point when he says, "Take that table."

- To *describe*. A person may use her hands to indicate size as she says, "The ball is about three inches in diameter."

- To *mimic*. A person may nod his head as he says, "Did you see the way he nodded?"

5   **3. Body motions can display the verbal expression of feelings.** These *affect (emotional) displays* will take place automatically and are likely to be quite noticeable. For instance, if you stub your toe on a chair as you drag yourself out of bed in the morning, you are likely to grimace in pain. Occasionally we are fooled by these displays when people purposely deintensify or overreact. For example, a baseball player may remain stone-faced when he is hit by a wild pitch and refuse to rub the spot where he has been struck; conversely, a youngster may howl "in pain" when her older sister bumps her by accident.

6   **4. Body motions may be used to control or regulate the flow of a conversation or other communication transaction.** We use shifts in eye contact, slight head movements, shifts in posture, raising of eyebrows, and nodding of the head to tell a person when to continue, to repeat, to elaborate, to hurry up, or to finish. Effective communicators learn to adjust what they are saying and how they are saying it on the basis of such cues.

7   **5. Body motions may be used to relieve tension.** As we listen to people and watch them while they speak, they may scratch their head, tap their foot, or wring their hands.

—From *Communicate!* 9th edition by Verderber. 1999. Reprinted with permission of Wadsworth, a division of ThomsonLearning.

The Write Connection

Directions *Write a paragraph about three things you learned or that you think are most important in the reading selection.*

_____

_____

_____

_____

_____

Comprehension Check

Directions: *See how many questions you can answer without referring to the selection. Then, review the selection to write more complete responses.*

1. What body motion is the emblem for peace or victory?

_____

_____ 2. According to the author, body motions can take the place of
     a. emblems.   c. sign language.
     b. a system of body movements.   d. words.

_____ 3. A woman who rolls her eyes as she says, "Yeah, sure I believe you," is using body motions to
     a. describe an event.
     b. show the position of an object.
     c. show direction.
     d. emphasize the content of her speech.

_____ 4. A child who uses his hands to show the size of a monster he saw in a dream as he says, "It was twenty gazillion feet tall," is using body motions to
   a. describe what he saw.
   b. show the position of the monster.
   c. show the path or direction of his thoughts.
   d. symbolize the content of his speech.

_____ 5. An usher who extends his arm to a row of seats and says, "This aisle," is using body motions to
   a. include the audience.
   b. show the position of the seat.
   c. show what he is thinking.
   d. emphasize the content of his speech.

_____ 6. An example of an _affect (emotional) display_ of body motion used to express feelings would be
   a. yelling at the person who cut ahead of you in a long line.
   b. using caution when changing lanes on the freeway.
   c. opening your mouth wide with shock after hearing some surprising news.
   d. tilting your head toward a person as you say, "Who does he think he is?"

7. What is one body motion that may be used to tell a person when to continue, to repeat, to elaborate, to hurry up, or to finish a conversation?

_____

8. What are two examples of body motions that can be used to relieve tension?

_____

9. What information does the author want to present about body motions?

_____

_____ 10. The pattern of organization of this selection is
   a. enumeration or listing.
   b. comparison and contrast.
   c. sequence of events/process.
   d. definition and example.

Critical Thinking Questions

_____ 1. Which of the following conclusions can be drawn from the selection?
   a. Body motions reveal the speaker's personality.
   b. Body motions and gestures are necessary in order to get a message across to others.
   c. Body motions and gestures can help to convey meaning.
   d. It is impossible to misread the meaning of a message that is accompanied by body motions and gestures.

_____ 2. Which of the following statements supports the author's contention that we can be fooled by affect displays?
   a. A man pounds the table and says, "Don't bug me. Can't you see I'm busy?"
   b. A woman uses her hands to indicate the size of her waist before losing weight.
   c. A youngster howls "in pain" when her older sister accidentally bumps her.
   d. We scratch our heads or tap our feet while listening to others speak.

_____ 3. The author's tone can be described as
   a. sorrowful.   c. humorous.
   b. matter-of-fact.   d. excited.

Vocabulary Check

Directions: _See if any of the words you underlined in the selection are among the list of words below. If not, write your words in the spaces provided. Guess the meaning of the words from the way they were used in the selection. Then, look up the definition of each word in the dictionary to see if you were right._

affect (_n_): Your guess: _____

   Dictionary Definition: _____

mimic (_vb_): Your guess: _____

   Dictionary Definition: _____

Your word: _____ Your guess: _____

   Dictionary Definition: _____

Your word: _____ Your guess: _____

   Dictionary Definition: _____

♟♟♟ Skills in Practice ► Reading Selection 2

VIOLENT VIDEO GAMES CAN INCREASE AGGRESSION
Diana Zuckerman

Accessing Prior Knowledge

Questions for Discussion

1. Do you think that playing violent video games can cause violent behavior? Why or why not?

2. Why do you think violent video games are so popular?

Preview and Predict

Directions *Look at the title of the selection. Think about what you already know about the subject. Then, write a couple of predictions about what you are going to read. For instance, what do you think the author will discuss about violent video games?*

1. _____

2. _____

Word Search and Discovery

Directions: *Skim through the selection to find the two words below. Underline both words in the selection. Then, use a dictionary to write their definitions in the spaces provided. As you read and encounter these words, see if the definitions you wrote fit the way each word is used in the selection.*

interactive (*adj*): _____

_____

Nazi (*n*): _____

_____

Also, underline two new words as you read the selection and write your guesses as to their meanings in the right margin of the text.

VIOLENT VIDEO GAMES CAN INCREASE AGGRESSION

Diana Zuckerman

1   Playing violent video games can increase aggressive thoughts, feelings, and behavior in real life, according to two new studies. Violent video games may be more harmful than violent television and movies because they are interactive and engrossing, requiring the player to identify with the aggressor.

2   The first study involved 227 male and female college students, who were asked about their recent delinquent behaviors as well as their video game playing habits. Students who reported playing more violent video games in junior high and high school had more aggressive personalities, behaved more aggressively, and were more likely to report delinquent behavior in real life. In addition, students who spent more time playing video games had lower grades in college.

3   The second study was designed to determine if violent games really do cause violent behavior. The 210 college students played either a violent or nonviolent video game. In the violent game (*Wolfenstein 3D*) the human hero chooses from an array of weapons to kill Nazi guards with the ultimate goal of killing Adolph Hitler. The game was chosen because it is blatantly violent, realistic and has human characters. The nonviolent game was *Myst*. As part of the study, the students were "tested" on three different days to see how well they played the game. On the third day, they were told to punish their opponent with an unpleasant blast of noise when the opponent lost. The students who played the violent game punished their opponent for a longer period of time than did students who had played the nonviolent video game. (To protect the students in the experiment, the opponents did not actually hear the noise, but the students thought they did).

4   The authors explain that violent video games teach kids to practice aggressive solutions to conflict. In the short run, playing a violent video game appears to affect aggression by encouraging a child to think violent thoughts. Over a long period of time, the player learns and practices new aggressive strategies and ways of thinking during the games, and he or she becomes more likely to use these strategies when real-life conflicts arise.

5   Why does this happen? Many violent video games involve learning how to be more effective at destroying the opponent. According to the researchers, this makes video games potentially more dangerous than exposure to violent television and movies, which are known to have substantial effects on aggression and violence.

6   I interviewed Karen Dill, one of the authors, who told me that parents and youth workers should be concerned if someone is spending a lot of time playing violent computer games. "They aren't just games—they can have a serious effect, so consider it a red flag, and take it seriously" she emphasized. She pointed out that the

military uses video games to train troops for combat. Perhaps most important, she reminded us that it is easier to prevent a child from becoming violent than to rehabilitate one who is already violent.

—This summary, written by Diana Zuckerman, PhD, is available on the National Research Center for Women & Families web site at www.center4research.org/V-media.html#ViolentVideo <http://www.center4research.org/v-media.html#ViolentVideo> and is based on an article by Craig A. Anderson, PhD, and Karen E. Dill, PhD and Published in the *Journal of Personality and Social Psychology*, April 24, 2000, Vol. 78, No. 4, pp. 772–790

The Write Connection

Directions: *Write a paragraph about the three things you learned or that you think are most important in the reading selection.*

_____

_____

_____

_____

_____

Comprehension Check

Directions: *See how many questions you can answer without referring to the selection. Then, review the selection to write more complete responses.*

_____ 1. The title of the selection implies that the author will present the _____ of video games.
   a. events
   b. differences
   c. effects
   d. similarities

_____ 2. The pattern of organization of the selection is
   a. listing or enumeration.
   b. comparison.
   c. cause and effect.
   d. sequence of events/process.

_____ 3. In which publication did the study appear?
   a. *Journal of Personality and Social Psychology*
   b. *Journal of International Video Games and Gaming*
   c. *Game World*
   d. *Games Gone Wild*

_____ 4. The first study found that college students who had played more violent video games in junior high and high school
   a. had an increased likelihood of visual impairments.
   b. were more likely to report delinquent behavior in real life.
   c. indicated that they participated in chat room discussions.
   d. were disruptive in school settings.

_____ 5. Which violent video game was used in the second study?
   a. *Myst*   c. *Wolfenstein 3D*
   b. *Grand Theft Auto*   d. *Adolph Hitler*

6. The violent video game used in the second study was selected because

_____

_____

_____ 7. The second study found that the students who played the violent video game
   a. also played a number of other violent video games that were not designated for use in the study.
   b. were more likely to have difficulty performing successfully in an academic setting than those who played the nonviolent video game.
   c. were unable to decrease the amount of time they spent playing violent video games after the study was completed.
   d. punished their opponent for a longer period of time than did students who had played the nonviolent video game.

_____ 8. According to the researchers, one reason why violent video games may be more harmful than violent television and movies is
   a. the player can become skilled in military combat.
   b. the player can identify with the aggressor in the game.
   c. the aggressor and the player share similar physical characteristics.
   d. the player is damaging key areas of the brain associated with tactile movements.

9. What is another reason why violent video games may be more harmful than violent television programs or movies? _____

_____

_____

_____ 10. What is the meaning of the word *engrossing* as it is used in paragraph 1?
   a. disgusting   c. absorbing
   b. punishing   d. insulting

Critical Thinking Check

_____ 1. Which of the following statements best supports Dr. Karen Dill's contention that playing violent computer games can have a serious effect on someone who spends a lot time playing them?
   a. Parents and youth workers are not aware of the effect of violent video games.
   b. The military uses video games to train troops for combat.
   c. It is easier to prevent an adult from becoming violent than it is a child.
   d. The military has banned violent video games.

_____ 2. Which of the following conclusions can be drawn from the information contained in the selection?
   a. Violent video games may increase aggression by encouraging a child to think violent thoughts.
   b. Action should be taken to insure that all video games with violent content are banned from the market.
   c. Parents are ultimately responsible for the types of video games their children are able to gain access to.
   d. The number of violent video games on the market will continue to increase.

3. Do you believe that playing violent video games can cause a child to develop aggressive behaviors? Why or why not? _____

_____

Vocabulary Check

Directions: _See if the words you underlined in the selection are among the list of words below. If not, write your words in the spaces provided. Guess the meaning of the words below from the way they were used in the selection. Then, look up the definition of each word in the dictionary to see if you were right._

blatantly (_adv_): Your guess: _____

   Dictionary Definition: _____

delinquent (_adj_): Your guess: _____

   Dictionary Definition: _____

Your word: _____ Your guess: _____

   Dictionary Definition: _____

Your word: _____ Your guess: _____

   Dictionary Definition: _____

PART 3

7 Lecture Notes and Learning Strategies

> *There is only one good, knowledge, and one evil, ignorance.*

— Socrates

In this chapter you will learn how to:

Take Lecture Notes for Effective Study

Use Memorization Techniques for Learning Important Lecture Information

You will learn the following strategies:

RODEO Attention Plan for Note Taking and Test Preparation

Recall to Mind

List, Label, and Repeat

▲ **Your interest paid over time will yield great dividends.**

Preview and Predict ▶ What do you know so far?

- How many of the following questions can you answer before you read the chapter?

- Why are listening and note-taking skills important to your success in college?

_____

- How do you decide which information is most important to study for an exam?

_____

251

- What do you think you will learn in this chapter?

  _____

- Think of one way in which the picture relates to this chapter's objectives.

  _____

Now, as you read the chapter, look for the answers to see if you were right.

WHY YOU NEED TO TAKE LECTURE NOTES

There are two reasons why you should take notes for every lecture. First, taking notes helps you to pay attention during class because you are listening for important information to write down or thinking of questions that will make your notes more accurate and more complete. Second, taking notes helps you to perform well on college exams. College courses tend to have few exams, making each one worth a large portion of your grade. You will find that it is difficult to remember the large amount of information presented each day unless you take notes. You may remember some of the details of a lecture for a day or so, but three or four weeks later when the test is given, how much will you recall? Some students actually decide that they *want* to fail a class by refusing to take notes. In this way, they create a situation where they do not have what they need to succeed.

It can be difficult to decide what's essential to write down and to study because there is so much information presented in each college lecture. The following guidelines will help you decide what information is important to include in your notes for study.

First, think like your instructor. For instance, if you were the instructor, what would you want your students to learn from the course? What questions would you ask your students on an exam? Thinking like the instructor prepares your mind for taking good notes because it helps you understand what information is important to study. Second, use the RODEO Attention Plan for Note Taking and Test Preparation. It serves as a guide to the five most important items of information that are most likely to appear as questions on an exam.

Memory Check 1 How much do you remember?

1. What are two reasons why it is important to take notes in college courses?

   a. _____

   b. _____

2. What do some students do when they want to fail? _____

_____

3. What are two guidelines that will help you decide which information is important to include in your notes for study?

a. _____

b. _____

The RODEO Attention Plan: A Strategy for Note Taking and Test Preparation

The RODEO Attention Plan provides a guide for determining which information is most important to include in your lecture notes for later study. If you include these five items in your notes, you will have the information you need to be more prepared for exams.

R–**Repeated information**: Write all information that has been repeated, reviewed, or emphasized by instructors.

O–**On the board**: Write all information that has been written on the board.

D–**Definitions**: Write any definitions or key terms that have been presented in class.

E–**Examples**: Write any examples that have been presented to illustrate a definition.

O–**Outlines**: Write any outlines that have been presented in class.

 ## 1. Repeated Information (R)

Instructors repeat or emphasize information they think is important. If they think it's important enough to repeat, you can bet it will appear on an exam. For instance, you will notice that instructors often review the most important information to see how much you remember. Sometimes instructors will also emphasize important information by raising their voice or walking across the room. They may use words or phrases such as "the best way" or "the most important," or words like "key," "requires," or "crucial" to stress the importance of what they are saying.

You should highlight, underline, or place a star next to any information that is repeated, reviewed, or emphasized in class. Then, make sure you know the information because it will most likely appear on an exam.

2. On the Board (O)

If any information is on the board, write it down. When instructors take the time to write something on the board so that everyone is sure to see it, you know they think it is important. Be prepared to see it again on an exam. This includes any information that is projected on a screen for presentation.

You should also learn any information provided in a handout or worksheet. This information is already written down for you. When instructors take the time to prepare these materials, it means the information they are presenting is important for you to study.

3. Definitions (D)

Definitions and key terms form the language of a course. When you take a college course, it's like learning a new language. Different definitions and key terms form the language of a mathematics course, a biology course, or a course in psychology. For instance, in a computer class, a *mouse* refers to an input device with buttons controlling a curser on a monitor. Instructors want you to know the definitions or key terms of the subject they are teaching so you can understand as well as discuss what you are learning using the language of the discipline you are studying.

You should underline, highlight, or place the abbreviation *def* next to any definition or key term you write down in your notes. Then, make sure you know the meaning of each one because they will almost always appear on an exam.

4. Examples (E)

Instructors provide examples to help you understand a definition or key term. Examples often appear as test questions on exams. For instance, imagine that you are taking a psychology class and have written the following information in your notes:

> Agoraphobia—the fear of crowded places; victims may avoid all social interactions— symptoms may last a few months to a life time if not properly treated.
> ex. Emily Dickinson may have had agoraphobia. (Rarely left her father's house.)

A possible question on an exam might be: "Which of the following phobias is associated with the avoidance of all social interactions?"

You should write down any examples presented in class underneath or beside the new words they illustrate. Doing this helps you to remember the meanings of new words or terms more easily. You can place the abbreviation *ex* next to each example to make it stand out in your notes.

♟ 5. Outlines (O)

You should make certain to write down *all* of the details of any outline presented in class. An outline starts with a topic, followed by a list of major details that support the topic.

For instance, you might see an outline like the one in Figure 7.1 on the board in a world history class. Notice that each major detail is underlined. Doing this helps you to see how the major details support the topic. You should underline, highlight, or number the major details to make them stand out. You also want to be able to see very clearly the difference between the major details and the examples or minor details in your notes.

Why are outlines so important? First, instructors can easily turn the topic as well as the major details of an outline into questions on an exam. For instance, consider the *topic* of the example outline below. An instructor could ask the question, "What are the four reasons for the fall of the Roman Empire?" Then, you would need to recall the four reasons on the exam. Second, it is easy for an instructor to create questions about each *major detail* or *example* in an outline such as "How did the expansion of the Roman Empire contribute to its downfall?" Then, you would

Figure 7.1 Example Outline

Four Reasons for the fall of Roman Empire — (Topic)

Too large: From Mesopotamia to Scotland, difficult to administer

Corrupt governors: Became greedy; the rich got richer, the poor got poorer

Foreign mercenaries used to protect borders: War. Roman army too busy.

Romans lost national pride: Easier take-over by foreign tribes. ie. Huns.

↑   ↑

Major details = four reasons (underlined)   Minor details = (examples)

need to respond that because the Roman Empire became too large, it was difficult to administer.

There is another reason outlines are important to include in your notes. Outlines are often *repeated* or reviewed, they usually appear *on the board*, and they frequently contain *definitions* and *examples*, which make them important to study. Since outlines contain the most RODEO items, all of their information is likely to appear as questions on an exam.

Memory Check 2 How much do you remember?

1. What are two ways that an instructor can emphasize or *repeat* important information?

   a. _____

   b. _____

2. Why is it important to write and study information that appears on the board? _____

3. What important information forms the language of a course? _____

   _____

4. Why do instructors provide examples for definitions or key terms? _____

   _____

5. What are two reasons outlines are so important to include in your lecture notes?

   a. _____

   b. _____

   _____

Additional Suggestions for Taking Effective Lecture Notes

1. **Put the date on the top of the page so you can refer back to the lecture more easily.** It's also a good idea to keep your notes in chronological order.

2. **Use a folder to keep all your notes together or use separate notebooks for each class.** Your notes will be much easier to find.

3. **Listen and look for RODEO information.**

4. **Attend class early enough to write down anything the instructor has put *on the board* such as homework assignments, lecture discussion topics, or test dates.** Then, you can concentrate more easily on what the instructor is saying when the lecture begins.

5. **As soon as you can, after class, review your notes to make sure they are complete and accurate while the information is still fresh in your mind.**

6. **Use your lecture notes to create a study guide.** You can do this by writing questions in the left margin of your notes next to the information you want to know for an exam. Then, you can test yourself by covering your notes and asking the questions in the margin to see how much you can recall.

Using the Cornell Method

The Cornell Method of Note Taking has been used successfully by students for decades; it provides a format for taking notes that can also serve as a study guide. There are four steps to remember: First, write your notes on the right side of your paper so you will have a margin on the left (approximately 2½ inches wide). (See Figure 7.2 on page 258.) After the lecture, use the left side margin to write questions beside the information in your notes. Then, test yourself by covering your notes, asking the questions in the margin, and answering them in your own words to see how much you can recall. Finally, in the Cornell Method, you leave a space at the bottom of your notes to summarize key information for each page. When you can summarize the information, you will find that it is easier to remember it during an exam because you are using your own words to condense the material.

How can you apply the Cornell Method to create a study guide? Figure 7.2 shows an example of student notes from a lecture on the *RODEO Attention Plan*. The student has added questions in the left margin to test herself on the most important information. Now, look at the first question in the margin. It says, "What is the RODEO Attention Plan?" Can you see the answer in the notes next to the question? Yes. What is the next margin question?

How long do you think it would take you to learn the answer to this question for an exam? It would probably not be much time at all. You will soon find that many of your margin questions appear on exams. Using the Cornell Method will help you to be better prepared to answer them.

Figure 7.2 Student Example of Study Guide Using Cornell Method for Taking Lecture Notes

Date: April 1, 2009

QUESTIONS	NOTES FROM LECTURE ON RODEO ATTENTION PLAN
What is the RODEO Attention Plan? What are two things it will help you to do?	The RODEO Attention Plan—tells you which information is important to write in your lecture notes for study. Helps you to: 1) improve quality of information in notes 2) be better prepared for exams
R—stands for what? How do instructors emphasize or repeat what's important?	R—Repeated Instructors raise their voices, walk across room, and use phrases like "most important" or "best way"
O—stands for what? Includes what 2 things? Why is it important?	O—On the Board Includes worksheets and handouts Instructors take extra time to prepare or write info that they think is important—will be on a test.
D—stands for what? Why are they important?	D—Definitions They form the language of the course
E—stands for what? Why are they important?	E—Examples Help you to remember the definition
O—stands for what? What are they? Why are they important?	O—Outlines A topic with a list of supporting details 1 Topic of outline can be easily turned into a question 2 Instructor might ask questions about examples that support each major detail

Summary: The RODEO Attention Plan includes information that is Repeated, On the Board, Definitions, Examples, and Outlines. RODEO information is most likely to appear on an exam.

Memory Check 3 How much do you remember?

1. Why should you put the date on the top of your lecture notes? _____
   _____

2. Why should you write assignments or test dates that appear on the board before class begins? _____
   _____

3. What should you do as soon as possible after class? _____

_____

_____

4. What are steps for using the Cornell Method to create a study guide from your lecture notes?

a. _____

b. _____

c. _____

_____

d. _____

Activity 7.1 ▶ RODEO in the Classroom

Directions: *Apply the RODEO Attention Plan for Note Taking and Test Preparation for one class you are currently taking until the day of your next exam. After the exam, look at your lecture notes. Identify how many RODEO items appeared as questions on the exam. You will soon begin to see the value of including RODEO items in your lecture notes for effective study.*

Internet Activity ▶ Additional Note-Taking Methods

Directions: *Explore the note-taking methods contained in each of the websites below.*

Then, answer the questions that follow.

http://www.studygs.net: Study Guides and Strategies by studygs.net: Go to "Classroom Participation" and select "Taking Notes in Lectures."

http://www.dyslexia-college.com/notes.html: Dyslexia at college edited by John Bradford.

1. What did you learn from each website that was helpful? _____

_____

_____

_____

_____

2. Which website was the most useful and why? _____

_____

_____

_____

Mind Mapping and Diagramming

A mind map or a diagram is a way to take notes by drawing a visual representation of the relationships among ideas presented in a lecture or in written material. Some students find that they can better understand important ideas by drawing a map or diagram that shows how each idea is connected to the topic. Figure 7.3 shows an example of a mind map on the four reasons for the fall of the Roman Empire.

Figure 7.4 shows a diagram of the same information.

Figure 7.3 Example Mind Map

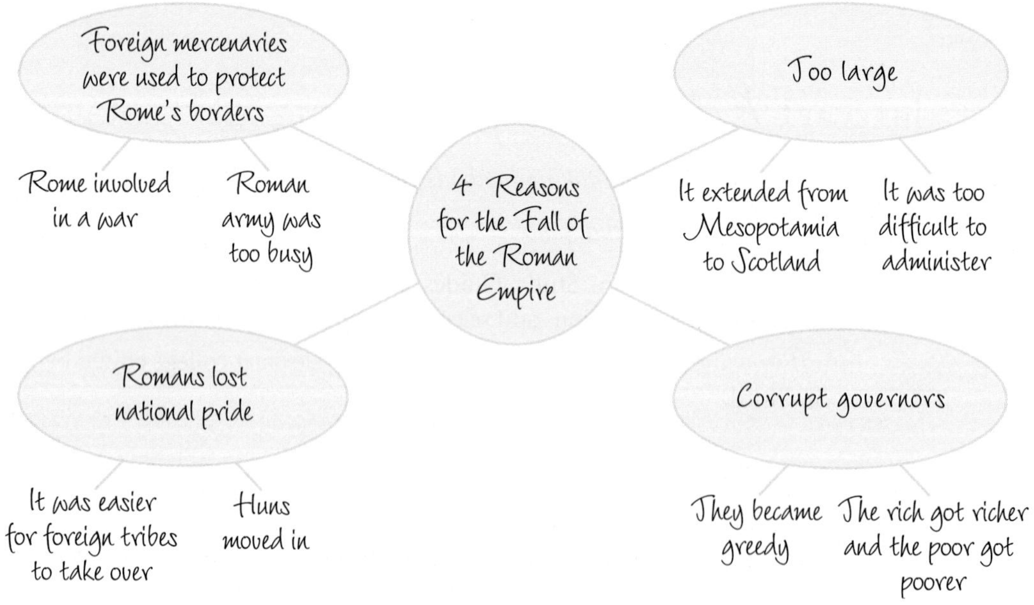

Foreign mercenaries were used to protect Rome's borders

Too large

Rome involved in a war

Roman army was too busy

4 Reasons for the Fall of the Roman Empire

It extended from Mesopotamia to Scotland

It was too difficult to administer

Romans lost national pride

Corrupt governors

It was easier for foreign tribes to take over

Huns moved in

They became greedy

The rich got richer and the poor got poorer

Figure 7.4 Sample Diagram

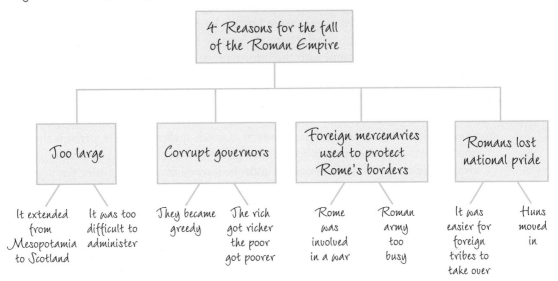

MEMORIZATION STRATEGIES FOR EFFECTIVE LEARNING

Recall to Mind: A Strategy for Creating Recall Words or Recall Sentences for Study

Recall to Mind is a strategy that will help you to learn the major details of an outline for effective study. For instance, what question would you expect to see on an exam about the Roman Empire? You might expect the following question: "What are the four reasons for the fall of the Roman Empire?" Would you be able to remember the four reasons? There are two useful ways to memorize a list of major details in an outline. You can create a *recall word* or a *recall sentence*.

1. Creating a Recall Word

A **recall word** is an *acronym* in which each letter of the word represents a set of information. A recall word, or acronym, is a word you can use as a memory device. For example, ASAP is an acronym or recall word that represents **A**s **S**oon **A**s **P**ossible. RODEO is a "recall word" that stands for **R**epeated, **O**n the Board, **D**efinitions, **E**xamples, and **O**utlines.

To create a recall word, use the first letters of the most important word in each major detail in an outline to form a word you can easily remember. By doing this, you can increase the amount of information you are able to memorize and reduce the amount of time you need for study. For instance, when you see the acronyms ASAP or RODEO, you know what is represented by the letters in each word. You don't have to try and recall each major detail separately because the letters that form the recall word are associated in your mind with the information. A recall word works best when the major details in an outline can be arranged in any order to spell a word.

♟ 2. Creating a Recall Sentence

Some major details in an outline, however, may not spell a word. Or, perhaps the outline presents a list of steps in a sequence, a process, or event. In this case, you can't re-arrange the major details because they must be learned in a specific order. For instance, what if you had to learn the order of the planets in the solar system? How would you remember Mercury, Venus, Earth, Mars, Jupiter, Saturn, Uranus, and Neptune? You can't create a recall word using the first letters in the names of each planet.

If the list of major details you are trying to memorize is very long or if the first letters of the major details do not spell a word, you can create a recall sentence. In a **recall sentence**, the first letters of the most important information in a list of major details are used, *in order*, as the first letters of the words in the sentence. Here is an example:

My **V**ery **E**lderly **M**other **J**ust **S**howed **U**s **N**intendo.

This sentence could help you to remember the order of the planets because it has a logical order and meaning. It would probably be much harder to remember the order of the planets if you created the list of words, **M**ary, **V**ase, **E**mily, **M**oses, **J**erry, **S**ally, **U**ncle, and **N**eville, because they don't make sense as a sentence. Your recall sentence needs to make sense *to you* so that it will be easy to associate with the information you want to learn or memorize.

If you can create a meaningful sentence using the first letters of the most important information in each major detail, you will find it much easier to remember what each letter represents when you want to recall the entire outline. Then, you will reduce the amount of notes you need to carry around for study, because when you see each letter of the recall word or sentence, your mind will automatically fill in the rest of the information. Applying the *Recall to Mind* strategy can cut your study time in half.

Memory Check **4** How much do you remember?

1. What is one example of an acronym or *recall word?* _____

2. What is a *recall word?* _____

_____

3. What is a *recall sentence?* _____

_____

_____

4. What is an example of a *recall sentence?* _____

_____

_____   5. If the outline you want to learn contains a list of steps or events, you would probably need to create:

    a. a recall word   b. a recall sentence

Activity 7.2 ▶ Creating Recall Words and Sentences I

Directions: *Answer the questions that follow each of the outlines below. Then, create a recall word or recall sentence using the first letter of each major detail in the outlines below.*

Outline 1	Outline 2	Outline 3
Grocery Store List	Dance Steps	Trees
Eggs	Stomp	Oak
Apples	Slide	Maple
Vitamins	Together	Cedar
Rice	Clap	Elm
Cheese	Turn	Pine

___ 1. The major details are arranged in:
  a. any order.
  b. a specific order.
	___ 1. The major details are arranged in:
	  a. any order.
	  b. a specific order.
		___ 1. The major details are arranged in:
		  a. any order.
		  b. a specific order.

2. Your *recall word* or *recall sentence:* _____ _____ _____	2. Your *recall word* or recall *sentence:* _____ _____ _____	2. Your *recall word* or *recall sentence:* _____ _____ _____

Outline 4	Outline 5
The Great Lakes <u>H</u>uron <u>O</u>ntario <u>M</u>ichigan <u>E</u>rie <u>S</u>uperior	Presidents since 1980 <u>C</u>arter <u>R</u>eagan <u>B</u>ush Sr. <u>C</u>linton <u>B</u>ush Jr.

___ 1. The major details
    are arranged in:
    a. any order.
    b. a specific order.
 	
   2. Your recall word or
    recall sentence:
 	
   _____
 	
   _____
 	
   _____
	___ 1. The major details
	    are arranged in:
	    a. any order.
	    b. a specific order.
	
	   2. Your recall word or
	    recall sentence:
	
	   _____
	
	   _____
	
	   _____

List, Label, and Repeat: A Strategy for Learning Outlines When Studying

List, Label, and Repeat is another effective strategy for learning outlines when studying. If you want to be prepared for an exam, it is important to memorize the entire outline, including the examples, so that any questions pertaining to the topic will be easy to answer. *List, Label, and Repeat* will help you to learn an entire outline.

List, Label, and Repeat is an effective technique because it involves the use of a variety of senses at one time. You are Listing (touching), Labeling (looking), and Repeating (hearing). *The more senses you combine as you study, the more ways your memory will have for recalling information.* For instance, during an exam, you may recall information because you remember the way it looked on the page, what you were doing when you wrote it, or the way it sounded when you repeated it. If you apply List, Label, and Repeat, you will find that you have created several ways to recall the information you need to remember.

In order to apply the List, Label, and Repeat strategy, you should follow these steps:

♟ 1. List

List the entire outline including the topic heading, major details, and the examples that support each major detail on the right side of the page. Make sure that your list of major details stands out in some way. You want to be able to *see* the relationship between the topic and each major detail as well as the relationship between each major detail and its supporting information.

Look at the example of student notes in Figure 7.5 Imagine you are taking an exam in a world history class. How would you learn all of the information in this outline? You should ask yourself questions that help you relate to each major detail, such as "*In what way* was the Roman Empire too large?" or, "*Why* were foreign mercenaries used to protect borders?"

Now think of a who, what, or why question to write in the spaces provided in the left margin next to where the answers appear in the example below.

♟ 2. Label

Choose a word in each major detail that you think will best help you to remember the supporting details. Then, label the word by circling the first letter. Then use the circled letters to create a *recall word* or *recall sentence*.

For instance, look at the first major detail in the student notes below. Would you circle the word "too" or "large" to help you remember the first major detail?

Figure 7.5 Example of a Student's Notes from a World History Class

What are the four reasons for the fall of the Roman Empire? In what way was the Roman Empire too large? Why did it cause the fall of the Roman Empire?	Four reasons for the fall of Roman Empire Too large: From Mesopotamia to Scotland, difficult to administer Corrupt governors: Became greedy, The rich got richer, the poor got poorer Foreign mercenaries used to protect borders: Roman army too busy because of war. Romans lost national pride: Easier take-over by foreign tribes. ex. Huns.
How were they corrupt? Why were foreign mercenaries used to protect borders?	
Recall sentence: _____	

"Large" (L) might be a better signal to help you remember that Mesopotamia to Scotland is a "large" area. Which word would you circle for the next major detail, "Corrupt"? or "governors"? Which word would help you to remember greedy, the rich got richer, the poor got poorer? You might choose the word "corrupt" (C), since the examples illustrate corrupt behavior. Perhaps you would choose the word "mercenaries" (M) to help you remember who was protecting the borders and "pride" (P) to represent the pride that the Romans lost.

Once you have labeled the word in each major detail that you think is most important, you can decide whether you want to form a recall word or a recall sentence. Remember, the recall phrase or recall sentence you create should be meaningful to you. Before you create a recall word or recall sentence you should ask yourself, "Do the reasons or major details have to be listed in a specific order or could they be listed in any order?" The reasons for the fall of the Roman Empire can appear in any order.

Can you form a recall word from the example letters LCMP? No. So, you would create a recall *sentence*. What recall sentence could you create for the letters,

L, C, M, and P? _____

_____

You might come up with a recall sentence, such as **Larry Called My Parents**, to remember the four reasons for the fall of the Roman Empire. Write your recall sentence in the student example in Figure 7.5.

♟ 3. Repeat

First, look at the letters you labeled as you *repeat* the major details of the outline aloud two or three times. Then, turn the topic of the outline into a question and see if you can use only your recall word or sentence to remember the major details that answer the question—without looking at your notes. Finally, see how many of the supporting details you can recall each time you ask the question. You can ask yourself the questions you wrote in the margin to help you recall the information that supports each major detail.

For example, what are the four reasons for the fall of the Roman Empire? Larry "L" stands for _____. In what way was the Roman Empire too large? It spanned from Mesopotamia to Scotland. Called "C" stands for _____. The governors were greedy. My "M" stands for _____. Why were foreign mercenaries used to protect borders? _____

MyReadingLab

Memory and
Concentration:
To practice your skills
go to
>Study plan
>Reading skills
>Memory and
concentration

Parents "**P**" stands for _____. What happened when the Romans lost national pride? (It was easier for foreign tribes to take over. Ex. Huns.) Now do you understand why the Roman Empire fell?

You will soon find that you are able to recall an entire outline without looking. You will see how much easier it is to recall all of the information an hour later, the next day, or whenever you study for an exam.

Memory Check 5 — How much do you remember?

1. Why should you make sure your major details stand out when you *list* an outline?

   _____

   _____

2. How do you decide which information to *label?*

   _____

   _____

3. What question should you ask before you create a *recall word* or *recall sentence?*

   _____

   _____

4. What are the three steps in the *repeat* process?

   a. _____

   _____

   b. _____

   _____

   _____

   c. _____

   _____

Activity 7.3 ▶ Creating Recall Words and Sentences 2

Directions: *Create a recall word or a recall sentence that you can use to memorize each outline below. Circle the most important word that will help you to remember each item.*

1. The Goals of the United Nations created in 1945:

   - maintain international peace

   - remove threats to peace in other countries

   - develop friendly relations among nations

   - promote respect for human rights

   - promote international cooperation to solve economic and social problems

   Write your own recall word or recall sentence: _____

   _____

2. Maslow's Hierarchy of Needs: Needs that must be met in order of importance:

   - physiological needs—such as food and shelter

   - safety needs—physical security and freedom from pain and fear

   - belonging and love needs—being accepted and having one's own territory

   - esteem needs—to appreciate oneself and others

   - self-actualization needs—to reach for one's own highest potential

   Write your own recall word or recall sentence: _____

   _____

3. Multiplication of Polynomials: Order of multiplication for $(6x + 7)(4x - 5)$

   - First: Multiply the first terms

   - Then: Multiply the outer terms

   - Next: Multiply the inner terms

   - Last: Multiply the last terms

   Write your own recall word or recall sentence: _____

   _____

4. The Steps in the Scientific Process:

   - name the problem or question

   - form a guess (hypothesis) for the cause of the problem and predict results

- test your hypothesis through controlled experiments or observations

- check and interpret your results

- report your results to the scientific community

Write your own recall word or recall sentence: _____

_____

5. The Hierarchy of Living Things:

- kingdom

- phylum

- class

- order

- family

- genus

- species

Write your own recall word or recall sentence: _____

_____

MyReadingLab

Note Taking/
Highlighting: To practice
your skills go to
>Study plan
>Reading skills
>Note taking/
highlighting

? Test Yourself Review Quiz

Chapter Review Questions

1. What are two reasons you should take lecture notes?

_____

2. What five items of information should you include in your notes using the *RODEO Attention Plan for Note Taking?* _____

_____

3. What can you write in the left margin of your notes to test yourself on information that may appear on an exam? _____

4. What should you ask yourself before you create a *recall word* or *recall sentence*?

_____

Use the recall words or sentences you created earlier in the chapter to recall and answer the following questions.

5. What are the names of the five Great Lakes?

   _____

6. What are the names of the five Presidents of the United States since 1980?

   _____

7. What are the four steps for multiplying polynomials?

   _____

   _____

8. What are four reasons for the fall of the Roman Empire?

   _____

   _____

Application Questions

1. Complete the study guide provided for the following paragraph. Add any additional RODEO items of information from the paragraph underneath each major detail. Then, add questions in the margin that would help you recall the information.

The Mexican War

What Americans call the Mexican War was actually the final armed struggle in a sequence of conflicts lasting more than a decade. The first phase was the war of Texas independence, which took place in 1835–1836. Then, in 1841, a second, brief war was fought between the Republic of Texas and Mexico as a result of Texan efforts to occupy even more Mexican territory. The third and final phase was a declared war between the United States (now including Texas as a state) and Mexico in 1846–1847.

—From *The Pursuit of Liberty: A History of the American People*, 3rd ed. vol. I
by R. Jackson Wilson [et al.] p. 486. © 1996 Addison-Wesley
Educational Publishers Inc.

Margin Questions	Notes
What events led to the Mexican War? _____ _____	**Topic:** The sequence of conflicts which led to the Mexican War The war of Texas independence It took place in 1835–1836
What was the second conflict? When did the war take place? _____ _____	_____ _____ Texans wanted to occupy even more Mexican territory A declared war between the United States (including the State of Texas) and Mexico
When did the war take place?	_____ _____

2. Create a recall sentence or recall word to help you remember the sequence of conflicts leading to the Mexican War.

   _____

3. On a separate piece of paper, create a mind map or diagram that represents the sequence of conflicts that led to the Mexican War and includes the information you identified about each one.

Summarization Activity

Directions: *Write the major headings in this chapter. Under each heading, write a couple of sentences about the most important topics presented in the section of text that follows that heading.*

First heading _____

What information is most important? _____

_____

_____

Second heading _____

What information is most important? _____

_____

_____

Third heading _____

What information is most important? _____

_____

_____

Combine the information you wrote in this outline into a paragraph to summarize what you have learned in this chapter.

Reflection Activity

How am I am going to apply what I have learned in this chapter?

Directions: *Write a paragraph about the two or three things you learned about taking notes and learning strategies that were most helpful to you and how you plan to use what you have learned.*

_____

_____

_____

_____

_____

_____

_____

_____

♟♟♟ Skills In Practice ▶ Reading Selection 1

"CONVERSATIONS WITH EASE," FROM *SOCIAL SAVVY: A HANDBOOK FOR TEENS WHO WANT TO KNOW WHAT TO SAY, WHAT TO DO, AND HOW TO FEEL CONFIDENT IN ANY SITUATION*
Judith Re

Accessing Prior Knowledge

Questions for Discussion

1. What is the longest friendship you have ever had? Why do you think you have been friends for so long?

2. What do you think is the best way to disagree with someone you care about?

Preview and Predict

Directions: *Look at the title of the selection. Think about what you already know about the subject. Then, write a couple of predictions about what you are going to read. For instance, what do you think the author will discuss about conversation?*

1. _____

2. _____

Word Search and Discovery

Directions: *Skim through the selection to find the two words below. Underline both words in the selection. Then, use a dictionary to write their definitions in the spaces provided. As you read and encounter these words, see if the definitions you wrote fit the way each word is used in the selection.*

compromise (*n*): _____

savvy (*n*): _____

Also, underline at least one new word as you read the selection and write your guess as to its meaning in the right margin of the text.

CONVERSATIONS WITH EASE
Judith Re

1   [S]ome emotions, like sympathy or excitement, can actually help a conversation flow. But if you're feeling very nervous, it can be awfully difficult to have a nice "chat"!

2   This is not to say, of course, that emotions are the only things that muddy up a clear conversation. Shaky communication skills can cause a lot of trouble as well. Unfortunately, most of us are not aware of our weaknesses in this area. After all, we do have some skills. We know, for example, that it's not polite to interrupt or to point and laugh. We know when to say hello, thank you, excuse me, and good-bye and when to introduce one person to another. We easily carry on in-depth conversations with close friends. But there is a whole lot more to good conversation skills than just the simple basics.

3   The truth is, I can't do much about your nervousness in approaching a new person, but I can help you feel a bit more confident that you will have things to say. I can't keep you from forgetting a few people's names, but I can show you how to get through the awkward period of not remembering with a smile. And I can't keep the hurt away if someone is clearly not listening to a thing you have to say. But I can suggest a few ways to walk away that will save you from any more bad feelings.

You Don't Agree

4   Conversations should never come to a grinding halt over a disagreement. But often they do. This is largely because most people don't know how to disagree. Some stubbornly state their opinion, insist they are right, assure the other person he or she is being silly or dumb, and then feel surprised when they have a fight on their hands. Others, afraid of an argument, say they agree when they really don't and then, because they are not telling the truth, find themselves in a very stilted and awkward conversation that soon ends. "What happened?" they think. "I didn't cause a fuss!"

5   Disagreements are as natural as rain. They can sometimes even be interesting! Here are some savvy guidelines on how to manage them.

- Be honest. State your opinion, but not as fact. "I feel . . ." or "In my opinion . . ." is the way to go. That way you won't sound like a know-it-all. You simply know how *you* feel. No one will get offended at that.

- Listen carefully to what your partner is saying and don't interrupt. He or she has the same right as you to express an opinion.

- Avoid making judgmental remarks no matter how tempted you are to blurt them out. "I can't believe you mean that!" or "That's the silliest thing I ever heard" or "That's ridiculous" will do nothing but quite understandably enrage your partner.

- When your partner is through, explain why you think he or she is wrong, using expressions like "Well, I disagree because . . ." or "I don't think that's true because . . ." or "I don't feel that way one bit. After all . . ." It's a very *respectful* way of letting someone know they have a right to their feelings but you disagree.

- Don't expect to agree after you have disagreed. Sometimes you will want to *compromise.* "I finally see what you mean, but surely you can see why I . . ." Other times you may simply have to respect each other's opinions and let it go. "I don't agree, but I still think of you as my friend." Disagreements don't mean you shouldn't be friends or that you have nothing in common. In fact, they mean quite the opposite.

6   Two friends gain the most from each other when they bring different thoughts and feelings to the relationship. They learn from each other. They make each other think. So when disagreements spring up, go with them! It may be an opportunity to learn something!

Expressing Anger

7   Anger is a very difficult emotion to express. This is true largely because it can be so overwhelming. It can influence the way you see everything and make you lose sight of reason. It can force you to lose control of yourself and further confuse the situation. And it can feel just plain awful. But, and this is a big but, it doesn't have to.

8   Anger is a natural emotion. You simply need to control it instead of the other way around. Expressing anger carefully is very important. Here are some basic guidelines.

- Find a period of time during which you can really talk it out with your friend. Rushing isn't good. Nor is having to stop an angry conversation in the middle. Pick a time when you can really focus together.

- Before speaking, take a few deep breaths. Feel the tension leave your body. Doing this will help you gain some control over your emotions.

- If you are angered by something someone has done, first ask them why or how it happened. This is critical, because sometimes we may misunderstand a situation. We may not know all the details, which would clarify why a hurtful situation arose. Give your friend a chance to explain.

- If the explanation is not satisfactory, don't attack. That will only put your friend on the defensive, making it impossible for him or her to hear *you* out. Instead, remember to couple whatever you have to say that is negative with something positive. For instance, "You have been such a good friend. Why did you do this?"

- As your friend continues to explain his or her position, *really listen*. Don't just concentrate on your own negative feelings. Even if you are still angry with your friend, you might find out something that will help you understand him or her a little better. That can only serve to improve your friendship.

- Never leave the conversation hanging. It's fine for each of you to part still feeling angry at each other. But it isn't okay to part not knowing where you go from here. Will you talk again tonight? Tomorrow? Do you still want to be friends? Do you each need a little time to cool off? Establish what you're going to do at the end of the conversation. It's cruel for either one of you to keep the other one in a state of limbo.

9   If you are the one with whom someone is angry, there are definitely a few additional things you need to keep in mind.

- Hear your friend out. Don't interrupt with defensive remarks like "That's not true!" or "You have no right to say that!" He or she has the same right as you to be heard—even if he or she is wrong.

- If you think your friend is wrong to be angry with you, don't be afraid to stick up for yourself. But do acknowledge his or her feelings. "I can see you are really upset and I'm sorry, but I'm not to blame" is one example. Pretending you think you're wrong just to keep the peace will never work. That will end up making you feel angry, and sooner or later you'll get into another unpleasant confrontation.

- If you are wrong, just admit it. It's a lot easier to forgive someone who fesses up to their mistakes than it is someone who refuses to accept responsibility for them. Saying you're sorry takes a lot of strength. It is also an expression of *respect*. Your friend will appreciate that you were willing to acknowledge an error. It is a way of saying you honor the friendship.

The Write Connection

Directions: *Write a paragraph about three things you learned or that you think are most important in the reading selection.*

_____

_____

_____

_____

_____

Comprehension Check

Directions: *See how many questions you can answer without referring to the selection. Then, review the selection to write more complete responses.*

_____ 1. According to the author, some people may respond to a disagreement by insisting that they are right, while others:
   a. assure the other person that he or she is being silly or dumb.
   b. look for a solution to the argument.
   c. agree with the other person just to avoid a fight.
   d. act surprised that the other person was offended.

_____ 2. What can you say if you want to disagree with your partner in a respectful way?
   a. Listen without interrupting and say, "Well, I disagree because . . ."
   b. State your emotions honestly and say, "That's ridiculous!"
   c. Listen without interrupting and say, "Let's take a short break from each other."
   d. Stand up for yourself and say, "I'm not comfortable with this conversation."

_____ 3. Statements such as "I finally see what you mean, but surely you can see why I . . ." and "I don't agree, but I still think of you as my friend" are examples of:
   a. savvy.   c. disagreement.
   b. compromise.   d. disrespect.

_____ 4. According to the author, friends gain the most from each other when they:
   a. share the same thoughts and feelings.
   b. share the same friends.
   c. have known each other for many years.
   d. bring different thoughts and feelings to the relationship.

_____ 5. What can you say when your friend is angry and you want to stick up for yourself in a way that acknowledges his or her feelings?
   a. I can see you're really upset and I'm sorry, but I'm not to blame.
   b. I'm not to blame, despite what you think.
   c. I can see you're upset, but try to get over it.
   d. If you are really my friend, you will see that I'm not to blame.

6. Why is it a bad idea to pretend you are wrong just to avoid a fight?

_____

_____

7. Why should you admit when you are wrong?

_____

_____

8. Write a main idea sentence for the selection. _____

_____

_____ 9. The author's pattern of organization is:
   a. cause and effect.   c. sequence of events/process.
   b. comparison and contrast.   d. listing or enumeration.

Critical Thinking Check

1. Have you, or someone you know, ever lost a good friend because of an argument? In what way could you have acted differently?

_____

_____

_____

_____

_____ 2. Which of the following statements best supports the author's contention that disagreements can provide friends with an opportunity to learn from each other?
   a. A friend is a person who avoids doing things that make you angry.
   b. As your friend continues to explain his or her position, really listen.
   c. Shaky conversation skills can cause a lot of trouble.
   d. Explain the cause of your negative emotions until your friend understands how you feel.

3. Suppose you hear that a friend has been saying negative things about you. Provide two examples that illustrate how you would use what you have learned in

the selection to handle the situation. _____

_____

_____

_____

Vocabulary Check

Directions: *See if any of the words you underlined in the selection are among the list of words below. If not, write your words in the spaces provided. Guess the meaning of the words from the way they were used in the selection. Then, look up the definitions of each word in the dictionary to see if you were right.*

enrage (*v*): Your guess: _____

    Dictionary Definition: _____

halt (*v*): Your guess: _____

    Dictionary Definition: _____

Your word: _____ Your guess: _____

    Dictionary Definition: _____

Your word: _____ Your guess: _____

    Dictionary Definition: _____

♟♟♟ Skills In Practice ▶ Reading Selection 2

"UNDERSTANDING ACTIVE LISTENING," FROM
THE CHALLENGE OF EFFECTIVE SPEAKING
Rudolph Verderber

Accessing Prior Knowledge

Questions for Discussion

1. What do you think is the difference between listening and hearing?

2. How can you tell when someone is listening to you?

Preview and Predict

Directions: Look at the title of the selection. Think about what you already know about the subject. Then, write a couple of predictions about what you are going to read. For instance, what will you learn about active listening?

1. _____

2. _____

Word Search and Discovery

Directions: *Skim through the selection to find the two words below. Underline both words in the selection. Then, use a dictionary to write their definitions in the spaces provided. As you read and encounter these words, see if the definitions you wrote fit the way each word is used in the selection.*

decode (*v*): _____

deficit (*n*): _____

Also, underline at least one new word as you read the selection and write your guess as to its meaning in the right margin of the text.

UNDERSTANDING: ACTIVE LISTENING
Rudolph Verderber

1   Understanding requires active listening. Active listening means using specific techniques to ensure your understanding. Active listening skills take advantage of the fact that we can think faster than a speaker can talk. As a result we can process information while it is being given. Active listening involves determining the organization of the message, asking questions to anticipate material, silently para-phrasing the meanings we have understood, and paying attention to nonverbal cues: Let's consider these four procedures of active listening.

2   **1. Determine the organization.** Determining the organization helps listen-ers establish a framework for the information. In any extended message, the speaker is likely to have an overall organizational pattern for the in-formation that includes a goal, key ideas (or main points) to develop the goal, and details to explain or support the main points. Effective listeners mentally outline the organization so that when the speech is over they can cite the goal, main points, and some of the key details. For instance, during a parents' meeting Gloria raises the subject of teenage crime. As Gloria talks, she mentions three apparent causes: poverty, permissiveness, and broken homes. She includes information she has read or heard that relates to each of these points. When Gloria finishes speaking, her listen-ers will understand the message if they distinguish Gloria's view of the causes of teenage crime (her goal), the three specific factors she sees as causes (her main ideas), and the evidence she has provided to support each factor (details).

3   Sometimes, people organize their speeches so that it is easy to identify their goal, key points, and details. At other times, however, we must work to be sure that we have a grasp of the organization. You can sort out the pur-pose, key points, and details of a complex message, and thus increase your understanding of the message, by mentally outlining the message. Asking "What am I supposed to know/do because I listened to this?" will allow you to determine purpose. Asking "What are the categories of information?" and "Why should I do/think this?" will enable you to identify key points. Asking "What's the support?" will enable you to identify the details.

4   **2. Ask questions.** Mentally asking questions helps listeners identify key as-pects of the speech. Such questions as "What am I supposed to know/do because I listened to this?" allow you to determine the goal. Answers to such questions as "What are the steps/topics?" and "Why should I do/think this?" help to identify key points. The parts of the message that elaborate or sup-port ideas are the details.

5   Asking questions also helps you to determine whether enough information was presented. For instance, if a person says "Swimming is an activity that provides exercise for almost every muscle," active listeners might inwardly question "How?" and then pay attention to the supporting material offered or request it if the speaker does not supply it.

6   **3. Silently paraphrase.** Silent paraphrases help listeners understand material. A paraphrase is a statement in your own words of the meaning you have assigned to a message. After you have listened to a message, you should be able to summarize your understanding. For example, after a person has spent a few minutes explaining the relationship between ingredients and amounts in recipes and the way a mixture is achieved, you can say to yourself, "In other words, how the mixture is put together may be more important than the ingredients used." If you cannot paraphrase a message, either the message was not well encoded or you were not listening carefully enough.

7   **4. Attend to nonverbal cues.** Listeners interpret messages more accurately when they observe the nonverbal behaviors accompanying the words, for meaning may be shown as much by the nonverbals as by the spoken words. So, whether you are listening to a politician explaining her stance on deficit reduction or the director of parking explaining the system of priorities for obtaining parking passes for the new garage, you must pay attention to tone of voice, facial expression, and gestures. For instance, the director of parking might tell a freshman that he stands a good chance of getting a parking sticker for the garage, but the sound of the person's voice may suggest that the chances are not really that good.

—From Verderber, R., *The Challenge of Effective Speaking,* 10E. © 1997 Wadsworth, a part of Cengage Learning, Inc. Reproduced by permission. www.cengage.com/permissions

The Write Connection

Directions: *Write a paragraph about three things you learned or that you think are most important in the reading selection.*

_____

_____

_____

_____

_____

Comprehension Check

Directions: *See how many questions you can answer without referring to the selection. Then, review the selection to write more complete responses.*

1. According to the author, what is "active listening"? _____

   _____

2. What are the four procedures involved in active listening?

   a. _____

   b. _____

   c. _____

   d. _____

_____ 3. Why do effective listeners mentally outline the organization of what they are listening to?
   a. to reveal what they have understood
   b. to attend to nonverbal cues
   c. to cite the goal, main idea, and key details
   d. to review the order of the information that was presented

4. What are two reasons you should mentally ask questions as you listen?

   a. _____

   b. _____

_____ 5. What question can you ask yourself to determine the goal of a speech?
   a. What am I supposed to know/do because I listened to this?
   b. Who is the main character of the story they are telling?
   c. What do I think the speaker will say next?
   d. How could I present the details more effectively?

_____ 6. Paraphrasing means that you are:
   a. revealing what you understood.
   b. restating what you understood.
   c. sharing what you understood.
   d. choosing what you want to understand.

———— 7. According to the author, what should you be able to do after you have listened to a message?
   a. You should be able to provide an appropriate response.
   b. You should be able to summarize your understanding.
   c. You should be able to identify the speaker's point of view.
   d. You should be able to determine the truthfulness of the speaker.

8. What are three examples of nonverbal cues that you should pay attention to as a person is speaking? _____

9. Create a recall word or recall sentence that will help you to remember the four procedures involved in active listening. _____

10. Underline the main idea of the selection.

———— 11. The author's pattern of organization is:
   a. cause and effect.   c. sequence of events/process.
   b. comparison and contrast.   d. listing or enumeration.

Critical Thinking Check

1. Provide an example to illustrate how you could apply one of the four procedures of active listening during a lecture in order to improve your note-taking skills. _____

_____

———— 2. Which of the following conclusions can be drawn from the example of a college freshman who is told that he has a good chance of getting a parking sticker?
   a. Nonverbal cues are not as essential to a message as the words that are spoken.
   b. It is important to ask the right person if you need a parking sticker.
   c. Nonverbal cues may reveal a message that conflicts with a speaker's words.
   d. A speaker who uses nonverbal cues is more likely to be lying than a speaker who does not use gestures while speaking.

3. In the selection, the author provides examples to illustrate how active listeners "ask questions." Write a question after each of the following statements that will help you to clarify or to gain additional information about them.

- There will be a test next week. _____
  _____

- Chemicals found in some common foods have been shown to cause cancer.
  _____

- If you register on the national "No Call List," then telemarketers will be prevented from calling your cell-phone number.
  _____

Vocabulary Check

Directions: *See if any of the words you underlined in the selection are among the list of words below. If not, write your words in the spaces provided. Guess the meaning of the words from the way they were used in the selection. Then, look up the definition of each word in the dictionary to see if you were right.*

framework (*n*): Your guess: _____

    Dictionary Definition: _____

stance (*n*): Your guess: _____

    Dictionary Definition: _____

Your word: _____ Your guess: _____

    Dictionary Definition: _____

Your word: _____ Your guess: _____

    Dictionary Definition: _____

8 Text Notes

> *Knowledge is, indeed, that which, next to virtue, truly and essentially raises one man above another.*

– Joseph Addison

▲ Capture the most important text information for effective study.

Preview and Predict ▶ What do you know so far?

How many of the following questions can you answer?

• Why is it important to take notes for a text assignment?

_____

• What information from the text do you think is most important to write in your notes?

_____

- Think of one way in which the picture relates to this chapter's objectives.

Now, as you read the chapter, look for the answers to see if you were right.

WHY YOU NEED TO TAKE TEXT NOTES

When college instructors assign chapters, selections, or articles to read, do they say, "Don't forget to take notes?" No. They assume that, as a college student, you will automatically write text notes while reading.

Why should you take text notes? First, you will be better prepared to listen during class discussions because you are already familiar with the topic. You will be able to ask questions to clarify what you have studied so far. Second, you will be better prepared for exams because you will have a record of all the important details contained in the text assignment. You can go directly to the most important information when you study.

A typical college textbook assignment contains large amounts of information. For instance, look at the following excerpt about memory from a psychology text. How would you write text notes on this excerpt? Could you create a study guide that would contain the information you need to learn before an exam?

The Three Memory Stages

As the information from a sensory experience (such as reading this sentence) becomes a permanent memory, it must be processed in three stages: first in *sensory memory*, then in *working memory*, and finally in *long-term memory*. At each stage, information receives additional processing. In general, the three stages work together to convert a barrage of initially meaningless incoming stimuli into meaningful patterns that can be stored for later use. Figure A shows the flow of information through these stages. We will focus our attention on each stage in turn.

FIGURE A: A Simplified Memory Model
The "standard model" says that memory is divided into three stages. Everything that goes into long-term storage must first be processed by sensory memory and working memory.

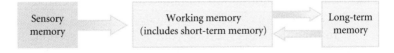

| Sensory memory | → | Working memory (includes short-term memory) | ⇄ | Long-term memory |

SENSORY MEMORY   Sights, sounds, smells, textures, and other sensory impressions persist only fleetingly in **sensory memory.** You may have experienced a sensory memory trace as you watched a moving Fourth-of-July sparkler that seemed to leave a fading trail of light. The function of these brief images is to store incoming sensory information long enough to be screened for possible access to working memory.

WORKING MEMORY   The second stage of memory, known as **working memory,** takes information from sensory memory and connects it with items already in long-term storage. It also holds information temporarily, making working memory a useful buffer for items such as a phone number you have just looked up. Thus, this stage is sometimes also called **short-term memory (STM)** (Beardsley, 1997; Goldman-Rakic, 1992).

It is noteworthy that everything entering consciousness must also pass into working memory. Likewise, we are conscious of everything that working memory considers. Because of this intimate relationship between working memory and consciousness, some psychologists have suggested that working memory *is* the seat of consciousness (LeDoux, 1996).

LONG-TERM MEMORY   The final stage of processing, known as **long-term memory (LTM),** receives information from working memory and preserves it for retrieval at any later time—sometimes for the rest of a person's life. Information in long-term memory constitutes our knowledge about the world and includes such varied material as the lyrics to your favorite song and the year that Wilhelm Wundt established the first psychology laboratory. (Do you remember what year that was? 18??) Long-term memory constitutes each person's total knowledge of the world and of the self. Material in long-term memory enables you to solve new problems, reason, keep future appointments, and use a variety of rules to manipulate abstract symbols—allowing you to think about situations you have never experienced or that might be impossible.

—From Zimbardo, Philip G. et al., *Psychology: Core Concepts*, 4e. Published by Allyn and Bacon, Boston, MA. Copyright © 1997 by Pearson Education. Reprinted by permission of the publisher.

The SQUARE Textbook Study Strategy

The SQUARE Textbook Study Strategy is a step-by-step method for identifying the most important information contained in a textbook chapter or narrative selection, so you can create an effective study guide.

To use this strategy, divide your reading into sections for easier study. Next, *annotate* or mark the most important details in each section of your reading. Then write the information you marked underneath each heading or section in which it appeared. Doing this will help you to create an organized study guide. Finally, review the content of your study guide after the exam in order to evaluate what you did well and what you could do better so you can improve your future performance. Here are the steps in the process:

Step 1: **S—Survey**: Look for the structure and emphasis of the chapter or selection before you read it.

Step 2: **Q—Question**: Turn each heading or main idea into a question.

Step 3: **U—Underline** the *best* answers to each question.

Step 4: **A—Add RODEO items** and marginal notes.

Step 5: **R—Review**: Use headings or main ideas to create a study guide.

Step 6: **E—Evaluate**: How you can improve your study guide?

After you learn about each step in the process, apply it to the sample excerpt you just read. You will have an opportunity to practice what you have learned at the end of the chapter in Reading Selection 1 on page 309.

 1. Survey

Look for the structure and emphasis of the chapter or selection *before* you read it. Think about the title and what it suggests about the topic to be discussed. Then, as you skim the entire chapter or selection, you will see how the author has organized his or her ideas about the topic and the way these ideas are emphasized. There are four things you should do before you read a textbook chapter or selection.

Think about the Title

Ask yourself, "What do I already know about the topic?" and "What might be discussed about the topic?" For instance, look at the sample text excerpt above. What do you already know about the three stages of memory? What might be discussed about each stage of memory? Then, as you skim the titles of each heading listed in the chapter, you can see if you were right about what you thought the chapter was going to discuss.

If you are reading a selection that does not contain headings, read the *first and last sentences* of each paragraph to see if they answer the questions you have asked about the title.

Look at the Way the Headings or Major Details Are Organized

Ask yourself, "Are the chapter or selection ideas organized *in a specific order* step by step as in a sequence of events? Or does the author present major details in *any order?*" For instance, could the headings about the stages of memory be arranged in *any order* or must they be presented in a *specific order*, step by step? The stages of memory must be arranged in _____ because they relate to steps in a process.

If you are reading a selection that does not contain headings, look for transition words. Transition words such as *next, then, after,* or *last* indicate steps in a sequence of events pattern of organization. For instance, a story would likely contain transition words that indicate a sequence of events. On the other hand, an essay about the *types* of drivers on the highway would likely contain transition words like *one, another,* and *also* to indicate that the major details are organized in *any order.* You will maintain concentration more efficiently if you know how the author's ideas will be presented as you read.

Study Visual Aids

Visual aids, which include pictures, cartoons, graphs, data boxes, and diagrams, are provided to illustrate the most important ideas in a chapter or selection. When authors take the time to provide an example "on the board" of the page, then they consider the information to be important and an instructor may include it on an exam. You should try to understand *why* the visual aid is being presented. For instance, you might ask yourself, "Why did the author include a diagram of *A Simplified Memory Model?* What information is being emphasized by this visual aid?" In this case, the author wants to be sure you understand the *process* of how information is stored in long-term memory. (See online Appendix C for additional information about how to read visual aids.)

Study Preview or Summary Points

Textbook authors often add preview or summary points at the beginning or end of chapters to emphasize the most important ideas they have discussed. By reading this information you will have the advantage of knowing what the author thinks is important before you study the chapter.

Memory Check **1** How much do you remember?

1. What is a synonym for the word *annotate?* _____

2. What are two reasons why you should write text notes before class?

   a. _____

   b. _____

3. What are four things you should do before you read?

   a. _____

   b. _____

   c. _____

   d. _____

4. What are two questions you should ask yourself when you think about the title?

   a. _____

   b. _____

5. Why should you look at the way headings or major details are organized before you read?

   _____

6. What is one question you should ask about visual information?

   _____

7. Why should you study preview or summary points?

   _____

   _____

♟ 2. Question: Turn Each Heading or Main Idea into a Question

Use the list of chapter headings to divide your reading into more manageable parts. Start with the title of a chapter and turn it into a *question*. Then, look for *the best answer* to that question as you read. When you reach the first heading of the chapter, *stop*. You have finished one section of reading.

For instance, the title of the text excerpt is "The Three Stages of Memory." Now, turn it into a question in the space provided below.

What are _____

Find the best answer to your question as you read to the first heading, "Sensory Memory." When you reach this first heading, stop reading. Now, see if you can answer the question in your own words. What are the three stages of memory?

There are two good reasons for doing this. First, you will be able to identify and summarize the most important information contained under each heading. You will learn how the three stages of memory work together. Second, it will be easier to relate what you are reading to what you have already learned in previous sections. Then, repeat this process for each heading that follows in the chapter. For instance, you might turn the next heading, "Sensory Memory," into the question, "What is sensory memory?" As you look for the best answer to your question, you will also learn how sensory memory works in the memory process.

Next, see if you can explain sensory memory and how it works using your own words. Then, when you read the next section, "Working Memory," you can compare the new information with what you have just learned about sensory memory. You might ask yourself, "What is the difference between sensory memory and working memory?" By summarizing what you have learned after each section of reading, asking questions about how it relates to previous sections, and integrating the information from each section, you will find that you are able to understand and learn more information as you study.

For narrative selections, use paragraphs to divide your reading into sections. Then identify the main event in each paragraph of a story or the main idea in each paragraph of an article or essay. You can apply the Make Your Own Main Idea strategy to help you locate the main point of each paragraph more easily.

To create your own main idea, you should ask the following three key questions: "What is the topic?" "What is listed about the topic?" and "What do the major details have in common?" Once you find the main idea sentence, you can apply the Main Idea Test. To test your main idea sentence, turn it into a question. If you see the answer to your question in the major details of the paragraph, then you will know you have found the main idea (see Chapter 4, page 132, for a detailed explanation of this strategy).

Once you have identified the key event or main idea in each paragraph, see if you can summarize in your own words what you have learned. Then, you can integrate that information with what you learned in previous paragraphs.

3. Underline the Best Answers to Each Question

It is easy to make the mistake of underlining too many sentences the first time you read a selection. Then later, you may be unable to find the most important information to study because you have underlined too many sentences. Instead, you should read to the end of a section or to the beginning of a new paragraph *before* you decide which information provides the *best*, most complete answers to your question. That way, you will only underline what is most important, and you will be able to go directly to the information you need when you write text notes to create a study guide. For instance, turn the heading "Working Memory" in the text excerpt into a question. What is the best answer to the question, "What is working memory?"

Notice what is underlined in the following student example:

WORKING MEMORY   The second stage of memory, known as **working memory,** takes information from sensory memory and connects it with items already in long-term storage. It also holds information temporarily, making working memory a useful buffer for items such as a phone number you have just looked up. Thus, this stage is sometimes also called **short-term memory (STM)** (Beardsley, 1997; Goldman-Rakic, 1992).

It is noteworthy that everything entering consciousness must also pass into working memory. Likewise, we are conscious of everything that working memory considers. Because of this intimate relationship between working memory and consciousness, some psychologists have suggested that working memory *is* the seat of consciousness (LeDoux, 1996).

In the example above, the student has only underlined the information that best answers the question. When he is ready to write notes for this section, he will easily be able to find the information he needs to study. Here are the student's notes on the passage above. Notice what he has written about working memory.

Example: Student Text Notes for Memory Passage

Working Memory (Short-Term Memory STM) The second stage of memory

1. takes information from sensory memory and connects it to items already in long-term storage
2. holds information temporarily
3. psychologists suggest that it is the seat of consciousness because everything entering consciousness must also pass through it

If you are reading a story, you should underline the most important event that occurs in each paragraph or section. If you are reading an essay or an article, you should underline the sentence that best summarizes what the paragraph or section is about.

Memory Check 2 How much do you remember?

1. If you are reading a textbook chapter, what can you use to divide your reading into sections?

    _____

2. What should you do to each heading in a textbook chapter? _____

    _____

    _____

3. If you are reading a narrative selection, what can you use to divide your reading into sections?

    _____

4. When you reach the next section or heading, you should _____

5. What are two reasons why you should stop after each section of a reading to see if you can answer your heading question in your own words?

    a. _____

    _____

    b. _____

    _____

6. What can happen if you underline too many sentences in the text while you are reading?

    _____

    _____

7. Why should you read to the end of the paragraph or section *before* you underline the best answers to your question? _____

    _____

8. What should you underline in each paragraph or section of an essay or article?

    _____

    _____

9. What should you underline in each paragraph or section of a story?

    _____

♟ 4. Add RODEO Items and Marginal Notes

Once you have underlined the best answer to your question in each section, look for RODEO items of information that you need to learn before an exam (see Chapter 7, page 253). You should highlight each RODEO item so it will stand out from the information you have already underlined. You might use a highlighter or you could place a star (*) in the left side margin next to the repeated or emphasized information. Look for and highlight the following RODEO items in each section of a chapter or selection:

- **Information that was also *repeated* or *reviewed* in class**. For instance, instructors often preview important details that will be discussed in a text assignment. You should highlight this information when it appears in the text because the instructor is telling you it is important and therefore likely to appear on an exam.

- **Points the author has *repeated* in the text or emphasized by such phrases as "most important," "the best," "essential," "key," "must," or "critical."** You should highlight this information because the author is telling you what he or she thinks is most important. For instance, complete the following sentence

  using the sample excerpt on page 293: "It is *noteworthy* that _____

  _____

  The information you wrote above should be highlighted because the author is telling you that it is noteworthy or important. Later, when you write text notes, you might write the following question in the margin: "What does everything entering consciousness pass into?" Then, you can easily test your ability to recall this information for study.

- **Information that is supported by pictures, graphs, diagrams, or data boxes**. Visual aids are used by authors to emphasize or illustrate the most important information in the chapter. You should highlight the title of the visual aid as well as any *conclusions* the author states about the data. For pictures, think about the title of the chapter or selection. Next, write a few words under the picture about why you think it was used to emphasize the topic.

- **Definitions or key terms that usually appear in bold lettering or *italics.*** Authors often include an example (or examples) to help you understand a definition. You should highlight the definition. Then, to avoid highlighting too many sentences in the text, you should write *ex* in the left margin next to where each example appears. For instance, look at the sample excerpt. What is an example of "long-term memory"? Instead of highlighting the phrase ". . . the lyrics to your favorite song," write *ex* in the left margin next to where this example of long-term memory appears in the text.

- **Information that appears as an outline.** Outlines, which appear as a list of details under a topic, make perfect test questions on an exam. So, you should make sure that you identify and mark them in the text wherever they appear.

  There are four ways to identify outlines in a selection or chapter so that you can make sure to include them in your text notes:

  1. **Look for bullets or dots used to list major details in an outline.**

  2. **Look for a list of short paragraphs that contain a key phrase, step, or term in bold or *italic* lettering.** These are major details in an outline. The author usually discusses each detail more fully in the rest of the paragraph. For instance, look at the sample text excerpt. What are the three key terms

     listed in bold lettering? _____

     _____ These are the major details in an outline about the three stages of memory.

  3. **Look for transition words used to list major details in an outline.** Transition words like *first, also, second, next, last,* or *finally* tell you when the author is presenting an outline with a list of details. You should highlight transition words to help you find the major details more easily when you need to study.

  4. **Look at the sentence that appears *before* the word *first* or the first detail, bullet, or dot.** This sentence usually contains the topic of the outline. Turn this sentence into a question to see if it passes the Main Idea Test. If the list of details that follows answer the question, then you have found the topic or main idea of the outline.

Notice how the student in the following example has marked or annotated the text excerpt about the three stages of memory.

The Three Memory Stages

As the information from a sensory experience (such as reading this sentence) becomes a permanent memory, it must be processed in three stages: first in *sensory memory*, then in *working memory*, and finally in *long-term memory*. At each stage, information receives additional processing. In general, the three stages work together to convert a barrage of initially meaningless incoming stimuli into meaningful patterns that can be stored for later use. Figure A shows the flow of information through these stages. We will focus our attention on each stage in turn.

MAIN IDEA How the three stages work together

Barrage: a bunch?

* Know Process

FIGURE A: A Simplified Memory Model
The "standard model" says that memory is divided into three stages. Everything that goes into long-term storage must first be processed by sensory memory and working memory.

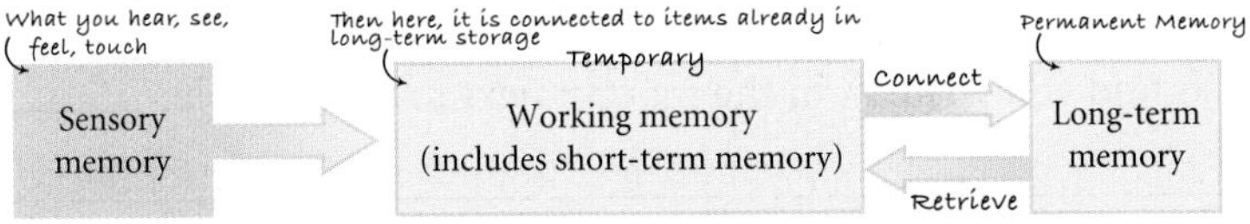
What you hear, see, feel, touch
Then here, it is connected to items already in long-term storage
Temporary
Permanent Memory
Sensory memory
Working memory (includes short-term memory)
Connect
Retrieve
Long-term memory

At each stage, information receives additional processing

(First) **SENSORY MEMORY** Sights, sounds, smells, textures, and other sensory impressions persist only fleetingly in **sensory memory.** You may have experienced a sensory memory trace as you watched a moving Fourth-of-July sparkler that seemed to leave a fading trail of light. The function of these brief images is to store incoming sensory information long enough to be screened for possible access to working memory.

Fleetingly: a short time?

EX.

What it does

(Then) **WORKING MEMORY** The second stage of memory, known as **working memory,** takes information from sensory memory and connects it with items already in long-term storage. It also holds information temporarily, making working memory a useful buffer for items such as a phone number you have just looked up. Thus, this stage is sometimes also called **short-term memory (STM)** (Beardsley, 1997; Goldman-Rakic, 1992).

Also called short-term memory (STM)

EX.

Buffer: holder?

☆ It is noteworthy that everything entering consciousness must also pass into working memory. Likewise, we are conscious of everything that working memory considers. Because of this intimate relationship between working memory and consciousness, some psychologists have suggested that working memory *is* the seat of consciousness (LeDoux, 1996).

(Last) **LONG-TERM MEMORY** The final stage of processing, known as **long-term memory (LTM),** receives information from working memory and preserves it for retrieval at any later time—sometimes for the rest of a person's life. Information in long-term memory constitutes our knowledge about the world and includes such varied material as the lyrics to your favorite song and the year that Wilhelm Wundt established the first psychology laboratory. (Do you remember what year that was? 18??) Long-term memory constitutes each person's total knowledge of the world and of the self. Material in long-term memory enables you to solve new problems, reason, keep future appointments, and use a variety of rules to manipulate abstract symbols—allowing you to think about situations you have never experienced or that might be impossible.

Retrieval: remembering?

Constitutes: makes?

EX.

Repeated ☆

What it does

—From Zimbardo, Philip G. et al. *Psychology: Core Concepts,* 4e. Published by Allyn and Bacon, Boston, MA. Copyright © 1997 by Pearson Education. Reprinted by permission of the publisher.

Memory Check 3 How much do you remember?

1. Why should you highlight instead of underline RODEO items in the text?

   _____

2. What is an example of a phrase used by an author to emphasize important information? _____

3. How does an author write something "on the board"? _____

4. Why should you write *ex* in the margin next to an example? _____

   _____

5. What are four ways to identify outlines in a text assignment?

   a. _____

   b. _____

   _____

   c. _____

   d. _____

   _____

5. Review: Use Headings to Write Text Notes

Now that you have identified the most important information in the text, you can create text notes for review. Use the following steps:

- Write the title of the chapter or selection at the top of the page.

- Create margin spaces on the left and right sides of your paper.

- Write the first heading of the chapter. For an article or story, write the sentence that summarizes the main idea or major event of the first paragraph. In this case, you should underline or highlight it to make it stand out.

- Underneath the heading, *write only what you underlined or marked in that section* (including margin notes) up to the next heading. Then, repeat this process for all the headings or sections in the assignment.

- Write questions, recall words, or recall sentences for self-testing in the left side margin of your paper, For instance, when you write your text notes, you can write the question, "What is long-term memory?" in the margin beside the term. Then, you will be able to test your ability to recall the definition and its example.

- Use the right side margin of your paper to apply the Words in Mind strategy (Chapter 3, page 97) to learn additional definitions or key terms and their meanings.

To review a textbook chapter, cover the notes on the right side and use the questions on the left side to see if you can remember the answers. You can also quiz yourself on the additional definitions or key terms that you wrote in the right side margin.

To review a narrative selection or story, leave a space at the bottom of your paper. Then, you can write a short summary of the major events you have written in the margin next to each paragraph of the story. By following these steps, you will create an effective study guide that you can use to learn the most important information in a text assignment.

Activity 8.1 ▶ Creating Margin Questions for Self-Testing I

Directions: *Below is an example of the kind of text notes and margin questions a student would write for the excerpt "The Three Memory Stages." Some of the questions are missing. Fill in the blanks in the left margin with questions that will help you to recall the related material on the right.*

Margin Questions	Text Notes	Additional Definitions and Key Terms
What are the three stages of memory? (SWL) How is everything that goes into long-term memory processed? How do the three stages work together? What is sensory memory?	The Three Stages of Memory - Everything that goes into long-term memory must first be processed by sensory memory and working memory. - They work together to convert initially meaningless stimuli into meaningful patterns that can be stored for later use. **Sensory Memory** It is information stored long enough to be screened for possible access to working memory.	Convert-change Stimuli-causes something to act

Margin Questions	Text Notes	Additional Definitions and Key Terms
Ex. of sensory memory	EX. sights, sounds, smells, textures, impressions	
Working memory is also called what? What are two things working memory does?	**Working Memory (also called Short-Term Memory)** 1) Takes info from sensory memory and connects it with items already in long-term memory 2) Holds information temporarily EX. A phone number you just looked up	
Ex. of _____ Why is it called the "seat of consciousness"?	Called the "seat of consciousness" because everything we are conscious of must also pass through working memory	
What is _____ What are three things _____	**Long-Term Memory** It constitutes a person's total knowledge of the world. 1) Receives information from working memory and preserves it for retrieval at a later time—sometimes for the rest of your life 2) Helps you solve problems, reason, keep future appointments 3) Allows you to think about situations you never experienced	
Ex. of _____	EX. The lyrics to your favorite song	

Activity 8.2 ▶ Creating Margin Questions for Self-Testing II

Directions: *On the next page is a student example which illustrates how to mark the major events in a story. Some of the margin summary notes are missing. Write margin notes that would help you recall the most important event for each paragraph where spaces are provided. Then combine only the sentences written in the left side margin to create a summary of "The Perfect Purse" in the space provided at the bottom of the story.*

The Perfect Purse

Sara loved purses.	Sara loved purses. In fact, Sara had such a penchant for purses that she had a closet full of handbags in every color and style. Some of them had not been used for years. Yet, she continued to look for that "perfect purse." This purse would be the one that she would use exclusively forever.	Penchant: _____

She wants the perfect purse.

Sara sees a "perfect purse" but it costs $100.

One day, Sara saw "the perfect purse" in the window of Groban's Department Store. It was gold with black velvet trim and jeweled pockets. It was large without being too bulky and had a long shoulder strap. Yet, when she went inside to inquire about the cost, Sara was stunned. The "perfect purse" would cost a hundred dollars.

Immediately, Sara went home to devise a plan for raising the money she needed. She decided to sell some of her beloved purses on e-Bay. Yet, which purses would she sell?

Sara sells two designer purses. One was a gift from Grandma.

Sara had two designer purses. She had a Harry's original that she won years ago but it was out of style. It would sell for at least fifty dollars. The other designer purse was a gift from her grandmother which she had never used. "Grandma won't mind if I sell her gift," she thought. "Besides, Grandma doesn't know my style."

Sara got $135 from the sale of her designer purses and was very excited when she was able to buy her "perfect purse." She promptly transferred all of her necessities to each pocket. She wore the purse to her closet and imagined how fine it would look with her clothes.

Grandma calls.

Just then, the phone rang. It was Grandma.

"Hello, dear one."

"Hi Grandma." Sara replied, suddenly feeling a bit guilty.

"Your birthday is coming up again and I wanted to get you something that you'll really like. I know you love purses."

"I love the purse that you got me last time, Grandma," Sara lied.

"Well, I'm so glad. I wasn't sure what you would like. That's why I put that hundred dollar bill in the pocket in case you wanted to buy something more appropriate." But for this birthday . . . I . . . . ."

Sara couldn't concentrate on what Grandma was saying after that.

Summary

♟ 6. Evaluate: How Can I Improve My Performance?

You should evaluate your study guide to see how well it prepared you for an exam. One of the best ways to evaluate your study guide is to identify missing information. For instance, did your study guide contain all the information that appeared as questions on the exam? If not, you need to know why you left out this important information so you can make sure to incorporate it when you write future study guides.

If you apply the SQUARE Textbook Study Strategy to your text assignments, you will learn the most important information more easily and you will have exactly what you need to perform well on any exam.

Memory Check 4 How much do you remember?

1. Why should you leave spaces in the left side margin? _____

   _____

2. Why should you leave spaces in the right side margin? _____

   _____

3. What is the only thing you need to write under each heading to create text

   notes? _____

4. How should you use your study guide to review a textbook chapter? _____

   _____

   _____

5. How should you use your study guide to review a narrative selection or story?

   _____

   _____

6. What is one of the best ways to evaluate your study guide? _____

   _____

7. You need to know why you might have omitted important information so

   that you can _____

Internet Activity 8.3 ▶ Evaluating Additional Text/Study Methods

Directions: *Explore some other study methods using the websites below. Then, answer the questions that follow.*

- http://www.studygs.net/texred2.htm Study Guides and Strategies by studygs.net: Go to "Reading Skills" and select "Taking Notes from a Textbook."

- http://www.rio.maricopa.edu/distance_learning/tutorials/study/textbook.shtml Rio Solado College Distance Learning site

1. Which website was the most helpful and why? _____

   _____

   _____

2. Which study method mentioned in each website would you use and why?

   _____

   _____

   _____

MyReadingLab

Reading Textbooks:
To practice your skills
go to
>Study plan
>Reading skills
>Reading textbooks

? Test Yourself Review Quiz

Chapter Review Questions

1. What is one reason why you should take text notes?

   _____

2. What are four things you should do before you read a text assignment?

   a. _____

   b. _____

   c. _____

   d. _____

3. What can you use to divide your reading into sections in a textbook chapter?

_____

4. What can you use to divide your reading into sections in a narrative selection or story? _____

5. What should you do after you turn a heading in a textbook chapter into a question?

_____

6. What should you do after you read to the end of each section?

_____

_____

7. Why should you read to the end of the section *before* you underline the best answer to your question? _____

_____

_____   8. You should look for a list of transition words or a list of key phrases or terms that form the major details of _____ in a selection or chapter.

   a. repeated information   c. an example

   b. an outline   d. a visual aid

9. Write a paragraph that explains the steps you should follow to create a study guide based on information you have marked in a text.

_____

_____

_____

_____

10. To review a textbook chapter, you should _____

_____

11. Why should you leave a space at the bottom of your paper to review a story?

_____

_____

12. Why should you evaluate your study guide after an exam? _____

_____

13. The SQUARE Textbook Study Strategy involves what six steps?

_____

_____

_____

_____

_____

_____

Application Questions

1. Use the SQUARE Textbook Study Strategy to identify and mark the most important information in the following excerpt from an interpersonal communications textbook.

The Needs of Friendship

In the *Psychology Today* survey, the 40,000 respondents selected from a wide number of activities the ones they had shared with friends over the previous month. Table 8.1 presents the ten activities most frequently noted by these respondents. As can be appreciated from this list, friendship seems to serve the same needs that all relationships serve (lessening loneliness, providing stimulation, and encouraging self-knowledge).

You develop and maintain friendships to satisfy those needs that can only be satisfied by certain people. On the basis of your experiences or your predictions, you select as friends those who will help to satisfy your basic growth needs. Selecting friends on the basis of need satisfaction is similar to choosing a marriage partner, an employee, or any person who may be in a position to satisfy your needs. Thus, if you need to be the center of attention or to be popular, you might select friends who allow you, and even encourage you, to be the center of attention or who tell you, verbally and nonverbally, that you are popular.

As your needs change, the qualities you look for in friendships also change. In many instances, old friends are dropped from your close circle to be replaced by new friends who better serve these new needs.

We can also look at needs in terms of the five values or rewards we seek to gain through our friendships (Wright 1978, 1984). First, friends have a **utility value.** A friend may have special talents, skills, or resources that prove useful to us in achieving our specific goals and needs. We may, for example, become friends with someone who is particularly bright because such a person might assist us in getting better grades, in solving our personal problems, or in getting a better job.

Table 8.1 The Ten Most Frequently Identified Activities Shared with Friends

> Before reading this table, consider the activities you share with friends. How similar are the activities you engage in with those identified here? No. 1 = the most frequently identified activity.
>
>   1. Had an intimate talk
>   2. Had a friend ask you to do something for him or her
>   3. Went to dinner in a restaurant
>   4. Asked your friend to do something for you
>   5. Had a meal together at home or at your friend's home
>   6. Went to a movie, play, or concert
>   7. Went drinking together
>   8. Went shopping
>   9. Participated in sports
> 10. Watched a sporting event

Second, friends have an **affirmation value.** A friend's behavior toward us acts as a mirror that affirms our personal value and helps us to recognize our attributes. A friend may, for example, help us to see more clearly our leadership abilities, athletic prowess, or sense of humor.

Third, friends have an **ego-support value.** By behaving in a supportive, encouraging, and helpful manner, friends help us to view ourselves as worthy and competent individuals.

Fourth, friends have a **stimulation value.** A friend introduces us to new ideas and new ways of seeing the world and helps us to expand our worldview. A friend brings us into contact with previously unfamiliar issues, concepts, and experiences—for example, modern art, foreign cultures, new foods.

Fifth, friends have a **security value.** A friend does nothing to hurt the other person or to emphasize or call attention to the other person's inadequacies or weaknesses. Because of this security value, friends can interact freely and openly without having to worry about betrayal or negative responses.

—From *The Longman Textbook Reader.* 5th ed. pp. 182–183.
Addison-Wesley © 1999.

2. Using the grid on the next page, create a study guide that will help you learn the most important information you have identified in the excerpt above. Create at least eight margin questions or annotations to test yourself on the information you have written in your text notes. Also, write at least three additional

definitions to help you learn new words contained in the excerpt. Some of the answers have been provided for you.

Margin Questions	Text Notes	Additional Definitions
	The Needs of Friendship	
_____ _____	Lessening loneliness, providing stimulation, and encouraging self-knowledge.	
Most frequently shared activity with friends?	Table 8.1 shows that the most frequently identified activity shared with a friend was an intimate talk.	
How does the table relate to the needs of friendship?	The most frequently shared activities are most likely to lessen loneliness, provide stimulation, and encourage self-knowledge because they are one-on-one activities.	
What are the five _____ _____ _____	Five Values or Rewards Gained Through Friendship	
What is the utility value of friendship?	1. Utility Value: Has special talents, skills or resources that are useful to us in achieving our specific goals and needs.	Utility: Usefulness
Ex. of _____ _____ _____	Ex. A friend who helps you get better grades	
	2. Affirmation Value: Helps us to recognize our attributes.	
	Ex. A friend who helps you see your leadership abilities.	
What is the ego-support value of friendship?	3. Ego-Support Value: Helps us to view ourselves as worthy and competent individuals.	
_____	Ex. A friend who is supportive, encouraging and helpful.	
_____	4. Stimulation Value: Helps us to expand our worldview.	
Ex. of stimulation value	Ex. A friend who brings us into contact with previously unfamiliar issues, concepts, and experiences such as new foods.	
_____ _____	5. Security Value: Does nothing to hurt the other person or to emphasize or call attention to the other person's inadequacies or weaknesses.	

Summarization Activity

Directions: *Write the major headings in this chapter. Under each heading, write a couple of sentences about the most important topics presented in the section of text that follows that heading.*

First Heading _____

What information is most important? _____

_____

_____

_____

_____

_____

Second Heading _____

What information is most important? _____

_____

_____

_____

_____

_____

      Combine the information you wrote in this outline into a paragraph to summarize what you have learned in this chapter.

Reflection Activity

How am I am going to apply what I have learned in this chapter?

Directions: *On a separate sheet of paper, write a paragraph discussing the two or three things you learned about taking text notes that were most helpful to you and how you plan to use what you have learned.*

"Wʜᴀᴛ Is Mᴇᴍᴏʀʏ" Fʀᴏᴍ *Psʏᴄʜᴏʟᴏɢʏ: Cᴏʀᴇ Cᴏɴᴄᴇᴘᴛs*
Philip G. Zimbardo, Ann Weber, and Robert L. Johnson

Accessing Prior Knowledge

Questions for Discussion

1. What is your best strategy for memorizing information you want to learn?

2. What are two things that computers do that are similar to what you are able to do?

Preview and Predict

Directions: *Look at the title of the selection. Think about what you already know about the subject. Then, write a couple of predictions about what you are going to read. For instance, what will the author discuss about memory?*

1. _____

2. _____

Word Search and Discovery

Directions: *Skim through the selection to find the two words below. Underline both words in the selection. Then, use a dictionary to write their definitions in the spaces provided. As you read and encounter these words, see if the definitions you wrote fit the way they are used in the selection.*

cognitive (*adj*): _____

encode (*vb*): _____

Also, underline two new words as you read the selection and write your guesses as to their meanings in the right margin of the text.

Text Notes in Practice

Directions: *Use a textbook study method such as SQUARE to identify the most important information in the selection. Then, create a study guide that you can use to prepare for the questions that follow the selection.*

WHAT IS MEMORY?

Philip G. Zimbardo, Ann Weber, and Robert L. Johnson

1   Cognitive psychologists define **memory** broadly as any system that encodes, stores, and retrieves information—a definition that applies equally to an organism or a computer. Unlike a computer's memory, however, human memory is a *cognitive* system—closely related to *perception*.

> Human memory is a cognitive system composed of three stages that work together constructively to encode, store, and retrieve information.

2   And how is memory related to learning? You might think of human memory as the biological and mental system that allows us to retain what we have learned for later use.

3   In general, psychologists have found that human memory usually makes the most accurate records for:

- Information on which we have focused our attention—such as a friend's words against the background of a noisy restaurant.

- Information in which we are interested—such as the courses in your major field.

- Information that arouses us emotionally—such as an experience that is especially enjoyable or painful.

- Information that fits with our previous experience—such as a physician learning about a new treatment for a familiar disease.

- Information that we rehearse—such as memory for material reviewed the night before an exam.

As you can see, cognitive psychologists use an information-processing approach that takes into consideration the psychological nature of human memory—the ties that memory has to other cognitive processes, such as learning and perceptual processing. In the following pages we will examine this model of memory closely, beginning with the three essential functions that we rely on memory to perform.

Memory's Three Essential Functions

4   Any memory system, whether in a computer, a laboratory rat, or a person, must perform three essential functions. It must *encode* information in a useful

format; it must *store* the information; and it must have a means of *accessing and retrieving* the stored data. We will look at each of these operations in more detail.

5   **Encoding** requires that you first *select* some stimulus event from among the vast array of inputs assaulting your senses. Next you *identify* the distinctive features of that input. Is it a sound, a visual image, or a smell? If it's a sound, is it loud, soft, or harsh? Does it fit into some pattern that forms a name, a melody—or a cry for help? Is it a sound you have heard before? Finally, you mentally tag, or *label*, an experience. Some labels are specific and unique ("It's Minerva"), others describe a general category or class ("She's our cat"). These steps involved in encoding are usually so automatic and rapid that you are unaware you are performing them.

6   Further encoding entails a process called **elaboration,** which relates the new input to other information you already have in memory or to goals or purposes for which it might later prove useful. Such connections make memories more meaningful. And, because memory is a system built on meaningful connections, elaboration strengthens memories.

7   **Storage,** a second essential function of memory, involves the retention of encoded material over time. As we have noted, information is best retained when it has been linked to information already stored. Otherwise it is usually lost. Occasional rehearsal of the material also helps. In general, the more meaningful some item of information is and the more often it is rehearsed, the more likely it is to be retained.

8   **Access and retrieval** involve the recovery of stored information, the payoff for your earlier effort involved in encoding and storage. When all goes well, you gain access—sometimes in a split second—to information you stored earlier in your memory banks. (Let's see if your access and retrieval mechanisms are working for the material we just covered. Can you remember which of the three memory functions comes before *storage?*) When a memory is accessed with the appropriate cues, retrieval is usually automatic.

The Three Memory Stages

9   As the information from a sensory experience (such as reading this sentence) becomes a permanent memory, it must be processed in three stages; first in *sensory memory*, then in *working memory,* and finally in *long-term memory*. At each stage, information receives additional processing. In general, the three stages work together to convert a barrage of initially meaningless incoming stimuli into meaningful patterns that can be stored for later use. Figure A shows the flow of information through these stages. We will focus our attention on each stage in turn.

FIGURE A: **A Simplified Memory Model**
The "standard model" says that memory is divided into three stages.
Everything that goes into long-term storage must first be processed by
sensory memory and working memory.

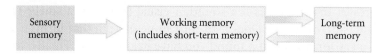

10   SENSORY MEMORY Sights, sounds, smells, textures, and other sensory impressions persist only fleetingly in **sensory memory.** You may have experienced a sensory memory trace as you watched a moving Fourth-of-July sparkler that seemed to leave a fading trail of light. The function of these brief images is to store incoming sensory information long enough to be screened for possible access to working memory.

11   WORKING MEMORY The second stage of memory, known as **working memory,** takes information from sensory memory and connects it with items already in long-term storage. It also holds information temporarily, making working memory a useful buffer for items such as a phone number you have just looked up. Thus, this stage is sometimes also called **short-term memory (STM)** (Beardsley, 1997: Goldman-Rakic, 1992).

12   It is noteworthy that everything entering consciousness must also pass into working memory. Likewise, we are conscious of everything that working memory considers. Because of this intimate relationship between working memory and consciousness, some psychologists have suggested that working memory is the seat of consciousness (LeDoux, 1996).

13   LONG-TERM MEMORY The final stage of processing known as **long-term memory (LTM),** receives information from working memory and preserves it for retrieval at any later time—sometimes for the rest of a person's life. Information in long-term memory constitutes our knowledge about the world and includes such varied material as the lyrics to your favorite song and the year that Wilhelm Wundt established the first psychology laboratory. (Do you remember what year that was? 18??) Long-term memory constitutes each person's total knowledge of the world and of the self. Material in long-term memory enables you to solve new problems, reason, keep future appointments, and use a variety of rules to manipulate abstract symbols—allowing you to think about situations you have never experienced or that might be impossible.

The Write Connection

Directions: *Write a paragraph about three things you learned or that you think are most important in the reading selection.*

_____

_____

_____

_____

_____

Comprehension Check

Directions: *Use your study guide to see how many questions you can answer without referring to the selection. Then, review the selection to write more complete responses.*

1. What is the definition of human memory? _____

   _____

2. The author provides five types of information most accurately recorded by human memory. Provide two types below.

   a. _____

   b. _____

_____ 3. Cognitive psychologists use _____ approach when they consider human memory.
   a. a natural-processing
   b. a functional-processing
   c. an emotional-response
   d. an information-processing

4. What are the three essential functions that we rely upon memory to perform?

   _____

_____ 5. Encoding involves the ability to:
   a. retrieve and process stored information.
   b. preserve, store, and retrieve information.
   c. select, identify, and label information.
   d. access and preserve information.

6. The encoding process that involves making meaningful connections to strengthen memory is called _____

7. The more meaningful some item of information is and the more often it is rehearsed, the more likely it is to be _____

8. The third function of memory involves the _____ and retrieval of stored information.

9. What are the three stages of the memory process?

   _____

_____ 10. Everything that goes into long-term memory must first be processed by:
   a. sensory and retrieval memory.   c. short-term memory.
   b. working memory   d. sensory and working memory.

_____ 11. A phone number you have just looked up for temporary use is an example of:
   a. sensory and retrieval memory.   c. short-term memory.
   b. long-term memory.   d. sensory and working memory.

_____ 12. Remembering the lyrics to your favorite song is an example of:
   a. sensory response.   c. working memory.
   b. sensory memory.   d. long-term memory.

Critical Thinking Check

_____ 1. The author has written the selection in order to:
   a. show the importance of long-term memory in the memory process.
   b. discuss the three functions of memory and the three stages in the memory process.
   c. illustrate several ways in which memory techniques can improve learning.
   d. define the types of memory and the relationship between each one.

2. The author gives the example of a phone number you have just looked up in order to illustrate working memory. Write your own example of working memory. Then, discuss what you would do in order to store that information in long-term memory so you can remember it at a later time.

   _____

   _____

   _____

3. Discuss the difference between working or short-term memory and long-term memory using examples from your own experience. _____

_____

_____

Vocabulary Check

Directions: *See if any of the words you underlined in the selection are among the list of words below. If not, write your words in the spaces provided. Guess the meaning of the words from the way they were used in the selection. Then, look up the definition of each word in the dictionary to see if you were right.*

barrage (*n*) Your guess: _____

    Dictionary Definition: _____

convert (*vt*): Your guess: _____

    Dictionary Definition: _____

stimuli (*n*) your guess: _____

    Dictionary Definition: _____

Your word: _____ Your guess: _____

    Dictionary Definition: _____

Your word: _____ Your guess: _____

    Dictionary Definition: _____

"CROWD BEHAVIOR," FROM *SOCIOLOGY: AN INTRODUCTION*, 4TH ED.

J. Ross Eshleman, Barbara G. Cashion, and Laurence A. Basirico, Addison-Wesley

Accessing Prior Knowledge

Questions for Discussion

1. Have you or anyone you know ever been in a crowd that became violent? What happened and how did you or the person you know respond to the situation?

2. Why do you think that some people believe it is okay to loot stores during a riot?

Preview and Predict

Directions: *Look at the title of the selection. Think about what you already know about the subject. Then, write a couple of predictions about what you are going to read. For instance, what will the author discuss about crowd behavior?*

1. _____

2. _____

Word Search and Discovery

Directions: *Skim through the selection to find the three words below. Underline both words in the selection. Then, use a dictionary to write their definitions in the spaces provided. As you read and encounter these words, see if the definitions you wrote fit the way each word is used in the selection.*

arouse (*vb*): _____

_____

impulse (*n*): _____

_____

proximate (*adj*) _____

_____

Also, underline at least one new word as you read the selection and write your guess as to its meaning in the right margin of the text.

CROWD BEHAVIOR

J. Ross Eschleman, Barbara G. Cashion,
and Laurence A. Basirico

1 The nonemotional, unstructured crowd is known as a **casual crowd.** People who stop to look at an animated holiday display or who gather to watch a street musician would be of this type. Another type of crowd, sometimes called a **conventional crowd**, is more highly structured and occurs, for example, when spectators gather at a baseball game, attend a concert, or ride on an airplane. Although the participants are generally unknown to one another (anonymous), they have a specific goal or common purpose and are expected to follow commonly accepted norms and procedures. At symphony concerts, for example, people applaud at the end of the music (a commonly accepted procedure). When the music is being played, however, they do not run up and down the aisles or call out to a friend at the opposite side of the concert hall (a commonly accepted procedure).

2 The . . . crowds that attract the most public attention are called **acting crowds,** the behavior of which is centered around and typifies aroused impulses. The two most dramatic forms of acting crowds are mobs and riots.

3 **Mobs** are groups that are emotionally aroused and ready to engage in violent behavior. They are generally short-lived and highly unstable. Their violent actions often stem from strong dissatisfaction with existing government policies or social circumstances; extreme discontentment with prevailing conditions is used to justify immediate and direct action. Disdainful of regular institutional channels and legal approaches, mobs take matters into their own hands.

4 Most mobs are predisposed to violence before their actions are triggered by a specific event. When feelings of frustration and hostility are widespread, leaders can easily recruit and command members. With aggressive leadership, an angry, frustrated mob in an atmosphere of hostility can be readily motivated to riot, commit lynchings, throw firebombs, hang people in effigy, or engage in destructive orgies.

5 Mob violence has erupted in many different circumstances. During the French Revolution of the 1780s and 1790s, angry mobs stormed through Paris, breaking into the Bastille prison for arms and calling for the execution of Louis XVI. In nineteenth-century England, enraged workers burned the factories in which they worked. Lynchings of blacks in the United States for real or imagined offenses continued into the twentieth century, often with little or no opposition from the formal agencies of control—police, courts, and public officials. Although lynch mobs are uncommon today, occasional instances of mob behavior take place over civil rights issues such as busing or housing, during political conventions and

rallies, and among student or labor groups angry about perceived injustices. In 1987, for example, mob violence erupted in all-white Forsyth County, Georgia, when a white mob disrupted a march by whites and blacks protesting discriminatory antiblack housing policy.

6   **Riots** are collective actions involving mass violence and mob actions. The targets of their hostility and violence are less specific than those of mobs, and the groups involved are more diffuse. Most riots result from an intense hatred of a particular group with no specific person or property in mind. Destruction, burning, or looting may be indiscriminate, and unfocused anger can lead to violent acts against any object or person who happens to be in the wrong area at the wrong time. Like mobs, rioters take actions into their own hands when they feel that institutional reactions to their concerns about war, poverty, racial injustices, or other problems are inadequate.

The Write Connection

Directions: *Write a paragraph about three things you learned or that you think are most important in the reading selection.*

_____

_____

_____

_____

_____

Comprehension Check

Directions: *See how many questions you can answer without referring to the selection. Then, review the selection to write more complete responses.*

1. What is the topic of the selection? _____

2. What do the major details have in common about the topic? (*ways? types? steps?*)

    _____

3. What are two types of acting crowds? _____

4. How many major categories of crowds are listed in the selection? _____

5. Make your own main idea sentence for the selection.

_____

_____ 6. An example of a conventional crowd would be:
   a. a crowd that gathers at the scene of an accident.
   b. a crowd that gathers at city hall to protest the high cost of gasoline.
   c. a crowd that gathers at an arena to watch a football game.
   d. a riot.

_____ 7. The difference between a casual crowd and a conventional crowd is that:
   a. casual crowds are structured and nonemotional and follow established procedures.
   b. the behavior of a conventional crowd is centered around aroused impulses.
   c. a conventional crowd is less structured and less emotional than a casual crowd.
   d. a casual crowd is less structured and less emotional than a conventional crowd.

_____ 8. An example of a casual crowd would be:
   a. a crowd that gathers at the scene of an accident.
   b. a crowd that gathers at city hall to protest the high cost of gasoline.
   c. a crowd that gathers at an arena to watch a football game.
   d. a riot.

_____ 9. An example of a mob would be:
   a. a crowd that begins looting stores after losing a basketball championship.
   b. a crowd that turns violent in a courtroom after a child molester is convicted.
   c. a crowd that is stabilized by violent leadership.
   d. a crowd that is short-lived and highly stable.

_____ 10. The difference between a mob and a riot crowd is:
   a. as opposed to a mob, a riot involves violent acts against any object or person who happens to be in the wrong area at the wrong time.
   b. most riots are short-lived and less destructive than mobs.
   c. a riot is more stable than a mob because the people involved are already prone to violence, having an intense hatred of a specific group or person.
   d. unlike a riot, a mob may engage in violent acts against any object or person who happens to be in the wrong place at the wrong time.

_____ 11. An example of a mob would be:
   a. a crowd that begins burning the courthouse after a suspected child molester is found innocent.
   b. a crowd that gathers outside a courtroom during the trial of a famous person.
   c. a crowd that is highly structured.
   d. a crowd that is short-lived and highly stable.

_____ 12. What is the meaning of the word *indiscriminate* as it is used in paragraph 6?
   a. random   c. illegal
   b. prejudiced   d. responsible

_____ 13. Which of the following outlines best organize the information presented in the excerpt?
   a. casual crowds   c. acting crowds
      conventional crowds   mobs
      mobs   riots
      riots
   b. casual crowds   d. casual crowds
      conventional crowds   acting crowds
      acting crowds

Critical Thinking Check

1. Give examples from your own experience that illustrate the difference between commonly accepted procedures and those procedures that are not commonly accepted in a conventional crowd. _____

   _____

   _____

_____ 2. The author's tone can be described as:
   a. concerned.   c. formal.
   b. melancholy.   d. sarcastic.

3. Do you think that people who commit acts of violence during a riot are justified in their actions, if the reason they are rioting is related to unjust treatment

(for example, low wages and lack of benefits, loss of civil rights, or mistreatment of a specific racial group)? Why or why not? _____

_____

_____

Vocabulary Check

Directions: *See if any of the words you underlined in the selection are among the list of words below. If not, write your words in the spaces provided. Guess the meaning of the words below from the way they were used in the selection. Then, look up the definitions of each word in the dictionary to see if you were right.*

disdainful (*adj*): Your guess: _____

Dictionary Definition: _____

effigy (*n*): Your guess: _____

Dictionary Definition: _____

Your word: _____ Your guess: _____

Dictionary Definition: _____

Your word: _____ Your guess: _____

Dictionary Definition: _____

9 Test-Taking Strategies

"I count him braver who overcomes his desires than he who conquers his enemies; for the hardest victory is the victory over self."

— Aristotle

In this chapter you will learn how to:

Reduce Test Anxiety

Determine Your Learning Style

Prepare for and Take Various Types of Exams

You will learn the following strategy:

♟ **The Eight-Day Action Plan**

▲ **Prepare to succeed.**

Preview and Predict ▶ What do you know so far?

How many questions can you answer before you read the chapter?

• What is the best way to reduce test anxiety?

_____

- What strategies do you use to prepare for an exam?

  _____

- What do you think you will learn in this chapter?

  _____

- Think of one way in which the picture relates to this chapter's objectives.

  _____

Now, as you read the chapter, look for the answers to see if you were right.

TEST ANXIETY

Do you get nervous before an exam? Does your memory erase when you are trying to think of an answer? Then you probably have test anxiety. Everyone experiences test anxiety. It's a normal response to the idea that your grade depends upon your performance. You want to do well on an exam and yet, you're afraid you won't know the answers.

In most cases some test anxiety is actually good because it can motivate you to be more prepared. On the other hand, if you believe that a bad performance will mean something negative about who you are, then test anxiety can interrupt your ability to answer questions on an exam. For instance, "If I don't do well on this exam, it means I am stupid." Or, "If I don't pass this test, it means I am a bad student."

How can you reduce test anxiety and feel more comfortable about your performance?

Reducing Test Anxiety

When you take a test, you are like a fighter in a boxing ring, facing an opponent. The test is your opponent. To be ready for a boxing match, you have to train. You train by practicing your moves. You study your opponent by looking at videos and you work out to stay in shape before the fight. When you are prepared, no matter what kind of punch your opponent throws at you, you are more likely to respond with the right moves because you have trained for the fight.

The same applies to taking exams. When you know you have prepared for an exam, you will gain the confidence you need to reduce the negative effects of test anxiety. You are more likely to recall the most correct response to a test question. Being prepared is the best way to reduce test anxiety.

KNOW YOUR LEARNING STYLE

A learning style refers to the way a person prefers to learn new information. There are three main learning styles: **auditory** (hearing the information), **visual** (viewing the information), and **tactile** (working with the information in a physical way). Understanding your learning style can improve your test performance because you can review the information in the way that you learn best.

What is your learning style? Imagine that someone is giving you a phone number, but you don't have a pen or a pencil. How would you remember the phone number? If you need to *picture* the number in your mind, then you might be a *visual* learner. If you need to *repeat* the number aloud so you can *hear* it, you might be an *auditory* learner. If you need to *write* it with your finger on your hand or *dial* it on an imaginary key pad, then you might be a *tactile* learner.

Auditory Learners

Auditory learners understand information best when they hear it or when someone tells them what they need to know. If you are an auditory learner:

- **Read aloud** when testing yourself on exam information.

- **Ask someone to test your knowledge** of exam information by asking you to answer questions out loud.

- **Participate in a study group** where you can discuss information that will be covered on an exam.

Visual Learners

Visual learners understand information best when they can see how details relate to each other. If you are a visual learner:

- **Write information on flash cards** that you can look at throughout the day to see how much you can recall.

- **Organize information into a chart, graph, or map** to create a picture that will help you understand how the details relate to each other.

- **Use colors to highlight and identify different types of information.** For instance, you might use red for definitions, green for examples and so on.

Tactile Learners

Tactile learners understand information best when they have an opportunity to work with the details in a hands-on way. They need to touch or feel the information in order to understand how the details relate to each other. If you are a tactile learner:

- **Trace the information you have written** in your study guide with a pencil as you read and review.

- **Create an object or a model** that provides an example of what you are learning.

- **Use movement to emphasize and identify different types of information.** For instance, you might put your hands together when reviewing synonyms and move your hands apart when reviewing antonyms.

- **Memorize information while walking or exercising.**

Studies show that the more senses you use when you review, the more you will remember. So, whether you are an auditory, visual, or tactile learner, it is a good idea to develop and use other senses as you study. Then, you will have several ways to recall the information when it is needed on an exam.

Activity 9.1 ▶ Know your Learning Style

Directions: *Go to http://www.engr.ncsu.edu/learningstyles/ilsweb.html and take the Learning Styles Questionnaire. Then, write a paragraph that begins with the following sentences. "I am a _____ learner. I am going to do the following things when I study so I will learn more efficiently."*

Memory Check ✓ **1** How much do you remember?

1. _____ T/F Very few people experience test anxiety.

2. What is the best way to reduce test anxiety? _____

3. What are learning styles? _____

    _____.

4. An auditory learner learns best by _____

    _____.

5. If you need to work with new information in a hands-on way, then you
   might be a _____ .

6. What is one way to prepare for an exam if you are a visual learner?

   _____

   _____

PREPARE TO SUCCEED

If you want to perform well on an exam, you need to prepare to succeed. You can prepare to succeed by following these steps: find out about the exam, identify what you need to study, create an effective study guide, and use study strategies like Recall to Mind and List, Label, and Repeat. Finally, you need to review regularly before an exam and evaluate how well you prepared after an exam. The Eight-Day Action Plan discussed later in this chapter will help you to improve the way you prepare for future exams.

Find Out about the Exam

When an exam is announced, there are several things you can do to prepare in order to be successful.

1. Find out how many questions will appear on the exam. Knowing how many questions are on the exam will help you to determine how much information from your lecture and text notes you will need to learn.

2. Find out what kinds of questions will appear on the exam. You need to ask the following questions:

- **Will the exam include multiple-choice questions?** If it will, then make certain you learn the differences and similarities between definitions or key terms. Doing this will help you to select the best answer among the choices given in a multiple-choice question. For instance, if you were taking a test in biology, you would need to know the differences and similarities between a *solution*, a *solvent*, a *solute*, and an *aqueous solution* in order to choose the correct definition among the choices in a multiple-choice question.

- **Will the exam include a reading selection?** If so, make certain to review any selections that were assigned during the period being tested. You should also find out if the instructor will allow you to make notes on the selection during the exam. Taking notes as you read will help you find key information needed to answer questions about the selection.

- **Will the exam contain essay questions?** Information that was provided in an outline form is most likely to appear as a short-essay response question on an exam. Be sure to memorize the outlines in your text and lecture notes that were repeated or that appeared on the board most often.

Once you know the number and the type of questions that will appear on an exam, you will need to know what information to study.

Identify What You Need to Study

There are two steps you can take to determine what you need to study in order to be successful when taking an exam.

Step One: Gather together all the relevant information. Gather all of your text notes and lecture notes for the period of time that is going to be tested.

Step Two: Use the RODEO Attention Plan for note taking to identify the most important information presented by the instructor during each lecture (Chapter 7, p. 253). Place a check mark next to any RODEO items contained in your lecture and text notes to find the topics and supporting information most emphasized during the period that is to be tested. For instance, you would place a check mark next to the following:

- Information from the textbook that was repeated or reviewed in class.

- Information you copied from the board, including definitions, examples, or an outline.

The information with the most check marks is most likely to appear as a question on an exam. You can use this information to create an effective study guide.

Create an Effective Study Guide

To create an effective study guide for an exam you should:

1. Identify the entries from your text and lecture notes that have the most check marks beside them.

2. Write the information with the most check marks on the right side of a sheet of paper.

3. Leave a 1½ inch margin on the left side.

4. Turn the information on the right into questions. Write each question in the left margin next to the information it relates to.

Figure 9.1 shows an example of a student's study guide on the topic of Bloom's Taxonomy based on notes taken during a psychology lecture. Look at the questions written next to each important detail in Figure 9.1.

This student has created an effective study guide containing the information most likely to appear as questions on an exam on the topic of Bloom's Taxonomy.

Figure 9.1 Example Student Study Guide

Margin Questions	Text Notes
What is Bloom's Taxonomy?	Bloom's Taxonomy — The Six Levels of Thinking
What are the six levels of Bloom's Taxonomy?	The ability to: Remember, Understand, Apply, Analyze, Evaluate, and Create
Ability needed for Remembering? What is an example question?	1. Remember — Ability to recognize information appearing in a selection. Ex. "What was the name of the main character?"
Ability needed for Understanding? What is an example question?	2. Understand — Ability to understand information by doing something with it (summarizing or interpreting). Ex. "Summarize the major events of the selection."
Ability needed for Application level? What is an example question?	3. Apply — Ability to use the information in a different way from the way it is presented in the selection. Ex. "Write a dialogue between the main character and the father he never knew."
What ability is needed for the Analysis level? What is an example question?	4. Analyze — Ability to break down certain parts of the information presented in a selection. Ex. "Compare and contrast the main character and his father."
What ability is needed for the Evaluation level? What is an example question?	5. Evaluate — Ability to judge, criticize, or defend the information presented in a selection by using the information to support possible alternatives. Ex. "Defend or criticize the following statement: 'Boys are more likely to have psychological problems when their fathers are not in their lives.'
What ability is needed for the Creation level? What is an example question?	6. Create — Ability to do something new or different with the information presented in a selection but in a way that is opposite from analysis. Ex. "Write a different ending to the story."

Source: Anderson and Krathwohl © 2001

Use Study Strategies

There are several ways to practice learning and remembering the information contained in your study guide that will allow you to use a variety of learning styles.

Test Yourself Using Margin Questions

Use the questions you wrote in the margin of your study guide to test yourself on the information it contains. Simply cover the information on the right, ask the questions you wrote in the margin on the left, and see if you know the answers. This method is most effective for learning definitions and examples of key terms.

For instance, use the study guide in Figure 9.1 to answer the following questions.

1. What ability is needed at the Remembering Level of Bloom's Taxonomy?

    _____

2. What is an example question at the Understanding Level of Bloom's Taxonomy?

    _____

3. What is an example question at the Creation Level of Bloom's Taxonomy? _____

    _____

You should practice asking yourself each margin question in your study guide until you can answer them all correctly without looking at your notes.

Create Recall Words or Sentences

Use the Recall to Mind strategy (Chapter 7, page 261) to create a recall word or sentence to help you remember the major details in the outlines of your study guide. Ask yourself whether the information you are learning has to be listed in a specific order, or whether it can be arranged in any order. If it can be listed in any order, you can use the first letters of each major detail to make a recall word. For example, many people use the word HOMES to remember the names of the Great Lakes: Huron, Ontario, Michigan, Erie, and Superior.

If the major details in the outline have to be listed in a *specific order*, you could use the first letter of each entry to create a *recall sentence*. For example, the six levels of thinking in Bloom's Taxonomy (Remember, Understand, Apply, Analyze, Evaluate, and Create) must be listed in a specific order. To remember the order of each level in the taxonomy, you might create the sentence **R**eview **U**nknown **A**nswers **A**fter **E**very **C**lass.

Apply List, Label, and Repeat to Learn Outline Details

Once you decide upon a recall word or sentence that makes sense to you, you can use the List, Label, and Repeat strategy to learn the details about each major idea in the most important outlines of your study guide. (See Chapter 7, page 264, to review this strategy in detail.) For instance, let's say you like the recall sentence **R**eview **U**nknown **A**nswers **A**fter **E**very **C**lass. First, *list* each level of thinking and write what you learned under each level. Then, *label* the first letter of each level by circling it or highlighting it in some way. Finally, *repeat* the six levels of the taxonomy while you think about the recall sentence you created. You want to understand how each letter of your recall sentence relates to each level in Bloom's Taxonomy so that you can re-peat each level from memory using your recall sentence.

When you have memorized the major details in the outline, you can use your recall sentence to ask yourself questions that will help you learn the information listed under each major detail. For instance, you would look at the letter R in **Review Unknown Answers After Every Class**. You know that the letter R stands for Remem-ber, which is the first level of Bloom's Taxonomy. Now, look at the information you need to learn, such as the kinds of thinking involved at the remembering level. Then, turn the information into questions such as "What ability is required at the remem-bering level of thinking?" and "What is an example question at the remembering level of Bloom's Taxonomy?" until you can answer each question without looking at the material. Repeat this process with every major detail until you can recall the en-tire outline about the six levels of Bloom's Taxonomy using your recall sentence.

To test yourself, repeat your recall word or sentence later in the day to see how many details you can remember. By using recall words and sentences, you will soon find you are able to remember information quickly.

Memory Check 2 How much do you remember?

1. To create an effective study guide for the exam, you should:

   a. _____

   _____

   b. _____

   _____

   c. _____

   d. _____

   _____

2. What question will help you decide whether to create a recall word or a re-call sentence?

   _____

   _____

3. What are the six levels of Bloom's Taxonomy? Hint: **Review Unknown Answers After Every Class.** _____

   _____

The Eight-Day Action Plan

You may know someone who says, "I didn't even study, and I passed." Or, "I just looked over the information before the exam and I made a C." While it is possible to cram important details during one review session, the information is more likely to be lost very quickly after the exam. As college courses build on one another, you want to be able to remember the information from each course, not just for exams, but so you are prepared for future courses. Daily review of important information for *at least* a week is the best way to prepare successfully for a college exam. The **Eight-Day Action Plan** will help you review more effectively.

First, divide your study guide into four sections. Then, **beginning eight days before the exam,** review each section using the following step-by-step guide:

	The Eight-Day Action Plan
Day One	Test yourself on the information contained in the first section until you can answer all of the margin test questions without looking at the answers.
Day Two	See how much you can remember from the day before. Review until you feel confident in your ability to recall all of the information in the first section. Then, see how much you can recall when you ask yourself the margin questions in the second section. If you can recall at least half of the information, then stop.
Day Three	See how much you can recall from section one and review anything that you missed or forgot. Then, test yourself on the information contained in the second section until you feel confident.
Day Four	See how much information you can recall from section two. Review until it is easy to answer all of the margin questions without looking.
Day Five	See how much you can remember from sections one and two. Review anything that you missed or forgot. Then, see how much you can recall when you ask yourself the margin questions in section three. If you can recall at least half of the information, then stop.
Day Six	See how much you can recall from sections one, two, and three. Then, test yourself on the information contained in section three until you feel confident. Test yourself on the margin questions contained in section four. If you can recall at least half of the information, then stop.
Day Seven	See how much you can remember from sections one through four. Review anything that you missed or forgot until you feel confident in your ability to recall the information.

| Day Eight | Test yourself on all of the margin questions in all four sections. Review anything that you missed or forgot until it is easily recalled. |

Preparing for an exam will be much easier if you review regularly. Also, if you review consistently, you will be able to see connections between what you have learned and what you are learning. These connections allow you to retain and use information more easily.

Memory Check 3 How much do you remember?

1. What is the first step you should take to create your Eight-Day Action Plan before an exam? _____

2. What can happen if you cram information into one study session?

   _____

3. What are two important ways you can gain an advantage through regular review?

   a. _____

   b. _____

   _____

PREPARE PHYSICALLY FOR THE DAY OF THE EXAM

1. **Go to bed early on the night before the exam**. You know how much sleep your body requires to be alert. Make sure you get the sleep you need to give you a physical advantage.

2. **Eat small meals prior to the exam**. Studies show that concentration and test performance are reduced when a person is hungry. Eating a small amount of protein such as cheese, bacon, or eggs before an exam can provide the energy your brain needs to function more efficiently on tasks that require concentration.

3. **Avoid consuming larger than usual amounts of caffeine before the exam**. Some students think that drinking more coffee will improve their test performance. While a small amount of caffeine can improve concentration, increasing your intake of caffeine can also increase your anxiety.

If you follow these rules before an exam, you will have the physical advantage that you need to succeed.

TEST-TAKING TIPS

There are several things you can do to improve your performance when you are taking an exam.

Know the Instructor's Rules for the Exam

If you know the instructor's rules for an exam, you can be certain to bring the materials you need to succeed. For instance, you need to know if you are allowed to mark or write notations on the exam. If so, are you allowed to use a pen or should you bring a pencil? If not, are you allowed to have a blank sheet of paper for writing notes during the exam? Are calculators allowed and so on? You also need to know how you will be graded on the exam. For example, will you also lose points for questions that you do not answer?

Skim the Exam to Budget your Time

If you skim the exam, you can review the number of questions, the type of questions, and the value of each question you will need to answer in order to complete the exam on time. For instance, if a short-essay response question is included, you will need to budget your time so that you can both write an essay and answer the other questions on the exam. Instructors often divide exam questions into sections. Usually, the value of the questions in each section is indicated on the exam. If not, find out this information before the exam so that you can be certain to spend enough time on these questions to earn a higher score.

Answer the Easiest Questions First

Read each question *very* carefully, answering the easiest questions first. If you skip a question that is more difficult, put a light check mark next to it in pencil in the margin. After you have answered the last question on the exam, go back to the first question that you marked or skipped.

Think Before Answering Multiple-Choice Questions

There is no strategy that can take the place of consistent review in preparing for an objective exam. However, there are several tips you can use to improve your performance on multiple-choice questions:

- **Look for the best answer to the question.** Many students answer incorrectly because they choose the first correct answer they see among the list of items.

Instructors may include several choices that are partially correct, but are not the most complete or accurate answers to the question they have asked. Make sure the answer you choose is the one that best answers the question. In addition, instructors may include the choice *all of the above* at the end of a list of correct responses to a question in order to test whether you have read all of the choices before you made a decision.

- **Eliminate the answers you know are incorrect.** Carefully read all of the choices in a multiple-choice question. Then, eliminate those you know are incorrect. You can mark through them lightly in pencil if you are allowed to write on the exam. The best answer will be easier to find if you reduce the number of choices.

- **Look for the longest answer.** The correct answer often contains the most complete information, which can make it longer than the other items.

- **Consider eliminating answers that contain words such as *always, never, every*, or *all*.** There is usually a situation in which something that supposedly "never" happens actually does occur. If you have studied, you will know when the answer refers to situations that *always* or *never* occur in a certain way, or when something occurs *none* or *all* of the time, or *every* time.

- **Look for answers that contain words like *may, usually*, or *can*.** Multiple-choice responses that contain these types of words are more likely to be correct because there is a possibility that the statement is true.

Handling Reading Selection Questions

- **Read exam passages carefully before reviewing the questions that follow them.** When you read the questions first, you are more likely to miss important details because you are skimming the selection for the answers instead of focusing on everything the author has to say and the way that it is written.

- **If you are allowed to mark exam passages, underline main ideas, number lists of major detail sentences, and label definitions and examples.** This will make answering the questions that follow easier.

- **When a question asks for specific facts, go back and check the selection before answering.** If you have read the selection before reviewing the questions that follow, these facts will be much easier to find.

Handling Short-Essay Response Questions

Outlines about topics that have been repeated or emphasized by the instructor are more likely to appear as short-essay response questions on an exam. Unlike formal, five-paragraph essays often required in an English class, a short-essay response usually consists of one or more paragraphs *without* an introduction or conclusion.

Instructors include a short-essay response question to test your ability to present what you know about a topic in more detail. Therefore, it is a good idea to ask the instructor or use the RODEO Attention Plan for note taking method discussed earlier to determine what topics will be likely to appear as an essay question. Then, you can prepare by organizing the information about the topic in an outline using transition words to distinguish each major detail from the minor details that support each one. Finally, use List, Label, and Repeat to create a recall word or recall sentence that you can use to memorize the major details and help you remember the entire outline.

On the day of the exam, you can improve your performance on a short-essay response question if you apply the following five steps.

Step One: Create a Main Idea Sentence That Responds Directly to the Essay Question

Short-essay response questions contain certain words that tell you what you should write about. For instance, consider the essay question "**Compare** one-celled and two-celled animals." Your response should rephrase the question in the form of a main idea sentence as follows: "*There are several* **similarities** between one-and two-celled animals."

In this case, the word *similarities* in the main idea sentence shows that you understand the question and the type of information being asked for in the essay. If you read essay questions carefully, you will know how to respond. Figure 9.2 is a guide you can use to answer short-essay response questions.

Figure 9.2 Common Short-Essay Response Question Words and Example Questions

Question Words	What You Should Write about and Example Questions
compare	• Similarities between two things, people, places, events, or ideas • Ex: "*Compare* one-celled and two-celled animals." 　**Main idea:** There are several similarities between . . .
contrast/ distinguish	• Differences between two things, people, places, events, or ideas • Ex. "*Distinguish* between a plutocracy and a democracy." 　**Main idea:** There are a few differences between a . . .
define	• The meaning of a key term or concept using specific examples

	• Ex. "*Define* the terms, *gentleman* and *lady*."
	Main idea: The term, gentleman is defined as . . .
	Main idea: Webster defines a lady as a woman who . . .
describe/ illustrate	• Key features of a person, place, thing, event, or idea using specific examples
	• Ex. "*Describe* an ideal fitness program."
	Main idea: An ideal fitness program would possess the features:
discuss	• Strengths and weaknesses on both sides of an issue, or the specific facts that show your complete understanding of a person, event, or idea
	• Ex. "Should public schools require a course in Bible studies? *Discuss.*"
	Main idea: Public schools should not require . . . for the following reasons:
	Main idea: Public schools should require . . . for the following reasons:
enumerate	• List major points using specific examples
	• Ex. "*Enumerate* the location of each of the five Great Lakes."
	Main idea: There are five Great Lakes.
explain	• Reasons for or against a particular issue using specific examples
	• Ex. "Do you think the main character will achieve his goal?" *Explain.*
	Main idea: There are several reasons why I believe Joel will achieve his goal.
summarize	• A brief overview of main points
	• Ex. "*Summarize* the main events in the selection."
	Main idea: The story is about a man who is so stressed because of his work that he quits and takes a job on a secluded island where he encounters other forms of stress.
trace	• Steps, stages, or events in the development of something
	• Ex. "*Trace* the development of the Civil Rights Act."
	Main idea: There are several events that led to the Civil Rights Act.

Activity 9.2 ▸ Creating a Main Idea Sentence
for a Short-Essay Response

Directions: *Study the example below. Then write a main idea sentence that begins a short-essay response for each of the following questions.*

Example

Essay Question: Should marijuana be legalized? Explain.

Write a main idea sentence: There are several reasons for the legalization of marijuana.

Or: There are several reasons against the legislation of marijuana.

1. Essay Question: *Contrast* one-celled and two-celled animals.

   Main idea sentence: There are several *differences* _____

   _____

2. Essay Question: *Enumerate* the disorders associated with drug abuse.

   Main idea sentence: There are several _____

   _____

3. Essay Question: *Explain* what motivates students to achieve good grades.

   Main idea sentence: There are several *reasons* why _____

   _____

4. Essay Question: *Describe* the childhood of the main character.

   Main idea sentence: There are several *features* that describe _____

   _____

5. Essay Question: *Trace* the development of the first telephone.

   Main idea sentence: There are several events that led to _____

   _____

Step Two: Outline the Major and Minor Details of Your Response Before You Write the Essay

Use a separate sheet of paper or margin space to write the outline you memorized about the topic. By outlining your response before you write the actual essay, you will be less likely to forget important details.

Example

Essay Question: Discuss the six types of love.

Main idea sentence: There are six types of love.

Outline of response: (On a separate sheet of paper or margin space)

Mania: Elation and Depression

    —extreme highs and lows

    —obsession, jealousy, and worry about loss of love

    —low self-image, nothing else matters except love

Agape: Compassionate and Selfless

    —loves everyone on a spiritual level, without expectation of reward.

    ex. Jesus, Buddha, and Gandhi

Pragma: Practical and Traditional

    —careful selection based on long-term usefulness and compatibility.

Ludus: Entertainment and Excitement

    —love is a game not taken seriously

    —needs to control love and emotions

    —changes partners when no longer interested or amused, unfaithful

Eros: Beauty and Sexuality

    —sensitive to physical imperfections instead of inner qualities

    ex. Narcissus who fell in love with the beauty of his own image

Storge: Peaceful and Slow

    —sex is not as important as shared interests, activities, and feelings

    —lacks passion and intensity

    —difficult to define the status of the relationship

If you have used List, Label, and Repeat, you will be able to write the entire outline so you can use it as a guide to keep you focused on your answer to the short essay response question.

Activity 9.3 ▶ Using List, Label, and Repeat to Prepare for Short-Essay Response Questions

Directions: *Use List, Label, and Repeat to create a recall word or recall sentence that will help you memorize the entire outline about the six types of love. Next, see how long it takes you to memorize all of the details in the outline.*

1. What is your recall word or sentence for memorizing the six types of love?

    ————————————————————————————————

2. How many minutes did it take you to memorize all of the details in the outline?

_____

3. On a separate sheet of paper, test your memory by writing the entire outline about the six types of love.

Step Three: Use Appropriate Transition Words to List Major Details in Your Outline Response

Transition words help you to emphasize the major details in your essay response. But, it is important to use transition words that are appropriate to the pattern of organization you are presenting.

For instance, must the major details in the example outline about the six types of love be presented in a specific order? Or, can they be arranged in any order? The six types of love can be arranged in *any order*. So, it wouldn't make sense to use transition words such as *next, then,* or *after* because the major details are not presented in a sequence of events/process pattern of organization. Instead, you would use transition words, such as *first, second, third,* or *another* to show that each *type* of love can be listed in *any order,* as in a classification pattern of organization.

Step Four: Turn Each Major Detail of Your Outline Response Into a Complete Sentence

Be sure to use the transition words you have selected for each major detail.

Example

Mania, consisting of elation and depression, is the *first* type of love.

The *second* type of love is agape, which is compassionate and selfless.

Step Five: Write Your Response Beginning With the Main Idea

Next, write the first major detail sentence. Then, write the information you listed about the detail using complete sentences. Finally, repeat the process for all of the remaining major details in your outlined response.

Example

There are six types of love. Mania, consisting of elation and depression, is the *first* type of love. It is characterized by extreme highs and lows. People who fall into this category of love tend to be obsessive and jealous, often worrying about the loss of love. They may have low self-image and believe that nothing else matters except love. The *second* type of love is agape, which is compassionate and selfless. . . .

EVALUATE YOUR PERFORMANCE

Preparing for exams and reducing test anxiety take time and practice. If you performed well, you want to think about what you did so you can repeat the process on the next exam. If you are not happy with the result, you want to know what you could have done to improve your performance. So, it is important to evaluate your performance after an exam. Successful students learn from their mistakes. Here are some questions you can ask to evaluate your performance on an exam.

Test Performance Evaluation Questions
_____ Did I regularly attend classes?
_____ Did I complete all my homework assignments?
_____ Did I take lecture notes?
_____ Did I take text notes?
_____ Did I create a study guide?
_____ Did I use learning strategies?
_____ Did I review consistently for at least one week before the exam?
_____ Did I get enough sleep before the exam?
_____ Did I eat small meals throughout the day before the exam?
_____ Did I increase my intake of caffeine before the exam?
_____ What information was included in the exam that I did not study?

If you make a habit of evaluating your performance after every exam, you will be able to learn from your mistakes. You will be able to improve upon the way you prepare for the next exam.

Activity 9.4 ► Chapter Application: Preparing for the Test Yourself Review Quiz

Directions: *Before answering the questions in the Test Yourself Review Quiz, create a study guide containing the most important information found in Chapter 9. Then, apply the Eight-Day Action Plan to learn the information you have written in your study guide. Finally, see how many questions you can answer without referring to your study guide in order to evaluate how much you have learned about test-taking techniques.*

Test Yourself Review Quiz

_____ 1. If you learn information more easily if it is spoken to you, then you are:
   a. an informal learner.   c. a visual learner.
   b. a tactile learner   d. an auditory learner.

_____ 2. The best way to reduce test anxiety is to:
   a. speak to the instructor.   c. be prepared.
   b. be organized.   d. write down your fears.

_____ 3. According to the author, what is one thing you should find out about an up-coming exam?
   a. the time of the exam
   b. the number of questions on the exam
   c. the instructor's learning style
   d. where the exam will be given.

4. What are two steps you can take to identify what you need to study for an exam?

   a. _____

   b. _____

   _____

5. The first step in creating an effective study guide is to identify the entries in

   your text and lecture notes that have the most _____.

_____ 6. You should create a margin space on the left side of your study guide so you can:
   a. organize your notes into manageable parts.
   b. create a summary of the most important information in the text.
   c. write margin questions next to the information in your study guide.
   d. write information about the date and time of the exam.

7. What are three study strategies you can use to learn the information in your study guide?

   a. _____

   b. _____

   c. _____

_____ 8. What is the first step you should take in order to apply the Eight-Day Action Plan?
   a. Find out what type of questions will appear on the exam.
   b. Create an effective recall word or recall sentence for outlined information.
   c. Form a study group.
   d. Divide your study guide into four sections.

9. What should you do on the first day of the Eight-Day Action Plan?

   _____

   _____

_____ 10. If you review consistently, you will be able to:
   a. see connections between what you have learned and what you are learning.
   b. increase the amount of information in your study guide.
   c. recognize errors contained in your text and lecture notes.
   d. answer multiple-choice questions without having to read all of the possible responses.

11. What is one question you should ask in order to know the instructor's rules for

   the exam? _____

12. If you skip a difficult question on the exam, you should

   _____

   _____

_____ 13. Which of the following is a strategy for answering multiple-choice questions?
   a. Never select answers that contain words such as _may_ or _often_.
   b. Always select answers that contain words such as _all_ or _every_.
   c. Eliminate answers you know are incorrect.
   d. Eliminate all of the longest answers.

14. What can happen if you review the selection questions before you read the selection?

   _____

   _____

_____ 15. In order to evaluate your performance on an exam, why would you ask yourself if you attended class regularly?
   a. If you miss class, you miss important information necessary to perform well.
   b. Perfect attendance is always used by instructors to evaluate test performance.
   c. Without perfect attendance, it is impossible to pass an exam.
   d. Instructors never include questions from lecture material on an exam.

16. What are the five steps for handling a short-essay response question?

    a. _____

    b. _____

    c. _____

    d. _____

    e. _____

17. Why should you outline the major and minor details of your response before you write the essay? _____

    _____

18. Successful students learn from their _____.

Use the recall words or sentences you created in the chapter activities to answer the following questions.

19. What are the six types of love? _____

20. What are the six levels of thinking in Bloom's Taxonomy? _____

    _____

Summarization Activity

Directions: *Write the major headings in this chapter. Under each heading, write a couple of sentences about the most important topics presented in the section of text that follows that heading.*

First Heading _____

What information is most important? _____

_____

_____

Second Heading _____

What information is most important? _____

_____

_____

Third Heading _____

What information is most important? _____

_____

_____

Fourth Heading _____

What information is most important? _____

_____

_____

Fifth Heading _____

What information is most important? _____

_____

_____

Sixth Heading _____

What information is most important? _____

_____

_____

Seventh Heading _____

What information is most important? _____

_____

_____

Combine the information you wrote in this outline into a paragraph to summarize what you have learned in this chapter.

Reflection Activity

How am I am going to apply what I have learned?

Directions: *On a separate sheet of paper write a paragraph discussing two or three things you learned about test-taking strategies that were most helpful to you and how you plan to use what you have learned.*

SEVEN SECRETS TO COLLEGE SUCCESS
Bruce Gibbs

Accessing Prior Knowledge

Questions for Discussion

1. What are some things that students do that cause them to fail a class?

2. What are some things that students do when they want to perform well in a class?

Preview and Predict

Directions: *Look at the title of the selection. Think about what you already know about the subject. Then, write a couple of predictions about what you are going to read. For instance, what will the author discuss about college success?*

1. _____

2. _____

Word Search and Discovery

Directions: *Skim through the selection to find the two words below. Underline both words in the selection. Then, use a dictionary to write their definitions in the spaces provided. As you read and encounter these words, see if the definitions you wrote fit the way each word is used in the selection.*

embarking (*vb*): _____

_____

punctual (*adj*): _____

_____

Finally, underline at least one new word as you read the selection and write your guess as to its meaning in the right margin of the text.

Text Notes in Practice

Directions: *Use a textbook study method such as SQUARE to identify the most important information in the selection. Then, create a study guide that you can use to prepare for the questions that follow the selection.*

SEVEN SECRETS TO COLLEGE SUCCESS
Bruce Gibbs

1   Congratulations. You have made the decision to pursue higher education and to meet your goal of obtaining a college degree. You are embarking on a journey that can take you places you may have only dreamed of. Being in college can be fun but it can also be challenging. In this article I have put together seven steps that can help you to be successful at your collegiate goals.

2   **1. Be punctual:** Being late for class is a sign of disrespect. It tells the instructor you don't want to be in his class or that you don't take the class seriously. You also miss important information when you are late. Do you like it when people are late for something you've planned? Of course not. The instructor has spent time preparing for the class and you should give the instructor the time you have scheduled for his class. Besides, you have spent money for the class so you should show up on time to get what you paid for. Being punctual also helps when it comes time for grading. Grading is subjective and you want to do everything you can to leave a positive impression in your instructor's mind so he can remember you this way doing grading. Being late for class doesn't make a positive impression. So if you are habitually late, why should he sweat over your grade? Take my word for it, show up on time.

3   **2. Do the homework:** It is a waste of your time and the instructor's time if you just sit in class but never do the assignments. Not doing class assignments is a guaranteed way to fail. Instructors use assignments to determine your knowledge and your grade. Assignments also help you to learn more about your field of study. Instructors can also tell if you half-heartedly completed an assignment. And don't wait until the last minute to do your assignment. If you start early you will have a better product than if you waited until the due date to start on it.

4   **3. Ask questions:** Some people think asking questions is dumb. In reality it's just the opposite. Instructors like students who ask questions. It shows you are interested in the class and that you really want to learn more about the subject the instructor is an expert in. The question you ask is probably the same question several other students in the class want answered so you'll be doing them a favor.

5   **4. Be confident:** As an instructor, I like students who are confident in their abilities and act on them. Many times students are afraid to speak up in class or write a paper about an interesting subject because they are afraid what the instructor or their fellow students may think. As a result research

papers or projects are sometimes dull and boring because they cover "safe" topics. It's okay to be afraid. It's not okay to let fear keep you from doing something you really want to do. So go ahead and write that paper you've been longing to write or start on that project that you truly believe in. Be confident and be able to back up your findings or conclusions with evidence.

6 **5. Volunteer:** College instructors like students who volunteer. Volunteerism shows you really want to get involved in your major or your school. You don't have to volunteer for something big. It could be something as simple as agreeing to be a group discussion leader or leading a class project. It could be volunteering to be on a student committee or to be on the board of a student chapter of an organization. Find ways to volunteer. This will not only help your grades but it can also enhance your studies.

7 **6. Be prepared for tests:** Depending on your instructor, you may not know when she may call a pop quiz. Successful students are prepared and always ready. You can be prepared by reading the class material before the class, participating in class discussions, and by doing the assignments and exercises in your textbook.

8 **7. Get to know people:** Successful people network. You have to do the same too, even on a college campus. When you get to know people on campus they share with you information that they have. This information can help you in a class, help you to save money on a purchase, assist you in choosing a class, or even choosing a major. Networking is a very important tool in the world of business so you might as well practice the skill while you are in college.

9 Remember that you can be a success in college. Yes it's hard but you can do it!

The Write Connection

Directions: *Write a paragraph about three things you learned or that you think are most important in the reading selection.*

_____

_____

_____

_____

Comprehension Check

Directions: *See how many questions you can answer without referring to the selection. Then, review the selection to write more complete responses.*

_____ 1. The author compares being in college to:
    a. basketball game.   c. his own personal experience.
    b. a long trip.   d. a dream.

_____ 2. According to the author, you will miss important information:
    a. when you are punctual.   c. when you are disrespectful.
    b. when you are not prepared.   d. when you are late.

_____ 3. To demonstrate your desire to be involved in your major, you should:
    a. get tutoring.   c. speak up in class.
    b. volunteer for something.   d. ask questions.

_____ 4. According to the author, what is a guaranteed way to fail?
    a. not doing class assignments.   c. being late.
    b. being disrespectful.   d. not asking questions.

_____ 5. The author suggests that you do your assignments early because:
    a. your instructor may call a pop-quiz at any time.
    b. it shows that you want to complete a project that you truly believe in.
    c. you will turn in a better product than if you waited until the last minute.
    d. you will learn more about your field of study if you start early.

_____ 6. A research paper or a project can be boring if:
    a. it covers an uninteresting topic without much thought.
    b. it is assigned after the mid-term exam or mid-term break.
    c. it is completed at the last minute.
    d. it is a dull topic that needs to be supported by lots of evidence.

_____ 7. To determine your knowledge and your grade in a course, instructors use:
    a. their impression of you as a person.
    b. discussion questions.
    c. study modules.
    d. assignments.

_____ 8. According to the author, what will "help your grades and enhance your studies"?
    a. getting some extra tutoring   c. doing your assignments on time
    b. volunteerism   d. showing confidence

_____ 9. Which of the following best describes the main idea of the selection?
   a. There are seven differences between successful and non-successful college students.
   b. There are several reasons why students fail to be successful in college.
   c. There are seven ways to improve your performance in college courses.
   d. There are steps you can take to improve your performance on exams.

10. List the seven secrets to college success.

_____

_____

Critical Thinking Check

_____ 1. Which of the following conclusions can be drawn from the information in the selection?
   a. Students who appear confident make the most positive impression on college instructors.
   b. Students who are habitually late make the most negative impression on college instructors.
   c. Students who ask too many questions are viewed negatively by most college instructors.
   d. Students who have a positive relationship with their college advisors tend to perform well on exams.

_____ 2. The author has written the selection for the purpose of
   a. stating the importance of good study habits.
   b. persuading the reader to be on time for every class.
   c. providing suggestions for improving the likelihood of success in college.
   d. encouraging volunteerism.

_____ 3. Which of the following statements can be inferred from the article?
   a. Grades may be affected by an instructor's positive or negative impressions of the student.
   b. The author is disapproving of students who ask too many questions.
   c. The author prefers students who volunteer over those who network.
   d. The author has failed students who have submitted boring research papers.

Vocabulary Check

Directions: *See if any of the words you underlined in the selection are among the list of words below. If not, write your words in the spaces provided. Guess the meaning of the words from the way they were used in the selection. Then, look up the definition of each word in the dictionary to see if you were right.*

dull (*adj*) Your guess: _____

    Dictionary Definition: _____

subjective (*adj*): Your guess: _____

    Dictionary Definition: _____

Your word: _____ Your guess: _____

    Dictionary Definition: _____

Your word: _____ Your guess: _____

    Dictionary Definition: _____

♟♟♟ Skills in Practice ▶ Reading Selection 2

"Love," From *The Interpersonal Communication Book*, 11th ed.

Joseph A. DeVito

Accessing Prior Knowledge

Questions for Discussion

1. What do think are the most important elements of an intimate relationship?

2. How has your view of intimate relationships changed over the past five years? Why?

Preview and Predict

Directions: *Look at the title of the selection. Think about what you already know about the subject. Then, write a couple of predictions about what you are going to read. For instance, what will the author discuss about lovers?*

1. _____

2. _____

Word Search and Discovery

Directions: *Skim through the selection to find the two words below. Underline both words in the selection. Then, use a dictionary to write their definitions in the spaces provided. As you read and encounter these words, see if the definitions you wrote fit the way each word is used in the selection.*

characterization (*n*): _____

deteriorate (*vb*): _____

    Finally, underline one new word as you read the selection and write your guess as to its meaning in the right margin of the text.

Text Notes in Practice

Directions: *Use a textbook study method such as SQUARE to identify the most important information in the selection. Then, create a study guide that you can use to prepare for the questions that follow the selection.*

LOVE

Joseph A. DeVito

1   Of all the qualities of interpersonal relationships, none seems as important as love. "We are all born for love," noted famed British prime minister Benjamin Disraeli. "It is the principle of existence and its only end." **Love** is a feeling characterized by closeness and caring and by intimacy, passion, and commitment. It's also an interpersonal relationship developed, maintained, and sometimes destroyed through communication. And at the same time a relationship that can be greatly enhanced with communication skills (Dindia & Timmerman, 2004).

2   Although there are many theories about love, the one that captured the attention of interpersonal researchers and continues to receive research support is a conceptualization proposing that there is not one but six types of love (Lee, 1976; Kanemasa, Taniguchi, Daibo & Ishimori, 2004). View the descriptions of each type as broad characterizations that are generally but not always true. As a preface to this discussion of the types of love, you may wish to respond to the self-test "What Kind of Lover Are You?"

TEST YOURSELF: What Kind of Lover Are You?

Respond to each of the following statements with T for true (if you believe the statement to be a generally accurate representation of your attitudes about love) or F for false (if you believe the statement does not adequately represent your attitudes about love).

_____ 1. My lover and I have the right physical "chemistry" between us.

_____ 2. I feel that my lover and I were meant for each other.

_____ 3. My lover and I really understand each other.

_____ 4. I believe that what my lover doesn't know about me won't hurt him or her.

_____ 5. My lover would get upset if he or she knew of some of the things I've done with other people.

_____ 6. When my lover gets too dependent on me, I want to back off a little.

_____ 7. I expect to always be friends with my lover.

_____ 8. Our love is really a deep friendship, not a mysterious, mystical emotion.

_____ 9. Our love relationship is the most satisfying because it developed from a good friendship.

_____ 10. In choosing my lover, I believed it was best to love someone with a similar background.

_____ 11. An important factor in choosing a partner is whether or not he or she would be a good parent.

_____ 12. One consideration in choosing my lover was how he or she would reflect on my career.

_____ 13. Sometimes I get so excited about being in love with my lover that I can't sleep.

_____ 14. When my lover doesn't pay attention to me, I feel sick all over.

_____ 15. I cannot relax if I suspect that my lover is with someone else.

_____ 16. I would rather suffer myself than let my lover suffer.

_____ 17. When my lover gets angry with me, I still love him or her fully and unconditionally.

_____ 18. I would endure all things for the sake of my lover.

How Did You Do?

This scale, from Hendrick and Hendrick (1990), is based on the work of John Alan Lee (1976), as is the discussion of the six types of love that follows. The statements refer to the six types of love that we discuss below: eros, ludus, storge, pragma, mania, and agape. "True" answers represent your agreement and "false" answers your disagreement with the type of love to which the statements refer. Statements 1–3 are characteristic of the eros lover. If you answered true to these statements, you have a strong eros component to your love style. If you answered false, you have a weak eros component. Statements 4–6 refer to ludus love, 7–9 refer to storge love, 10–12 to pragma love, 13–15 to manic love, and 16–18 to agapic love.

What Will You Do?

What things might you do to become more aware of the different love styles and to become a more well-rounded lover? How might you go about incorporating the qualities of effective interpersonal communication—for example, being more flexible, more polite, and more other-oriented—to become a more responsive, more exciting, more playful love partner?

Source: From "A Relationship Specific Version of the Love Attitude Scale" by C. Hendrick and S. Hendrick. *Journal of Social Behavior and Personality 5,* 1990. Reprinted by permission of Select Press.

Love Types

3   Let's look at each of Lee's (1976) six types of love:

4   *Eros: Beauty and sexuality.* Like Narcissus, who fell in love with the beauty of his own image, the erotic lover focuses on beauty and physical attractiveness, sometimes to the exclusion of qualities you might consider more important and more lasting. Also like Narcissus, the erotic lover has an idealized image of beauty that is unattainable in reality. Consequently, the erotic lover often feels unfulfilled. Not surprisingly, erotic lovers are particularly sensitive to physical imperfections in the ones they love.

5   *Ludus: Entertainment and excitement.* Ludus love is experienced as a game, as fun. The better you can play the game, the greater the enjoyment. Love is not to be taken too seriously; emotions are to be held in check lest they get out of hand and make trouble; passions never rise to the point where they get out of control. A ludic lover is self-controlled, always aware of the need to manage love rather than allow it to be in control. Perhaps because of this need to control love, some researchers have proposed that ludic love tendencies may reveal

tendencies to sexual aggression (Sarwer, Kalichman, Johnson, Early, et al., 1993). Not surprisingly, the ludic lover retains a partner only as long as the partner is interesting and amusing. When interest fades, it's time to change partners. Perhaps because love is a game, sexual fidelity is of little importance. In fact, recent research shows that people who score high on ludic love are more likely to engage in "extradyadic" dating and sex than those who score low on ludus (Wiederman & Hurd, 1999). And, not surprisingly, ludic lovers score high on narcissism (Campbell, Foster, & Finkel, 2002).

6   *Storge: Peaceful and slow.* Storge love (a word that come from the Greek for "familial love") lacks passion and intensity. Storgic lovers don't set out to find lovers but to establish a companionable relationship with someone they know and with whom they can share interests and activities. Storgic love is a gradual process of unfolding thoughts and feelings; the changes seem to come so slowly and so gradually that it's often difficult to define exactly where the relationship is at any point in time. Sex in storgic relationships comes late, and when it comes, it assumes no great importance.

7   *Pragma: Practical and traditional.* The pragma lover is practical and seeks a relationship that will work. Pragma lovers want compatibility and a relationship in which their important needs and desires will be satisfied. They're concerned with the social qualifications of a potential mate even more than with personal qualities; family and background are extremely important to the pragma lover, who relies not so much on feelings as on logic. The pragma lover views love as a useful relationship that makes the rest of life easier. So the pragma lover asks such questions about a potential mate as "Will this person earn a good living?" "Can this person cook?" "Will this person help me advance in my career?" Pragma lovers' relationships rarely deteriorate. This is partly because pragma lovers choose their mates carefully and emphasize similarities. Another reason is that they have realistic romantic expectations.

8   *Mania: Elation and depression.* Mania is characterized by extreme highs and extreme lows. The manic lower loves intensely and at the same time intensely worries about the loss of the love. This fear often prevents the manic lover from deriving as much pleasure as possible from the relationship. With little provocation, the manic lover may experience extreme jealousy. Manic love is obsessive; the manic lover must possess the beloved completely. In return, the manic lover wishes to be possessed, to be loved intensely. The manic lover's poor self-image seems capable of being improved only by love; self-worth comes from being loved rather than from any sense of inner satisfaction. Because love is so important, danger signs in a relationship are often ignored; the manic lover believes that if there is love, then nothing else matters.

9   *Agape: Compassionate and selfless.* Agape is a compassionate, egoless, self-giving love. The agapic lover loves even people with whom he or she has no close ties. This lover loves the stranger on the road even though the two of

them probably will never meet again. Agape is a spiritual love, offered without concern for personal reward or gain. This lover loves without expecting that the love will be reciprocated. Jesus, Buddha, and Gandhi preached this unqualified love, agape (Lee, 1976). In one sense, agape is more a philosophical kind of love than a love that most people have the strength to achieve. Not surprisingly people who believe in *yuan*, a Chinese concept that comes from the Buddhist belief in predestiny, are more likely to favor agapic (and pragmatic) love and less likely to favor erotic love (Goodwin & Findlay, 1997).

10 Each of these varieties of love can combine with others to form new and different patterns (for example, manic and ludic or storge and pragma). These six, however, identify the major types of love and illustrate the complexity of any love relationship. The six styles should also make it clear that different people want different things, that each person seeks satisfaction in a unique way. The love that may seem lifeless or crazy or boring to you may be ideal for someone else. At the same time, another person may see these very same negative qualities in the love you're seeking.

11 Love changes. A relationship that began as pragma may develop into ludus or eros. A relationship that began as erotic may develop into mania or storge. One approach sees this developmental process as having three major stages (Duck, 1986):

First stage: Eros, mania, and ludus (initial attraction)
Second stage: Storge (as the relationship develops)
Third stage: Pragma (as relationship bonds develop)

12 In reading about the love styles, you may have felt that certain personality types are likely to favor one type of love over another. Here are personality traits that research finds people assign to each love style (Taraban & Hendrick, 1995). Which personality characteristics do you think go with which love style (eros, ludus, storge, pragma, mania, or agape)?

1. inconsiderate, secretive, dishonest, selfish, dangerous
2. honest, loyal, mature, caring, loving, understanding
3. jealous, possessive, obsessed, emotional, dependent
4. sexual, exciting, loving, happy, optimistic
5. committed, giving, caring, self-sacrificing, loving
6. family-oriented, planning, careful, hard-working, concerned

13 Very likely you perceived these personality factors in the same way as did the participants in the research from which these traits were drawn: 1 = ludus, 2 = storge, 3 = mania, 4 = eros, 5 = agape, and 6 = pragma. Do note, of course, that these results do not imply that ludus lovers are inconsiderate, secretive, and dishonest; they merely mean that people in general (and perhaps you in particular) *think* of ludus lovers as inconsiderate, secretive, and dishonest.

—From DeVito, Joseph A. *Interpersonal Communication: Relating to Others*, 11e. Published by Allyn and Bacon, Boston, MA. Copyright © 2007 by Pearson Education. Reprinted by permission of the publisher.

The Write Connection

Directions: *Write a paragraph about three things you learned or that you think are most important in the reading selection.*

_____

_____

_____

_____

_____

Comprehension Check

Directions: *See how many questions you can answer without referring to the selection. Then, review the selection to write more complete responses.*

_____   1. The *erotic* lover:
   a. has an idealized image of beauty that is unattainable in reality.
   b. focuses on beauty and physical attractiveness to the exclusion of more lasting qualities.
   c. is particularly sensitive to physical imperfections in the ones he or she loves.
   d. all of the above.

_____   2. A person who tends to be obsessive, jealous, and fearful about the loss of love demonstrates which of the following love styles?
   a. storge   c. agape
   b. pragma   d. mania

_____   3. Jesus, Buddha, and Gandhi exemplify which of the following love styles?
   a. storge   c. agape
   b. pragma   d. mania

   4. What question might be asked by a *pragma* type of lover who is seeking a

   relationship? _____

_____   5. The author refers to Narcissus as an example of the *Eros* type of lover because in Greek mythology, Narcissus:
   a. flew so high that he was burned by the sun.
   b. fell in love with a queen.
   c. continually tried to push a heavy rock up a hill.
   d. fell in love with the beauty of his own image.

_____ 6. According to research on personality traits and love styles, *ludus* lovers are seen as:
   a. jealous, possessive, and dependent.
   b. committed, giving, and self-sacrificing.
   c. honest, loyal, mature, and loving.
   d. inconsiderate, secretive, and dishonest.

_____ 7. Which of following best fits the meaning of the term "extradyadic" dating as it is used in paragraph 3 of the selection?
   a. dating without the benefit of marriage.
   b. dating only one person.
   c. dating others outside of the relationship.
   d. dating for the purpose of having children.

8. According to the author, the six styles show that different people want different things and that each person _____

9. List the six love styles: _____

10. What is an approach to love styles that represents three major stages in the development of a relationship?

   a. _____

   b. _____

   c. _____

Critical Thinking Check

1. Take the Self-Test, "What Kind of Lover Are You?" Then, answer the following questions:

   Were you surprised by the result? Why or why not? _____

   _____

2. Which type of lover described in the selection do you think would be the most difficult to handle as your significant other in a relationship? Explain your response. _____

   _____

Vocabulary Check

Directions: *See if any of the words you underlined in the selection are among the list of words below. If not, write your words in the spaces provided. Guess the meaning of the words from the way they were used in the selection. Then, look up the definition of each word in the dictionary to see if you were right.*

deriving (*vb*): Your guess: _____

    Dictionary Definition: _____

provocation (*n*) : Your guess: _____

    Dictionary Definition: _____

reciprocated (vb): Your guess: _____

    Dictionary Definition: _____

Your word: _____ Your guess: _____

    Dictionary Definition: _____

Your word: _____ Your guess: _____

    Dictionary Definition: _____

PART 4

10 Evaluating Arguments and Critical Thinking

> "It is undesirable to believe a proposition when there is no ground whatever for supposing it true."
>
> – Bertrand Russell

In this chapter you will learn how to:

Distinguish between Statements of Fact and Opinion

Evaluate the Evidence Supporting an Argument

Support Your Point of View

Recognize Bias

Recognize Deductive and Inductive Reasoning

Recognize Errors in Reasoning

▲ There are two sides to every argument.

Preview and Predict ▶ What do you know so far?

How many of the following questions can you answer before you read the chapter?

- What is the difference between a statement of fact and a statement of opinion?

_____

- What is bias?

_____

- What do you think you will learn in this chapter?

  _____

- Think of one way in which the picture relates to this chapter's objectives.

  _____

Now, as you read the chapter, look for the answers to see if you were right.

THE ADVANTAGES OF CRITICAL THINKING

Have you ever wondered why certain people are able to command the respect and attention of others? It seems that whenever they speak, others listen. What makes them appear to be so wise? They have mastered the art of critical thinking.

Critical thinking is a term that refers to a wide range of skills used in the process of solving problems and evaluating information. In reading, critical thinking involves the ability to distinguish facts from opinions; to recognize an author's purpose, tone, and bias; and to make inferences from evidence in order to reach reasonable conclusions. In addition, critical thinking involves the ability to evaluate the strength of an author's argument by looking at the way it is supported. Critical thinking is the cutting edge technology of the mind.

Mastering the art of critical thinking will give you certain advantages. First, you will be able to defend your point of view or argument more effectively. You will know how to find and evaluate the facts presented on both sides of an issue and be ready to use them. As a result, you will be able to demonstrate that you know what you are talking about. Second, you will be able to recognize an author's purpose for writing. When you can do this, you will know when an author is trying to persuade you to agree with his or her point of view. Finally, you will be less likely to be fooled by an author's argument about an issue because you have learned how to verify the facts. You will be less likely to jump to inaccurate conclusions.

In this chapter, you will learn how to distinguish between fact and opinion so you can evaluate the strength of an author's argument. You will also learn to recognize an author's bias as well as common errors in reasoning. As a result, you will learn how to support your own arguments more effectively.

DISTINGUISHING BETWEEN FACT AND OPINION

What Is a Fact?

A **fact** is a statement that can be *proven* to be true or false. A fact isn't *true* until it is proven in an **objective** or unbiased way (without personal prejudice).

Read the following note:

> Jennifer,
>
> I didn't come home again last night because I was at David's house. I'm not cheating on you.
>
> Brad

These are statements of fact, but are they true? You want to know how to prove whether a statement of fact is true because an author may use false statements that only sound like facts. You want to know how to prove a statement of fact so that you will not be wrongly persuaded to agree with an author's particular point of view.

A statement of fact can be proven true or false using any of the following objective sources of evidence.

- It can be measured.

- It can be found in historical records, archives, or government databases.

- It can be supported by statistics from scientific research.

- It can be verified by *eyewitness accounts or quotes from those directly involved. (*If at least two eyewitnesses say the same thing)

By using these objective sources, you can verify whether a statement of fact is actually true or whether it is a lie and false.

Many people use the Internet to find facts about a topic. However, information found on the Internet may not be accurate; you should verify information found on the Internet by looking at two or more alternative, objective web sources. Government web-sites which have a .gov suffix such as, www.BLS.gov (Bureau of Labor Statistics) and educational institution web sites, which have a .edu suffix can be reliable alternate sources of information on the Internet.

Can you prove whether the following statements are true or false?

Statements

1. Joe is taller than Tony.

2. The courthouse is older than the federal building.

3. "Seinfeld" was on television for eight seasons.

Yes. Each statement is a fact that can be proven to be true or false. You can measure the height of both Joe and Tony to see who is taller. If Joe is taller, then statement 1 is *true and is a fact*. If Tony is taller, then you can prove that statement 1 is false. Where can you find proof that the courthouse is older than the federal building? Historical records would tell you which building is older. Television archives would provide documentation of the number of seasons the sitcom "Seinfeld" appeared on television.

Memory Check 1 How much do you remember?

1. What is critical thinking? _____

_____

2. What are three advantages of mastering the art of critical thinking?

   a. _____

   b. _____

   c. _____

3. What is a fact? _____

4. What are four objective sources of evidence that you can use to prove a statement of fact?

   a. _____

   b. _____

   c. _____

   d. _____

5. What does it mean to be objective? _____

6. Why should you verify information found on the Internet? _____

   _____

What Is an Opinion?

If a fact is a statement that can be proven to be true or false, then an *opinion* is a statement that _____ be proven. There are three ways to identify an opinion.

1. Ask yourself, "Can I prove it?" If the answer is **no**, then it is an opinion. An opinion *cannot be proven* in an objective way because it is based on personal preference. For instance, suppose you have a personal preference for vanilla ice cream. Someone else cannot prove that your preference is true or false. It's just a matter of personal opinion. There is no way to measure personal preference in an objective way that can be verified. Therefore, you cannot prove an opinion to be true or false.

2. Ask yourself, "Could someone else have an *opposite* point of view?" If the answer is **yes**, then it is an opinion. While others may agree with an opinion, there will always be someone who has an *opposite point of view*. If it is possible for someone to have an opposite point of view about a particular statement, then it is an *opinion*. An opinion is based upon the way a person views the world. If you find yourself agreeing or disagreeing with a particular statement, then it is an opinion.

3. Ask yourself, "Can I tell how the author *feels* about the issue?" If the answer is **yes**, then it is an opinion. There is an *emotional quality* to the way people express their opinions. An author who conveys emotion when writing about an issue is being subjective. **Subjective** is a term that refers to a personal judgment about a subject. It means that the author is showing a personal preference in the support of *one side* of an issue.

The emotional quality of an author's opinion can be found in *value* words. Value words are used to express emotion for one side of a particular issue. Examples of value words may include *best, worst, beautiful, ugly, smart, dumb, better, good, great, wonderful,* or *terrible.* You will know when an author has a subjective or emotional point of view when value words are used. For instance, notice the difference in the following example statements when value words (in italics) are used.

Statements

1. Joe is more *handsome* than Frank.
2. The courthouse is not as *beautiful* as the bank building.
3. Seinfeld is the *funniest* show on television.

Can you prove any of these statements in an objective or unbiased way? No. You can't prove an opinion to be true or false. Could someone have an opposite point of view about each statement? Yes. Is there any emotion in the statements that conveys what the authors are feeling? Yes. The authors convey an emotional or *subjective* point of view in the use of value words in their statements.

Some people incorrectly identify an opinion as a statement of fact because they *agree* with the statement. For instance, consider the following opinion: "We are as guilty as the murderer if we allow executions." If you *agree* with this statement, you may be more likely to believe it is a fact because of the emotion you have regarding the issue. By recognizing the difference between fact and opinion, you will be able to evaluate an author's statements more objectively.

Memory Check 2 How much do you remember?

1. What is an opinion? _____

_____

2. What three questions can you ask yourself to identify an opinion?

a. _____

b. _____

c. _____

3. Write a recall word that will help you remember the three questions for identifying an opinion. _____

4. What are two examples of value words used to express feelings and attitudes?

_____

5. What does it mean when an author is being subjective? _____

_____

6. What can happen if you agree with an author's opinion?

_____

Activity 10.1 ▶ Fact or Opinion?

Directions: *Identify each statement below as a fact* (F) *or an opinion* (O).

_____ 1. The president is doing a great job of running this country.

_____ 2. The president is doing a poor job of running this country.

_____ 3. The president makes decisions that can affect the country.

_____ 4. Classical music is the best example of musicianship.

_____ 5. You must be more creative to play jazz than rock and roll.

_____ 6. The Beatles came from Liverpool in England.

_____ 7. Violence on TV is out of control.

_____ 8. Parents shouldn't worry about TV; the Internet is more dangerous.

_____ 9. Violence on TV has increased 70% since the 1960s.

_____ 10. Violence on TV has led to the downfall of American society.

Activity 10.2 ▶ Fact or Opinion? Using Objective Sources to Prove Statements of Fact

Directions: *Identify each statement below as an opinion or a fact by asking yourself: "Can I prove it?" If the statement is a fact, write two of the Objective Sources (listed below) that you could use to prove the statement true or false in the space provided.*

> **Objective Sources:** historical records, government databases, news articles, textbooks, scientific research, research, measurement, eyewitness accounts, or quotes from people directly involved.

Example 1

Diet soda contains more sodium than regular soda.

_____ A) This is a statement of opinion that cannot be proven true or false.

___✓___ B) This statement of fact can be proven true or false through (provide two objective sources) <u>measurement and scientific research.</u>

You can compare the amount of sodium in a can of diet soda with the amount of sodium in a can of regular soda by looking at the lists of Nutrition Facts on the sides of the cans. You can also find research that compares the levels of sodium in diet soda and regular soda.

Example 2

Diet soda tastes *better* than regular soda.

___✓___ A) This is a statement of opinion that cannot be proven true or false.

_____ B) This statement of fact can be proven true or false through: (provide two objective sources) <u>You would leave this space blank if</u> <u>the statement is an opinion.</u>

1. Herbert Hoover was President during the Great Depression.

   _____ A) This is a statement of opinion that cannot be proven true or false.

   ___✓___ B) This statement of fact can be proven true or false through: (provide two objective sources) _____

   _____

2. The Great Depression started with the stock market crash that occurred on October 29, 1929.

_____ A) This is a statement of opinion that cannot be proven true or false.

_____ B) This statement of fact can be proven true or false through: (provide two objective sources) _____

_____

3. Wendy told me that she believes in witchcraft.

_____ A) This is a statement of opinion that cannot be proven true or false.

_____ B) This statement of fact can be proven true or false through: (provide two objective sources) _____

_____

4. Mary is a lovely girl.

_____ A) This is a statement of opinion that cannot be proven true or false.

_____ B) This statement of fact can be proven true or false through: (provide two objective sources) _____

_____

5. That show is so stupid.

_____ A) This is a statement of opinion that cannot be proven true or false.

_____ B) This statement of fact can be proven true or false through: (provide two objective sources) _____

_____

EVALUATING THE EVIDENCE

Authors who are presenting an opinion or argument usually state their point of view in their main idea sentence. The main idea sentence tells you whether an author is _for_ or _against_ a particular issue. Authors may use the following words or phrases when they state their opinions: _I think, in my opinion, I believe, should, should not, must,_ or _must not._ The major details are used to list the reasons that support their argument.

A strong argument is one that is supported by facts or by logical reasoning which provides enough evidence for you to make an informed decision about an issue. You can evaluate the strength of an argument by looking at the kinds of evidence or reasons presented in the major details which are used to support it. For instance, the outline of an author's argument might look like this:

The Main Idea Is an Opinion ➝ I think that *we should* build a new auditorium.

Reason (Major Detail)   Because the old one is too small.
Reason (Major Detail)   Because it doesn't have central air and heat.
Reason (Major Detail)   Because it needs too many costly repairs.

Once you have identified the outline of a paragraph or essay, you can look at the list of reasons used by an author to support his or her position and decide if the evidence is strong enough for you to make an informed decision on the subject.

Four Ways to Evaluate the Evidence for an Argument

There are four ways you can evaluate the evidence supporting an author's point of view.

1. Find the number of facts listed in the major details. An author's list of reasons may include both statements of fact as well as statements of opinion. Facts, however, add more strength to an author's arguments. By looking at the number of facts, you can decide if an author has provided a strong enough argument.

2. Find out if the facts are accurate or able to be verified. In order to persuade the reader, an author's list of reasons may include statements of fact that are not true. For instance, consider the following argument: "Bill Jefferson is the best candidate for city council." Now suppose the author has used the following fact as a reason to support his or her argument: "He was a member of President Clinton's Better Business Team." You will want to find out if this statement is true before you decide whether you should agree with the author. You can do this by searching the Internet to find actual news stories about President Clinton's Better Business Team that list the members of the team. Then find a separate source that verifies the accuracy of facts presented on the Internet.

Authors may also use the following phrases to persuade readers of the accuracy of their statements: *studies show* or *three out of ten doctors agree that* . . . . Ask yourself, "What studies?" "Who are the doctors?" These are statements of fact that cannot be proven unless the author provides specific information you can use to verify them. For example, suppose an author wants to prove his or her point by referring to a study conducted by Dr. Robertson and reported in *The Journal of American Medicine* in June of 2005. You can check to see if the study exists and what results the study reported.

3. Consider the trustworthiness of the source.   In other words, how would the author *benefit* from persuading you to believe his or her point of view? What are the author's possible motives for using certain facts? Is the author using facts from sources you can trust? For instance, consider the following opinion: "Tobacco companies *should not* be held responsible for the increase in lung cancer among smokers." Suppose the author has used research conducted by scientists who were *paid* by a tobacco company to show other factors such as pollution are the main causes of lung cancer. Should you trust the evidence? No, not necessarily. Scientists who are *paid* by the people they are defending may not provide objective or unbiased evidence.

4. Find out if an author has the knowledge and experience to speak with authority about the subject.   For instance, suppose you were involved in an accident and the other party claimed it was your fault. Whom would you ask for advice about what to do: a doctor, your best friend, or a lawyer? While you may trust your friend or doctor, neither one has the credentials or expertise to provide the information you need. The best advice would come from a lawyer.

Look at following outline of a paragraph below. Then, see if you can evaluate the author's argument by filling in the spaces provided as you read.

Opinion	Main idea: Corina's is the best Mexican restaurant in town. (Why?)
Reason	It maintains health department standards.
Reason	The service is good.
Reason	It earned an "A-One Rating" from the Food Critics Guild.

Notice the reasons the author provides to support the opinion in the main idea sentence above. Do the reasons contain mostly facts or opinions? _____ You should expect an author to provide these kinds of facts before deciding whether to agree that a particular restaurant is the best in town. You want to know if the restaurant is clean, if the service is good, or if the restaurant has won any awards.

Would you be able to verify the accuracy of the facts? _____ You can check the health department's database. You can also check the official Food Critics Guild website for a list of restaurants that have earned an "A-One Rating."

Always consider the trustworthiness of the source. Is the author a professional food critic? Or is he or she the owner of the restaurant? Which one would be more likely to present objective or unbiased evidence? _____ The food critic would also have the knowledge and experience to speak about the qualities of a good restaurant.

Now consider this outline of a paragraph that contains a similar argument.

Opinion	**Main idea: Manny's is the best Mexican restaurant in town. (Why?)**
Reason	The waiters are cute.
Reason	It's easy to find a parking space in front of the restaurant.
Reason	It is beautifully decorated.

Do the author's reasons contain mostly facts or opinions? _____ Do the reasons provide you with the facts you need to decide if a restaurant is the best in town? No. You have no objective reasons to agree with the author's opinion.

Memory Check 3   How much do you remember?

1. Where is the author's opinion or argument usually found? _____

    _____

2. The major details provide a list of the _____ that support the author's opinion.

3. What are two examples of words or phrases that authors use to state their opinions? _____

4. What are four ways to evaluate the support of an argument?

    a. _____

    b. _____

    c. _____

    d. _____

    _____

5. Create a recall word or sentence to help you remember the four ways to evaluate an opinion. _____

When you hear or read an opinion, it is important to ask yourself how it is supported. If the opinion is only supported by more opinions, then there are no reasons you can use to make an informed decision. By recognizing the difference between facts and opinions, you will be able to evaluate an author's arguments or opinions more effectively.

Learn how to evaluate an argument by answering the questions that follow the paragraph below.

Cameras should be installed at every intersection to catch people who run red lights. They do this in other cities, such as Fenwood and Grendle. Why can't we do it here? Also, it would generate money for the city. Fenwood saves over a million dollars on manpower each year because the police don't have to be at every intersection. The picture of the license plate is the only proof needed. The police just send a ticket to the person who owns the car. Finally, it would save lives. Grendle has reduced the number of accident-related fatalities by 50%. Apparently, drivers in Grendle think twice before running a red light.

Argument	**Main idea:** _____
	_____
Reason	Other cities have cameras.
Reason	_____
Reason	_____

1. Is the author's opinion supported mostly by statements of fact or opinion?

   _____

2. Can you prove that other cities have cameras? _____ You can call other cities to find out.

3. Can you prove that cameras would generate money for the city? _____ You can look at Fenwood Police Department records to see how much money they saved on manpower.

4. Can you prove that it would save lives? _____ How? You can find the data about Grendle's accident fatalities in the state's department of safety records.

5. Who is the author? A private citizen? A city council member who proposed the law? The owner of the company who would provide the cameras if the law is passed? Do you know who the author is? _____ In this case, you are not able to check the knowledge or experience of the author because you don't know who Author 1 is.

Activity 10.3 ▶ Evaluating an Argument

Directions: *Complete the outline of this paragraph. Then, answer the questions that follow it.*

Cameras should be installed at every intersection to catch people who run red lights. First of all, these people make me sick. Who do they think they are?

Also, the police are doing a terrible job of catching these criminals. There's never a cop around when someone runs a red light. Finally, it's obvious that the city doesn't care about our safety. Otherwise, the council members would have installed the cameras a long time ago.

Argument	**Main idea: Cameras should be installed at every intersection to catch people who run red lights.**
Reason	_____
Reason	The police are doing a terrible job of catching these criminals.
Reason	_____

1. What facts does the author provide so that you can make a decision about

   the issue? _____

2. Can you prove any of the statements used to support the opinion? _____

   Why or why not? _____

Objective vs. Subjective Points of View

In college courses you are often asked to read opposing arguments or opinions about a particular issue. You are then asked either to write about your **subjective,** or personal, point of view on a topic to persuade a reader to agree with you or to discuss both sides of an issue from an **objective,** or unbiased, point of view. When you are asked to write objectively, you need to present the facts without adding your opinion so that the reader will be unable to tell which side of the issue you support.

When you are asked to write a persuasive essay or argument paper, you will need to use the facts you have gathered in order to persuade the reader to support your subjective point of view about a particular issue.

Supporting Your Point of View

How can you use facts to present either an objective or a subjective point of view about an issue? Here are four steps you can use to support your point of view more effectively.

1. List the reasons why you are *for* or *against* a particular issue.   For instance, consider the following issue: violent video games and teen violence. Do you think that violent video games cause teen violence? You can list the reasons why you agree (or disagree) that violent video games cause teen violence. For instance, if you agree, you might list the following reasons to support your point of view: "They can make you think that being violent is fun," and "Teens who commit violent acts probably play a lot of violent video games."

2. List the reasons why someone would support the *opposite* point of view.   You want to know what someone who disagrees with you would say about the issue. You want to be ready to defend yourself against the opposing arguments. For instance, if you believe that video games cause teen violence, you can list the following reasons why someone might disagree with your point of view: "Children need to be better supervised," and "Just because one kid who played video games becomes violent doesn't mean all kids will become violent."

3. Gather the facts.   You can gather the facts about an issue from the objective sources mentioned previously such as news articles, eyewitness accounts, quotes from people directly involved, textbooks, interviews, scientific research data, government databases, or historical records. Then, you can add these facts to your own list of reasons to strengthen the support for your argument. You can also look in *editorials*, which are articles that present the opinions of the editors or publishers of newspapers and magazines, to see how authors on both sides of the issue use facts to persuade their readers. You can write questions or comments in the margin when you identify misleading or inaccurate statements. Then, you can plan to find or verify the facts you need to support your own point of view in a more persuasive way. In Figure 10.1 the student has written comments in the margin of an article about video game violence. Notice how the student evaluates the author's reasoning and how he plans to strengthen his or her own argument.

Figure 10.1 Student Example of Notation about Video Game Violence

Pa Leeze Who are <u>you</u> anyway?	Video games are turning our children into violent criminals. I'm a single mother who had to work two jobs to feed my family. My son played Mortal Combat and Grand Theft Auto every day after school from the time he was eight years old until he was arrested for murder at the age of eighteen. I was glad that he was staying at home after school. I thought that these games were just entertaining. I never knew they were training my son how to kill and steal. I would never have purchased these video games for my son had I known the amount of violence they contained.
So? Just because your son became a criminal doesn't mean every child will become one. It's not the video games' fault.	
I guess you didn't supervise your child.	
You should have checked them out before you bought them. DUH!	

I need to:
1. Look up—Facts about Video Games & Violence   2. Find opinions for and against children playing these kind of video games.   3. Look up—Facts about parents' responsibility and video games.

Figure 10.2 shows a paragraph from a paper written by the same student who found a couple of facts to support an opposing point of view to the one in Figure 10.1 on the effects of video game violence. Read the paragraph and answer the questions that follow.

Figure 10.2 Student Example: Opposing Point of View (Subjective)

Violent video games are not responsible for an increase in crime among teenagers. While the Compton study showed that kids responded more aggressively after playing a violent video game, it does not show the long term effects. Just because one child who played violent video games grows up to commit a crime does not mean that all kids will do the same. Also, if parents are concerned about the violence in video games, then they need to do their homework. They should find out what is contained in a particular video game before buying it for their kids. They should monitor what their kids are doing. According to a study reported by Parents Action Magazine "Children who are consistently supervised are less likely to commit crime as teenagers."

1. What is the student's point of view? _____

_____

2. Underline the two facts the student found to include in his argument.

4. Evaluate the facts on both sides of the issue. Did you list more facts on *one side* of the issue than the other? If you need to discuss an issue in an objective way, you should make certain to mention an equal number of facts to support both sides of the argument. In Figure 10.3, the same student has gathered an equal number of facts and reasons to support each side of the issue in an *objective* manner. Read the paragraph then answer the questions that follow it.

Figure 10.3 Student Example: Discussion of Opposing Points of View (Objective)

> There are several reasons why people are for and against the idea that violent video games increase crime among teenagers. Those who believe that violent video games are to blame cite the Compton Study which shows an increase in aggression among children who have just played a violent video game. The study also found that teenagers who play violent video games are 35% more likely to drop out of school before the 11th grade. On the other hand, those who do not believe violent video games are to blame refer to the Parent's Action Magazine study which cites a lack of parental supervision as the primary cause for increased teen violence. In addition, the study linked a lack of "emotionally-supportive communication between parent(s) and child" as a common characteristic of teenagers who commit crime.

1. Is the main idea sentence a statement of fact or opinion? _____

2. The reasons or major details contain mostly facts or opinions? _____

_____ 3. The student presents a point of view that is:
     a. objective.   b. subjective.

Memory Check 4 How much do you remember?

1. What are the four ways to support your arguments more effectively?

    a. _____

    b. _____

    c. _____

    d. _____

2. What are three places where can you find facts about an issue?

    _____

3. What are two places where can you find opposing points of view about an issue?

    _____

4. What is an editorial?

    _____

    _____

Activity 10.4 ▶ Supporting Arguments I

Directions: *Choose ONE of the statements of opinion below. Make a list of three (3) reasons why you agree with the statement or three (3) reasons why you disagree. You can use the objective sources mentioned on p. 361 as well as the* Internet Site List for Factual Sources *below to find at least one fact to support your argument. Then, write a paragraph using your reasons to support the statement you selected.*

- The execution of convicted murderers should be made public.

- A woman does not have the right to kill her unborn child.

- Marijuana is harmless and should be legalized.

Internet Site List for Factual Sources:

www.reference.com Provides factual source references by topic

www.encyclopedia.com Provides factual source references by topic www.cdc.com Website of the Centers for Disease Control

www.bls.gov Website of the U.S. government's Bureau of Labor Statistics

Tips for Reading Visual Aids and Graphics can be found online (URL to come)

1. Why did you choose this topic? _____

2. Were your reasons mostly statements of fact or opinion? _____

3. Where did you find the fact(s) used to support your point of view? _____

_____

_____

Activity 10.5 ▶ Supporting Arguments II

Directions: *Choose one of the opinion statements from Activity 10.4. Find an article on the Internet that supports the author's point of view about the issue. Then, answer the following questions about the article you found on the Internet.*

1. Which statement did you select? _____

2. What is the title of the Internet article and the name of the author who wrote it?

_____

3. How do you know that the author of the Internet article would agree with the

author of the statement you selected? _____

_____

BIAS

The prefix *bi* means "two." There are two sides to every issue. **Bias** is a judgment based on personal preference or opinion. When people are biased, they are "stuck" on one side of an issue. They only present one side of an argument, or they present the other side in a weak or negative way. When authors show preferences in their arguments for one side of an issue or are unable to present both sides equally and fairly, they are showing bias.

We all have our personal preferences and opinions, but when bias interferes with decisions such as hiring or the way the law is applied, it is called *discrimination*. You want to be sure that you can recognize an author's bias as you read. Then, you can develop the ability to discuss an issue objectively and fairly. When you discuss an issue objectively, the reader will be unable to tell which side you prefer.

Read the following paragraph. Is the author presenting both sides of the issue objectively?

> America should not have bombed Iraq. President Bush only went to war because he wants the oil. His friend, Vice President Cheney, has ties to the Halliburton Company. Halliburton was given the contract to rebuild Iraq even before the war began. Now, the innocent lives of our soldiers are being lost every day and all for oil and greed.

What is the issue? Bombing Iraq. What is the main idea of the paragraph?

_____ Is the main idea a statement of opinion or a statement of fact? It is an opinion. Is the author *for* or *against* the bombing in Iraq?

The author is _____ the bombing. Does the author present both sides of the issue equally or objectively? No. You can tell the author is against the bombing of Iraq. So there is bias.

Now read this paragraph.

> Bombing Iraq was the best way to protect the Iraqi people. Saddam Hussein was the most dangerous leader in the Middle East. He and his sons killed thousands of their fellow Iraqi citizens. The CIA had evidence that there were weapons of mass destruction that could be used in terrorist attacks. Removing Saddam Hussein was the best way to protect the Iraqi people as well as the world.

The issue is the same, but this time you can tell the author is *for* the bombing of

Iraq. The main idea is a statement of _____. Does the author present both sides equally or objectively? No. The author only lists the reasons *for* bombing Iraq. So, there is bias.

Look at the way the issue is discussed in the following paragraph.

> America bombed Iraq on March 19, 2003. There are reasons for and against this act. First, President Bush based his decision upon CIA intelligence that indicated Iraq had weapons of mass destruction. This meant that Iraq had violated an agreement with the United Nations not to have such weapons. The United Nations as well as some Americans opposed the attack because the actual weapons were not found. Yet other Americans, as well as the British Prime Minister, Tony Blair, were convinced that Saddam Hussein posed too great a danger to risk what they saw as his ability to use weapons of mass destruction at any time. Secondly, some Americans believed the president acted in America's self-interest to gain control of the rich oil reserves in Iraq. Others felt that it was his duty to protect our country, the world, and the Iraqi people from a leader who seemed to be a possible terrorist threat.

What is the main idea of the paragraph? _____

_____ Is the main idea a statement of fact or opinion?

It is a statement of _____. Does the author present one side as being better than the other side of the issue? No. Both sides of the issue are presented equally. You can't tell which side the author favors. The author has presented the issue objectively without an opinion. There is no bias.

Recognizing Bias

If you can identify an author's opinion, then you can recognize bias. To recognize bias, you should ask the following questions as you read about an issue.

1. Is the main idea sentence a statement of opinion? If the main idea sentence is an opinion, then you know you have found bias. When authors have a preference for one side of an issue, they often make it known in their main idea sentence. For example, suppose you are reading about the issue of abortion and the main idea sentence is: "Abortion should be illegal because it kills innocent babies." Is the main idea an *opinion*? Yes. Could someone have an *opposite* viewpoint? Yes. Then, the author is showing bias.

Now consider the difference in the following main idea sentence about the same issue. "There are several reasons for the controversy surrounding the issue of abortion." Is this main idea sentence a statement of fact or opinion? It is a statement of fact. There is no bias.

2. Is the author for or against one side of an issue? Often, the main idea sentence tells you when the author is for or against one side of an issue. You can also look for value words such as *best, better*, or *worse* in the list of major details. If you can tell that the author is for one side of an issue, then you have found bias. If you can tell that the author is against one side of an issue, then you have found bias.

3. Are both sides presented objectively? When authors are presenting an issue objectively, without bias, you should not be able to tell which side of the issue they prefer. The main idea sentence is a statement of *fact*. The major details present an equal number of *facts* on both sides of the issue. There is no emotion in the statements used to support the main idea.

On the other hand, when authors show bias they will only present one side of an issue. They don't present both sides equally. Also, when authors are being subjective or emotional about which side of an issue they prefer, they may criticize anyone who disagrees with them. If both sides are not treated equally, then you have found bias. For example, here is a statement about the legalization of marijuana:

People who think that marijuana should be legalized have been smoking pot too long.

Is the author is treating both sides equally? No. The author is showing bias by criticizing those who disagree with his or her opinion on the issue.

Now consider the difference in the following sentence:

Some people believe the legalization of marijuana would benefit those with medical needs, while others believe legalization would encourage the use of more dangerous drugs.

Is the author treating both sides equally and fairly? Yes. There is no bias.

Memory Check 5   How much do you remember?

1. What is bias? _____

2. What are three questions that will help you to recognize bias?

    a. _____

    b. _____

    c. _____

Activity 10.6 ▶ Thinking on Both Sides 1

Directions: *Read the arguments below. List two reasons to support each side of each argument. Identify each reason as a statement of fact (F) or as an opinion (O). Then, answer the questions that follow.*

1. Welfare is another form of slavery.

Reasons for Welfare	**Reasons against Welfare**
A. _____	A. _____
_____ F/O _____	_____ F/O _____
B. _____	B. _____
_____ F/O _____	_____ F/O _____

2. A woman does not have the right to kill her unborn child.

Reasons for Abortion

A. _____

_____ F/O _____

B. _____

_____ F/O _____

Reasons against Abortion

A. _____

_____ F/O _____

B. _____

_____ F/O _____

3. Marijuana is harmless and should be legalized.

Reasons for Legalization of Marijuana

A. _____

_____ F/O _____

B. _____

_____ F/O _____

Reasons against Legalization of Marijuana

A. _____

_____ F/O _____

B. _____

_____ F/O _____

4. The execution of convicted murderers should be made public.

Reasons for Public Executions

A. _____

_____ F/O _____

B. _____

_____ F/O _____

Reasons against Public Executions

A. _____

_____ F/O _____

B. _____

_____ F/O _____

5. Do your reasons contain mostly statements of fact or opinion? _____

_____

6. On a separate sheet of paper, list two objective sources where you could find facts to strengthen the support for each of your arguments.

Activity 10.7 ▶ Thinking on Both Sides 2

Directions: *Choose ONE of the statements from Activity 10.6 and write an objective paragraph comparing the facts or reasons you have listed on both sides of the issue using the format below. See if you can discuss the issue without showing which side of the issue you prefer.*

The issue of _____ has been debated for years. Some
people believe that (state one reason for the issue) _____
They also refer to (source of fact) which states that (state a fact for the issue)
_____ Those who disagree with the issue of (issue)
believe that (state one reason against the issue) _____
They cite (source of fact) which states that (state a fact against the issue)
_____

In college, you will be asked to write objectively about a variety of issues. By
recognizing bias, you will be able to present the facts that support both sides of an
issue equally and fairly.

DEDUCTIVE AND INDUCTIVE REASONING

Deductive Reasoning

The prefix *de* means "down" or "away." The root *duct* means "to lead." In **deductive**
reasoning, you are *leading down* from a list of reasons to prove the claim of an
argument.

Here is a variation of a famous example of deductive reasoning.

Since all men die	Reason 1
and	+
since Joe is a man	Reason 2
what will happen to Joe?	=
_____	Conclusion

In deductive reasoning, the evidence is used to prove what you claim to be true. The
evidence is *necessary* to support the argument.

Inductive Reasoning

Inductive means to "lead into." In **inductive** reasoning you are *led into* a conclusion
as the evidence or facts come together. The conclusion depends upon the amount of
evidence you have so far. Finding the cause of a problem or inferring who might
have killed the butler in a mystery novel are examples of inductive reasoning. In
inductive reasoning, however, you infer probable conclusions that you test as the
evidence is being presented. Here is an example of someone who used inductive
reasoning to reach a conclusion.

Last year I got sick after eating the shrimp at Crazy Joe's. I thought I was
allergic to shrimp. Or, maybe I had the flu. In March, I got sick again after

having a hamburger at Crazy Joe's. When Della held her bachelorette party there, I only had drinks. Everyone else became violently ill.

What can you conclude about Crazy Joe's? _____

_____ How did you form this conclusion? You inferred a conclusion from the series of events. These events lead you to the conclusion that Crazy Joe's is a dirty, unsafe place to eat.

Deductive and inductive reasoning skills work together in the critical thinking process. You use inductive reasoning to test the possible solutions to solve a particular problem. Then, you use deductive reasoning to support what you think using logic and evidence.

ERRORS IN REASONING

The ability to use sound reasoning to support an argument is at the foundation of all academic studies. These studies are based upon the idea that thinking is an art. Your ability to recognize common errors in reasoning can help you to evaluate the arguments of others, as well as your own, more effectively.

As you progress through college, you will become more involved in analyzing the reasoning of authors, especially the deductive reasoning they use to support arguments. You will need to know how an author got from point A to point B to arrive at a particular conclusion. You will also need to be able to recognize when the process of someone's reasoning is logical and when it is not. Did the author add one and one and get two? Or did the author get fifteen?

You can identify errors in reasoning by looking closely at each reason an author uses to lead you to a particular conclusion. Here is an example of deductive reasoning used to support an argument:

Reason 1	because the service is excellent
Reason 2	because they only use fresh ingredients
Conclusion	Tony's is a great restaurant.

The reasoning is logical because the reasons or facts directly support the conclusion. Can you correctly deduce that Tony's is a great restaurant from the reasons given? Sure. Errors in reasoning occur in an argument or conclusion when it is not supported in a logical way. The reasons do not lead to the conclusion in a way that makes sense.

For instance, notice the reasoning used in the following example:

Reason 1	because it's called "Italiano's"
Reason 2	because it's a great restaurant
Reason 3	because we went to an Italiano's in another city and it was good
Conclusion	Italiano's is the best Italian restaurant in town.

Look at the reasons used to support the previous conclusion or argument. Do they support the conclusion or argument in a logical way? No. There are errors in reasoning.

Look at the first reason and ask yourself Why is Italiano's the best Italian restaurant in town? Can you say Italiano's is the best Italian restaurant in town just because it's called *Italiano's*? No. The author assumes all restaurants with an Italian name have the best Italian food.

Now look at the second reason and ask yourself Why is Italiano's the best Italian restaurant in town? Can you say Italiano's is the best Italian restaurant in town because it is a great restaurant? No. The author just says the same thing as the conclusion or argument.

Finally, look at the third reason. Can you say Italiano's is the best Italian restaurant in town because someone went to another restaurant with the same name in another city and it was a good place to eat? No. The author assumes one situation will apply in the same way to another.

Recognizing Common Errors in Reasoning

How can you develop the ability to recognize errors in reasoning when you read? Look at each reason and ask yourself the following questions:

1. Does the author assume *all* people act the same way?

2. Does the author just *restate* the argument?

3. Does the author use reasons that support one situation as if they apply *equally* to another situation?

4. Does the author assume there is only one *choice*?

Here are four of the most common errors in reasoning and the questions you should ask to find them.

1. Hasty Generalizations

Question to ask: Does the author assume *all* people act the same way?

Hasty means "fast, quick, or without much thought." A **hasty generalization** is a conclusion based on one or two examples usually referring to a group as if all members are alike in some way. Stereotypes are a good example of hasty generalization. For example: *All* blonds are dumb, *everyone* of Asian descent is good in math, *everyone* who is gay would make an excellent fashion designer, *all* African Americans can sing and dance, *all* people of Scottish origin are cheap, *all* men cheat on their wives, or *all* women are money hungry.

What's wrong with the reasoning in these conclusions or argument? Notice the words in italics in each statement. When authors make such statements, they are assuming that since they know or have heard of a few people who fit a certain description, it must be true for *everyone* in that group.

Racial profiling is based on stereotypes and is another form of hasty generalization. Racial profiling can be seen in law enforcement when certain people are suspected of a crime based upon the way they look or because they fit a stereotype or profile of a criminal.

When authors use the words *all* or *everyone* to refer to a particular group, ask yourself: Do all people act the same way? If the answer is NO, then you have found hasty generalization.

Memory Check 6 How much do you remember?

1. What is hasty generalization? _____

   _____

2. What is one example of hasty generalization? _____

   _____

3. What two words will help you recognize hasty generalizations? _____

4. What should you ask when an author uses the words *all* or *everyone* to refer

   to a particular group? _____

---

2. Circular Logic

Question to Ask: Does the author only *restate* the argument?

Circular logic refers to reasoning that says the same thing as the conclusion of the argument. The reasoning leads the reader around in a circle without saying anything new. For instance,

Abortion should remain a legal choice for women, because it's not against the law.

Abortion is against God's law, because it's a sin.

What's wrong with the reasoning in these arguments? The reasons just restate the argument claims. When authors make such statements, it usually means they have not thought about facts to support their arguments. Ask yourself: Does the author only restate the claim of the argument? If so, then it is circular logic.

3. False Comparison

Question to Ask: Does the author use reasons that support one situation as if they apply *equally* to another situation?

False comparison refers to using a reason that applies to one situation to support another, different one. Here is an example of false comparison.

Sara tells her parents, *I should be allowed to go out of town* with my boyfriend because *Marsha's parents let her go out of town* with her boyfriend.

What's wrong with the reasoning in this argument? In this reasoning, two different situations are treated as being the same in order to support an argument. Marsha's parents and their decision have nothing to do with the decisions Sara's parents should make. Just because it's okay in another situation doesn't mean it's okay in this situation. You cannot apply the same reasons to both situations equally.

Some people use false comparison when they want to justify doing something they shouldn't be doing. For instance, a person who smokes may use the following reasoning:

I know a smoker who lived to be one hundred years old.

Or

My brother, Richard has smoked for years and he's never gotten lung cancer.

So, it's okay if I smoke.

The person has wrongly compared one situation to their own in order to support the argument that it's okay to smoke. Just because Richard never got cancer doesn't mean someone else won't get lung cancer.

When an author supports an argument by referring to a separate situation, you should ask yourself: Does the author use reasons that support a separate situation as if they apply *equally* to this situation? If the answer is yes, then you have found a false comparison.

Memory Check 7   How much do you remember?

1. What is circular logic? _____

   _____

2. What is an example of circular logic? _____

   _____

3. What should you ask if a reason sounds very similar to the point an author is

   trying to make? _____

4. What is false comparison? _____

   _____

5. What is one example of false comparison? _____

_____

6. What should you ask if an author refers to a separate situation to support

his or her argument? _____

_____

4. Either/Or Fallacy

Question to ask: Does the author assume there is *only one option available*?

Fallacy means "false" or "incorrect." An **either/or fallacy** refers to a conclusion that assumes there is only one choice available in the reasoning process. For instance,

Either I pass this test, *or* I am a failure.

Either he asks me out to dinner, *or* he doesn't, which means that I am worthless.

You are *either* against the war in Iraq, *or* you are foolish and misinformed.

The *only* way to get hired at that company is to lie on the application."

(In other words, *either* lie on the application *or* don't get hired.)

What's wrong with the reasoning that supports these arguments? The reasons assume that there is only one option available. When people make such statements, they are showing that they have not considered other solutions or possibilities. When an author presents an all-or-nothing point of view, you should ask yourself: "Does the author assume there is only one choice?" If the answer is yes, then you have found an either/or fallacy.

Now see if you can identify the errors in reasoning made by the members of a group in an English class assigned to complete the parts of an essay. They need one more person and are trying to decide if they should ask Joe.

Argument: We should ask Joe to join our essay writing group for English class.

Jesse's Reason: He got an A on the last algebra exam.

    1. Error: _____

Jeremy's Reason: We really need Joe in our group.

    2. Error: _____

Cammy's Reason: Either he joins our group, or we will fail.

    3. Error: _____

Teri's Reason: He's from England.

4. Error: _____

Lena's Reason: We need one more person to complete our group.

5. Error _____

What does Joe's performance on an algebra exam have to do with his performance on an essay writing assignment? Does the reason apply equally to this situation? No. So it is a false comparison. Reason two is a restatement of the opinion and is an example of circular logic. Look at reason three. Does the reason assume there is only one choice? Yes. Reason three is an example of either/or fallacy. Are all people from England good writers? No. So, reason four is an example of hasty generalization. Reason five just restates the conclusion, so it is an example of circular logic.

Memory Check 8   How much do you remember?

1. What is an either/or fallacy? _____

_____

2. What is one example of an either/or fallacy? _____

_____

3. What question should you ask when an author provides only one solution?

_____

Match the four common errors in reasoning with the questions you can ask to identify each one.

_____ 4. Circular Logic

_____ 5. Hasty Generalization

_____ 6. Either/Or Fallacy

_____ 7. False Comparison

a. Does the author use reasons that support one situation as if they apply equally to another situation?

b. Does the author assume all people act the same way?

c. Does the author assume there is only one option available?

d. Does the author just restate the claim of the argument?

8. What is an example of deductive reasoning? _____

_____

9. What is an example of inductive reasoning? _____

_____

Activity 10.8 ▶ Identifying Errors in Reasoning

Directions: *Read each statement. Then, identify the errors in reasoning as being hasty generalization, circular logic, false comparison, or either/or fallacy.*

1. Spanking is the only way to teach a child the difference between right and wrong.

   _____

2. Everything on the Internet is true.

   _____

3. We should not have executions because it is wrong to put people to death.

   _____

4. I can't go to the party because I'm not able to go.

   _____

5. You can't trust a man to be faithful.

   _____

6. I can miss class because Doris missed two days and got a B on the test.

   _____

7. Either Ramon calls me tonight, or I'll know that he doesn't care about me anymore.

   _____

8. Kathy tried cocaine and she didn't become an addict.

   _____

9. China Hop is the best Chinese restaurant in town because it has an Asian name.

   _____

10. Little Vienna's is the best Italian restaurant in town because it's a great restaurant.

   _____

Activity 10.9 ▸ Recognizing Statements of Fact and Opinion: Textbook Applications

Directions: *Apply the concepts you have learned in this chapter to answer the questions after each of the following paragraphs.*

Paragraph 1

No love relationship comes with a guarantee, no matter how many promises have been made by partners to be together forever. Losing a love is as much a part of life as falling in love. That being said, the uncoupling process can be very painful. Whenever we risk getting close to another, we also risk being hurt if things don't work out. Remember that knowing, understanding, and feeling good about oneself before entering a relationship is very important.

—From *Access to Health*, 10th ed. by Rebecca J. Donatelle. p. 163.

1. What is the author's main point or conclusion? _____

_____

2. List three reasons that support the author's main point or conclusion.

Reason 1: _____

Reason 2: _____

Reason 3: _____

_____ 3. The author supports her main point or conclusion by using mostly statements of:
   a. fact.   b. opinion.

Paragraph 2

As you look around, you can see that the living world is constantly changing. You see changes with the seasons. In most parts of the country, there are lots of houseflies in summer and few in winter. You see changes over the years. Houseflies may be much more numerous in one summer than in another. And you know that changes have occurred over still longer periods of time. The dinosaurs and flying reptiles of the past have given way to the mammals and birds of the present. Some changes are the result of human activity. We build cities, plant forests, and harvest crops.

—From *Biological Science: An Ecological Approach.* 4th ed.
BSCS Green Version. p. 5.

4. What is the author's main point or conclusion? _____

_____

5. List three reasons that support the author's main point or conclusion.

Reason 1: _____

Reason 2: _____

Reason 3: _____

_____ 6. The author supports his or her main point or conclusion by using mostly statements of:
   a. fact.   b. opinion.

Paragraph 3

Burr's lawyers were brilliant and cutting in their cross-examination of government witnesses. Burr, acting as his own counsel, was even more brilliant and more cutting. One by one, the prosecution witnesses were broken. One had to admit, under Burr's questioning, that he had just been paid $10,000 by the government. Another ended by testifying for Burr; he admitted that, as far as he knew, Burr's force had been gathered for use only if the United States declared war against Spain. A third testified against Burr, only to have his own son follow him to the stand to swear that his father was "old and infirm, and like other old men, told long stories and was apt to forget his repetitions." Another witness, who knew Blennerhassett well, revealed that Blennerhassett was so nearsighted that it was ridiculous to imagine his participating in a military action.

—From *The Pursuit of Liberty: A History of the American People.* 3rd ed. vol. I
p. 268. R. Jackson Wilson, et al.

7. What is the author's main point or conclusion? _____

_____

8. List three reasons that support the author's main point or conclusion.

Reason 1: _____

Reason 2: _____

_____

Reason 3: _____

_____

_____

_____ 9. The author supports his or her main point or conclusion by using mostly statements of:

    a. fact.   b. opinion.

Paragraph 4

    The electronic revolution may well change the role of public space in stimulating communication (Drucker & Gumpert, 1991; Gumpert & Drucker, 1995). For example, home shopping clubs make it less necessary for people to go downtown or to the mall, and shoppers consequently have less opportunity to run into other people and to talk and exchange news. Similarly, electronic mail permits us to communicate without talking and without leaving the house to mail a letter. Perhaps the greatest change is telecommuting (Giordano, 1989), in which workers can go to work without leaving their homes. The face-to-face communication that normally takes place in an office is replaced by communication via computer.

> —From *Human Communication: The Basic Course*, 10th Ed. by
> Joseph A. DeVito p. 143. New York, NY: Allyn and Bacon, 2006

10. What is the author's main point or conclusion? _____

_____

11. List three reasons that support the author's main point or conclusion.

    Reason 1: _____

_____

_____

    Reason 2: _____

_____

    Reason 3: _____

_____

_____ 12. The author supports his main point or conclusion by using mostly statements of:

    a. fact.   b. opinion.

Paragraph 5

Viruses that have appeared suddenly or have recently come to the attention of medical scientists are referred to as **emerging viruses.** HIV, the AIDS virus, is a classic example: This virus appeared in San Francisco in the early 1980s, seemingly out of nowhere. The deadly Ebola virus, recognized initially in 1976 in central Africa, is one of several emerging viruses that cause hemorrhagic fever, an often fatal syndrome characterized by fever, vomiting, massive bleeding, and circulatory system collapse. A number of other dangerous new viruses cause encephalitis, inflammation of the brain. One example is the West Nile virus, which appeared for the first time in North America in 1999 and had spread to all 48 contiguous U.S. states by the end of 2004.

—From *Biology: Concepts & Connections.* 5th ed. by Neil A. Campbell, Jane Reece [et al] p. 202.

13. What is the author's main point or conclusion? _____

_____

14. List three reasons that support the author's main point or conclusion.

Reason 1: _____

_____

Reason 2: _____

Reason 3: _____

_____ 15. The author supports his main point or conclusion by using mostly statements of:
    a. fact.   b. opinion.

? Test Yourself Review Quiz

Chapter Review Questions

1. A fact is a statement that can be _____ to be true or false.

2. An opinion is a statement that _____ be proven.

3. _____ is a judgment or opinion based on personal preference.

4. What are four ways to evaluate the support of an argument?

    a. _____

    b. _____

    c. _____

    d. _____

    _____

5. What are four ways to support your arguments more effectively?

    a. _____

    b. _____

    c. _____

    d. _____

Identify the following as statements of fact (F) or opinion (O).

_____ 6. Slim Jay is the only rapper who knows how to bust a rhyme.

_____ 7. The Players are performing at the City Arena on Saturday night.

_____ 8. Two hundred security guards were hired for the Slim Jay concert.

_____ 9. Rap is better than jazz.

_____ 10. Poetry forms the foundation of rap.

Identify the error in reasoning in the following statements.

_____ 11. Unfortunately, because we are females, we don't know anything about cars.

    a. either/or fallacy.   c. hasty generalization

    b. false comparison   d. circular logic

_____ 12. If I don't get this job, my life is ruined.

    a. either/or fallacy   c. hasty generalization

    b. false comparison   d. circular logic

Application Questions

A. *Read the following editorial. Then answer the questions that follow.*

We should impose a 10 P.M. curfew for all children under the age of eighteen. First of all, children need to be off the streets after 10 P.M. They need to be home, safe with their families. Second, the curfew would reduce crime. The cops would be able to spot teenagers after 10 P.M. more easily. Grendle reduced crime by 30% in the first six months after they imposed their curfew.

1. What is the author's opinion? _____

_____

2. List the reasons that support the author's opinion.

   Reason 1: _____

   Reason 2: _____

3. Which of the author's reasons is an example of circular logic? _____

_____ 4. The author:

   a. presents both sides objectively.   b. shows bias.

_____ 5. T/F The author has a subjective point of view.

B. *Read the following textbook excerpt. Then, answer the questions that follow.*

Gender Inequality in Everyday Life

Of the many aspects of gender discrimination in everyday life that we could examine, we have space to look only at two: the general devaluation of femininity in U.S. society, and male dominance of conversation.

General Devaluation of Things Feminine

Leaning against the water cooler, two men—both minor executives—are nursing their cups of coffee, discussing last Sunday's Giants game, postponing for as long as possible the moment when work must finally be faced.

A [male] vice president walks by and hears them talking about sports. Does he stop and send them back to their desks? Does he frown? Probably not. Being a man, he is far more likely to pause and join in the conversation, anxious to prove that he, too, is "one of the boys," feigning an interest in football that he may very well not share at all. These men—all the men in the office—are his troops, his comrades-in arms.

Now, let's assume that two women are standing by the water cooler discussing whatever you please: women's liberation, clothes, work, any subject—except football, of course. The vice president walks by, sees them, and moves down the hall in a fury, cursing and wondering whether it is worth the trouble to complain—but to whom?—about all those bitches standing around gabbing when they should be working. "Don't they know," he will ask, in the words of a million men, "that this is an office?" (Korda 1973: 20–21)

Gender Inequality in Conversation   You may have noticed that men are more likely than women to interrupt conversations. They also are more likely to control changes in topics. Sociologists note that talk between a man and a woman is often more like talk between an employer and an employee than between social equals (West and Garcia 1988; Smith-Lovin and Brody 1989; Tannen 1990, 2003). In short, conversations between men and women mirror their relative positions of power in society.

—From Henslin, James M. *Sociology: A Down-to-Earth Approach,*
Core Concepts, 1e. Published by Allyn and Bacon, Boston, MA.
Copyright © 2006 by Pearson Education. Reprinted by
permission of the publisher.

6. What is the author's main point or conclusion? _____

_____

_____

_____ 7. The author supports his main point or conclusion by using mostly statements of:

    a. fact.   b. opinion.

_____ 8. The examples provided in the excerpt may be used to illustrate which of the following errors in reasoning?

    a. circular logic   c. hasty generalization

    b. either/or fallacy   d. false comparison

Summarization Activity

Directions: *Write the major headings in this chapter. Under each heading, write a couple of sentences about the most important topics presented in the section of text that follows that heading.*

First Heading _____

What information is most important? _____

_____

_____

Second Heading _____

What information is most important? _____

_____

_____

Third Heading _____

What information is most important? _____

_____

_____

Fourth Heading _____

What information is most important? _____

_____

_____

Fifth Heading _____

What information is most important? _____

_____

_____

Combine the information you wrote in this outline into a paragraph to summarize what you have learned in this chapter.

Reflection Activity

How am I am going to apply what I have learned in this chapter?

Directions: *On a separate sheet of paper, write a paragraph about the two or three things you learned about evaluating arguments and critical thinking that were most helpful to you and how you plan to use what you have learned.*

WHAT DOES SPANKING TEACH YOUR CHILD?
Mark Brandenburg

Accessing Prior Knowledge

Questions for Discussion:

1. Were you spanked as a child? If you were, do you think it had a positive effect in your upbringing or do you think it was used too often for the wrong reasons?

2. If you were not spanked as a child, would you support a law that would make spanking illegal? Why or why not?

3. Do you think that there is a growing trend against spanking? If so, what would you say is the reason, or reasons, for this trend?

Preview and Predict

Directions: *Look at the title of the selection. Think about what you already know about the subject. Then, write a couple of predictions about what you are going to read. For instance, is the author for or against spanking?*

1. _____

2. _____

Word Search and Discovery

Directions: *Skim through the selection to find the two words below. Underline both words in the selection. Then, use a dictionary to write their definitions in the spaces provided. As you read and encounter these words, see if the definitions you wrote fit the way each word is used in the selection.*

condone (*vt*): _____

rod (*n*): _____

Also, underline at least one new word as you read the selection and write your guess as to its meaning in the right margin of the text.

Text Notes in Practice

Directions: *Use a textbook study method such as SQUARE to identify the most important information in the selection. Then, create a study guide that you can use to prepare for the questions that follow the selection.*

WHAT DOES SPANKING TEACH YOUR CHILD?
Mark Brandenburg

Spare the rod, spoil the child.

1   This philosophy's been around a long time. In fact, a study done by *Zero to Three*, a nonprofit child development group, found that 61 percent of the adults who responded condone spanking as a regular form of punishment. The percentage of parents who actually use spanking is believed to be much higher. And when my five-year-old son's behavior went beyond annoying a few days ago, I felt inclined to join the majority and swat him to "teach him a lesson."

2   Most parents reach this point with their kids. We feel as though we can't take any more of what our kids are dishing out. It usually happens when we're tired, stressed and overdone.

3   So what are our choices when we reach this point?

What Are You Teaching?

4   Spanking certainly can take care of things quickly and can temporarily change your kids' behavior. But there are many reasons to question the practice of spanking your kids. Here are five of them.

Do You Really Want Your Kids to Be Afraid of You?

5   Kids will sometimes obey more readily when they're afraid of you. Is this what you really want? What happens when they're six feet two inches and 200 pounds? Effective parenting is based on love and respect, not fear.

Spanking Shows Your Kids That You Lack Self-Control

6   The huge majority of spanking incidents happen when a parent is angry. What is quite clear to your child is this: when my Dad and Mom get angry, they hit me. So when the same child hits his sister when he gets angry, do you demand that he show better self-control? Something's wrong with this picture. We teach our kids best through our own actions.

You May Breed Resentment and Anger in Your Kids

7   Kids who are spanked usually don't learn a great deal about "correcting" their misbehavior. They don't usually sit in their rooms and say, "Gosh, I can really see after getting spanked that I was wrong. I'll do better now." They do think about how angry their Dad or Mom is, and they can develop a good deal of resentment for their parents.

Spanking Shows Your Kids That "Might Makes Right"

8   Adults make mistakes in their lives too, right? Can we use our imaginations and feel what it would be like for someone four times our size to pick us up and

swat us on the butt? What would we learn from that? Would we feel any injustice? You can bet that your kids are feeling some.

Spanking Isn't Effective in the Long Run

9   Parents who are asked why they spank report that they use spanking to "teach their kids a lesson" or so that they won't misbehave again. Many kids who are spanked go underground with their misbehavior and become more cunning to avoid being caught. (Wouldn't you?) If you're spanking your kids fairly often, doesn't this show that it's not working very well?

Alternative Solutions

10   I don't believe that kids who are spanked occasionally are ruined for life, nor do I believe that spanking is necessary to discipline a child. There are countless examples of disciplined and responsible young people who were never spanked by their parents.

11   Parents who don't spank their kids use time outs, re-directing or distraction with their kids. They pick their kids up and let them cool down, or simply leave the area themselves so they don't do something they'll regret later. While these methods aren't always perfect, they help to form the foundation of a certain kind of household— one in which violence is not "taught" as a means to better behavior.

12   After all, we live in a world that's filled with violence. Can't we provide a place for our kids where there isn't any?

Mark Brandenburg, MA, CPCC, CSC, is an author, speaker, and certified relationship coach. He has worked with individuals, teams, and families to improve their lives for more than 20 years. He is the author of a number of books for men, including *25 Secrets of Emotionally Intelligent Fathers*. Mark coaches parents from around the country through weekly telephone coaching sessions on balancing their lives and improving their parenting. He runs workshops and gives presentations for fathers and for parents that are enthusiastically received, as well as teleclasses for parents at MarkBrandenburg.com.

The Write Connection

Directions: *Write a paragraph about three things you learned or that you think are most important in the reading selection.*

_____

_____

_____

_____

_____

Comprehension Check

Directions: *See how many questions you can answer without referring to the selection. Then, review the selection to write more complete responses.*

1. What is the topic of the selection? _____

2. Is the author for or against spanking children? _____

_____ 3. Which of the following statements represents an opinion rather than a fact?
   a. A study done by *Zero to Three*, a nonprofit child development group, found that 61 percent of the adults who responded condone spanking as a regular form of punishment.
   b. Mark Brandenburg, MA, CPCC, CSC, is an author, speaker, and certified relationship coach.
   c. If you're spanking your kids fairly often, doesn't this show that it's not working very well?
   d. Parents who are asked why they spank report that they use spanking to "teach their kids a lesson" or so that they won't misbehave again.

4. What knowledge or experience does the author have about the issue? _____

   _____.

_____ 5. According to the author, what is one alternative solution to spanking?
   a. use a rod   c. teach them a lesson
   b. time out   d. corporal punishment

6. What is the author's argument against parents wanting their children to be

   afraid of them? _____

   _____

7. What is the error in reasoning contained in the following statement? "Children

   who are spanked will grow up to hurt their parents." _____

Critical Thinking Check

1. Do you believe that parents are abusing their children when they use spanking

   as a form of punishment? Why or Why not? _____

   _____

   _____

2. Has your point of view about spanking changed after reading the selection? Provide at least two examples from the selection to support your reasons why

or why not. _____

_____

_____

Vocabulary Check

Directions: *See if any of the words you underlined in the selection are among the list of words below. If not, write your words in the spaces provided. Guess the meaning of the words from the way they were used in the selection. Then, look up the definition of each word in the dictionary to see if you were right.*

cunning (*adj*): Your guess: _____

    Dictionary Definition: _____

distraction (*n*): Your guess: _____

    Dictionary Definition: _____

Your word: _____ Your guess: _____

    Dictionary Definition: _____

Your word: _____ Your guess: _____

    Dictionary Definition: _____

"Seven Forms of Bias" From *Teachers, School, and Society*, 6th ed.

Myra Pollack Sadker and David Miller Sadker

Accessing Prior Knowledge

Questions for Discussion

1. Do you know someone who can persuade others to dislike a particular person? If so, what kinds of things does this person do?

2. How do you think a history text could make a particular culture, race, or heritage seem unimportant, powerless, or undesirable?

Preview and Predict

Directions: *Look at the title of the selection. Think about what you already know about the subject. Then, write a couple of predictions about what you are going to read. For instance, what will the author discuss about bias?*

1. _____

2. _____

Word Search and Discovery

Directions: *Skim through the selection to find the two words below. Underline both words in the selection. Then, use a dictionary to write their definitions in the spaces provided. As you read and encounter these words, see if the definitions you wrote fit the way each word is used in the selection.*

exclusion (*n*): _____

perpetuate (*vb*): _____

Also, underline at least one new word as you read the selection and write your guess as to its meaning in the right margin of the text.

Text Notes in Practice

Directions: *Use a textbook study method such as SQUARE to identify the most important information in the selection. Then, create a study guide that you can use to prepare for the questions that follow the selection.*

SEVEN FORMS OF BIAS

Myra Pollack Sadler and David Miller Sadler

1   Many Americans are passionate about how various groups are portrayed in textbooks. In the 1970s and 1980s, textbook companies and professional associations, such as the American Psychological Association, issued guidelines for nonracist and nonsexist books; as a result, textbooks became more balanced in their description of underrepresented groups. Today, educators work to detect underrepresentation of those groups.

2   Following is a description of seven forms of bias, which can be used to assess instructional materials. Although this approach has been used to identify bias against females and various racial and ethnic groups, it can also help identify bias against the elderly, people with disabilities, non-English speakers, gays and lesbians, limited English speakers, and other groups.

Invisibility

3   Perhaps the most fundamental form of bias in instructional materials is the complete or relative exclusion of a particular group or groups from representation in text narrative or illustrations. Research suggests, for example, that textbooks published prior to the 1960s largely omitted any consideration of African-Americans within contemporary society and, indeed, rendered them relatively invisible in accounts of or references to the United States after Reconstruction. Latinos, Asian-Americans, and Native Americans were largely absent from most resources as well. Many studies indicate that women, who constitute more than 51 percent of the U.S. population, represented approximately 30 percent of the persons or characters referred to throughout the textbooks in most subject areas.

Stereotyping

4   By assigning rigid roles or characteristics to all members of a group, individual attributes and differences are denied. While stereotypes can be positive, they are more often negative. Some typical stereotypes include:

5
- African-Americans as servants, manual workers, professional athletes, troublemakers

- Asian-Americans as laundry workers, cooks, or scientists

- Mexican-Americans as non-English speakers or migrant workers

- Middle-class Americans in the dominant culture as successful in their professional and personal lives

- Native Americans as "blood-thirsty savages" or "noble sons and daughters of the earth"

- Men in traditional occupational roles and as strong and assertive

- Women as passive and dependent and defined in terms of their home and family roles

Imbalance and Selectivity

6   Curriculum may perpetuate bias by presenting only one interpretation of an issue, a situation, or a group of people. These imbalanced accounts simplify and distort complex issues by omitting different perspectives. Examples include:

7   • The origins of European settlers in the New World are emphasized, while the origins and heritage of other racial and ethnic groups are omitted.

- The history of the relations between Native Americans and the federal government is described in terms of treaties and "protection," omitting broken treaties and progressive government appropriation of Native American lands.

- Sources refer to the fact that women were "given" the vote but omit the physical abuse and sacrifices suffered by the leaders of the suffrage movement that "won" the vote.

- Literature is drawn primarily from Western male authors.

- Math and science courses reference only European discoveries and formulas.

Unreality

8   Many researchers have noted the tendency of instructional materials to ignore facts that are unpleasant or that indicate negative positions or actions by individual leaders or the nation as a whole. By ignoring the existence of prejudice, racism, discrimination, exploitation, oppression, sexism, and intergroup conflict and bias, we deny children the information they need to recognize, understand, and perhaps some day conquer the problems that plague society. Examples of unreality may be found in programs that portray:

9   • People of color and women as having economic and political equality with white males.

- Technology as the resolution of all our persistent social problems.

Fragmentation and Isolation

10   Bias through fragmentation or isolation primarily takes two forms. First, content regarding certain groups may be physically or visually fragmented and delivered separately (for example, a chapter on "Bootleggers, Suffragettes, and Other Diversions"). Second, racial and ethnic group members may be depicted as interacting only with persons like themselves, isolated from other cultural communities. Fragmentation and isolation ignore dynamic group relationships and suggest that nondominant groups are peripheral members of society.

Linguistic Bias

11   Language is a powerful conveyor of bias in instructional materials, in both blatant and subtle forms. Written and verbal communication reflects the discriminatory nature of the dominant language. Linguistic bias issues include race or ethnicity, gender, accents, age disability, and sexual orientation—for example,

12   • Native Americans are frequently referred to as "roaming," "wandering," or "roving" across the land. These terms might be used to apply to buffalo or wolves; they suggest a merely physical relationship to the land, rather than a social or purposeful relation. Such language implicitly justifies the seizure of native lands by "more goal-directed" white Americans who "traveled" or "settled" their way westward.

   • Such words as *forefathers, mankind,* and *businessman* deny the contribution and existence of females.

13   The insistence that we live in an English only, monolingual society creates bias against non-English speakers in this country and abroad. An imbalance of word order ("boys and girls") and a lack of parallel terms ("girls and young men") are also forms of linguistic bias.

Cosmetic Bias

14   Cosmetic bias offers the appearance of an up-to-date, well-balanced curriculum. The problem is that, beyond the superficial appearance, bias persists. Cosmetic bias emerges in a science textbook that features a glossy pullout of female scientists but includes precious little narrative of the scientific contributions of women. A music book with an eye-catching, multiethnic cover that projects a world of diverse songs and symphonies belies the traditional white male composers lurking behind the cover. This "illusion of equity" is really a marketing strategy directed at potential purchasers who *flip* the pages and might be lured into purchasing books that appear to be current, diverse, and balanced.

—From *Teachers, School, and Society,* 6th ed. by Myra Pollack Sadker and David Miller.
Copyright © 2003. Reprinted by permission of The McGraw-Hill Companies, Inc.

The Write Connection

Directions: *Write a paragraph about the three things you learned or that you think are most important in the reading selection.*

_____

_____

_____

_____

_____

Comprehension Check

Directions: *See how many questions you can answer without referring to the selection. Then, review the selection to write more complete responses.*

_____ 1. The authors have written the selection in order to:
   a. discuss various forms of stereotyping and their characteristics.
   b. present key differences between African Americans and Asian Americans.
   c. influence change in the way various groups are portrayed in new textbooks.
   d. illustrate the forms of bias that can be used to assess instructional materials.

_____ 2. Which of the following sentences from the selection is a statement of opinion?
   a. Many Americans are passionate about how various groups are portrayed in textbooks.
   b. Bias through fragmentation or isolation primarily takes two forms.
   c. An imbalance of word order ("boys and girls") and a lack of parallel terms ("girls and young men) are also forms of linguistic bias.
   d. Many studies indicate that women represent approximately 30 percent of the persons or characters referred to throughout textbooks in most subject areas.

_____ 3. Choose the statement that represents the best main idea sentence or thesis of the selection:
   a. Curriculum may perpetuate bias by presenting only one interpretation of an issue, or a group of people.
   b. There are seven forms of bias used to reflect the discriminatory nature of the dominant language, race or ethnicity, or gender found in many instructional materials.
   c. Bias should be banned as a component of instructional materials.
   d. The seven forms of bias can be used to identify the underrepresentation of various groups in instructional materials and to provide a means to assess these materials.

4. Invisibility, in instructional materials, is: _____

_____

5. Give one example of a stereotype that could appear in a biased textbook.

_____

6. If a textbook emphasizes the accomplishments of one group while minimizing or leaving out the accomplishments of another group, it demonstrates which form of bias? _____

_____ 7. Referring to a group of teenagers as "girls and young men" illustrates which form of bias?
   a. unreality
   b. fragmentation and isolation
   c. linguistic bias
   d. cosmetic bias

_____ 8. The tendency of instructional materials to ignore unpleasant facts about society illustrates which form of bias?
   a. unreality
   b. fragmentation and isolation
   c. linguistic bias
   d. cosmetic bias

_____ 9. When a textbook shows pictures of Mexican Americans in successful positions, but fails to discuss their contributions to the business world, it illustrates which form of bias?
   a. unreality
   b. fragmentation and isolation
   c. linguistic bias
   d. cosmetic bias

_____ 10. Which form of bias portrays racial and ethnic groups as interacting only with persons like themselves?
   a. unreality
   b. fragmentation and isolation
   c. linguistic bias
   d. cosmetic bias

Critical Thinking Check

1. While educators are working to detect and remove these biases from instructional materials, bias can still be seen in movies or on television shows. Describe a stereotype portrayed about a particular ethnic group or gender that you have found in a recent movie or on the news. _____

_____

_____

2. Why do you think it would be important to be able to identify one of the seven types of bias described in the selection as you read a textbook or other kind of

instructional material? _____

_____

_____

_____ 3. Which of the following conclusions can be drawn from the information in the selection?
   a. Most textbook authors intentionally use language to represent certain groups of people unfairly.
   b. Educators are becoming more aware of the ways in which bias can appear in instructional materials.
   c. Educators are looking for the most effective way to assess textbooks and other instructional materials.
   d. All textbooks contain bias.

Vocabulary Check

Directions: *See if any of the words you underlined in the selection are among the list of words below. If not, write your words in the spaces provided. Guess the meaning of the words below from the way they were used in the selection. Then, look up the definitions of each word in the dictionary to see if you were right.*

distort (*vb*): Your guess: _____

   Dictionary Definition: _____

exploitation (*n*): Your guess: _____

   Dictionary Definition: _____

fragmentation (*n*): Your guess: _____

   Dictionary Definition: _____

underrepresented (*adj*): Your guess: _____

   Dictionary Definition: _____

Your word: _____ Your guess: _____

   Dictionary Definition: _____

Your word: _____ Your guess: _____

   Dictionary Definition: _____

11 Recognizing the Author's Purpose and Tone

In Aristotelian terms, the good leader must have ethos, pathos, and logos. The ethos is his moral character, the source of his ability to persuade. The pathos is his ability to touch feelings, to move people emotionally. The logos is his ability to move people intellectually.

– Mortimer Adler

In this chapter you will learn how to:

Recognize the Author's Purpose

Recognize Figurative Language

▲ An author may write to persuade, to inform, or to entertain the reader.

Preview and Predict ▶ What do you know so far?

How many of the following questions can you answer before you read the chapter?

• Why do you think an author might choose to write a story about a dangerous experience instead of an article listing the facts about how to avoid danger?

- What are three basic reasons or purposes for writing?

_____

- What are some ways to recognize the emotion or tone of an author as you read?

_____

- Think of one way in which the picture relates to this chapter's objectives.

_____

Now, as you read the chapter, look for the answers to see if you were right.

THE AUTHOR'S PURPOSE

Authors have a **purpose** or reason for writing. The purpose depends upon the effect they want to have on the reader. For instance, the author who writes a funny story wants the reader to be *entertained*. The author who writes a textbook chapter wants the reader to be *informed* about a particular topic. The author who writes a letter to the editor of a newspaper wants to *persuade* the reader to agree with his or her opinion about a particular issue. By recognizing the author's purpose for writing, you will gain a greater understanding of what you are reading.

RECOGNIZING AN AUTHOR'S PURPOSE

Authors have three basic purposes or reasons for writing: to persuade, to inform, or to entertain the reader. Here are some ways to recognize an author's purpose as you read.

Writing to Persuade

To **persuade** means to convince, to sway, or to influence. For instance, if you are trying to persuade others, you are usually attempting to get them to agree with your opinion about a particular issue. You make an argument for your point of view and back it up with reasons, facts, and other information. While other people could have an opinion opposite to yours, you want to convince them to agree with your side of the issue.

When authors state an opinion, they often use words or phrases like *I think, I believe, should,* or *must*. Sometimes, when stating an opinion, authors reveal their feelings about the issue and use words that have an emotional effect. Advertisements, movie or music reviews, political speeches, editorials or letters to the editor, and blogs or Internet commentary are examples of the kinds of writing in which the author's purpose is to persuade the reader.

The author of the following example is trying to *persuade* the reader to agree with her point of view on the issue of building an adult video store next to a baseball field.

Letter to the Editor

I am outraged by the recent vote by the city council to allow an adult video store to be built next to the ballpark. Baseball is supposed to be a family affair, not a place where men will be tempted to view obscene material. These places often attract the more dangerous elements of society. Now families will have to walk right past the video store on the way to the ballpark. I think the citizens of the city should find out who voted for this sleazy attack on our families and make sure that they do not have a chance to be reelected.

Does the author have an opinion about the adult video store? Yes. The main idea in the first and last sentences state her opinion. Could someone have an *opposite* opinion? Yes. Is the author *for* or *against* the adult video store? _____

_____ You can tell that the author is against the adult video store. What kind of *emotion* does the author have about the issue? She seems to be _____ (happy? sad? angry? or without emotion?) about the issue. You can tell the author's emotion in such phrases as *I am outraged by* and *this sleazy attack on our families.* You can almost imagine the author yelling or at least raising her voice in *anger.*

Here are three ways you can tell when an author is trying to persuade you to agree with a particular point of view.

How to Recognize When an Author Is Writing to Persuade

1. **Ask yourself, "Can I agree or disagree with the author?"** By asking this question, you will be able to tell if the author has a point of view about a particular issue. If an author does have a point of view, then he or she is writing to persuade you.

2. **Look for opinion words and phrases in the main idea sentence of a paragraph or passage.** Authors who are trying to persuade you often use opinion words or phrases such as *I think, I believe, should,* or *must* to show that they are expressing their point of view about an issue. Therefore, if you find opinion words in the sentence that expresses the author's main point, you can be reasonably sure his or her purpose is persuasion.

3. **Look for emotional statements that support an author's point of view.** When authors are strongly opposed to a particular issue, they often use words and phrases that express their emotions.

Here are some examples of the kinds of emotional statements used by authors who are writing to persuade the reader:

. . . it is a disgusting way to . . .

. . . the attack was a hopeless attempt . . .

. . . but it was far better than the other song . . .

. . . the performance was embarrassingly bad . . .

. . . this sleazy attack on our families . . .

Standardized reading tests often include questions that ask you to recognize an author's purpose for writing. You should be familiar with common synonyms for the word *persuade* so that you can identify them among the choices on the exam. Synonyms for persuade include *convince, sway, propose,* and *influence.*

Memory Check 1 How much do you remember?

1. What are three ways to recognize when the author's purpose is to persuade the reader?

   a. _____

   b. _____

   _____

   c. _____

2. Give two examples of opinion words or phrases found in persuasive writing.

   _____

3. What are two synonyms for the word *persuade?* _____

   _____

4. Write a recall word for the three types of purpose that an author may have for writing. _____

5. What is one kind of writing in which the author's purpose is to persuade?

   _____

Writing to Inform

To **inform** means to teach or to explain. If you inform someone about how to register for classes, would you use mostly statements of fact or opinion? _____ You probably wouldn't use any statements of opinion to teach someone about the registration process. And you wouldn't have any emotion about the topic. Instead, you would present the topic in an objective or nonemotional manner. Examples of the kinds of writing in which the author's purpose is to inform the reader might include textbook excerpts, news articles, technical manuals, cookbooks, dictionaries, and video game directions.

The author of the following example is writing *to inform* the reader about what took place during a council meeting.

Newspaper Article

> The City Council has granted Smith Jones and Dave Smith of The Bare Necessities Adult Video Stores approval to build their newest adult video store, The Bare Necessities Video Bonanza in the former Granton Theater. The approval was granted by a vote of 7–6 on Monday night. The proposed video store has raised concern by family advocate groups due to its location next to Common's Ballpark. In response, Councilman Jerry Bacchas proposed an alternate family parking and admissions area on the other side of the video store to reduce public exposure among park patrons.

Does the author have an opinion about the adult video store? No. The author is not for or against the adult video store. The author seems to be _____ (happy? sad? angry? objective?) about the issue. The author is objective and nonemotional. Authors who are writing to inform use statements of *fact* to present their main idea and major details. The main idea in the first sentence of the paragraph and the major details in the sentences that follow provide facts regarding the approval to build a new adult video store. Here are two ways you can tell when an author is informing you about a topic.

How to Recognize When an Author Is Writing to Inform

1. **Ask yourself, "Can I agree or disagree with the author?"** By asking this question, you will distinguish whether the author is writing to inform or to persuade. If you can agree or disagree with the author, then you can be sure that the author is writing to persuade, rather than inform the reader. For instance, can you agree or disagree with the information presented in a dictionary? No. The author of a dictionary is writing to inform or teach you about the meanings of words and their origins.

2. **Look for statements of fact.** An author who wants to inform the reader will provide factual, objective information about the topic being discussed. The main idea and the major details that support it present the facts in order to teach or inform the reader. For instance, an author will use statements of fact to explain the steps in a process, the parts of an idea, or the facts concerning a specific event. If you find this kind of information presented in a straightforward, unemotional manner, you know the author is writing to inform.

Here are some examples of factual statements used by authors who are writing to inform the reader:

. . . whereas 28% of the . . .

. . . On the 22nd of May . . .

. . . The first step is . . .

. . . is another factor . . .

. . . The approval was granted by a vote of 7–6 on Monday . . .

. . . During the 1970s and 1980s . . .

. . . The research shows that . . .

You should be familiar with common synonyms for the word *inform* so that you can identify them among the choices on a standardized reading test. Synonyms for *inform* include *teach, explain,* and *discuss.*

Writing to Entertain

To **entertain** means to amuse or to interest. Examples of writing in which the author is trying to entertain the reader include novels, poetry, cartoons, jokes, or types of stories such as mystery, horror, humorous, or inspirational. When authors write to entertain, their goal might be to make the reader laugh, to express their feelings about an experience, or to describe a significant place, person, or event in their lives. They are more interested in the *emotion* they are trying to make the reader feel about the experience than in persuading or informing the reader.

For instance, the author of the following example is writing to *entertain* the reader by telling a story about how the town he lives in has changed since his childhood.

The city has grown so large since the days when I was a young boy. Then it was just a small town with a population of 2,500. I knew everyone in the neighborhood. I remember when Jimmy Watkins, Tim Rodriguez, and I would take our gloves down to the field where the ball park stadium is now and join the other boys in a game. We'd play for hours. Sometimes we would walk over to the orchard afterwards and pick a few apples to eat on the way home. Now, the orchard is gone and soon they will build an adult video store there instead. Hey, maybe *these are* the good old days.

Is the author of the example paragraph trying to persuade you to agree with his or her opinion? _____ Is the author trying to inform you about the facts regarding the adult video store? _____ The emotion he wants the reader to have in response to the story is more important than the issue surrounding the building of the adult video store or the facts concerning when and where it will be located. You can almost imagine the author laughing in the last sentence, "Hey, maybe *these* are the good old days." He is writing about the adult video store situation in a funny or humorous way to entertain the reader.

Here are two ways you can tell when an author is writing to entertain.

How to Recognize When an Author Is Writing to Entertain

1. **Ask yourself, "Can I agree or disagree with the author?"** Satire is a form of humor in which a person's mistakes are made fun of in some way. Humor and satire are used by authors to make political or social points in order to persuade the reader. For instance, *Doonesbury* is a cartoon that uses humor to express opinions about political issues. On the other hand, the cartoon *Calvin and Hobbes* uses humor to explore relationships. By asking this question, you will be able to distinguish whether the author is writing to entertain, persuade, or inform the reader.

2. **Look for narration and description.** Authors who are writing to entertain often use narration and description to paint a picture of a person, place, or event, or to tell a story. Authors who are writing to entertain use descriptions of people, places, things, or events to help the reader have a particular emotional response. For instance, an author may describe a person using details that help the reader feel a particular emotion. The author might want the reader to feel inspired, or to laugh, cry, or be scared after reading his story. So, instead of writing "the girl was five years old," an author who wants to entertain the reader may write, "the girl was thin, with dark eyes empty of the joy one usually expects to see in a five year old."

Here are some examples of descriptive or narrative statements used by authors who are writing to entertain:

Once upon a time . . .

One day, I was . . .

The wind howled through the dark cave . . .

I remember when . . .

We would walk over to the orchard and pick apples . . .

You should be familiar with common synonyms for the word *entertain* so that you can identify them among the choices on a standardized reading test. Synonyms for *entertain* include *amuse*, *humor*, or *engage*.

Memory Check 2 How much do you remember?

1. What are two ways to identify when the author's purpose is to inform the reader?

   a. _____

   b. _____

2. What are two synonyms for the word *inform?* _____

3. What does it mean if you are being objective? _____

   _____

4. What is one kind of writing in which the author's purpose is to persuade?

   _____

5. What are two ways to identify when the author's purpose is to entertain the reader?

   a. _____

   b. _____

6. What is a synonym for the word *entertain?* _____

7. What is satire? _____

   _____

8. Authors who are trying to entertain are concerned with the _____ they want the reader to feel.

9. What is one kind of writing in which the author's purpose is to entertain?

   _____

10. Fill in the blanks with the appropriate information about the different purposes for writing.

Author's Purpose	How do you know?	What are some examples?
To persuade	Contains mostly opinions	_____ _____
To inform	_____	Textbooks, news article, technical manuals
_____	Concerned with making the reader feel a specific emotion	Stories, poetry, novels

Activity 11.1 ▶ Identifying the Author's Purpose I

Directions: *Look at each type of writing below and identify whether the author's purpose is to persuade (P), to inform (I), or to entertain (E).*

_____   1. a textbook

_____   2. a funny story

_____   3. a review of a movie

_____   4. an advertisement

_____   5. a political speech

_____   6. a poem

_____   7. a technical manual

_____   8. a news article

_____   9. a medical book

_____   10. an editorial

Activity 11.2 ▶ Identifying the Author's Purpose II

Directions: *Identify the author's purpose in each of the following paragraphs and answer the questions that follow them.*

Paragraph 1

Bay City—A Beachview man was arrested Tuesday evening for vandalism and destruction of private property. The suspect, Mike Smith, 19, of Port Allen was apprehended at approximately 11:30 P.M. in the 1800 block of Seaport

Road after a surveillance camera captured him writing graffiti on the windows and doors of several businesses in the area. Surveillance cameras were recently installed in response to an increase in vandalism as well as robberies in the area. Mr. Smith is scheduled to appear in court on Monday. Five suspects have been arrested for vandalism since the surveillance cameras were installed.

_____ 1. Paragraph 1 contains mostly:
   a. fact.   c. description.
   b. opinion.

_____ 2. What is the author's purpose for writing Paragraph 1?
   a. to persuade the reader to agree with an opinion
   b. to inform the reader about the facts of a topic
   c. to entertain the reader in a way that inspires a particular emotion

Paragraph 2

To replay the previous segment, make sure that the Stop mechanism is on the OFF position. Press Rewind until at least five seconds from the start of the segment. Then, press PLAY. Increase or decrease sound quality by adjusting the Volume Moderator Synthesizer located below the RECORD button. To insure optimum sound quality, use the Frequency Indicator Bars located on the face of the recorder (Refer to Sound Adjustment, p. 4).

_____ 3. Paragraph 2 contains mostly:
   a. fact.   c. description.
   b. opinion.

_____ 4. What is the author's purpose for writing paragraph 2?
   a. to persuade the reader to agree with an opinion
   b. to inform the reader about the facts of a topic
   c. to entertain the reader in a way that inspires a particular emotion

Paragraph 3

Gigli is the romantic hit of the season. Ben Affleck and Jennifer Lopez give the audience nothing but non-stop fireworks. Gorman and Sands gave *Gigli* a "two-thumbs up." According to Frank Gorman, "We haven't seen this caliber of romantic comedy since Doris Day and Rock Hudson won our hearts in *Pillow Talk*. J Lo should win the Oscar for her performance!" Watch the exciting chemistry between two stars that happen to be a couple in real life. Four-star entertainment. A masterpiece!

_____ 5. Paragraph 3 contains mostly
    a. fact.   c. description.
    b. opinion.

_____ 6. What is the author's purpose for writing paragraph 3?
    a. to persuade the reader to agree with an opinion
    b. to inform the reader about the facts of a topic
    c. to entertain the reader in a way that inspires a particular emotion

Paragraph 4

I could feel the warmth of a loving family when I walked into the home of Joe and Minerva Aragon. All four of their children were sitting in the living room laughing and talking with one another. The aroma of delicious food filled the air. "Are you hungry?" Minerva asked. "I made chile rellenos." How could I refuse? So, we all moved to the dinner table located in their sunny kitchen. Joe and Minerva Aragon have raised four medical doctors. Dr. Ernesto Aragon, the couple's oldest son, is a pediatrician at Kent Clinic. Dr. Rodrigo Aragon, is a cardiologist at University General Hospital. Dr. Sandra Aragon is a cardiologist who has her own practice in nearby Newton. The youngest, Dr. Teresa Aragon, is an anesthesiologist at University General Hospital. When I asked Mr. and Mrs. Aragon what they did to raise such accomplished children, they smiled modestly. After a silence, Minerva said, "They always liked to learn. But, we encouraged them to do their studies together, right here at the table after dinner every night." "Pop used to quiz us on what we learned. Remember that?" Sandra said, laughing. "I know," Rodrigo recalled. "Then we would quiz Pop, and he would make up the craziest answers. And we'd be like, _is that true_? And he'd always say, look it up." "Look it up," Joe echoed proudly, and everyone laughed. "Although they were immigrants who spoke little English, my parents spent every penny and all of their time making sure that we had a good education," Teresa said. "We all knew that, next to a loving family, education was our most important goal."

_____ 7. Paragraph 4 contains mostly
    a. fact.   c. description.
    b. opinion.

_____ 8. What is the author's purpose for writing paragraph 4?
    a. to persuade the reader to agree with an opinion
    b. to inform the reader about the facts of a topic
    c. to entertain the reader in a way that inspires a particular emotion

Paragraph 5

The Squealing Worms performed at the Rocket Arena Friday night to a packed house. Unfortunately, the opening set, which included the hits, "Feast the Sky" and "Aisle of You," was a disappointment. Guitarist Zip Pity performed miserably at best and the garbled singing of Pete Dilly was embarrassing. The light show seemed only to entertain the screaming booze-hounds and groupies that danced in mindless glee in front of the stage throughout the entire concert.

_____ 9. Paragraph 5 contains mostly
    a. fact.   c. description.
    b. opinion.

_____ 10. What is the author's purpose for writing paragraph 5?
    a. to persuade the reader to agree with an opinion
    b. to inform the reader about the facts of a topic
    c. to entertain the reader in a way that inspires a particular emotion

TONE

Tone refers to the emotion an author conveys when writing about a topic. Remember, when you read it is as if an author is talking to you through the words on the page. If you can imagine an author speaking to you as you read, you can hear the emotion in the "tone of voice" used. (The words an author chooses to use often provide clues to how he or she feels about a topic. They can also tell you what an author's attitude is towards an issue.

By recognizing an author's tone, you enhance your ability to understand the author's purpose. For instance, an author writing about his or her opinion on a particular issue may have an angry or *bitter* tone of voice. An author who is writing a cookbook will probably have an objective or *impartial* tone of voice, while a poet may convey sadness, happiness, or anger in his or her tone.

Recognizing an Author's Tone of Voice

Your ability to recognize an author's tone of voice also helps you to visualize what is being described more clearly. For instance, imagine that you were writing about visiting someone you hadn't seen in a long time.

"I knocked on the door. When she opened the door she said, 'Oh, it's you.'"

How did she say it? What was her tone of voice? How does your reader know if the person was happy to see you, angry at seeing you, afraid to see you, or sad at seeing you? You can recognize the author's tone of voice by looking for the words he or she uses to describe a particular emotion. For instance, consider the difference that the addition of descriptive words makes in the author's tone in the examples below even when the statement stays the same:

"Oh, it's you," she cried, joyfully.

"Oh, it's you," she sneered.

"Oh, it's you," she screamed.

"Oh, it's you," she said, slowly, looking down to hide her tears.

You can recognize the author's tone of voice by the words that are added to describe a particular emotion. You are able to see the picture of what you are reading more clearly because you recognize the author's tone of voice.

Tone and Vocabulary Development

There are as many tones of emotion as there are shades of color. The more tone words you know, the more clearly you can describe as well as recognize an author's emotions or tone of voice. Consider the following basic emotions that an author's tone can convey: happy, sad, afraid, objective, and angry. Each one can be described using words with various shades of meaning. Here are some examples.

A boy has earned an "A" on an English exam. Is he just happy? Or is he *joyful, elated,* or *amazed?*

A girl is talking about a fellow student in a negative way. Is the girl just angry? Or is she *arrogant, vindictive, mocking,* or *bitter?*

Someone is walking alone in a parking lot after dark. Is the person just afraid? Or, is the person *apprehensive, terrified,* or *filled with trepidation?*

A person is discussing the steps necessary to create a website. Is the person speaking in an objective, matter-of-fact manner? Or is the person *impartial* or *detached?*

A woman is talking about missing a former boyfriend. Is the woman just sad? Or is the woman *grim, depressed, melancholy,* or *nostalgic?*

You can improve your vocabulary if you learn alternate words or synonyms that describe basic emotions. You can use these synonyms to create a clearer picture of what you want to say. In addition, you will be able to identify with more accuracy the shade of emotion used in an author's tone of voice. Table 11.1 on the next page contains a list of common tone words used to describe emotion.

Table 11.1 Common Tone Words

absurd, ridiculous: laughable or a joke

amazed, shocked: filled with surprise

ambivalent: having conflicting feelings

anxious: expecting a fearful outcome

apprehensive: feeling uneasy

arrogant, condescending: acting better than

bitter, hateful: feeling anger about a result; blaming

compassionate: understanding the feelings of others

congratulatory: honoring an achievement

cruel, malicious: hateful or mean-spirited

cynical: expecting the worst from others

depressed, somber: unhappy

disapproving, critical: judging negatively

elated, gleeful: joyful, happy

evasive: avoiding an issue

formal: using an official style

grave, sober: serious, not joking

humorous, jovial: funny or feeling joyful

impartial, objective, matter-of-fact: without emotion

incredulous: doubtful, not believing

indecisive: unable to decide

indignant: angry, resentful

ironic: saying the opposite of what was meant or anticipated

irreverent: disrespectful of something held sacred

melancholy: sad

mocking: making fun of

nostalgic: to recall or to dream about the past

objective, factual, impartial, formal: using facts, without emotion

optimistic: expecting a positive outcome

pessimistic: expecting a negative outcome

reticent: shy or not speaking out

reverent: showing respect; feeling awe

righteous: feeling morally correct or superior

romantic: expressing love or affection

sarcastic: saying one thing but meaning another in a mean-spirited way

sensational: over-dramatic

sentimental: very emotional

sincere, heartfelt: honest expression

subjective: expressing personal opinions or beliefs

terror: extreme fear

tragic: a terrible occurrence or mistake

trepidation, unease: feeling scared or uncertain

vengeful, vindictive: wanting to repay an attack

zealous: enthusiastic commitment

Memory Check 3 How much do you remember?

1. Tone refers to the _____

2. You can recognize an author's tone of voice by _____

   _____.

3. You can improve your vocabulary by learning _____

   _____.

Activity 11.3 ▶ Thesaurus Search

Directions: *Use a thesaurus to find a synonym for each tone word below. Then, look up the definition of each synonym.*

Tone	Synonym	Definition
Happy		
Sad		
Angry		
Afraid		
Impartial		

Activity 11.4 ▶ Matching Tones and Synonyms

Directions: *Match the tone on the left with the appropriate synonym on the right.*

Tone

_____ 1. melancholy

_____ 2. elated

_____ 3. terrified

_____ 4. objective

_____ 5. bitter

_____ 6. humorous

Synonym

a. very fearful

b. disappointed, resentful

c. joyful or happy

d. unemotional

e. funny

f. sad

Activity 11.5 ▶ Identifying Tone

Directions: *Identify the tone of the following passages.*

_____ 1. Sherry looked at the new student and said to her friends, "I can't stand her. She thinks she's so cute."
   a. melancholy
   b. elated
   c. bitter
   d. objective

_____ 2. At the funeral, Carmen placed her hand on her grandmother's cheek and whispered, "Goodbye Nana," for the last time.
   a. sorrowful
   b. gleeful
   c. vindictive
   d. impartial

_____ 3. Ruben told Tony and Ray what had happened to him the day before: "So he turns around and says, 'Hey, did you just call me a chicken?' And I said, 'Well, you turned around. So, I guess it's true.'" Suddenly the milkshakes that Tony and Ray were drinking came out of their noses.
   a. sentimental
   b. humorous
   c. bitter
   d. terrified

_____ 4. Sylvia awoke to the sound of breaking glass. It was two o'clock in the morning. When she jumped out of bed and picked up the telephone, there was no dial tone. Suddenly, Sylvia could hear familiar voices coming from behind the door at the end of the hallway. She couldn't tell exactly who it was. She only knew that it was the voices of two men. Slowly she walked to the door and heard footsteps crumbling shards of glass. Sylvia didn't run. She had to see who was behind the door. As she reached for the knob, she heard, "I know where she keeps her money." Sylvia recognized the voice, but by then it was too late.
   a. impartial
   b. melancholy
   c. sarcastic
   d. terrifying

_____ 5. "I can't believe it's finally happening," Libby said, as she stepped upon the stage to receive her diploma.
   a. terrified
   b. elated
   c. bitter
   d. mocking

Tone and an Author's Purpose

Tone is used to support an author's purpose for writing. For instance, an author who is trying to *persuade* you to agree with his or her opinion about an issue might have a tone of voice that could be described as *angry, bitter, arrogant, righteous,* or *critical.* An author who is trying to *inform* you may have a tone of voice that could be described as *impartial* or *formal*. An author who is trying to entertain will have a tone of voice that matches the emotion he or she wants to convey depending upon the form of entertainment. For instance, the author who writes a *funny* story may have a tone of voice that can be described as *humorous, absurd,* or *amusing.* The author who writes a *sad* story to entertain the reader may have a tone of voice that can be described as *melancholy, nostalgic,* or *grim.* An author's purpose is supported by the emotions conveyed in his or her tone of voice. Recognizing how an author's purpose and tone of voice work together will help you better understand what you read.

FIGURATIVE LANGUAGE

Figurative language refers to the figures of speech authors use to describe people, things, events, or behaviors. For instance, think of a number. That number is a figure that is used to represent an amount. In the same way, a figure of speech is used to represent meaning in an artistic way. For instance, how would you convey the message that a woman you know is an excellent dancer? You could use *literal* language and say, "She is an excellent dancer." But that is an ordinary description. Literal language merely presents the information. Notice how you can convey the same information using figurative language:

"She is music in motion."

You can identify the difference between literal and figurative language by the *way* a message is conveyed. Writers use figurative language to create an image that represents what they want to say. The message is conveyed in a descriptive or expressive way. For instance, an ordinary literal statement would be:

"John is a very smart young man."

Now, notice how figurative language is used in the following examples to convey the same message:

"John is as sharp as a tack."

"John is a computer."

"John can add a million numbers in his head at one time."

"John must have had razor soup for breakfast."

All of the statements convey the same idea as the first sentence—that John is smart—but they use figurative language. The more you use figurative language, the more you can recognize and appreciate the artistic way in which authors express their ideas. Some of the most common forms of figurative language include the following: hyperbole, analogy (metaphor and simile), idiom, and cliché.

Hyperbole

The prefix *hyper* means "over." For instance, a *hyper*active child is a child who is overactive. A **hyperbole** (pronounced hi PER bowly) is an *over*statement or an exaggeration used to make a point.

As you read the examples below, notice how the literal statements on the left are expressed using hyperbole on the right.

Examples of Hyperbole

Literal Statement	Hyperbole
She talked to me for 10 minutes.	She talked **my head off**. She talked **my ear off**. She talked **forever**.
I waited 20 minutes before you arrived.	I waited **forever** . . . I waited an **eternity** . . . I waited **one hundred years** . . .
I have a lot of work to do.	I have a **ton of work** . . . I have a **mountain of work** . . .

Activity 11.5 ▶ Figurative Language: Hyperbole

Directions: *Use the examples in the preceding list or think of your own to change each of the following literal statements into a hyperbole.*

1. *Literal statement*: The phone rang three times before you answered.

   Hyperbole: The phone rang _____ before you answered.

2. *Literal statement*: The teacher assigned a lot of homework.

   Hyperbole: The teacher assigned _____ of homework.

3. *Literal statement*: I am so tired that I could sleep all night.

   Hyperbole: I am so tired that _____

4. *Literal statement*: She is strong enough to lift 240 pounds.

   Hyperbole: She is strong enough _____

5. *Literal statement*: He would do almost anything to see her again.

   Hyperbole: He would _____ to see her again.

Analogy

An **analogy** is a comparison. It is an artistic way of comparing two things that are unrelated to one another. Simile and metaphor are two types of analogy or comparison.

Simile

A **simile** is a comparison of two unrelated things using the words *like* or *as*. For instance, consider the literal statement "Jim is a good swimmer." Is the way that Jim swims being compared to anything? No. On the other hand, if you want to use a simile to describe Jim as a good swimmer, you might say that Jim swims *like* a fish. Or, you could say that Jim swims *as smoothly as* a shark. You are comparing the *way* Jim swims to a fish or to the *way* a shark swims as if they are *similar*.

As you read the examples below, notice how the literal statements on the left are expressed as similes on the right.

Examples of Simile

Literal Statement	Simile
Sydney is not very affectionate.	Sydney is **as cold as ice**. (Sydney's behavior is compared to ice.)
Tina doesn't eat very much.	Tina eats **like a bird.** (The way Tina eats is compared to the way a bird eats.)
He is very busy.	He is **as busy as a bee**. (His busy behavior is compared to that of a bee.)
Andy cried.	Andy cried **like a baby**. (The way Andy cried is compared to the way a baby cries.)

Additional Examples of Simile

How many of the following examples have you used, or heard other people use, when describing something or someone's behavior?

as clear as a bell	like a bull in a china shop	as sly as a fox
as cute as a button	cheeks like a balloon	fits like a glove
as flat as a pancake	slept like a log	as dry as a bone
as hard as nails	worked like a dog	eyes like stars
as deep as the ocean	drinks like a fish	as strong as an ox

Activity 11.6 ▶ Figurative Language: Simile I

Directions: *Compare the subject in each of the following literal statements to something that has the same qualities.*

     Example: *Literal statement*: Della drinks too much.

                Simile: Della drinks like a thirsty dog

1. *Literal statement*: Joella makes a mess when she eats.

   Simile: Joella eats like a _____.

2. *Literal statement*: This room is too hot.

   Simile: This room is as hot as _____.

3. *Literal statement*: Loretta does not sing very well.

   Simile: Loretta sings like a _____.

4. *Literal statement*: Amanda runs fast.

   Simile: Amanda runs as fast _____.

5. *Literal statement*: My love has a beautiful smile.

   Simile: My love's smile _____.

Activity 11.7 ▶ Figurative Language: Simile II

Directions: *Create your own similes by choosing the phrases* sounds like, looks like, smells like, tastes like, *or* feels like *to write your own description of traffic, rain, and the one you love.*

     Example: The rain sounds like the white noise static of a TV when it's off-channel.

              The traffic looks like a parade of busy ants.

Choose one: sounds like   looks like   smells like   tastes like   feels like

1. Traffic _____

   _____

2. Rain _____

   _____

3. The one I love _____

_____

4. My friend _____

_____

5. My bedroom _____

_____

Metaphor

A metaphor is another type of analogy or comparison. The prefix *meta* means "to change." Unlike a simile, a **metaphor** compares two unrelated things as if they are equal or the same. For instance, consider the literal statement, "Jim is a good swimmer." Notice the difference between a simile and a metaphor in the following examples:

"Jim swims **like** a fish." (simile)

"Jim swims **as** smoothly **as** a fish." (simile)

"Jim **is** a fish." (metaphor)

What is the difference in the way that Jim is being compared to a fish? The similes use the words *like* or *as* to show the similarities in the way Jim swims to that of a fish. The metaphor uses the word *is* to compare Jim to a fish *as if they are equal or the same*. So, in the metaphor, Jim is no longer like or similar to a fish; he *is* a fish.

Metaphors often contain clue words such as ***are, is, were***, or ***am*** to compare two unrelated things as if they are equal or the same. As you read the following examples, notice how the literal statements on the left are expressed as metaphors on the right.

Examples of Metaphor

Literal Statement	Metaphor
My car is very old.	My car **is a dinosaur**.
I spend a lot of time watching television.	I **am a couch potato**.
He ate the entire five-course meal.	His stomach **is a bottomless pit**.
The stars were easy to see last night.	The stars **were diamonds in the sky**.
They are too skinny.	They **are toothpicks**.

These examples directly state a comparison between two unrelated things as if they are equal. Sometimes, however, a metaphor can be stated *indirectly*. In this case, a metaphor may not include the clue words *is, am, are,* or *were*. For instance, notice how metaphors can be expressed indirectly in the following examples:

Literal Statement	Metaphor (Indirectly Stated)
His cheeks are round and full.	He has **balloon cheeks**. (His cheeks *are* balloons.)
She has interesting eyes.	She has **cat eyes**. (She *is* a cat.)
Send it through the post office.	Send it using **snail mail**. (The postal service is a snail.)

Additional Examples of Metaphor

Notice how two unrelated things are being compared directly such as "Dan is a dog" or indirectly as in "Dan barked" in each of the following statements:

Directly Stated	Indirectly Stated
He is all that and a bag of chips.	He clammed up when the judge spoke.
You are the wind.	Jim has fins for feet.
You are my sunshine.	He barked orders at me.
Kenton is a dog.	There was a blanket of snow on the field.
Dan is a player.	He needed a napkin for his snout.

Activity 11.8 ▶ Figurative Language: Working with Metaphors

Directions: *Read the literal statements on the left. Then, rewrite each one as a metaphor.*

Example

He is a sloppy eater.   He is a *pig*.

Literal Statement	Your Metaphor
1. Mia is very pretty.	Mia is a _____
2. Andrea is always in a bad mood.	Andrea is a _____
3. Anita is always so nice to everyone.	Anita is a _____
4. Rueben likes to talk.	Rueben is a _____
5. Corey's car is very old.	Corey's car is a _____

Activity 11.9 ▶ Figurative Language: Metaphors in Motion

Directions: *Answer the questions that follow each of the passages below.*

Passage 1 From *As You Like It,* by William Shakespeare

All the world's a stage.

And all the men and women merely players.

They have their <u>exits</u> and their entrances.

And one man in his time plays many parts.

His acts being seven ages.

1. Shakespeare is comparing the world to a _____

2. Underline three words used by Shakespeare to illustrate this comparison. One of the words has been underlined for you.

3. How does the way people present themselves change as they get older?

   _____

   _____

   _____

Passage 2 *Dreams* by Langston Hughes

Hold fast to dreams
For if dreams die
Life is a broken-winged bird
That cannot fly.

Hold fast to dreams
For when dreams go
Life is a barren field
Frozen with snow.

1. In the first part of the poem, Langston Hughes is comparing life without

   dreams to a _____.

2. In the second part of the poem, Langston Hughes compares life without dreams to _____.

3. How would you describe what these two comparisons have in common?

   _____

4. How would you describe a life without dreams?

   _____

   _____

   _____

Memory Check **4** How much do you remember?

1. Figurative language refers to the _____

   _____

2. Hyperbole is an overstatement or _____.

3. An analogy is a _____.

4. What are two types of analogy? _____

5. _____ compares two unrelated things as if they are similar to one another.

6. A _____ compares two unrelated things as if they are equal or the same.

7. The prefix *meta* in the word *meta*phor means _____.

Activity 11.10 ▶ Identifying Figurative Language

Directions: *Identify the type of figurative language used in each of the statements below as follows: H (hyperbole), M (metaphor), or S (simile).*

_____ 1. My instructor assigns mountains of homework.

_____ 2. You are the wind beneath my wings.

_____ 3. He's as fast as lightning.

_____ 4. He's as sly as a fox.

_____ 5. Tony is a fox.

_____ 6. The phone rang a million times.

_____ 7. It took forever to finish that job.

_____ 8. He was as nervous as a cat in a room full of rocking chairs.

_____ 9. The baby had a button nose.

_____ 10. I'm so hungry I could eat a horse.

Activity 11.11 ▶ The Poetry Framework: Create Your Own Poetry

Directions: *Complete the spaces provided in the poetry framework below. Think of artistic ways to describe each of the topics and to create your own poetry.*

The City

Hear the _____

See the _____

Smell the _____

Touch the _____

"This is where I live."

My Neighborhood

Hear the _____

See the _____

Smell the _____

Touch the _____

"This is where I live."

My House

Hear the _____

See the _____

Smell the _____

Touch the _____

"This is where I live."

My Bedroom

Hear the _____

See the _____

Smell the _____

Touch the _____

"This is where I live."

Idioms

An **idiom** refers to an expression that people from a particular area or group use in conversation. For instance, if you said that you had "lost your temper," you would be using an *idiomatic expression*. But, its meaning might be lost to someone who does not speak English well or who is unfamiliar with that particular expression. For example, imagine that you and a friend are having lunch together. Your friend does not yet speak English very well. You have eaten too much. So, you laugh and say, "I guess my eyes were bigger than my stomach." Your friend might think you *literally* mean your eyes are bigger than your stomach, which could be very confusing. Idioms are often taken literally by those who are unfamiliar with them.

Some idioms are common throughout American culture. Others are particular only to one area of the country. Since many idioms are not understood by all people, their use is not usually considered appropriate in formal writing assignments. How many of the following idioms and their meanings are you familiar with?

Idiom	Meaning
Ed is *out to lunch*.	He is tired, crazy, or intoxicated.
He didn't go because he *got cold feet*.	He changed his mind due to fear.
Cindy *knows the ropes*.	She is an experienced worker.
Kyle *burned the midnight oil*.	He stayed up all night working.
It was *on the tip of my tongue*.	It was easily recalled.
She *lucked out*.	She was unexpectedly lucky.
Avery *caught some Z's*.	He went to bed or to sleep.
She *roots for the underdog*.	She supports the person least likely to win.
It was a *piece of cake*.	It was easy.

Activity 11.12 ▶ Figurative Language: Idiomatic Expressions

Directions: *See if you can guess the meaning of each of the idiomatic expressions below.*

1. He has the backbone of a chocolate éclair. _____

    _____

2. He thinks a seven-course meal is a six-pack and a toothpick. _____

    _____

3. The lights are on, but nobody's home. _____

    _____

4. Never wrestle with pigs. They enjoy it and you get dirty. _____

    _____

5. I have too much on my plate. _____

_____

6. She acts like the bride at every wedding and the corpse at every funeral.

_____

7. She could start a fight in an empty house. _____

_____

8. It sounds fishy to me. _____

_____

9. I wonder what she'd charge to haunt a house. _____

_____

10. She had nothing on but TV. _____

_____

Cliché

A **cliché** is a trite or overused expression that no longer has impact. For instance, the first time someone used the simile "slept like a log," it was probably considered a very creative way of saying the person got a good night's sleep. Today, few people would be impressed by its use. A cliché is a phrase that is no longer considered a creative use of language.

You want to recognize figurative language that is overused or cliché so you can avoid using it in your own writing. It is more effective to think of new and creative ways to express your ideas or to describe your world.

Clichés

Put your foot down.
He's taking the bait.
They're like two peas in a pod.
Keep your eye on the ball.
Six feet under
He's getting the red carpet treatment.
Cross that bridge when you come to it.
That's hot.
It was a media circus.
What a gut-wrenching event.

Sink or swim.
Break a leg.
She's pulling your leg.
Kick the bucket
That's water under the bridge.
You're driving me crazy.
Here is the bottom line.
They called it quits.
My old lady
The product is state of the art.

Activity 11.13 ▶ Recognizing Figurative Language: Textbook Application

Directions: *Read the following paragraphs. Then, answer the questions that follow.*

Paragraph 1

Some have said Disney's greatest gift was his ability to develop a concept and have others implement it, sometimes allegedly running his company with an iron first. But he was also a genius in his innovative use of technology in creating stories and entertainment. One can only imagine what Disney would have been able to create with digital technology. Walt Disney died on December 15, 1966, leaving behind one of the best-known media and entertainment empires in the world.

—From *Converging Media: An Introduction to Mass Communication* by
John V. Pavlik and Shawn McIntosh. p. 122. New York, NY:
Allyn and Bacon, 202

1. Write the phrase from paragraph 1 that contains an example of figurative language. _____

_____

2. What is another way to describe how Walt Disney ran his companies?

_____

_____

_____ 3. The type of figurative language used in paragraph 1 is:
   a. cliché.   c. simile.
   b. metaphor.   d. idiom

Paragraph 2

London was a powerfully exciting city at the end of the sixteenth century. Everyone felt it. The city was a magnet drawing the young in search of opportunities from all over England. Talented people came to find like-minded friends, and literary circles burgeoned. William Shakespeare and Ben Jonson created plays that drew high and low to the theater—a different play every day, sometimes two a day. Criers would travel through the city calling out the names of the plays, and fans would flock to the Globe Theatre and its rivals, where rich and poor jostled together.

—From *The Pursuit of Liberty: A History of the American People.* 3rd ed. vol. I
p. 4. R. Jackson Wilson, et al.

4. Write the phrase from paragraph 2 that contains an example of figurative language. _____

5. What is another way to describe the popularity of London?

_____

_____

_____ 6. The type of figurative language used in paragraph 2 is:
    a. cliché.   c. simile.
    b. metaphor.   d. idiom.

Paragraph 3

A final problem that mankind must solve in order to survive in the world house that we have inherited is finding an alternative to war and human destruction. Recent events have vividly reminded us that nations are not reducing but rather increasing their arsenals of weapons of mass destruction. The best brains in the highly developed nations of the world are devoted to military technology. The proliferation of nuclear weapons has not been halted, in spite of the limited-test-ban treaty.

—From "Where Do We Go From Here: Community or Chaos? by Martin
Luther King, Jr.

7. Write the phrase from paragraph 3 that contains an example of figurative language. _____

8. What is another way to describe the world that we have inherited?

_____

_____

_____ 9. The type of figurative language used in paragraph 3 is:
    a. cliché.   c. simile.
    b. metaphor.   d. idiom.

Paragraph 4

One nonproductive conflict strategy is **avoidance.** Avoidance may involve actual physical flight. You may leave the scene (walk out of the apartment or meeting room). Or you may simply psychologically tune out all incoming arguments or problems. In the United States men are more likely to use avoidance than women (Markman, Silvern, Clements, & Kraft-Hanak, 1993; Oggins, Veroff, & Leber, 1993), often additionally denying that anything is wrong (Haferkamp, 1991–92). **Nonnegotiation** is a special type of avoidance. Here you refuse to discuss the conflict or to listen to the other person's argument. At times nonnegotiation takes the form of hammering away at your own point of view until the other person gives in, a method referred to as steamrolling.

—From *Human Communication: The Basic Course,* 10th ed. by
Joseph A. DeVito, p. 255. New York, NY: Allyn and Bacon, 2006.

10. Write one phrase from paragraph 4 that contains an example of figurative language. _____

11. What is another way to describe nonnegotiation?

    _____

_____ 12. The type of figurative language used in paragraph 4 is:
    a. cliché.   c. simile.
    b. metaphor.   d. idiom.

Paragraph 5

Sociologist Erving Goffman (1922–1982) added a new twist to microsociology when he developed **dramaturgy** (or dramaturgical analysis). By this term he (1959) meant that social life is like a drama or a stage play: Birth ushers us onto the stage of everyday life, and our socialization consists of learning to perform on that stage. The self that we studied in the previous chapter lies at the center of our performances. We have ideas of how we want others to think of us, and we use our roles in everyday life to communicate those ideas. Goffman called these efforts to manage the impressions that others receive of us **impression management.**

—From Henslin, James M. *Sociology: A Down-to-Earth Approach,*
Core Concepts, 1e. Published by Allyn and Bacon, Boston, MA.
Copyright © 2006 by Pearson Education. Reprinted by
permission of the publisher.

13. Write one phrase from paragraph 5 that contains an example of figurative language. _____

14. What is another way to describe social life? _____

_____

_____ 15. The type of figurative language used in paragraph 5 is:
    a. cliché.
    b. metaphor.
    c. simile.
    d. idiom.

 Test Yourself Review Quiz

Chapter Review Questions

Match the author's purpose on the left with the tone words on the right.

Author's Purpose

1. _____ to persuade

2. _____ to inform

3. _____ to entertain

Tone

a. objective, impartial

b. humorous, melancholy

c. disapproving, zealous

Identify the author's purpose for each type of writing below.

4. a textbook chapter _____

5. a cartoon _____

6. a music review _____

Application Questions

Read the paragraphs and poems. Then, answer the questions.

Paragraph 1

My husband and I decided to try a new restaurant on our way out of town. When we arrived, we saw that the other customers were dressed in formal attire. The lights were low and romantic and there were candles at each table. We felt very out of place in our blue jeans and tee shirts even though no one seemed to notice or care how we were dressed. Nevertheless, we tried to maintain the most perfect posture and our best table manners throughout the entire meal so we wouldn't be mistaken for a couple of bums. After we left our payment on the table, I led the way through the restaurant toward the exit with my head held high. To my amazement, everybody seemed to stare and smile as I passed. They actually stopped talking to look at me as I walked by. "It's all in the attitude," I said to my husband with confidence. That's when I noticed the two pats of butter stuck to the front of my tee shirt.

_____ 1. Paragraph 1 contains mostly:
    a. fact.
    b. opinion.
    c. description.

_____ 2. What is the author's purpose for writing Paragraph 1?
    a. to persuade the reader to agree with an opinion
    b. to inform the reader about the facts of a situation
    c. to entertain the reader in a way that inspires a particular emotion

_____ 3. The author's tone of voice can be described as:
    a. bitter.
    b. humorous.
    c. impartial.
    d. melancholy.

Paragraph 2

Tens of thousands of 18-year-olds will graduate this year and be handed meaningless diplomas. These diplomas won't look any different from those awarded their luckier classmates. Their validity will he questioned only when their employers discover that these graduates are semiliterate. Eventually a fortunate few will find their way into educational repair shops—adult-literacy programs, such as the one where I teach basic grammar and writing. There, high-school graduates and high-school dropouts pursuing graduate-equivalency certificates will learn the skills they should have learned in school. They will also discover they have been cheated by our educational system.

—From "In Praise of the "F" Word," by Mary Sherry.

_____ 4. Paragraph 2 contains mostly:
    a. fact.
    b. opinion.
    c. description.

_____ 5. What is the author's purpose for writing Paragraph 2?
    a. to persuade the reader to agree with an opinion
    b. to inform the reader about the facts of a situation
    c. to entertain the reader in a way that inspires a particular emotion

_____ 6. The author's tone of voice can be described as:
- a. bitter.
- b. humorous.
- c. impartial.
- d. formal.

Paragraph 3

Expectations can affect supply in different directions. If oil prices are expected to rise in the future, oil producers may produce less oil today to have more available for the future. In other cases, more investment will be undertaken if high prices are expected in the future. This greater investment will cause supply to increase and may result in lower prices for the company's product.

—From _Principles of Economics_, 7th Ed. by Roy J. Ruffin
and Paul R. Gregory. p. 69.

_____ 7. Paragraph 3 contains mostly:
- a. fact.
- b. opinion.
- c. description

_____ 8. What is the authors' purpose for writing Paragraph 3?
- a. persuade the reader to agree with their opinion
- b. to inform the reader about the facts of a situation
- c. to entertain the reader in a way that inspires a particular emotion

_____ 9. The authors' tone of voice can be described as:
- a. bitter.
- b. humorous.
- c. impartial.
- d. sorrowful.

A Song for Mama

Mama, mama you know I love you

Oh you know I love you

Mama, mama you're the queen of my heart

Your love is like

Tears from the stars

Mama, I just want you to know

Lovin' you is like food to my soul.

—Chorus from _A Song for Mama_, by Boyz II Men.

10. Write an example of simile from the lyrics above.

_____

11. Write an example of metaphor from the lyrics above.

_____

_____ 12. The author's purpose for writing the lyrics is:
a. to inform
b. to persuade
c. to entertain

Fog

The fog comes

On little cat feet.

It sits looking

Over harbor and city

On silent haunches

And then moves on.

Carl Sandburg

13. Carl Sandburg is comparing the fog to a _____.

_____ 14. Which form of figurative language is used to make this comparison?
a. metaphor   c. stage
b. hyperbole   d. simile

_____ 15. Carl Sandburg uses which of the following words or phrases to illustrate his comparison?
a. harbor   c. cat feet
b. fog   d. city

Summarization Activity

Directions: _Write the major headings in this chapter. Under each heading, write a couple of sentences about the most important topics presented in the section of text that follows that heading._

First Heading _____

What information is most important? _____

_____

_____

Second Heading _____

What information is most important? _____

_____

_____

Third Heading _____

What information is most important? _____

_____

_____

Combine the information you wrote in this outline into a paragraph to summarize what you have learned in this chapter.

Reflection Activity

How am I am going to apply what I have learned?

Directions: _On a separate sheet of paper, write a paragraph about the two or three things you learned about recognizing the author's purpose and tone that were most helpful to you and how you plan to use what you have learned._

♟♟♟ Skills in Practice ▶ Reading Selection 1

"Salvation," From *The Big Sea*
Langston Hughes

Accessing Prior Knowledge

Questions for Discussion

1. Have you ever pretended to feel something just because everyone else was responding that way? If so, what was the situation and what did you do?

2. What do you think are two main reasons why people are willing to go against their own beliefs in order to follow the actions of a crowd?

Preview and Predict

Directions: *Look at the title of the selection. Think about what you already know about the subject. Then, write a couple of predictions about what you are going to read. For instance, what will the author discuss about salvation?*

1. _____

2. _____

Word Search and Discovery

Directions: *Skim through the selection to find the two words below. Underline both words in the selection. Then, use a dictionary to write their definitions in the spaces provided. As you read and encounter these words, see if the definitions you wrote fit the way each word is used in the selection.*

deacon (*n*): _____

knickerbockers (*n*): _____

Also, underline at least one new word as you read the selection and write your guess as to its meaning in the right margin of the text.

Text Notes in Practice

Directions: *Use a textbook study method such as SQUARE to identify the most important information in the selection. Then, create a study guide that you can use to prepare for the questions that follow the selection.*

SALVATION

Langston Hughes

1   I was saved from sin when I was going on thirteen. But not really saved. It happened like this. There was a big revival at my Auntie Reed's church. Every night for weeks there had been much preaching, singing, praying, and shouting, and some very hardened sinners had been brought to Christ, and the membership of the church had grown by leaps and bounds. Then just before the revival ended, they held a special meeting for children, "to bring the young lambs to the fold." My aunt spoke of it for days ahead. That night I was escorted to the front row and placed on the mourners' bench with all the other young sinners, who had not yet been brought to Jesus.

2   My aunt told me that when you were saved you saw a light, and something happened to you inside! And Jesus came into your life! And God was with you from then on! She said you could see and hear and feel Jesus in your soul. I believed her. I had heard a great many old people say the same thing and it seemed to me they ought to know. So I sat there calmly in the hot, crowded church, waiting for Jesus to come to me.

3   The preacher preached a wonderful rhythmical sermon, all moans and shouts and lonely cries and dire pictures of hell, and then he sang a song about the ninety and nine safe in the fold, but one little lamb was left out in the cold. Then he said: "Won't you came? Won't you come to Jesus? Young lambs, won't you come?" And he held out his arms to all us young sinners there on the mourners' bench. And the little girls cried. And some of them jumped up and went to Jesus right away. But most of us just sat there.

4   A great many older people came and knelt around us and prayed, old women with jet-black faces and braided hair, old men with work-gnarled hands. And the church sang a song about the lower lights are burning, some poor sinners to be saved. And the whole building rocked with prayer and song.

5   Still I kept waiting so *see* Jesus.

6   Finally all the young people had gone to the alter and were saved, but one boy and me. He was a rounder's son named Westley. Westley and I were surrounded by sisters and deacons praying. It was very hot in the church, and getting later now. Finally Westley said to me in a whisper: "God damn! I'm tired o' sitting here. Let's get up and be saved." So he got up and was saved.

7   Then I was left all alone on the mourners' bench. My aunt came and knelt at my knees and cried, while prayers and songs swirled all around me in the little church. The whole congregation prayed for me alone, in a mighty wail of moans and voices. And I kept waiting serenely for Jesus, waiting, waiting—but he didn't come. I wanted to see him, but nothing happened to me. Nothing! I wanted something to happen to me, but nothing happened.

8   I heard the songs and the minister saying: "Why don't you come? My dear child, why don't you come to Jesus? Jesus is waiting for you. He wants you. Why don't you come? Sister Reed, what is this child's name?"

9   "Langston," my aunt sobbed.

10   "Langston, why don't you come? Why don't you come and be saved? Oh, Lamb of God! Why don't you come?"

11   Now it was really getting late. I began to be ashamed of myself, holding everything up so long. I began to wonder what God thought about Westley, who certainly hadn't seen Jesus either, but who was now sitting proudly on the platform, swinging his knickerbockered legs and grinning down at me, surrounded by deacons and old women on their knees praying. God had not struck Westley dead for taking his name in vain or for lying in the temple. So I decided that maybe to save further trouble, I'd better lie, too, and say that Jesus had come, and get up and be saved.

12   So I got up.

13   Suddenly the whole room broke into a sea of shouting, as they saw me rise. Waves of rejoicing swept the place. Women leaped in the air. My aunt threw her arms around me. The minister took me by the hand and led me to the platform.

14   When things quieted down, in a hushed silence, punctuated by a few ecstatic "Amens," all the new young lambs were blessed in the name of God. Then joyous singing filled the room.

15   That night, for the last time in my life but one—for I was a big boy twelve years old—I cried. I cried, in bed alone, and couldn't stop. I buried my head under the quilts, but my aunt heard me. She woke up and told my uncle I was crying because the Holy Ghost had come into my life, and because I had seen Jesus. But I was really crying because I couldn't bear to tell her that I had lied, that I had deceived everybody in the church, and I hadn't seen Jesus, and that now I didn't believe there was a Jesus any more, since he didn't come to help me.

The Write Connection

Directions: *Write a paragraph about the three things you learned or that you think are most important in the reading selection.*

_____

_____

_____

_____

_____

Comprehension Check

Directions: *See how many questions you can answer without referring to the selection. Then, review the selection to write more complete responses.*

_____ 1. From the information presented in paragraph 1, you can conclude that:
   a. the revival was considered to be a very special event by the church members.
   b. Auntie Reed was a deacon in the church.
   c. most children are sinners.
   d. the church needed more members.

_____ 2. You can conclude from paragraph 2 that the author believed:
   a. in the power of prayer.
   b. that he would actually see Jesus.
   c. that the older people of the church were exaggerating.
   d. that a light would shine on the church.

_____ 3. What is meant by the word *fold* as it is used in paragraph 3?
   a. towel   c. bend
   b. group   d. saved

4. What was the preacher's song about?

   _____

   _____

_____ 5. When the preacher referred to the children as "young lambs of God," he was using which form of figurative language?
   a. simile   c. antonym
   b. idiom   d. metaphor

6. How were the children supposed to show that they had been saved?

   _____

   _____

_____ 7. Langston was the last one to go to up to the altar because he:
   a. did not believe the preacher.
   b. had lost the bet he had made with Westley.
   c. was still waiting for Jesus to appear.
   d. was afraid to walk in front of the church by himself.

_____ 8. Langston cried because he had lied, but also because he:
  a. had disappointed Auntie Reed.
  b. had been saved.
  c. really didn't want to join the church.
  d. was disappointed that Jesus hadn't come to save him.

_____ 9. The author's tone can be described as:
  a. somber.   c. humorous.
  b. impartial.   d. terrifying.

10. Write one sentence from the selection that describes the author's tone of voice.

_____

Critical Thinking Check

_____ 1. Langston Hughes has written the selection in order to:
  a. discuss proper behavior in church.
  b. illustrate how he became disillusioned with the idea of God.
  c. sway the reader in favor of a particular religion.
  d. explain various styles of religious praise as a measurement of faith.

2. Give one word or phrase from the selection that helped you to recognize Langston Hughes's purpose for writing this selection.

_____

_____

3. Do you think that Langston Hughes has presented a positive or negative view of religion? Explain your answer. _____

_____

_____

4. Write a different ending to the story and explain why you chose to write the ending in that particular way. _____

_____

_____

Vocabulary Check

Directions: *See if any of the words you underlined in the selection are among the list of words below. If not, write your words in the spaces provided. Guess the meaning of the words from the way they were used in the selection. Then, look up the definition of each word in the dictionary to see if you were right.*

dire (*adj*): Your guess: _____

    Dictionary Definition: _____

gnarled (*adj*): Your guess: _____

    Dictionary Definition: _____

rounder (*n*): Your guess: _____

    Dictionary Definition: _____

Your word: _____ Your guess: _____

    Dictionary Definition: _____

Your word: _____ Your guess: _____

    Dictionary Definition: _____

♟♟♟ **Skills in Practice ▶ Reading Selection 2**

"LANGUAGE AND MEANING," FROM *THE BASICS
OF INTERPERSONAL COMMUNICATION*
Scott McLean

Accessing Prior Knowledge

Questions for Discussion

1. What is an example of a phrase or expression that is only understood among people within your particular group of friends, generation, or culture?

2. Why do you like to use this particular phrase or expression?

3. Would you use this phrase or expression on the job or in front of a prospective employer? Why or why not?

Preview and Predict

Directions: *Look at the title of the selection. Think about what you already know about the subject. Then, write a couple of predictions about what you are going to read. For instance, what will the author say about language?*

1. _____

2. _____

Word Search and Discovery

Directions: *Skim through the selection to find the two words below. Underline both words in the selection. Then, use a dictionary to write their definitions in the spaces provided. As you read and encounter these words, see if the definitions you wrote fit the way each world is used in the selection.*

arbitrary (*adj*): _____

inherent (*adj*): _____

Also, underline at least one new word as you read the selection and write your guess as to its meaning in the right margin of the text.

Text Notes in Practice

Directions: *Use a textbook study method such as SQUARE to identify the most important information in the selection. Then, create a study guide that you can use to prepare for the questions that follow the selection.*

LANGUAGE AND MEANING
Scott McLean

1   Language is symbolic. This means the words stand for concepts and things but are not the things themselves. Words, by themselves, do not have any inherent meaning. We give meaning to them. The arbitrary symbols (letters, numbers, and punctuation marks, for example) stand for sound and concepts in our experience. One way to think of this concept is to ask yourself: What is the value of a clay pot? The pot may have value to you because you made it or for its beauty, but one main function of the pot is to contain something. Its emptiness is, in effect, its value to you. Words, like that clay pot, are empty until you give them life and meaning by using them. Imagine yourself giving someone else a clay pot. Will he initially know what is inside? He may not be able to see in the shadows, and the meanings you have placed in the pot will have to be brought to the light by you. The person you give the pot to may also be able to reach inside and grasp some of the meaning, but when he brings the contents to the light of his own experience, he may perceive your meaning in new ways you did not plan on. By providing context, and explaining why you are giving him the pot as well as what it means to you, you help bridge the gap of understanding between you.

2   The letter "S" has a sound associated with it. The letter could just have easily have been reversed, or a different character entirely, when the alphabet was created. Once it was created, it became a character we refer to as representing a sound or, in combination with other letters, a word that represents an idea or concept.

3   Once we have an agreed-upon vocabulary, often stored in a dictionary, it is then possible to interpret words and refer to the denotative meaning. The **denotative meaning** is the dictionary meaning, or common meaning, that is generally agreed upon. Does everyone always agree on the meaning of words? Of course not. Take the word "cool," for example. At first it referred to temperature, as seen in a scale from cold to hot, or to describe a color, as in paintings from Picasso's Blue Period.

4   After World War II, the Beat Generation of the 1950s used the word "cool" to mean "hip" or "fashionable." Mainstream society still used the standard, dictionary meaning and had disdain for the slang meaning. Over time, the beat meaning came to be generally accepted, and now it is in common usage. Once, only a small group of "nontraditional" people used cool to refer to hip, but now aging "boomers" and dot.com CEOs alike use the word without fear of embarrassment.

5   This example shows how a word can go from its denotative (dictionary) meaning to a **connotative meaning,** one that has meaning to an individual or group, and how that special meaning became common. Connotative meanings can also refer to emotions associated with words, but the association between the word and the emotion is an individual or personal one and not held by larger society.

6   It is important to note that while the arbitrary and symbolic nature of language is universal, culture plays a significant role in how language is used and interpreted. For example, as noted by *The New York Times* (reprinted in *Reader's Digest*, 2003), the title for the film *There's Something about Mary* proved challenging for many foreign audience to understand. The movie was renamed several times to adapt to local audiences. In Poland blonde jokes are popular, and the film title became *For the Love of a Blonde*. In France, it was retitled *Mary at All Costs*, and for Thailand it became *My True Love Will Stand All Outrageous Events*. Each time, the title was changed to capture the meaning within the local culture of the audience.

—From McLean, Scott, *The Basics of Interpersonal Communication*, 1e. Published by Allyn and Bacon, Boston, MA. Copyright © 2005 by Pearson Education. Reprinted by permission of the publisher.

The Write Connection

Directions: *Write a paragraph about the three things you learned or that you think are most important in the reading selection.*

_____

_____

_____

_____

_____

Comprehension Check

Directions: *See how many questions you can answer without referring to the selection. Then, review the selection to write more complete responses.*

_____   1. The author's tone can be described as:
   a. humorous.   c. bitter.
   b. impartial.   d. argumentative.

_____   2. Which of the following statements best illustrates the main idea of the selection?
   a. There is no understanding of words unless they are clearly stated.
   b. There are several differences between denotative and connotative meanings.
   c. Mainstream society still prefers to use slang rather than the dictionary meaning of words.
   d. Words are given meaning by the way they are used in a particular context or situation.

   3. The denotative meaning of a word refers to _____.

_____ 4. Which of the following statements illustrates the denotative usage of a word?
   a. The car is a *lemon* that has cost me a lot of money.
   b. The baby cried when she tasted the *lemon*.
   c. That's a really *cool* necklace.
   d. He's *hot*.

5. The connotative meaning of a word is one that has _____

_____

_____ 6. Which of the following statements illustrates the connotative usage of a word?
   a. The *witch* told my boss I was late even though I had arrived on time.
   b. She chose to dress as a *witch* for the costume party.
   c. I had a problem *which* he helped me to solve.
   d. I burned my finger because the frying pan was *hot*.

_____ 7. What is the meaning of the word *disdain* as it is used in paragraph 4?
   a. disapproval.   c. relations.
   b. dye.   d. interest.

8. How was the title of the film *There's Something about Mary* adapted for foreign audiences? (Give one example.)

_____

Critical Thinking Check

_____ 1. The author has written the selection in order to:
   a. amuse the reader by discussing various types of symbols.
   b. distinguish key differences between symbols and dictionary definitions.
   c. propose the use of a collegiate dictionary over a pocket dictionary.
   d. illustrate how meaning is given to words and phrases.

2. In your own words, write what you think is the main point the author is making in the selection.

_____

_____

_____ 3. Which of the following conclusions can be drawn from paragraph 4?
   a. The Beat Generation of the 1950s created most of the slang we use today.
   b. CEOs and aging "boomers," in general, do not use slang.
   c. Mainstream society prefers the use of slang.
   d. The use of slang is usually avoided by successful professionals.

4. Have you ever told a joke or a story that was funny to your friends, but not funny to someone of a different culture? What happened, and why do you think the person did not find your joke or story amusing?

_____

_____

_____

_____

Vocabulary Check

Directions: *See if any of the words you underlined in the selection are among the list of words below. If not, write your words in the spaces provided. Guess the meaning of the words from the way they were used in the selection. Then, look up the definition of each word in the dictionary to see if you were right.*

mainstream (*adj*): Your guess: _____

    Dictionary Definition: _____

universal (*adj*): Your guess: _____

    Dictionary Definition: _____

Your word: _____ Your guess: _____

    Dictionary Definition: _____

Your word: _____ Your guess: _____

    Dictionary Definition: _____

12 Inference

Liberty cannot be preserved without a general knowledge of the people.

—John Quincy Adams

In this chapter you will learn how to:

Make Reasonable Inferences

Recognize Propaganda

You will learn the following strategy:

The Sherlock Method: A Strategy for Making Reasonable Inferences

▲ Reading can reveal more than the eye can see.

Preview and Predict ▶ What do you know so far?

How many of the following questions can you answer before you read this chapter?

• How do you know that someone is in a hurry?

_____

• What is an inference?

_____

- What would your advertisement look like if you wanted other students to buy a product you created?

  _____

- What is propaganda?

  _____

- Think of one way in which the picture relates to this chapter's objectives.

  _____

Now, as you read the chapter, look for the answers, to see if you were right.

MAKING REASONABLE INFERENCES

Have you ever been able to figure out who committed the crime on a television murder mystery before it was solved at the end of the program? Have you ever felt as if someone was lying and then discovered you were right? These conclusions are called *inferences*. An **inference** is a conclusion based on *evidence* found in behaviors or events that have a common reference point.

Example

A woman is sitting at her desk in an office. She is filing her nails, frequently looking at the clock, and yawning.

What can you *infer* about the woman? Can you infer that she is bored? Yes. What

evidence supports your inference that the woman is bored? _____

_____ Most people would reach the same conclusion you did about the woman because her behaviors are commonly associated with boredom. In other words, these behaviors have a *common reference point*. So, most people would use the same evidence to form a reasonable conclusion that the woman is bored.

On the other hand, would you infer that the woman is the owner of the company? No, because there is no evidence to support such a conclusion. A reasonable inference is based on evidence. The better you become at assessing behaviors or events, the more reasonable your inferences will be.

Using the evidence from what you observe in order to make reasonable inferences is like being a detective. For instance, you may use what you have learned about the way people behave and what these behaviors usually mean from your own past experience to form inferences. You may use what you know about the world or the nature of things to arrive at a reasonable conclusion based on certain events. In the same way, you can apply these detecting skills to make reasonable inferences as you read.

Authors often use descriptive language when presenting an important person, place, or thing. These descriptions provide the evidence you need in order to make reasonable inferences as you read. For instance, the description of an important person's behavior in a story can be used to make reasonable inferences about his or her character. A history text might describe the house where Abraham Lincoln was raised. You might use this information to support a reasonable inference about the way people lived in America during the early 1800s. A chemistry text might describe the negative reaction caused when two chemicals are combined. This information can be used to support a reasonable inference about the care that should be taken when working with these chemicals.

The Sherlock Method: A Strategy for Making Reasonable Inferences

The character Sherlock Holmes is a famous detective created by the mystery author, Sir Arthur Conan Doyle. Sherlock Holmes was able to solve the most difficult crimes because of his ability to assess the evidence. When the crime was solved, he would explain the behaviors or events that helped him to arrive at his conclusion. The Sherlock Method is a strategy that will help you to sharpen your ability to assess the evidence you need to make reasonable inferences as you read. To apply The Sherlock Method you should take the following steps.

 ## 1. Investigate the Scene

As you read, look for details that stand out in same way. Notice the kinds of words or phrases that are used to describe or discuss a person, place, or thing. What words or phrases does the author use to describe or discuss a particular behavior or situation?

 ## 2. Look For a Suspect

Ask yourself "What do I think about or suspect is meant by what the author has said or about the way the author has presented his or her ideas? Doing this helps you to connect the information you are reading to details you have already read to form a reasonable conclusion or inference.

♟ 3. Confirm the Evidence

Look for additional evidence that confirms what you inferred from the information presented in the text. For instance, what specific words or phrases did the author use that support your conclusion?

An accurate inference is based on evidence. The more evidence you have the more accurate your inferences will be. Notice the difference between the following descriptions.

Example 1

Ginny was Rhonda's best friend and roommate. Brad was Rhonda's boyfriend.

Example 2

Rhonda had called her roommate, Ginny, to say that she would be home in an hour. "Please tell Brad to wait for me, okay?" Rhonda said, innocently. Soon, Ginny watched Brad walk up to the apartment door from the window. Her mind began to race just looking at the cocky way he moved in those tight blue jeans. Ginny could feel her heart pounding as his steps got closer and closer. "Stop it!" Ginny thought. "Brad belongs to Rhonda. Rhonda is your best friend." When she heard his strong rap on the door, Ginny whispered, "I don't care. He belongs with me."

The first example does not give you enough evidence to form any reasonable conclusions about the characters of Ginny, Rhonda, or Brad. The second example, however, provides enough evidence to support several inferences about Ginny, Brad, and Rhonda. For instance:

1. What can you infer about Ginny? _____

    _____

2. Write one word or phrase from the second example that supports your conclusion. _____

3. What can you infer about Brad? _____

    _____

4. Write one word or phrase from the second example that supports your conclusion. _____

5. What can you infer about Rhonda? _____

6. Write one word or phrase from the second example that supports your conclusion. _____

Were you able to make reasonable inferences about Brad, Ginny, and Rhonda from the second example? Compare your inferences with those of your classmates. You will find that they are very similar because an inference is based on evidence that has a common reference point.

Read the following example, and then answer the questions that follow.

Example 3

A baby is sitting on the lap of his mother at a fall festival held at an elementary school. A man sits next to the mother and begins to make faces at the baby and the baby smiles. Suddenly, the man puts on a mask and the baby begins to scream.

Write the word *yes* next to the inferences you could support using evidence from the example. If there is no evidence for the statement, write the word *no* in the space provided.

_____ 1. The baby was happy when the man made faces at him.

_____ 2. The baby is four months old.

_____ 3. The man is the baby's father.

_____ 4. The baby was frightened by the man's mask.

Statements 1 and 4 are reasonable inferences because there is evidence to support them. The baby *smiled* when the man made faces. The baby *screamed* after looking at the man's mask. On the other hand, Statements 2 and 3 are not reasonable inferences because there is no evidence in the example to support them. There is no evidence to support that the baby is four months old or that the man is the baby's father.

Read the cartoon. Then, answer the question that follows.

Example 4

Cleats

_____ You can infer from the cartoon that:

    a. the children who are talking have lost the juggling endurance contest.

    b. the children who are talking are best friends.

    c. Abby might win the contest because she is in the shade.

    d. the girl who is talking knows that Abby is a professional juggler.

Statement c is a reasonable inference because the evidence in the cartoon supports it. The girl is saying that she believes Abby will win. Then, we see Abby juggling a ball under the shade of a tree while Mondo is juggling in the sun.

A good detective knows how to assess the evidence before reaching a conclusion. If you apply The Sherlock Method, you will learn to see what is being described and use it to form reasonable inferences based on the evidence you identify as you are reading.

Activity 12.1 ▶ Using the Sherlock Method to Make Reasonable Inferences

Directions: *There are four reasonable inferences among the seven statements that follow each paragraph. Write the word* yes *next to each of the reasonable inferences.*

Paragraph 1

Joe invited Jenny to his apartment for dinner. He carefully set the table with his best dinnerware and candles. The wine was chilling and the meal was about to be served, when Joe said, "I have something I want you to hear." Then, Joe played the CD that had the name of his group on the cover. As the music began to play, Jenny frowned. She looked at the CD player and shook her head.

_____ 1. Joe likes Jenny.

_____ 2. Joe is in a band.

_____ 3. Joe is a world famous musician.

_____ 4. Joe wanted Jenny to like the CD.

_____ 5. Jenny is an executive in the music business.

_____ 6. Jenny does not like the music.

_____ 7. Joe broke up with Jenny after their date.

Paragraph 2

A crowd had formed on the street. A twisted bicycle was sticking out from underneath the front of a dented car. The police had blocked traffic from entering the side of the street where a white sheet had been placed to cover a small body. Two women in the crowd covered their mouths with their hands. Some people in the crowd stared at the blood on the pavement next to the white sheet. Other bystanders watched the two policemen who were talking to a woman who swayed back and forth next to her dented car. "I only had one or a couple of some beers. That's all. I promise, Mister, I mean, officer," she slurred.

_____ 1. There was an accident.

_____ 2. The child was riding a bicycle to school.

_____ 3. A child was killed.

_____ 4. The crowd was asked to leave.

_____ 5. Some of the people in the crowd were shocked by what they saw.

_____ 6. The woman by the dented car had been drinking.

_____ 7. The woman was later sentenced to life in prison.

Paragraph 3

A man and a woman came into the fast-food restaurant with two small children. The woman sat at a table with the children. When the man walked to the front of the restaurant to place an order, the children began to scream with excitement as they chased each other, hiding under tables where other customers were sitting. The other customers looked toward the woman and shook their heads when the children stood on top of chairs next to an empty booth and ate packets of sugar. Suddenly, one of the children hid under a table where a man was sitting. He asked the boy to get out. As the boy emerged from underneath the table, the man's cola fell over and spilled onto the floor. The child did not look back as he ran to hide under another table. The woman stared at the floor where the drink had spilled, then looked out of the window without expression.

_____ 1. The children have been abused by their father.

_____ 2. The children were not supervised.

_____ 3. The children enjoyed playing with each other in the restaurant.

_____ 4. The event happened at Burger King.

_____ 5. The woman was not concerned about what the children were doing.

_____ 6. The other customers in the restaurant disapproved of the children's behavior.

_____ 7. The children knew that they were causing a disturbance in the restaurant.

Paragraph 4

Walking to school had always been Sara's favorite part of the day. She would follow the winding narrow path along the tree-lined ditch bank and imagine herself in an African jungle. Clara's house was nestled beside the ditch on Major Avenue. Sara could hardly wait to run down the side of the ditch bank to Clara's front gate. From there she would smell the fragrance of honeysuckle, jasmine, and wisteria blooming in Clara's carefully tended garden. The aroma of fresh cinnamon toast and coffee would greet her like a kiss as she reached the front door. Then, she and Clara, who was in her eighties, would share milk and toast and a special friendship that had lasted six years since Sara was in the first grade. Today, there was no smell of toast. No one came to the door. There was an eerie silence behind the door as if the air had been removed from the house.

_____ 1. Sara enjoyed her visits with Clara.

_____ 2. Sara lives in an African jungle.

_____ 3. Clara didn't mind making toast for Sara.

_____ 4. Sara was in the sixth grade.

_____ 5. Something has happened to Clara.

_____ 6. Clara was placed in a nursing home.

_____ 7. Clara has passed away.

Paragraph 5

I grew up with Pam, but had not spoken to her in the five years since she married Bob. They had moved to another city. Whenever I called, Bob always answered the phone and said that Pam was not there. So, when I heard that they were in town visiting her mom, I decided to drop in. When her mom opened the door, she gave me an extra long hug and welcomed me inside. I could see Bob in the kitchen eating a sandwich. Pam was sitting on the living room couch looking at her hands. She barely looked up when her mom said, "Look who's here, PJ." Her body was stiff and when she did look up, there were tears in her eyes. "How are you, Pam?" I asked, "Are you doing okay?" Pam looked at me for a few seconds without saying a word. I noticed that she was wearing a long-sleeved blouse even though it was the middle of July. Yet, before she could say a word, Bob called from the kitchen, "Hey stupid. Get in here . . . Now!" Pam jumped up immediately at the sound of his voice and went into the kitchen. "What the hell are you doing in there?" he yelled.

_____ 1. Pam is in an abusive relationship.

_____ 2. Pam's father has passed away.

_____ 3. Pam rarely visits her mother.

_____ 4. Pam is afraid of her husband.

_____ 5. Pam and her husband live in Kansas.

_____ 6. The event takes place in the summer.

_____ 7. Pam is upset about something.

Your ability to make accurate inferences will improve your reading comprehension because you are using visualization skills that allow you to form conclusions that are based on evidence contained in the text.

Memory Check 1   How much do you remember?

1. What is an inference? _____

_____

2. What are the three steps to apply in The Sherlock Method?

a. _____

b. _____

c. _____

INFERENCES AND PROPAGANDA

Propaganda refers to methods used to spread ideas or beliefs to a wide audience. Propaganda is designed to persuade by using language or images that create an emotional response. Examples of the power of propaganda to influence people can be found in advertisements and political speeches where language or images are carefully presented to have a particular effect.

Advertisers and political speech writers know a great deal about psychology. They know that people are motivated by certain needs and emotions. For instance, that people have the need to feel safe, to feel comfortable or satisfied, to feel loved, to feel important, or to feel as if they belong. Advertisers and political speech writers have studied how to create an association between these emotional needs and what they want to sell. They use language and images to create an emotional "I need" response that will motivate people to buy what they are selling. Often the associations they create are so powerful that people are often unaware of their influence.

Some propaganda is relatively harmless. For instance, you might incorrectly infer from an advertisement that shows sexy models wearing a particular brand of clothing that you too will belong to a popular group or feel more important if you buy the clothing. Yet, propaganda can also have dangerous consequences when it is used to sway the opinions of people against a particular race or culture. Adolf Hitler used propaganda to promote himself as a savior of the German people during the 1930s and 1940s prior to World War II. He was able to convince the German people that anyone of Jewish origin was a threat to the safety of the country and that they would be good Germans if they hated the Jews. As a result, very few Germans were willing to stop Hitler's soldiers when they took whole families of Jewish citizens to concentration camps to be killed.

It is important to become familiar with the most common propaganda techniques so that you are not easily fooled by what you read or experience.

Common Propaganda Techniques

Bandwagon

This technique is named after the bandwagon that is part of many parades. A band plays from the trailer of a truck or wagon. As it moves down the street, the band invites the parade-goers to follow behind them to join the parade. "Come on, everybody! Hurry up! Get on the bandwagon. Don't be left out."

The **bandwagon technique** appeals to your fear of being left out as well as your desire to be like others. Here are some examples of the bandwagon technique.

- The polls show that Terry Blake is far ahead of his opponent, Joe Dunn. Mr. Blake is sure to win the election. Be on the winning side. Vote for Terry Blake. (Inference: I want to be like others who are voting for Mr. Blake.)

- If you call in the next ten minutes, you will receive a free psychic reading! Hurry! (Inference: I'd better call now, or I will miss out on the free psychic reading.)

- Supplies of Amego High-Def are limited. We only have a few items left in stock. Don't miss this amazing offer! Hurry! (Inference: Everyone wants Amego High-Def and I don't want to be the only one who doesn't have it.)

- Everyone is wearing the latest style of Gaga tennis shoes and jerseys. (Inference: I'd better get Gaga tennis shoes or I will be different from everyone else.)

Transfer

Certain symbols are used so often in our culture that they do not have to be explained. For instance, a beautiful or handsome model is used to represent sexual attractiveness and appeals to your need to feel desirable. Expensive cars and other glamorous items are used to represent wealth and status and appeal to your need to feel important. The American flag, American soldiers, famous presidents, or the American eagle are used to represent feelings of patriotism and appeal to your need for approval or protection as an American. Crosses and other religious symbols are used to represent spiritual values and appeal to your need for approval or protection by God.

The **transfer technique** refers to the use of symbols or images that represent or imply sex appeal, importance or status, patriotism, or spiritual values to influence your thinking. The emotions you feel in connection to these symbols are automatically transferred to the products or ideas associated with them. As a result, these symbols can be a very powerful tool for advertisers and political speech writers who want to appeal to your needs or desires. Here are some examples of the transfer technique in action.

- A sexy model is lying across the hood of car in an advertisement. (Inference: Maybe I'll attract someone like her if I buy that car.)

- The car in the advertisement has expensive leather seats and state-of-the-art stereo equipment. The man in the car is wearing a Rolex watch and an Armani suit. He is pulling into the driveway of his mansion. (Inference: If I buy that car, I will be important, rich, and successful.)

- A political candidate is described as an American hero who fought in the Iraq War. A picture shows the candidate wearing her uniform and standing in front of the American flag. (Inference: If I vote for this candidate, I will be a good American.)

- A law firm advertises that they are Christian lawyers who will use God's laws to defend you. (Inference: If I use this law firm, I will be protected by God.)

Memory Check 2 How much do you remember?

1. What are two phrases or words commonly used in the bandwagon technique?

   _____

2. The bandwagon technique appeals to your fear of being left out as well as

   your desire _____

3. The transfer technique refers to the use of symbols or images that _____

   _____

4. What is an example of a symbol that can be used to appeal to your need to

   feel important? _____

   _____

5. What is an example of a symbol that can be used to appeal to your need to

   feel sexually attractive? _____

Plain Folks

This technique refers to the use of language or images that are associated with safety, trust, or comfort. For instance, we trust people we know, such as family, friends, and significant others. We also trust people who are easy to relate to because they are similar to us, or because they make us laugh or feel at ease. Advertisers and politicians know you are more likely to buy a product or vote for a candidate if they use language or images that suggest trustworthiness. The **plain folks technique** appeals to your need to feel safe or comfortable.

For instance, trial lawyers know how to use the Plain Folks technique. Have you ever seen a suspected murderer who has just been arrested on television and looks like he just crawled out of a sewer? You might say to yourself, "Look at that monster. Yeah, he did it." Then, later at the trial, the suspect is brought into the courtroom looking like he just came from church. The lawyer knows that the jury can be influenced by the way the suspect looks. If the suspect looks like someone the jury members might trust, such as a family member, they might have more compassion for him or her. Here are some examples of the plain folks technique in use.

- An article shows a picture of a candidate in blue jeans, standing with his family and pets, holding a baby, and shaking the hand of an elderly person. (Inference: He is going to help the common people, not big business.)

- An advertisement shows three ordinary women standing in a very cozy kitchen with food cooking in the background, having a good time drinking Miracle Coffee. (Inference: Miracle Coffee will make me, my friends, or family members feel more comfortable in my home.)

- An advertisement shows Grandma standing in front of her family members, who are sitting at a table filled with food. Everyone at the table appears to be excited about a bowl of mashed potatoes that is lifted up in praise by her son. Grandma is smiling proudly, but looking upwards as if she has a secret. The family cannot see a box of Mother's Love Instant Potatoes hidden under a nearby table. Under the picture is the following sentence: "Nothing Says Love Like Mother's Love Instant Potatoes." (Inference: If Grandma trusts Mother's Love Instant Potatoes, then they must be good.)

- Three ordinary-looking men are watching a football game on television. They are jumping up and yelling at each play. Pizza, beer, and popcorn are quickly disappearing from the coffee table. Each time more food disappears, the bellies of the men begin to grow. When all of the food and beverages are gone, you see them jump up to yell at a play. Suddenly their pants split as they are sitting down. When cheering is heard again from the television, no one jumps up. "Comfort Jeans and Slacks. We've got your back." (Inference: I would feel safer knowing that the same thing won't happen to me if I buy Comfort Jeans and Slacks.)

Name Calling

Name calling is a technique that is used to make a person or product look undesirable or unsafe in some way. This technique is easy to recognize because the tone of the message is usually negative. Sometimes, however, humor is used in order to make fun of a person or product. Advertisers and political speech writers know you are more likely to avoid a person who is portrayed as weak or untrustworthy or a product that is described as poorly made or unsafe. Name calling appeals to your fear of being harmed, looking foolish, or being disliked. For instance, you may incorrectly infer that you will be considered foolish if you support a particular person who has been described as an undesirable candidate.

Like gossip, the name calling technique may be used to imply that all of the negative statements made about a person or product are true without providing evidence to support them. So, it is important to investigate the truthfulness of negative statements made about a person or product in order to make more informed decisions. Here are some examples of name calling.

- Joe Dunn says that he's a war hero, but he's not. He lied about the way he earned his awards and medals. Vote for an honest candidate. Vote for Terry Blake. (Inference: If I vote for Joe Dunn, I will be voting for a liar.)

- Terry Blake would like you to think that he's for the common man. Yet, if you look at his record, you will see that he only supports big businesses that cut jobs. Can you afford to vote for Terry Blake? No. Vote for Joe Dunn. (Inference: I might lose my job if I vote for Terry Blake.)

- An advertisement has two pictures side by side. The picture on the left shows a tall stack of hamburgers on a plate in a Dooley's Hamburger kitchen that looks dark and empty. The picture on the right shows a smiling fast-food cook wearing a Raymond's Burger Joint uniform frying a hamburger in a spotless kitchen. Happy customers are eating in the background of the picture. The advertisement says: "Don't take chances with your burger. Eat at Raymond's Burger Joint." (Inference: I might get sick if I eat at Dooley's.)

- My opponent, Jerry Rickheimer, voted against the Hawk Bill that would have increased military spending. (Inference: America will be unsafe if I vote for Jerry Rickheimer.)

Testimonial

The **testimonial technique** uses a famous person or celebrity to sell a product or to support a person or political candidate. Advertisers and political speech writers know that you are more likely to trust the "testimony" of a famous person. The testimonial technique appeals to your need for approval or to feel a connection to someone you admire or respect. Here are some examples of the testimonial technique.

- An article shows a presidential candidate with his hand on the shoulder of Will Smith. The title of the article is "The Fresh Prince visits the future president of the United States." (Inference: Since I like Will Smith and Will Smith likes the candidate, I like the candidate.)

- A famous basketball player is seen throwing a basketball on the court. The ball bounces off several chairs, a wall, and a bleacher to fall through the hoop in the remaining seconds of the game. The famous ball player picks up a bottle of Blastaide and drinks it while the crowd cheers. (Inference: I will be like my favorite basketball player if I drink Blastaide.)

- An advertisement shows famous singer, song-writer, Maja in a music studio wearing headphones. It says, "When I make recordings in the studio, I want the sound to be perfect. That's why I use Xina CD's." (Inference: If Maja uses Xina CD's, they must be good.)

- An actor who plays a lawyer on a famous television court drama is seen on an advertisement for the McGuffie law firm. (Inference: The McGuffie law firm must be good if the lawyer on *Crime and Misdemeanors* is on their side.)

Memory Check 3 How much do you remember?

1. The plain folks technique refers to _____
   _____

2. The plain folks technique appeals to your need to feel _____

3. Name calling is a technique that is used to make an opposing person or
   product appear _____

4. How is name calling similar to gossip? _____
   _____
   _____

5. Why do advertisers and political speech writers use famous people to sell a
   product or political candidate? _____
   _____

6. The testimonial technique appeals to your need for _____
   _____

Activity 12.2 ▶ Identifying Propaganda Techniques

Directions *Read each of the following items and identify whether it is an example of the bandwagon, testimonial, transfer, plain folks, or name calling technique. Write your answers on the lines provided.*

1. Joe Dunn's proposed bill is a joke. It will raise our taxes and take money away
   from federal programs. Terry Blake has a more intelligent solution. _____

2. We have the best furniture on the market at the lowest prices. Americans want
   a good deal. Get a good deal at Eagle Furniture Warehouse. _____

3. If you call in the next fifteen minutes, you'll receive the cookbook, plus the
   special utensils, and the no-stick pie pan! _____

4. Manny Rodriquez, quarterback for the Kingston Riders, picks up a Terryington Razor and shaves his cheek. "Terryington Razors are smooth, and take it from me, I know smooth." _____

5. Get your next loan at Invest Bank. At Invest Bank, you're family. _____

6. Run, don't walk to the Mega Byte Spring Cleaning Sale! Saturday Only from 10 A.M.–8 P.M. Come early. Supplies are limited. _____

7. Actress Lilly Langbush says, "'Purrfect Cat' gives my cat a healthy coat and lots of energy." _____

8. You wouldn't ask a boy to do a man's job. So, why would you buy a Windsong Truck when you could own a Magnum Super Cab Truck? Magnum Super Cab Trucks: Built to Last. _____

9. Glamorous: A word that describes the new Venus Coupe. Luxurious leather seats, surround-sound five-disc CD player, and a GPS system are just some of the features designed to accommodate the way you live. The Venus Coupe; The Mark of Success. _____

10. Mac Tasty Macaroni and Cheese. Tastes like home. _____

The people who write political speeches and advertisements are particularly clever in their use of propaganda to persuade you to buy their products or share their beliefs. In fact, as you become more familiar with these techniques, you will begin to notice that these writers often combine several techniques within one advertisement or speech to enhance the effect. For instance, a political article might promote a candidate using pictures of an American flag or eagles while making negative comments about the opposing candidate. If you can recognize each technique, you will reduce the powerful effect of propaganda upon the decisions you make in your life.

Activity 12.3 ▶ Recognizing Inferences: Textbook Applications

Directions: Answer the questions that follow each of the following paragraphs.

Paragraph 1

All matter is composed of *elements,* of which there are about 110 different kinds. Of the 88 elements that occur in nature, one or more is used to make all the substances in the universe. Many elements are already familiar to you. Perhaps you use aluminum in the form of foil or drink a soft drink from an aluminum can. You may have a ring or necklace made of gold, or silver, or perhaps platinum. If you play tennis or golf, your racket or clubs may be made from the elements titanium or carbon. In the body, calcium and phosphorus form the structure of bones and teeth, iron and copper are needed in the formation of red blood cells, and iodine is required for the proper functioning of the thyroid.

—From *Basic Chemistry*, 2nd ed. © Karen C. Timberlake
and William Timberlake. p. 94.

_____ 1. T/F Illness may result if certain elements are not present in a person's body.

_____ 2. T/F Aluminum is the most common element found in nature.

_____ 3. Which of the following conclusions can be drawn from the information contained in the paragraph?
   a. Elements are composed of matter found in nature.
   b. Most elements occur in nature.
   c. Man-made elements are becoming more common in our daily lives.
   d. Matter is composed of aluminum, titanium, silver, gold, platinum, and carbon.

Paragraph 2

Economists like to make a distinction between *preferences* and *demand*. A consumer's preferences are what he or she likes; a consumer's demands are what he or she buys. You might prefer a Porsche to a Chevrolet, but you buy the cheaper car because that is what your budget will allow. You buy the Chevrolet from the list of cars you can afford. Preferences and demand are different, yet what we demand depends on our preferences. The amount of goods and services that households purchase depends not only on prices and income, but also on preferences and tastes.

—From *Principles of Economics*, 7th Ed. by Roy J. Ruffin and
Paul R. Gregory. p. 118.

_____ 4. T/F Most people would prefer a Porsche to a Chevrolet.

_____ 5. T/F Purchases are largely based on consumer preferences.

_____   6. Which of the following conclusions can be drawn from the information contained in the paragraph?
   a. Consumer preferences determine the demand for goods and services.
   b. The economy is based on consumer preferences for particular goods and
   services.
   c. Consumer demand and preferences determine the amount of goods and
   services purchased per household.
   d. People are likely to demand more affordable goods and services depending
   upon the state of the economy.

Paragraph 3

When Europeans "discovered" America, they stumbled on continents that
had been occupied for thousands of years by people who had developed a
rich variety of cultures. The earliest explorers and colonists wondered who the
Native Americans were and how they had come to America. Some Europeans
thought they were the descendants of the Ten Lost Tribes of Israel. Modern
archaeology has demonstrated that the American Indians share a common
set of ancestors with modern Asian people.

—From *The Pursuit of Liberty: A History of the American People.* 3rd ed. vol. I
by R. Jackson Wilson [et al.] p. 24.

_____   7. T/F The Europeans were interested in the origin of the Native Americans.

_____   8. T/F The European settlers were the first to discover the origin of Native
Americans.

_____   9. Which of the following conclusions can be drawn from the information contained in the paragraph?
   a. Native Americans are descendants of the Ten Lost Tribes of Israel.
   b. The Europeans were afraid of the Native Americans.
   c. Native Americans most likely came to America from Japan or Vietnam.
   d. America was already inhabited when the Europeans arrived.

Paragraph 4

Around the world, the first group to have a major impact on humans is the
family. Unlike some animals, we cannot survive by ourselves, and as babies we
are utterly dependent on our family. Our experiences in the family are so intense

that they have a lifelong impact on us. They lay down our basic sense of self, establishing our initial motivations, values, and beliefs. The family gives us ideas about who we are and what we deserve out of life. It is in the family that we begin to think of ourselves as strong or weak, smart or dumb, good-looking or ugly—or somewhere in between. And as already noted, here we begin the lifelong process of defining ourselves as female or male.

—From Henslin, James M. *Sociology: A Down-to-Earth Approach,*
Core Concepts, 1e. Published by Allyn and Bacon, Boston, MA.
Copyright © 2006 by Pearson Education. Reprinted by
permission of the publisher.

———— 10. T/F A person who does not have a family is likely to feel unattractive.

———— 11. T/F Animals are unable to survive without a family.

———— 12. Which of the following conclusions can be drawn from the information contained in the paragraph?
  a. Family experiences can impact every aspect of our development.
  b. We are unable to form life-long motivations, values, and beliefs without a family.
  c. Our basic sense of self is formed by the input of both a mother and father in the home.
  d. Confusion regarding gender roles is more likely without a strong family relationship.

Paragraph 5

People who fall asleep suddenly and unexpectedly have a disorder known as *narcolepsy*. In addition to daytime sleepiness, people with narcolepsy experience muscle weakness as they fall uncontrollably into sleep, and their sleep stages do not follow the normal cycle. This disorder affects about 1 in 2,000 people and can cause them to have a very restricted life—they never know when they will have an attack. Narcolepsy has a genetic component (Takahashi, 1999), and an effective drug treatment has recently been developed (Dement, 1999).

—From Lefton, Lester A. & Linda Brannon, *Psychology,* 8e. Published by
Allyn and Bacon, Boston, MA. Copyright © 2002 by Pearson
Education. Reprinted by permission of the publisher.

———— 13. T/F A person who has narcolepsy may fall asleep while driving.

———— 14. T/F Narcolepsy is a relatively common disorder.

_____ 15. Which of the following conclusions can be drawn from the information contained in the paragraph?

    a. Psychotherapy has been shown to reduce narcolepsy.

    b. Advances in drug therapy may allow people with narcolepsy to lead normal lives.

    c. Many people with narcolepsy are concerned about spreading their disorder to others.

    d. It is possible to develop narcolepsy as a result of poor sleep habits.

 Test Yourself Review Quiz

Chapter Review Questions

1. What is an inference? _____

_____

2. What three steps should you follow to apply The Sherlock Method?

    a. _____

    b. _____

    c. _____

_____ 3. Which propaganda technique might use a sexy model to sell a product?

    a. bandwagon   c. plain-folk

    b. transfer   d. testimonial

_____ 4. Which propaganda technique might use the phrase, "Supplies are limited"?

    a. bandwagon   c. name calling

    b. transfer   d. plain folk

_____ 5. Which propaganda technique might show a candidate wearing blue jeans?

    a. bandwagon   c. transfer

    b. name calling   d. plain folk

_____ 6. Which propaganda technique might describe an opposing candidate in a negative way?

    a. bandwagon   c. testimonial

    b. name calling   d. plain folk

_____ 7. Which propaganda technique might use a famous person to sell a product?
   a. bandwagon   c. testimonial
   b. transfer   d. plain folk

Application Questions

Look at the following advertisements. Then, answer the questions that follow.

Advertisement 1

Don't
Miss IT!

**Look for your FIESTA GUIDE in the
Compton Daily News!
Subscribe Today**

1. Which propaganda technique is used in this advertisement? _____

Advertisement 2

EAGLE AUTOS

BE American
BUY American

2. Which propaganda technique is used in this advertisement? _____

Advertisement 3

3. Which propaganda technique is used in Advertisement 3? _____

   Support your response _____

   _____

4. Look at the picture below. Then, answer the question that follows it.

What can you infer from the picture? What evidence do you have to support your conclusion?

_____

_____

_____

_____

Summarization Activity

Directions: *Write the major headings in this chapter. Under each heading, write a couple of sentences about the most important topics presented in the section of text that follows that heading.*

First Heading _____

What information is most important? _____

_____

_____

Second Heading _____

What information is most important? _____

_____

_____

Third Heading _____

What information is most important? _____

_____

_____

Combine the information you wrote in this outline into a paragraph to summarize what you have learned in this chapter.

Reflection Activity

How am I am going to apply what I have learned in this chapter?

Directions: *On a separate sheet of paper, write a paragraph about the two or three things you learned about inference that were most helpful to you and how you plan to use what you have learned.*

"*Fear*," From *Living Up the Street*
Gary Soto

Accessing Prior Knowledge

Questions for Discussion

1. Have you ever been afraid of another classmate? If so, what happened and what did you do about it?

2. What do you think causes a person to become a bully?

Preview and Predict

Directions: *Look at the title of the selection. Think about what you already know about the subject. Then, write a couple of predictions about what you are going to read. For instance, what will the author discuss about fear?*

1. _____

2. _____

Word Search and Discovery

Directions: *Skim through the selection to find the two words below. Underline both words in the selection. Then, use a dictionary to write their definitions in the spaces provided. As you read and encounter these words, see if the definitions you wrote fit the way each word is used in the selection.*

backstop (*n*): _____

rifled (*vb*): _____

Also, underline at least one new word as you read the selection and write your guess as to its meaning in the right margin of the text.

Text Notes in Practice

Directions: *Use a textbook study method such as SQUARE to identify the most important information in the selection. Then, create a study guide that you can use to prepare for the questions that follow the selection.*

FEAR

Gary Soto

1 A cold day after school. Frankie T., who would drown his brother by accident that coming spring and would use a length of pipe to beat a woman in a burglary years later, had me pinned on the ground behind a backstop, his breath sour as meat left out in the sun. "*Cabron*," he called me and I didn't say anything. I stared at his face, shaped like the sole of a shoe, and just went along with the insults, although now and then I tried to raise a shoulder in a halfhearted struggle because that was part of the game.

2 He let his drool yo-yo from his lips, missing my feet by only inches, after which he giggled and called me names. Finally he let me up. I slapped grass from my jacket and pants, and pulled my shirt tail from my pants to shake out the fistful of dirt he had stuffed in my collar. I stood by him, nervous and red-faced from struggling, and when he suggested that we climb the monkey bars together, I followed him quietly to the kid's section of Jefferson Elementary. He climbed first, with small grunts, and for a second I thought of running but knew he would probably catch me—if not then, the next day. There was no way out of being a fifth grader—the daily event of running to teachers to show them your bloody nose. It was just a fact, like having lunch.

3 So I climbed the bars and tried to make conversation, first about the girls in our classroom and then about kickball. He looked at me smiling as if I had a camera in my hand, his teeth green like the underside of a rock, before he relaxed his grin into a simple gray line across his face. He told me to shut up. He gave me a hard stare and I looked away to a woman teacher walking to her car and wanted very badly to yell for help. She unlocked her door, got in, played with her face in the visor mirror while the engine warmed, and then drove off with blue smoke trailing. Frankie was watching me all along and when I turned to him, he laughed, "*Chale!* She can't help you, *ese*." He moved closer to me on the bars and I thought he was going to hit me; instead he put his arm around my shoulder, squeezing firmly in friendship. "C'mon, chicken, let's be cool."

4 I opened my mouth and tried to feel happy as he told me what he was going to have for Thanksgiving. "My Mamma's got a turkey and ham, lots of potatoes, yams and stuff like that. I saw it in the refrigerator. And she says we gonna get some pies. Really, *ese*."

5 Poor liar, I thought, smiling as we clunked our heads softly like good friends. He had seen the same afternoon program on TV as I had, one in which a woman in an apron demonstrated how to prepare a Thanksgiving dinner. I knew he would have tortillas and beans, a round steak maybe, and oranges from his

backyard. He went on describing his Thanksgiving, then changed over to Christmas— the new bicycle, the clothes, the G.I. Joes. I told him that it sounded swell, even though I knew he was making it all up. His mother would in fact stand in line at the Salvation Army to come away hugging armfuls of toys that had been tapped back into shape by reformed alcoholics with veined noses. I pretended to be excited and asked if I could come over to his place to play after Christmas. "Oh, yeah, anytime," he said, squeezing my shoulder and clunking his head against mine.

6   When he asked what I was having for Thanksgiving, I told him that we would probably have a ham with pineapple on the top. My family was slightly better off than Frankie's, though I sometimes walked around with cardboard in my shoes and socks with holes big enough to be ski masks, so holidays were extravagant happenings. I told him about the scalloped potatoes, the candied yams, the frozen green beans, and the pumpkin pie.

7   His eyes moved across my face as if he were deciding where to hit me—nose, temple, chin, talking mouth—and then he lifted his arm from my shoulder and jumped from the monkey bars, grunting as he landed. He wiped sand from his knees while looking up and warned me not to mess around with him any more. He stared with such a great meanness that I had to look away. He warned me again and then walked away. Incredibly relieved, I jumped from the bars and ran looking over my shoulder until I turned onto my street.

8   Frankie scared most of the school out of its wits and even had girls scampering out of view when he showed himself on the playground. If he caught us without notice, we grew quiet and stared down at our shoes until he passed after a threat or two. If he pushed us down, we stayed on the ground with our eyes closed and pretended that we were badly hurt. If he rifled through our lunch bags, we didn't say anything. He took what he wanted, after which we sighed and watched him walk away peeling an orange or chewing big chunks of an apple.

9   Still, that afternoon when he called Mr. Koligian, our teacher, a foul name— we grew scared for him. Mr. Koligian pulled and tugged at his body until it was in his arms and then out of his arms as he hurled Frankie against the building. Some of us looked away because it was unfair. We knew the house he lived in: The empty refrigerator, the father gone, the mother in a sad bathrobe, the beatings, the yearnings for something to love. When the teacher manhandled him, we all wanted to run away, but instead we stared and felt shamed. Robert, Adele, Yolanda shamed; Danny, Alfonso, Brenda shamed; Nash, Margie, Rocha shamed. We all watched him flop about as Mr. Koligian shook and grew red from anger. We knew his house and, for some, it was the same one to walk home to: The broken mother, the indifferent walls, the refrigerator's glare which fed the people no one wanted.

The Write Connection

Directions: *Write a paragraph about three things you learned or that you think are most important in the reading selection.*

_____

_____

_____

_____

_____

Comprehension Check

Directions: *See how many questions you can answer without referring to the selection. Then, review the selection to write more complete responses.*

1. What was "just a fact, like having lunch"? _____

_____

2. Why do you think the author followed Frankie T. to the monkey bars in the

   playground? _____

3. What did the author want to do when he saw the teacher in the parking lot?

_____

_____ 4. After moving closer to the author on the monkey bars Frankie T:
   a. hit the author in the mouth.
   b. yelled for help.
   c. hugged the author.
   d. pushed the author off of the monkey bars.

5. How did the author know that Frankie T. was lying about what he was going to

   have for Thanksgiving dinner? _____

_____

6. What did Frankie T. do to Mr. Koligian? _____

7. What did Mr. Koligian do to Frankie T? _____

Critical Thinking Check

1. Write one phrase from the story that supports the inference that the author was poor. _____

   _____

2. Write one phrase from the story that supports the inference that Frankie T was poor. _____

3. Why do you think the other kids felt shamed after witnessing what Mr. Koligan did? _____

   _____

   _____

4. Why do you think the author mentions what happened to Frankie T. later in life?

   _____

   _____

   _____

Vocabulary Check

Directions: *See if any of the words you underlined in the selection are among the list of words below. If not, write your words in the spaces provided. Guess the meaning of the words from the way they were used in the selection. Then, look up the definition of each word in the dictionary to see if you were right.*

halfhearted (*adj*): Your guess: _____

    Dictionary Definition: _____

manhandled (*vb*): Your guess: _____

    Dictionary Definition: _____

Your word: _____ Your guess: _____

    Dictionary Definition: _____

Your word: _____ Your guess: _____

    Dictionary Definition: _____

♟♟♟ Skills in Practice ▸ Reading Selection 2

"NAZISM IN GERMANY" FROM *THE WEST IN THE WORLD,
VOL II: FROM 1600*
Dennis Sherman and Joyce Salisbury

Accessing Prior Knowledge

Questions for Discussion

1. Do you know someone who can persuade others to dislike a particular person? If so, how is this person able to persuade others?

2. Have you ever been kicked out of a group because of negative gossip? If so, what happened and what did you do in response?

Preview and Predict

Directions: *Look at the title of the selection. Think about what you already know about the subject. Then, write a couple of predictions about what you are going to read. For instance, what will the author say about Nazism in Germany?*

1. _____

2. _____

Word Search and Discovery

Directions: *Skim through the selection to find the three words below. Underline the words in the selection. Then, use a dictionary to write their definitions in the spaces provided. As you read, you can see if the definitions you wrote fit the way each word is used in the selection.*

fascist (*n*): _____

Nazi (*n*): _____

swastika (*n*): _____

Also, *underline at least one new word as you read the selection and write your guess as to its meaning in the right margin of the text.*

Text Notes in Practice

Directions: *Use a textbook study method such as SQUARE to identify the most important information in the selection. Then, create a study guide that you can use to prepare for the questions that follow the selection.*

NAZISM IN GERMANY
Dennis Sherman and Joyce Salisbury

▲ **Adolf Hitler at Buckeburg, Germany, 1934.**

1   In 1928, Germany's fascist party, the Nazis (National Socialists), won less than 3 percent of the vote in national elections. Five years later, the party and its leader, Adolf Hitler, gained power and ended German democracy—all through legal means. How did this happen?

2   Hitler inspired and manipulated people with his stirring, inflammatory speeches, rallies, parades, and symbols. His organizers choreographed mass meetings such as the one at Buckeberg in 1934, shown above, to whip up excitement and a sense of belonging among the populace. In this photograph, Hitler leads a procession of Nazi elites between two lines of honor guards and swastika banners. At such rallies, Hitler made a carefully staged, dramatic entrance and delivered a long, emotionally charged speech. "It is the belief in our people that has made us small men great, that has made us poor men rich, that has made brave and courageous men out of us wavering, spiritless, timid fold," he proclaimed at the Nuremberg rally in 1936. Listeners described feeling "eternally bound to this man." The ministry of propaganda, under Joseph Goebbels (1897–1945), reinforced the psychological power of the rallies by controlling information and spreading Nazi ideology through the press, radio, films, textbooks, pamphlets, and posters. For example, the ministry

commissioned Leni Riefenstahl (1902–) to create the documentary film *Triumph of the Will* (1935), which portrayed the Nazis and their leaders as awe inspiring and gloriously on the match. Goebbels also painted an image of Hitler as the people's heroic leader, the one who could even be trusted to limit any excesses by overzealous extremists within the Nazi Party itself.

3   In addition to promoting enthusiasm for their leader and ideology, the Nazis attacked "decadent" modern art and the popular culture of the Jazz Age. Only those whose works conformed to Nazi tastes—usually sentimental, pro-Nazi subject matter—could exhibit, publish, or perform. Officials promoted the burning of liberal books, sometimes even those of Germany's greatest literary figures of the eighteenth and nineteenth centuries, such as Goethe and Schiller. The Nazi minister of culture told university professors, "From now on it will *not* be your job to determine whether something is true but whether it is in the spirit of the [Nazi] revolution." Although some intellectuals and artists supported these policies, many opposed them and left Germany.

4   Both to solidify their power and to carry out their racist ideas, the Nazis targeted many groups for repression. For example, they sent communists, socialists, resisting Catholics, Jehovah's Witnesses, and the Roma ("Gypsies") to concentration camps. Mixed-race children, criminals, prostitutes, alcoholics—all considered genetically inferior or "community aliens"—became candidates for sterilization. Homosexuality warranted at least incarceration or castration. A frightening glimpse of the future for all these groups came in 1939 when the Nazis created euthanasia programs designed to eliminate the mentally ill, handicapped, aged, and incurably ill.

5   No group, however, was more systematically repressed than the Jews. According to Joseph Goebbels, Jews had "corrupted our race, fouled our morals, undermined our customs, and broken our power." He blamed them as "the cause and the beneficiary of our misery." In 1933, the government excluded Jews from higher education and public employment. By 1935, most Jewish professionals in Germany had lost their jobs. That year the Nuremberg Laws took citizenship away from Jews, forced them to wear a yellow Star of David on their clothes, and forbade marriage or sexual relations between Jews and non-Jews. In 1938, an episode of unrestrained violence revealed the mounting intensity of the Nazis' anti-Semitism. Incited by Goebbels, who blamed Jews for the assassination of a German diplomat in Paris, Nazi stormtroopers vandalized Jewish residences, synagogues, and places of business, smashing windows and plundering shops during the night of November 9–10. The troops then attacked Jews themselves, killing dozens and imprisoning tens of thousands in concentration camps. After this attack—known as *Kristallnacht*, or Crystal Night, for its images of shattered glass—the Nazi government increasingly restricted Jews' movements, eliminated their jobs, and confiscated their assets. By 1939, over half of Germany's Jews had emigrated, even though they had to leave their possessions behind, pay hefty

emigration fees, and face rejection in other countries. Soon, though, it became too late to escape Germany.

—From *The West in the World, From the Renaissance to the Present* 2e by Dennis Sherman and Joyce Salisbury. Copyright © 2004. Reprinted by permission of The McGraw-Hill Companies.

The Write Connection

Directions: *Write a paragraph about the three things you learned or that you think are most important in the reading selection.*

_____

_____

_____

_____

_____

Comprehension Check

Directions: *See how many questions you can answer without referring to the selection. Then, review the selection to write more complete responses.*

_____ 1. The author's tone can be described as:
    a. humorous.   c. bitter.
    b. impartial.   d. sorrowful.

_____ 2. What is the meaning of the word *inflammatory* as it is used in paragraph 2?
    a. highly infectious   c. painful
    b. amusing   d. emotionally arousing

       3. How long did it take Adolf Hitler to gain power in Germany? _____

_____ 4. By leading dramatic entrances with the Nazi's elite through lines of Honor Guards who carried banners depicting the swastika symbol, Hitler was using which of the following propaganda techniques?
    a. plain folks   c. bandwagon
    b. name calling   d. transfer

_____ 5. After Hitler's speech at Nuremberg in 1936, listeners described feeling "eternally bound to this man." Hitler had successfully used plain folks propaganda by using which of the following words or phrases in his speech at Nuremberg in 1936?
    a. our people, us small men   c. wavering, spiritless, timid
    b. brave and courageous men   d. eternally great

6. What did Joseph Goebbels do as Hitler's Minister of Propaganda?
   a. He promoted German democracy at a time of economic disparity.
   b. He created swastikas and other symbols of propaganda for the Honor Guard.
   c. He controlled information and spread Nazi ideology.
   d. He caused a riot at the Nuremberg rally.

7. What was the name of the documentary that portrayed Hitler as a heroic leader?

   _____

8. Write one example that illustrates how the Nazis attacked "decadent" modern art and the popular culture of Germany?

   _____

9. Write one example that illustrates how the Nazis targeted certain groups in order to solidify their power and promote their racist beliefs. _____

   _____

10. Joseph Goebbels used name calling to portray Jews in a negative way to the German people by saying that: _____

    _____

11. Write one example that illustrates how the Nazis repressed the Jews in Germany.

    _____

12. During the Crystal Night of November 1938:
    a. the Nuremberg Laws were enacted that forbade marriage between Jews and non-Jews and restricted the emigration of Jews to other countries.
    b. many Jews lost their communities and religious affiliations.
    c. Jewish homes were vandalized, their shops were destroyed, and tens of thousands of Jews were imprisoned in concentration camps.
    d. they were forced to wear a Star of David.

Critical Thinking Check

1. Which of the following conclusions can be drawn from the last sentence of the excerpt?
   a. Some of Germany's Jews would not meet the deadline set for leaving the country.
   b. Without proper assistance, many people in Germany would soon go hungry.
   c. The Nazis would soon begin imprisoning all of the German people in concentration camps.
   d. Nazi Germany would soon be a deadly place for Jews who remained in the country.

2

2. The Nazis used propaganda that was designed to blame the Jews for all of Germany's problems in order to justify their destructive acts. Think of an example either from your own experience or from events in the news that illustrates the way in which propaganda is used to blame members of particular group for certain problems in society.

_____

_____

_____

3. If Adolf Hitler were an American politician, do you think that he would be able to influence us as effectively as he influenced the people of Germany? Why or why not?

_____

_____

Vocabulary Check

Directions: *See if any of the words you underlined in the selection are among the list of words below. If not, write your words in the spaces provided. Guess the meaning of the words from the way they were used in the selection. Then, look up the definition of each word in the dictionary to see if you were right.*

confiscated (*vb*): Your guess: _____

Dictionary Definition: _____

euthanasia (*n*): Your guess: _____

Dictionary Definition: _____

_____

_____

Your word: _____ Your guess: _____

Dictionary Definition: _____

Your word: _____ Your guess: _____

Dictionary Definition: _____

Additional Reading Selections

♟♟♟ READING SELECTION 1

THE EDUCATION OF AN AMERICAN
Arnold Schwarzenegger

Arnold Schwarzenegger (b. 1947), Governor of California, champion bodybuilder, author, and actor, was born in a small Austrian town. When Arnold was 14, he began bodybuilding training at a local gym. He went on to win the following bodybuilding titles: Mr. Europe, Mr. World, Mr. Universe (five times), and Mr. Olympia (seven times). Arnold Schwarzenegger became a U.S. citizen in 1984, the same year that he starred in his first *Terminator* movie. In 1990, he was named Chairman of President George Bush's Council on Physical Fitness. In 2003, he became the Governor of California.

Questions for Discussion

1. What is your best strategy for getting yourself interested in what you are reading?

2. Have you ever read something so interesting that you could imagine it as if you were watching a movie? If so, what were you reading and why was it so interesting?

3. Do you think it is possible for people to become successful despite not having some of the advantages that others have?

Preview and Predict

Directions: *Look at the title of the selection. Think about what you already know about the subject. Then, write a couple of predictions about what you are going to read. For instance, what will the author discuss about the education of an American?*

1. _____

2. _____

THE EDUCATION OF AN AMERICAN
Arnold Schwarzenegger

1   . . . Actually for me, going out into the "real world" meant "coming to America." And it wasn't really the "things" I wish I'd known before I came—because I always thought I knew everything already. That's part of my charm!

2   But you know, the truth is, some of the things I knew when I came here were right on the money—and served me well. But some of the things I thought were true turned out to be terribly wrong. . . .

3   The first thing I was dead right about was this: where you're from is not as important as where you're going. Take it from me: if you're too focused on where you started, you'll never get where you're headed.

4   Where I started was a little farm community outside the Austrian town of Graz. Now, that may make you think of sunny hillsides with buttercups dancing in the breeze, and happy children with rosy cheeks, eating strudel.

5   But that's not what I think of.

6   First of all, strudel was a luxury. It was right after World War II, and the country was absolutely devastated and destroyed. We had no flushing toilet in the house. No refrigerator. No television. What we did have was food rations—and we did have British tanks around to give us kids an occasional lift to the elementary school.

7   But you know what? My background has never held me back. Instead, I've used it to my advantage—to fuel the intense desire to get the hell out of there! It's that desire that powered a very strong will in me.

8   I always say, "If you starve someone, you only make them more hungry." And I definitely was hungry to break out and do something very special. . . .

9   So we move on to another principle I was dead right about: No one's ever been successful without having a goal—and a plan for how to achieve it. . . .

10   And finally: the American Dream.

11   Perhaps the thing I was most dead right about was this country—America.

12   Ever since childhood, I fantasized over the pictures of America I saw in the magazines, the movies, the newsreels. I loved the skyscrapers and the beaches—the huge cars with fins, zooming down five-lane highways. I said to myself, "I want to be there! I want to be part of it!"

13   Well, I came here in 1968 with $20 in my pocket. And I have to tell you that within a week, I had an apartment and dishes and silverware and a television—all from people I had just met that week in the gym.

14   And within six months, I was asked to star in a movie. All right, granted they didn't use my real name—I was billed as "Arnold Strong." And they didn't use my real voice. They dubbed it in. But I was in a movie! It's called *Hercules in New York*. And I know every one of you has seen it. And you can rent it at Blockbuster!

15   But I have to say, I called all my friends back in Europe and said: "It's true! You can do anything in this country! Come over here! It's everything you imagine—and more!"

16   I decided right then—very early on—that I wanted to weave myself right into the fabric of America. I wanted to become a citizen. I wanted to work hard. I wanted to go to college and study politics, economics, and culture.

17   Today I stand before you—an immigrant success story.

18   I am the living, breathing incarnation of The American Dream.

19   I became the leading bodybuilder in the world. I've made millions as a businessman many times over. My movies have hit more than $2 billion at the box office.

20   I was dead right about it: If you have the desire and the determination—and you are willing to be a part of this country and embrace it—it will embrace you. There is nowhere like it on Earth. . . .

21   Which brings me to the biggest thing I was dead wrong about: whose dream is it, anyway?

22   It was a great day for me in 1989, when I was called to Washington. President Bush named me Chairman of the President's Council on Physical Fitness. I traveled to all 50 states, promoting fitness and sports programs in schools.

23   I thought I could inspire kids with a powerful message—especially in the inner cities: "If a poor kid like me from a farm town in Europe can make it, then anyone can make it in this great country!"

24   This was where I got my biggest and rudest awakening.

25   Because as I went around from inner city to inner city, I saw firsthand that this is not the land of opportunity for those kids. Most of them don't get any of the tools that I got.

26   Look at everything I had in my childhood: two parents, a well-equipped school with terrific sports facilities, the same education and books for every kid in the country. After school, there was a parent to help with homework—and safe places to do sports like soccer, sledding and skating.

27   I was accountable to someone all the time: parents, teachers, mentors, and coaches. Around the clock, I had people taking care of me, encouraging, and nurturing me. All this gave me a strong foundation, which gave me the confidence, which gave me the inner strength to believe in myself and know I could make it.

28   And it worked.

29   You know, I used to go around saying: "Everybody should pull himself up by his own bootstraps—just like I did!"

30   What I learned about this country is this: Not everybody has boots.

31   I saw it firsthand, when I met the children in the inner cities. We think we're motivating them by beaming the American Dream in to them—on TV and in movies.

32   Wrong!

33   Most of them don't get the motivation. Instead, they hear: "You're a loser. You'll never make it out of the barrio or the ghetto. You'll never get out."

34   The more I saw, the more I realized I'd been wrong when I thought the American Dream was available to everyone. Because even though it is the Land of Opportunity for me, and the majority of Americans, millions are left behind. It's not a level playing field for them. . . .

35   So really, it's not just the bodybuilding and the business and the box office for me anymore. Helping the kids who need help is the most important goal I have.

36   This is what it means for me to be an American. Maybe that's what it could mean for you, too! No matter how much success you have, you can be more successful by reaching out to someone who needs you.

The Write Connection

Directions: *Write a paragraph about three things you learned or that you think are most important in the reading selection.*

_____

_____

_____

_____

_____

♟♟♟ READING SELECTION 2

WORD POWER
Malcolm X

Malcolm X (1925–1965), American minister, author, and activist, was born Malcolm Little and became one of the most powerful and controversial leaders of the Black Muslim Movement during the 1960s. Although he graduated at the top of his class, he dropped out of junior high and turned to crime. It was during his imprisonment for robbery that he converted to the Black Nation of Islam, pursued an education, and changed his name to Malcolm X. The X stood for the African name or identity he believed he had lost as an African American. After he left prison, he formed his own group, the Organization of Afro-American Unity. He was shot and killed by three Black Muslim loyalists in 1965 while he was giving a speech in Harlem.

Questions for Discussion

1. How would you educate yourself if there were no colleges, trade schools, or universities?

2. What is your best strategy for learning new words?

Preview and Predict

Directions: *Look at the title of the selection. Think about what you already know about the subject. Then, write a couple of predictions about what you are going to read. For instance, what will the author discuss about the power of words?*

1. _____

2. _____

WORD POWER

Malcolm X

1   It was because of my letters that I happened to stumble upon starting to acquire some kind of a homemade education.

2   I became increasingly frustrated at not being able to express what I wanted to convey in letters that I wrote, especially those to Mr. Elijah Muhammad. In the street, I had been the most articulate hustler out there—I had commanded attention when I said something. But now, trying to write simple English, I not only wasn't articulate, I wasn't even functional. How would I sound writing in slang, the way I would say it, something such as, "Look, daddy, let me pull your coat about a cat, Elijah Muhammad—"

3   Many who today hear me somewhere in person, or on television, or those who read something I've said, will think I went to school far beyond the eighth grade. This impression is due entirely to my prison studies.

4   It had really begun back in the Charlestown Prison, when Bimbi first made me feel envy of his stock of knowledge. Bimbi had always taken charge of any conversation he was in, and I had tried to emulate him. But every book I picked up had few sentences which didn't contain anywhere from one to nearly all of the words that might as well have been in Chinese. When I just skipped those words, of course, I really ended up with little idea of what the book said. So I had come to the Norfolk Prison Colony still going through only book-reading motions. Pretty soon, I would have quit even these motions, unless I had received the motivation that I did.

5   I saw that the best thing I could do was get hold of a dictionary—to study, to learn some words. I was lucky enough to reason also that I should try to improve my penmanship. It was sad. I couldn't even write in a straight line. It was both ideas together that moved me to request a dictionary along with some tablets and pencils from the Norfolk Prison Colony school.

6   I spent two days just rifling uncertainly through the dictionary's pages. I'd never realized so many words existed! I didn't know which words I needed to learn. Finally, just to start some kind of action, I began copying.

7   In my slow, painstaking, ragged handwriting, I copied into my tablet everything printed on that first page, down to the punctuation marks.

8   I believe it took me a day. Then, aloud, I read back, to myself, everything I'd written on the tablet. Over and over, aloud, to myself, I read my own handwriting.

9   I woke up the next morning, thinking about those words—immensely proud to realize that not only had I written so much at one time, but I'd written words that I never knew were in the world. Moreover, with a little effort, I also could remember what many of these words meant. I reviewed the words whose meanings I didn't remember. Funny thing, from the dictionary first page right now, that "aardvark" springs to my mind. The dictionary had a picture of it, a long-tailed, long-eared, burrowing African mammal, which lives off termites caught by sticking out its tongue as an anteater does for ants.

10   I was so fascinated that I went on—I copied the dictionary's next page. And the same experience came when I studied that. With every succeeding page, I also learned of people and places and events from history. Actually the dictionary is like a miniature encyclopedia. Finally the dictionary's A section had filled a whole tablet—and I went on into the B's. That was the way I started copying what eventually became the entire dictionary. It went a lot faster after so much practice helped me to pick up handwriting speed. Between what I wrote in my tablet, and writing letters, during the rest of my time in prison I would guess I wrote a million words.

11   I suppose it was inevitable that as my word-base broadened, I could for the first time pick up a book and read and now begin to understand what the book was saying. Anyone who has read a great deal can imagine the new world that opened. Let me tell you something: from then until I left that prison, in every free moment I had, if I was not reading in the library, I was reading on my bunk. You couldn't have gotten met out of books with a wedge. Between Mr. Muhammad's teachings, my correspondence, my visitors—usually Ella and Reginald—and my reading of books, months passed without my even thinking about being imprisoned. In fact, up to then, I never had been so truly free in my life.

12   The Norfolk Prison Colony's library was in the school building. A variety of classes was taught there by instructors who came from such places as Harvard and Boston universities. The weekly debates between inmate teams were also held in the school building. You would be astonished to know how worked up convict debaters and audiences would get over subjects like "Should Babies Be Fed Milk?"

13   Available on the prison library's shelves were books on just about every general subject. Much of the big private collection that Parkhurst had willed to the prison was still in crates and boxes in the back of the library—thousands of old books. Some of them looked ancient: covers faded, old-time parchment-looking binding. Parkhurst, I've mentioned, seemed to have been principally interested in

history and religion. He had the money and the special interest to have a lot of books that you couldn't have in general circulation. Any college library would have been lucky to get that collection.

14   As you can imagine, especially in a prison where there was heavy emphasis on rehabilitation, an inmate was smiled upon if he demonstrated an unusually intense interest in books. There was a sizable number of well-read inmates, especially the popular debaters. Some were said by many to be practically walking encyclopedias. They were almost celebrities. No university would ask any student to devour literature as I did when this new world opened to me, of being able to read and *understand*.

15   I read more in my room than in the library itself. An inmate who was known to read a lot could check out more than the permitted maximum number of books. I preferred reading in the total isolation of my own room.

16   When I had progressed to really serious reading, every night at about ten P.M. I would be outraged with the "lights out." It always seemed to catch me right in the middle of something engrossing.

17   Fortunately, right outside my door was a corridor light that cast a glow into my room. The glow was enough to read by, once my eyes adjusted to it. So when "lights out" came, I would sit on the floor where I could continue reading in that glow.

18   At one-hour intervals the night guards paced past every room. Each time I heard the approaching footsteps, I jumped into bed and feigned sleep. And as soon as the guard passed, I got back out of bed onto the floor area of that light-glow, where I would read for another fifty-eight minutes—until the guard approached again. That went on until three or four every morning. Three or four hours of sleep a night was enough for me. Often in the years in the streets I had slept less than that. . . .

19   I have often reflected upon the new vistas that reading opened to me. I knew right there in prison that reading had changed forever the course of my life. As I see it today, the ability to read awoke inside me some long dormant craving to be mentally alive. I certainly wasn't seeking any degree, the way a college confers a status symbol upon its students. My homemade education gave me, with every additional book that I read, a little bit more sensitivity to the deafness, dumbness, and blindness that was afflicting the black race in America. Not long ago, an English writer telephoned me from London, asking questions. One was, "What's your alma mater?" I told him, "Books." You will never catch me with a free fifteen minutes in which I'm not studying something I feel might be able to help the black man.

The Write Connection

Directions: Write a paragraph about three things you learned or that you think are most important in the reading selection.

_____

_____

_____

_____

_____

_____

♟♟♟ READING SELECTION 3

THE GETTYSBURG ADDRESS
delivered by Abraham Lincoln at Gettysburg, Pennsylvania, in 1863

Abraham Lincoln (1809–1865) was the sixteenth president of the United States and served during the Civil War from 1861 to 1865. Lincoln had opposed the expansion of slavery into American-owned territories. The Civil War began after Lincoln was elected and southern states decided to secede, or withdraw, from the Union. While the Southern states or "Confederacy" won many battles against the Northern states or "Union," the battle of Gettysburg, marked a turning point in the war. The South surrendered on April 9, 1865. On April 14, 1865, President Lincoln was shot by John Wilkes Booth, who was a Confederate sympathizer. Abraham Lincoln died the following day.

Questions for Discussion

1. Do you think that America is doing enough to honor its soldiers? Why or why not?

2. Under what circumstances do you think it would be appropriate to honor the soldiers who fought for the other side in a war as well as the soldiers from your side?

Preview and Predict

Directions: *Look at the title of the selection. Think about what you already know about the subject. Then, write a couple of predictions about what you are going to read. For instance, what will the author discuss about Gettysburg?*

1. _____

2. _____

ABRAHAM LINCOLN: THE GETTYSBURG ADDRESS

1   Four score and seven years ago our fathers brought forth on this continent, a new nation, conceived in Liberty, and dedicated to the proposition that all men are created equal.

2   Now we are engaged in a great civil war, testing whether that nation, or any nation so conceived and so dedicated, can long endure. We are met on a great battlefield of that war. We have come to dedicate a portion of that field, as a final resting place for those who here gave their lives that that nation might live. It is altogether fitting and proper that we should do this.

3   But, in a larger sense, we can not dedicate—we can not consecrate—we can not hallow—this ground. The brave men, living and dead, who struggled here, have consecrated it, far above our poor power to add or detract. The world will little note, nor long remember what we say here, but it can never forget what they did here. It is for us the living, rather, to be dedicated here to the unfinished work which they who fought here have thus far so nobly advanced. It is rather for us to be here dedicated to the great task remaining before us—that from these honored dead we take increased devotion to that cause for which they gave the last full measure of devotion—that we here highly resolve that these dead shall not have died in vain—that this nation, under God, shall have a new birth of freedom—and that government of the people, by the people, for the people, shall not perish from the earth.

The Write Connection

Directions: *Write a paragraph about the three things you learned or that you think are most important in the reading selection.*

_____

_____

_____

_____

_____

♟♟♟ READING SELECTION 4

"Changing the Design of Instruction" from *Essentials of Sociology*

James Henslin

Questions for Discussion

1. Can you recall one teacher who inspired you to do your best? If so, who was the teacher and what did he or she do?

2. What is one thing you would do to improve the way that children are educated in the United States?

Preview and Predict

Directions: *Look at the title of the selection. Think about what you already know about the subject. Then, write a couple of predictions about what you are going to read. For instance, what will the author discuss about classroom instruction?*

1. _____

2. _____

Changing the Design of Instruction

James Henslin

1   Jaime Escalante taught in an East Los Angeles inner-city school that was plagued with poverty, crime, drugs, and gangs. In this self-defeating environment, he taught calculus. His students scored so highly on national tests that officials suspected cheating. They asked his students to retake the test. They did. This time, they earned even higher scores.

2   How did Escalante do it?

3   First, Escalante had to open his students' minds to the possibility of success, that they *could* learn. Most Latino students were tracked into craft classes, where they made jewelry and birdhouses. "Our kids are just as talented as anyone else. They just need the opportunity to show it," Escalante said. "They just don't think about becoming scientists or engineers."

4   Students also need to see learning as a way out of the barrio, as the path to good jobs. Escalante arranged for foundations to provide money for students to attend the colleges of their choice. Students learned that if they did well, their poverty wouldn't stop them.

5   Escalante also changed the system of instruction. He had his students think of themselves as a team, of him as the coach, and the national math exams as a sort of Olympics for which they were preparing. To foster team identity, students wore team jackets, caps, and T-shirts with logos that identified them as part of the math team. Before class, his students did "warm-ups" (hand-clapping and foot stomping to a rock song).

6   Escalante's team had practice schedules as rigorous as a championship football team. Students had to sign a contract that bound them to participate in a summer program, to complete the daily homework, and to attend Saturday morning and after-school study sessions. To remind students that self-discipline pays of, Escalante covered his walls with posters of sports figures—Michael Jordan, Babe Ruth, Jackie Joyner-Kersee, and Scottie Pippin.

7   The sociological point is this: The problem was not the ability of the students. Their failure to do well in school was not due to something *within* them. The problem was the *system*, the way classroom instruction was designed. When Escalante changed the system of instruction—*and* brought in hope—both attitudes and performance changed.

The Write Connection

Directions: *Write a paragraph about three things you learned or that you think are most important in the reading selection.*

_____

_____

_____

_____

_____

♟♟♟ READING SELECTION 5

"FACTORS THAT INFLUENCE BEHAVIOR CHANGE" FROM *ACCESS TO HEALTH*, 10TH ED.
Rebecca Donatelle

Questions for Discussion

1. Think of a habit or behavior that you would like to eliminate. What are some things that you believe may have caused you to develop this habit?

2. What is your best strategy for finding the main idea in a longer reading selection?

Preview and Predict

Directions: *Look at the title and subtitles of the selection. Think about what you already know about the subject. Then, write a couple of predictions about what you are going to read. For instance, what will the author discuss about the factors that influence behavior change?*

1. _____

2. _____

FACTORS THAT INFLUENCE BEHAVIOR CHANGE
Rebecca Donatelle

1   Too many of us decide on New Year's Day that we are going to lose weight, exercise more, find more friends, and essentially reinvent ourselves overnight! Is it any wonder that we don't keep most of these resolutions?

2   Major factors influence behavior and behavior-change decisions. They can be divided into three general categories: predisposing, enabling, and reinforcing.

Predisposing Factors

3   Our life experiences, knowledge, cultural and ethnic inheritance, and current beliefs and values are all *predisposing factors* that influence behavior. Factors that may predispose us to certain conditions include age, sex, race, income, family background, educational background, and access to health care. For example, if your parents smoked, you are 90 percent more likely to start smoking than someone whose parents didn't. If your peers smoke, you are 80 percent more likely to smoke than someone whose friends don't.

Enabling Factors

4   Skills and abilities: physical, emotional, and mental capabilities; and resources and accessible facilities that make health decisions more convenient or difficult are *enabling factors*. Positive enablers encourage you to carry through on your intentions. Negative enablers work against your intentions to change. For example, if you would like to join a fitness center but discover that the closest one is four miles away and the membership fee is $500, those negative enablers may convince you to stay home. On the other hand, if your school's fitness center is two blocks away, stays open until midnight, and offers a special, low-priced student membership, those positive enablers will probably convince you to join. Identifying positive and negative enabling factors and devising alternative plans when the negative factors outweigh the positive are part of planning for behavior change.

Reinforcing Factors

5   *Reinforcing factors* include the presence or absence of support, encouragement, or discouragement that significant people in your life bring to a situation. For example, if you decide to stop smoking and your family and friends continue smoking in your presence, you may be tempted to start smoking again. In other words, your smoking behavior is reinforced. If, however, you are overweight, you lose a few pounds, and all your friends tell you how terrific you look, then your positive behavior will be reinforced and you will be more likely to continue your weight-loss plan.

6   The manner in which you reward or punish yourself also plays a role. Accepting small failures and concentrating on your successes can foster further achievements. Berating yourself because you binged on ice cream or argued with a friend may create an internal environment in which failure becomes almost inevitable. Telling yourself that you're worth the extra time and effort and giving yourself a pat on the back for small accomplishments are often overlooked factors in positive behavior change.

The Write Connection

Directions: *Write a paragraph about three things you learned or that you think are most important in the reading selection.*

_____

_____

_____

_____

_____

_____

♟♟♟ READING SELECTION 6

"HARD TIMES IN HOOVERVILLE" FROM
THE AMERICAN JOURNEY, 3RD ED.
David Goldfield et al.

The following selection is taken from a history text. It discusses a tumultuous period in American history. The Great Depression was a time of economic collapse which began at the end of the prosperous 1920s and lasted until America entered the second world war.

Questions for Discussion

1. Have you ever been faced with the possibility of being homeless? If so, how did you improve your situation?

2. If an economic disaster occurs in the United States, most of its citizens will probably lose their jobs. Do you think that Americans will form communities to help each other? Or, do you think Americans have become too selfish or too frightened to help strangers?

Preview and Predict

Directions: *Look at the title and subtitles of the selection. Think about what you already know about the subject. Then, write a couple of predictions about what you are going to read. For instance, what will the author discuss about Hooverville?*

1. _____

2. _____

HARD TIMES IN HOOVERVILLE
David Goldfield et al.

1   The prosperity of the 1920s ended in a stock market crash that revealed the flaws honeycombing the economy. As the nation slid into a catastrophic depression, factories closed, employment and incomes tumbled, and millions lost their homes, hopes, and dignity. Some protested and took direct action; others looked to the government for relief.

Crash!

2   The buoyant prosperity of the New Era collapsed in October of 1929 when the stock market crashed. After peaking in September, the market suffered several sharp checks, and on October 29, "Black Tuesday," panicked investors dumped their stocks at any price. The slide continued for months, and then years. It hit bottom in July 1932. By then, the stock of U.S. Steel had plunged from 262 to 22, Montgomery Ward from 138 to 4.

3   The Wall Street crash marked the beginning of the Great Depression, but it did not cause it. The depression stemmed from weaknesses in the New Era economy. Most damaging was the unequal distribution of wealth and income. By 1929, the richest 0.1 percent of American families had as much total income as the bottom 42 percent. With more than half the nation's people living at or below the subsistence level, there was not enough purchasing power to maintain the economy.

The Depression Spreads

4   By early 1930, factories had shut down or cut back, and industrial production plummeted; by 1932, it was scarcely 50 percent of its 1929 level. Steel mills operated at 12 percent of capacity, auto factories at 20 percent. Unemployment skyrocketed, as an average of 100,000 workers a week were fired in the first three years after the crash. By 1932, one-fourth of the labor force was out of work. Personal income dropped by more than half between 1929 and 1932; by 1933, industrial workers had average weekly wages of only $16.73. Moreover, the depression began to feed on itself in a vicious circle: Shrinking wages and employment cut into purchasing power, causing business to slash production again and lay off workers, thereby further reducing purchasing power.

5   The depression particularly battered farmers. Commodity prices fell by 55 percent between 1929 and 1932, stifling farm income. Unable to pay their mortgages, many farm families lost their homes and fields. "We have no security left," cried one South Dakota farm woman. "Foreclosures and evictions at the point of sheriff's guns are increasing daily."

6   Urban families were also evicted when they could not pay their rent. Some moved in with relatives; others lived in **Hoovervilles**—the name reflects the bitterness directed at the president—shacks where people shivered, suffered, and starved. Oklahoma City's vast Hooverville covered 100 square miles; one witness described its hapless residents as squatting in "old, rusted-out car bodies," orange crates, and holes in the ground.

7   Soup kitchens became standard features of the urban landscape, but charities and local communities could not meet the massive needs, and neither state nor federal governments had welfare or unemployment compensation programs. To survive, people planted gardens in vacant lots and back alleys and tore apart empty houses or tapped gas lines for fuel. In immigrant neighborhoods, social workers found a "primitive communism" in which people shared food, clothing, and fuel.

"Women's Jobs" and "Men's Jobs"

8   Gender segregation had concentrated women in low-paid service, sales, and clerical jobs that shrank less than the heavy industries where men predominated. But traditional attitudes also reinforced opposition to female employment itself, especially that of married women. As one Chicago civic organization complained, "They are holding jobs that rightfully belong to the God-intended providers of the household." The city council of Akron, Ohio, resolved that public agencies and private employers should stop employing wives. Three-fourths of the nation's school systems refused to hire married women as teachers, and two-thirds dismissed female teachers who married. Many private employers, especially banks and insurance companies, also fired married women.

9   Few men sought positions in the fields associated with women, so firing women simply aggravated the suffering of families already reeling from the depression. Despite hostility, the proportion of married women in the work force increased in the 1930s as women took jobs to help their families survive.

Families in the Depression

10   "I have watched fear grip the people in our neighborhood around Hull House," wrote Jane Addams as the depression deepened in 1931 and family survival itself seemed threatened. Divorce declined because it was expensive, but desertion increased, and marriages were postponed. Birthrates fell. Husbands and fathers, the traditional breadwinners, were often humiliated and despondent when laid off from work. One social worker observed in 1931: "Like searing irons, the degradation, the sheer terror and panic which loss of job brings, the deprivation and the bitterness have eaten into men's souls."

11   The number of female-headed households increased. Not only did some women become wage earners, but to make ends meet, many women sewed their own clothing and raised and canned vegetables. Some also took on extra work at home. In San Antonio, one in every ten families had boarders, and in Alabama, housewives took in laundry at 10 cents a week.

12   Some parents sacrificed their own well-being to protect their children. One witness described "the uncontrolled trembling of parents who have starved themselves for weeks so that their children might not go hungry." In New York City, 139 people, most of them children, died of starvation and malnutrition in 1933. Many teenagers who left home so that younger children would have more to eat suffered from starvation, exposure, illness, and accidents. The California Unemployment Commission concluded that the depression had left the American family "morally shattered. There is no security, no foothold, no future."

"Last Hired, First Fired"

13   With fewer resources and opportunities, racial minorities were less able than other groups to absorb the economic pain. African Americans, reported a sociologist at Howard University in 1932, were "the last to be hired and the first to be fired." Black unemployment rates were more than twice the rate for white people. Jobless

white workers now sought the menial jobs traditionally reserved for black workers, such as street cleaning and domestic service. Religious and charitable organizations often refused to care for black people. Local and state governments set higher requirements for black people than for white people to receive relief and provided them with less aid. The Urban League reported, "at no time in the history of the Negro since slavery has his economic and social outlook seemed so discouraging." African Americans were "hanging on by the barest thread."

14   Hispanic Americans also suffered. As mostly unskilled workers, they faced increasing competition for decreasing jobs paying declining wages. They were displaced even in the California agricultural labor force, which they had dominated. Other jobs were lost when Arizona, California, and Texas barred Mexicans from public works and highway construction jobs. Vigilantes threatened employers who hired Mexicans rather than white Americans. Economic woes and racism drove nearly half a million Mexican immigrants and their American-born children from the United States in the 1930s. Local authorities in the Southwest encouraged the federal government to deport Mexicans and offered free transportation to Mexico.

The Write Connection

Directions: *Write a paragraph about three things you learned or that you think are most important in the reading selection.*

_____

_____

_____

_____

_____

_____

♟♟♟ READING SELECTION 7

You Can Stop Normal Aging
Dr. Henry S. Lodge

Born in Boston, Massachusetts, Dr. Henry Lodge is on the teaching faculty of Columbia Medical School. A distinguished doctor of Internal Medicine, Dr. Lodge received the Robert Loeb Award for Excellence in Clinical Medicine and was named in surveys as one of the Best Doctors in New York and one of the Best Doctors in America. Dr. Lodge is a past president of the New York Clinical Society, and a past president of the Presbyterian Hospital Alumni Association. He coauthored *Younger Next Year for Women,* which was published in 2005.

Questions for Discussion

1. Do you take care of your body? If so, what do you do?

2. How long do you expect to live and why?

Preview and Predict

Directions: *Look at the title of the selection. Think about what you already know about the subject. Then, write a couple of predictions about what you are going to read. For instance, what will the author discuss about aging?*

1. _____

2. _____

You Can Stop Normal Aging

Dr. Henry S. Lodge

1   From your body's point of view, "normal" aging isn't normal at all. It's a choice you make by the way you live your life. The other choice is to tell your cells to grow—to build a strong, vibrant body and mind.

2   Let's have a look at standard American aging. Barbara D. had a baby when she was 34, gave up exercise and gained 50 pounds. Exhausted and depressed, Barbara thought youth, energy and optimism were all in her rearview mirror. Jon M., 55, had fallen even farther down the slippery slope. He was stuck in the corporate world of stress, long hours and doughnuts. At 255 pounds, he had knees that hurt and a back that ached. He developed high blood pressure and eventually diabetes. Life was looking grim.

3   Jon and Barbara weren't getting old; they had let their bodies decay. Most aging is just the dry rot we program into our cells by sedentary living, junk food and stress. Yes, we do have to get old, and ultimately we do have to die. But our bodies are designed to age slowly and remarkably well. Most of what we see and fear is decay, and decay is only one choice. Growth is the other.

4   After two years of misery, Barabara started exercising and is now in the best shape of her life. She just finished a sprint triathlon and, at 37, feels like she is 20.

Jon started eating better and exercising too—slowly at first, but he stuck with it. He has since lost 50 pounds, the pain in his knees and back has disappeared, and his diabetes is gone. Today, Jon is 60 and living his life in the body of a healthy 30-year-old. He will die one day, but he is likely to live like a young man until he gets there.

5   The hard reality of our biology is that we are built to move. Exercise is the master signaling system that tells our cells to grow instead of fade. When we exercise, that process of growth spreads throughout every cell in our bodies, making us functionally younger. Not a little bit younger—a lot younger. True biological aging is a surprisingly slow and graceful process. You can live out your life in a powerful, healthy body if you are willing to put in the work.

6   Let's take a step back to see how exercise works at the cellular level. Your body is made up of trillions of cells that live mostly for a few weeks or months, die and are replaced by new cells in an endless cycle. For example, your taste buds live only a few hours, white blood cells live 10 days, and your muscle cells live about three months. Even your bones dissolve and are replaced, over and over again. A few key stem cells in each organ and your brain cells are the only ones that stick around for the duration. All of your other cells are in a constant state of renewal.

7   You replace about 1% of your cells every day. That means 1% of your body is brand-new today, and you will get another 1% tomorrow. Think of it as getting a whole new body every three months. It's not entirely accurate, but it's pretty close. Viewed that way, you are walking around in a body that is brand-new since Christmas—new lungs, new liver, new muscles, new skin. Look down at your legs and realize that you are going to have new ones by the Fourth of July. Whether that body is functionally younger or older is a choice you make by how you live.

8   You choose whether those new cells come in stronger or weaker. You choose whether they grow or decay each day from then on. Your cells don't care which choice you make. They just follow the directions you send. Exercise, and your cells get stronger; sit down, and they decay. (see Figure A)

9   This whole system evolved over billions of years out in nature, where all animals face two great cellular challenges: The first is to grow strong, fast and fit in the spring, when food abounds and there are calories to fuel hungry muscles, bones and brains. The second is to decay as fast as possible in the winter, when calories disappear and surviving starvation is the key to life. You would think that food is the controlling signal for this, but it's not. Motion controls your system.

10   Though we've moved indoors and left that life behind, our cells still think we're living out on the savannah struggling to stay alive each day. There are no microwaves or supermarkets in nature. If you want to eat, you have to hunt or forage every single day. That movement is a signal that it's time to grow. So, when you exercise, your muscles release specific substances that travel throughout your bloodstream, telling your cells to grow. Sedentary muscles, on the other hand, let out a steady trickle of chemicals that whisper to every cell to decay, day after day after day.

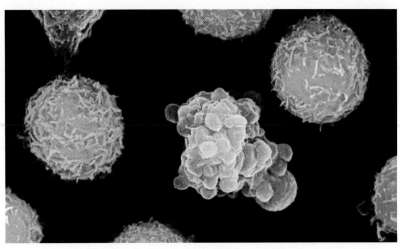

Figure A Scanning electron micrograph of cell death (apoptosis). Normal leukocytes are light blue color and apoptotic cells are light brown color.

11　Men like Jon, who go from sedentary to fit, cut their risk of dying from a heart attack by 75% over five years. Women cut their risk by 80%—and heart attacks are the largest single killer of women. Both men and women can double their leg strength with three months of exercise, and most of us can double it again in another three months. This is true whether you're in your 30s or your 90s. It's not a miracle or a mystery. It's your biology, and you're in charge.

12　The other master signal to our cells—equal and, in some respects, even more important than exercise—is emotion. One of the most fascinating revelations of the last decade is that emotions change our cells through the same molecular pathways as exercise. Anger, stress and loneliness are signals for "starvation" and chronic danger. They "melt" our bodies as surely as sedentary living. Optimism, love and community trigger the process of growth, building our bodies, hearts and minds.

13　Men who have a heart attack and come home to a family are four times less likely to die of a second heart attack. Women battling heart disease or cancer do better in direct proportion to the number of close friends and relatives they have. Babies in the ICU who are touched more often are more likely to survive. Everywhere you look, you see the role of emotion in our biology. Like exercise, it's a choice.

14　It's hard to exercise every day. And with our busy lives, it's even harder to find the time and energy to maintain relationships and build communities. But it's worth it when you consider the alternative. Go for a walk or a run, and think about it. Deep in our cells, down at the level of molecular genetics, we are wired to exercise and to care. We're beginning to wake up to that as a nation, but you might not want to wait. You might want to join Barbara, Jon and millions of others and change your life. Start today. Your cells are listening.

The Write Connection

Directions: *Write a paragraph about three things you learned or that you think are most important in the reading selection.*

_____

_____

_____

_____

_____

_____

♟♟♟ READING SELECTION 8

ISLAMIC FAITH
Palmira Brummet et al.

Questions for Discussion

1. What do you know about Islam and how did you learn about it?

2. What is your best strategy for taking notes from a text selection?

Preview and Predict

Directions: *Look at the title and subtitles of the selection. Think about what you already know about the subject. Then, write a couple of predictions about what you are going to read. For instance, what will the author discuss about Islam?*

1. _____

2. _____

ISLAMIC FAITH

Palmira Brummet et al.

The Qur'an

1   Muslims believe that the Qur'an contains the actual word of God as it was revealed to Muhammad through divine inspiration. These revelations to the Prophet

took place over a period of more than 20 years. Before Muhammad's death, many of these messages were written down. Muhammad himself began this work of preservation, and Abu Bakr, as caliph, continued the process by compiling revelations that up to that time had been memorized by the followers and passed on by word of mouth.

2   The Qur'an was intended to be recited aloud; anyone who has listened to the chanting of the Qur'an can testify to its beauty, melody, and power. Much of the power of the Qur'an comes from the experience of reciting, listening, and feeling the message. The Qur'an is never to be translated from the Arabic for the purpose of worship because it is believed that translation distorts the divine message. But over time, the Qur'an was indeed translated into many languages to facilitate scholarship and the spread of the Islamic message. As Islam spread, so too did the Arabic language. Arabic replaced many local languages as the language of administration, and gradually, some of the conquered territories adopted Arabic as the language of everyday use.

The Tenets of Islamic Faith

3   Monotheism is the central principle of Islam. Muslims believe in the unity or oneness of God; there is no other God but Allah, and this belief is proclaimed five times daily as the believers are called to prayer with these words:

> *God is most great. I testify that there is no God but Allah. I testify that Muhammad is the Messenger of Allah. Come to prayer, come to revelation, God is most great! There is no God but Allah.*

4   Islam also recognizes the significance and the contributions of prophets who preceded Muhammad. From the beginnings of human history, Allah has communicated with his people either by the way of these prophets or by written scriptures:

> *Lo! We inspire thee as We inspired Noah and the Prophets after him, as We inspired Abraham and Ishmael and Isaac and Jacob and the tribes, and Jesus and Job and Jonah and Aaron and Solomon and as We imparted unto David the Psalms. (Qur'an 4:164)*

5   Twenty-eight such prophets are mentioned in the Qur'an as the predecessors of Muhammad, who is believed to have been Allah's final messenger. Muhammad is given no divine status by Muslims; in fact, Muhammad took great care to see that he was not worshipped as a god. He told his followers, for example, that it was not appropriate for them to bow down before him.

6   The creation of the universe and of all living creatures within it is the work of Allah; harmony and balance in all of creation were ensured by God. In addition to humans and other creatures on the earth, angels exist to protect humans and to pray for forgiveness for the faithful. Satan, "the Whisperer," attempts to lead people astray, and mischievous spirits called *jinn* can create havoc for believers and unbelievers alike.

7   Men and women are given a special status in the pattern of the universe. They can choose to obey or to reject Allah's will and deny him. Allah's message includes

the belief in a Day of Resurrection when people will be held responsible for their actions and rewarded or punished accordingly for eternity.

. . .

The Five Pillars

8   Islam is united in the observance of the Five Pillars, or five essential duties that all Muslims are required to perform to the best of their abilities. These obligations are accepted by Muslims everywhere and thus serve further to unite the Islamic world. The first obligation is a basic *profession of faith,* by which a believer becomes a Muslim. The simple proclamation *(shahada)* is repeated in daily prayers. Belief in the One God and imitation of the exemplary life led by his Prophet are combined in the profession of faith.

9   Prayer *(salat)* is said five times a day, when Muslims are summoned to worship by the *muezzin,* who calls them to prayer from atop the minaret of the mosque *(masjid,* meaning "place of prostration"). During prayer, Muslims face Mecca and in so doing give recognition to the birthplace of Islam and the unity of the Islamic community. Prayer can be said alone, at work, at home, or in the mosque.

10   A Muslim is required to give *alms (zakat)* to the poor, orphans, and widows and to assist the spread of Islam. The payment of alms is a social and religious obligation to provide for the welfare of the **umma.* Muslims are generally expected to contribute annually in alms a percentage (usually 2.5 percent) of their total wealth and assets.

11   Muslims are requested to *fast (sawm)* during the holy month of Ramadan, the ninth month of the Islamic lunar calendar. From sunrise to sunset, adult Muslims in good health are to avoid food, drink, tobacco, and sexual activity. Finally, every Muslim able to do so is called to make a *pilgrimage (hajj)* to Mecca at least once in his or her lifetime, in the twelfth month of the Islamic year. The focus of the pilgrimage is the Ka'ba and a series of other sites commemorating events in the lives of the prophets Muhammad and Abraham. The *hajj* emphasizes the unity of the Islamic world community and the equality of all believers regardless of race or class.

*The Muslim community.

The Write Connection

Directions: *Write a paragraph about three things you learned or that you think are most important in the reading selection.*

_____

_____

_____

_____

_____

_____

♟♟♟ READING SELECTION 9

"WHAT IS MARRIAGE?" FROM *MARRIAGES AND FAMILIES: DIVERSITY AND CHANGE*

Mary Ann Schwartz and Barbara Marliene Scott

Dr. Mary Ann Schwartz is Professor Emeritus of Sociology and Women's Studies and former Chair of the Sociology Department at Northeastern Illinois University. Dr. Barbara Marliene Scott is a Professor of Sociology and Women's Studies and former Chair of the Criminal Justice, Social Work, Sociology, and Woman's Studies Department at Northeastern Illinois University.

Questions for Discussion

1. Is romance essential to a long-lasting relationship? Why or why not?

2. Why do you think some cultures believe it is a good idea to arrange marriages for their children?

Preview and Predict

Directions: *Look at the title and subtitles of the selection. Think about what you already know about the subject. Then, write a couple of predictions about what you are going to read. For instance, what will the author discuss about marriage?*

1. _____

2. _____

WHAT IS MARRIAGE?

Mary Ann Schwartz and Barbara Marliene Scott

1   Marriage has been defined in the United States as a legal contract between a woman and a man who are at or above a specified age and who are not already legally married to someone else. Although some people still regard this definition as adequate, increasing numbers of scholars and laypersons alike consider it too narrow.

Types of Marriages

2   Marriages across cultures generally have been either monogamous or polygamous. Monogamy involves one person married to a person of the other sex. Although,

legally, monogamy refers to heterosexual relationships, any couple can be monogamous if they are committed exclusively to each other sexually and otherwise during
the course of the relationship. Monogamy is the legally recognized marriage structure in the United States. However, approximately one-half of all marriages in this
country end in divorce, and the vast majority of divorced people remarry. Thus, the
U.S. marriage pattern is more accurately classified as **serial monogamy.** Individuals
may marry as many times as they like as long as each prior marriage was ended by
death or divorce.

3   In some societies, polygamy is the accepted marriage structure. **Polygamy** is
a broad category that generally refers to one person of one sex married to several
people of the other sex. It can take one of two forms: **polygyny,** in which one
male has two or more wives; and **polyandry,** in which one female has two or
more husbands. Although both forms of polygamy are illegal in the United
States, some religious groups here routinely practice polygyny. For example, despite the illegality of polygamy, it thrives in Utah, where an estimated 50,000 residents are part of families with more than one wife. One man in Salt Lake City is
believed to have fathered as many as 200 children by several wives. Although the
Church of Jesus Christ of Latter-day Saints renounced polygamy over 100 years
ago and excommunicates its practitioners, Mormons participating in plural marriages defend polygamy as a fulfillment of their religion as prescribed by their
ancestors (Janofsky, 2001).

4   A third form of marriage is **cenogamy,** or **group marriage,** in which all of the
women and men in a group are simultaneously married to one another. Like
polygamy, this form of marriage is also illegal in the United States. In the mid-
1800s, however, the Oneida Community, a communal group living in New York,
practiced cenogamy until they were forced to disband.

The Write Connection

Directions: *Write a paragraph about three things you learned or that you think are
most important in the reading selection.*

_____

_____

_____

_____

_____

_____

♟♟♟ READING SELECTION 10

LET'S TELL THE STORY OF ALL AMERICA'S CULTURES
Yuh Ji-Yeoh

Yuh Ji-Yeoh (b. 1965) is an American author and reporter who immigrated to America from Seoul, Korea, with her family when she was five years old. Yuh's writing focuses on U.S.–Korean relations and the oppression of people who struggle for liberation.

Questions for Discussion

1. Can you recall at least one important contribution to America that was made by a person or people of your particular race or culture? What did they do and where did you learn about it?

2. How do you think a history text could make a particular culture, race, or heritage seem unimportant, powerless, or undesirable?

3. What is your best strategy for determining an author's bias about an issue?

Preview and Predict

Directions: *Look at the title of the selection. Think about what you already know about the subject. Then, write a couple of predictions about what you are going to read. For instance, what will the author discuss about the story of all America's cultures?*

1. _____

2. _____

LET'S TELL THE STORY OF ALL AMERICA'S CULTURES
Yuh Ji-Yeoh

1   I grew up hearing, seeing and almost believing that America was white—albeit with a little black tinge here and there—and that white was best.

2   The white people were everywhere in my 1970s Chicago childhood: Founding Fathers, Lewis and Clark, Lincoln, Daniel Boone, Carnegie, presidents, explorers and industrialists galore. The only black people were slaves. The only Indians were scalpers.

3   I never heard one word about how Benjamin Franklin was so impressed by the Iroquois federation of nations that he adapted that model into our system of state and federal government. Or that the Indian tribes were systematically betrayed and massacred by a greedy young nation that stole their land and called it the United States.

4   I never heard one word about how Asian immigrants were among the first to turn California's desert into fields of plenty. Or about Chinese immigrant Ah Bing, who bred the cherry now on sale in groceries across the nation. Or that plantation owners in Hawaii imported labor from China, Japan, Korea and the Philippines to work the sugar cane fields. I never learned that Asian immigrants were the only immigrants denied U.S. citizenship, even though they served honorably in World War I. All the immigrants in my textbook were white.

5   I never learned about Frederick Douglass, the runaway slave who became a leading abolitionist and statesman, or about black scholar W.E.B. Du Bois. I never learned that black people rose up in arms against slavery. Nat Turner wasn't one of the heroes in my childhood history class.

6   I never learned that the American Southwest and California were already settled by Mexicans when they were annexed after the Mexican-American War. I never learned that Mexico once had a problem keeping land-hungry white men on the U.S. side of the border.

7   So when other children called me a slant-eyed chink and told me to go back where I came from, I was ready to believe that I wasn't really an American because I wasn't white.

8   America's bittersweet legacy of struggling and failing and getting another step closer to democratic ideals of liberty and equality and justice for all wasn't for the likes of me, an immigrant child from Korea. The history books said so.

9   Well, the history books were wrong.

10   Educators around the country are finally realizing what I realized as a teenager in the library, looking up the history I wasn't getting in school. America is a multicultural nation, composed of many people with varying histories and varying traditions who have little in common except their humanity, a belief in democracy and a desire for freedom.

11   America changed them, but they changed America too.

12   A committee of scholars and teachers gathered by the New York State Department of Education recognizes this in their recent report, "One Nation, Many Peoples: A Declaration of Cultural Interdependence."

13   They recommend that public schools provide a "multicultural education, anchored to the shared principles of a liberal democracy."

14   What that means, according to the report, is recognizing that America was shaped and continues to be shaped by people of diverse backgrounds. It calls for

students to be taught that history is an on-going process of discovery and interpretation of the past, and that there is more than one way of viewing the world.

15   Thus, the westward migration of white Americans is not just a heroic settling of an untamed wild, but also the conquest of indigenous people. Immigrants were not just white, but Asian as well. Blacks were not merely passive slaves freed by northern whites, but active fighters for their own liberation.

16   In particular, according to the report, the curriculum should help children "to assess critically the reasons for the inconsistencies between the ideals of the U.S. and social realities. It should provide information and intellectual tools that can permit them to contribute to bringing reality closer to the ideals."

17   In other words, show children the good with the bad, and give them the skills to help improve their country. What could be more patriotic?

18   Several dissenting members of the New York committee publicly worry that America will splinter into ethnic fragments if this multicultural curriculum is adopted. They argue that the committee's report puts the focus on ethnicity at the expense of national unity.

19   But downplaying ethnicity will not bolster national unity. The history of America is the story of how and why people from all over the world came to the United States, and how in struggling to make a better life for themselves, they changed each other, they changed the country, and they all came to call themselves Americans.

20   *E pluribus unum.* Out of many, one.

21   This is why I, with my Korean background, and my childhood tormentors, with their lost-in-the-mist-of-time European backgrounds, are all Americans.

22   It is the unique beauty of this country. It is high time we let all our children gaze upon it.

The Write Connection

Directions: *Write a paragraph about three things you learned or that you think are most important in the reading selection.*

_____

_____

_____

_____

_____

_____

♟♟♟ READING SELECTION 11

HUNGRY HOUNDS EAT UP ATTENTION
D. L. Stewart

D. L. Stewart is a native of Cleveland and a graduate of Ohio University. He joined the sports staff of Dayton Newspapers in 1966 as a sports writer. In 1975 he took over a general interest column about family life from a father's point of view. His columns are now nationally syndicated and have formed the basis of four books. D. L. Stewart has been featured in *Time, Redbook,* and *Reader's Digest.* He has appeared on Good Morning America and the CBS Morning News. He has been honored by the Atlantic City Press Club for "the most consistently outstanding local interest column in America." He is a four-time Pulitzer Prize nominee.

Questions for Discussion

1. Do you think that dogs make better pets than cats? Explain your answer.

2. What is your best strategy for determining the author's purpose for writing a particular selection?

Preview and Predict

Directions: *Look at the title and subtitles of the selection. Think about what you already know about the subject. Then, write a couple of predictions about what you are going to read. For instance, what will the author discuss about dogs?*

1. _____

2. _____

HUNGRY HOUNDS EAT UP ATTENTION
D. L. Stewart

1   A lot of people were amazed by the story of Elsie, the St. Bernard puppy in Fort Lauderdale, Fla., who swallowed a 13-inch knife and lived to bark about it.

2   Not me.

3   If Elsie had swallowed, say, a lawn mower, I would have been impressed. If X-rays revealed that her latest dinner had consisted of a set of golf clubs, plus half a dozen Titleists and a caddy, I would have been amazed. But, as nearly as I can tell, a 13-inch knife is not much more than an appetizer to a St. Bernard.

4   That's probably because my good friend, Paul, has two St. Bernards. Between them they have eaten a kitchen floor, a bathroom wall and a sizable chunk of his SUV's dashboard. One or two more bites, we estimated, and they would have been air-bagged through the rear window. St. Bernards, in other words, will eat just about anything that moves slower than they do. Which reminds me, I haven't heard from my good friend, Paul, in quite some time, and I'm not sure if I should be worried about that.

5   It's not that St. Bernards are gluttons. It's just that they are dogs.

6   And, as dogs, they will swallow just about anything. If you own a dog, you don't need a vacuum cleaner. Dogs spend most of the time that they are not sleeping—which frequently is as much as two hours a day—walking around with their noses to the ground looking for things to inhale.

7   Which is why I am puzzled when my wife makes a big deal about me giving pills to our dog while she is out of town for the weekend.

8   "The vet showed me how to do it," she says. "Now watch carefully."

9   While I watch carefully, she takes a slice of white bread and tears off a piece approximately the size of a garbanzo bean. Then she spreads butter on the bread. Then she wraps the buttered bread around the pill that is approximately the size of a lentil bean.

10   "Do you have all that, or do you want me to write it down for you?" she asks.

11   "Excuse me, but isn't this the same dog that swallowed my hearing aid, which didn't have anything on it but earwax?" I inquire.

12   I don't know what the pills are for, although I'm pretty sure they're not for constipation. And it's not that I don't appreciate her concern, because I still have the scars from the last animal I attempted to medicate. But that animal was a cat, so I'm probably lucky to be alive at all. As I remember it, giving him his medication involved wrapping him in a towel and prying open his mouth so my wife could use some sort of plunger device to ram the pill halfway down his throat. Which, as soon as we released him, he immediately projectile-vomited across the room.

13   But this is a dog.

14   So twice a day while my wife was gone I sat at the kitchen table and buttered some bread. While I ate the bread and butter, I tossed the pills over my shoulder.

15   They never reached the floor.

The Write Connection

Directions: *Write a paragraph about three things you learned or that you think are most important in the reading selection.*

_____

_____

_____

_____

_____

_____

♟♟♟ READING SELECTION 12

"Media and the Marketplace of Ideas" Adapted from *The Basics of American Politics*
Gary Wasserman

Dr. Gary Wasserman is a Visiting Professor at Johns Hopkins University's School of Advanced International Studies, teaching graduate students about American government, media, and political parties in Nanjing, China. He has taught at Columbia, Medgar Evers College CUNY, and George Mason University and is a Senior Vice President of the public affairs firm Bozell Sawyer Miller. Dr. Wasserman has written for the *New York Times*, *Foreign Policy*, and *Political Science Quarterly*.

Questions for Discussion

1. Do you think it is important to know what is happening in American politics? Why or why not?

2. Imagine that you own a TV station. You make money from companies that pay you to advertise their products. If you found out that one of these companies had a product that was harmful to the public, would you still run its advertisements? Why or why not?

Preview and Predict

Directions: *Look at the title of the selection. Think about what you already know about the subject. Then, write a couple of predictions about what you are going to read. For instance, what will the author discuss about the media?*

1. _____

2. _____

MEDIA AND THE MARKETPLACE OF IDEAS
Gary Wasserman

1   *Media are those means of communication that permit messages to be made public.* Media such as television, radio, newspapers, and, recently, the Internet provide important links connecting people to one another. But these are links with an important quality: They have the ability to communicate messages to a great many people at roughly the same time. The major forms of media we will concentrate on are television and newspapers.

2   The media provide three major types of messages. Through their *news reports,* *entertainment programs*, and *advertising*, the media help shape public opinion on many things—including politics. In news reports, the media supply up-to-date accounts of what journalists believe to be the most important, interesting, and newsworthy events, issues, and developments. But the influence of news reports goes well beyond relaying facts. The key to this power is *selectivity*. By reporting certain items (President Bush's jogging injuries) and ignoring others (President Roosevelt's crippled legs), the media suggest to us what's important. Media coverage gives status to people and events—a national television interview or a *Time* magazine cover creates a "national figure."

3   There are limits. Few people pay attention to political news. Most of us read the newspapers for the sports and comics and local events. Young people are notoriously indifferent to the news. Those under 30 are less likely than those over 30 to listen to or watch political news. This isn't because Generation Xers do not have enough time. Young people spend more time watching sports and entertainment on television than those over 30. One result of this is that the more they avoid coverage of politics, the less they know about American government. (See Figure A on page 523.)

4   The media perform two important political functions: agenda setting and framing. *Agenda setting is* putting together an agenda of national priorities—what should be taken seriously, what should be taken lightly, and what should be ignored altogether. "The media can't tell people what to think," as one expert put it, "but they can tell people what to think *about.*" The attention the media give to education

in the inner cities, environmental pollution, the budget deficit, or the war in Iraq will affect how important most people think these issues are.

5   *Framing* defines problems, explaining *how* we see issues. Media coverage can present, or frame, an issue in many ways. Is crime linked to unemployment, to lax immigration laws, or to poor police training? How the problem is understood may influence whether the solution is a jobs program or barriers on the border. During the 2004 presidential campaign, a major objective of the two sides was to present a convincing negative frame for their opponent—Kerry as a waffler, Bush as arrogant. The effort was then made in the press to explain what the candidates did or said within these negative frames. Media scholar Kathleen Hall Jamieson has written, "Frames tell us what is important, what the range of acceptable debate on a topic is, and when an issue has been resolved."

6   *Entertainment* programs offer amusement while giving people images of "normal" behavior. Whether this television behavior offers socially acceptable models is another question. Soap characters (such as Tony Soprano of *The Sopranos*) engage in immoral business practices that bring wealth and power. These media programs may substitute for learning from life's more complex experiences, and become as important as real life. As one analyst of television observed: "If you can write a nation's stories, you needn't worry about who makes its laws. Today, television tells most of the stories to most of the people most of the time."

7   Finally, the programs and news that media present are built around a constant flow of *advertisements*. Television programs are constructed to reach emotional high points just before the commercials so that the audience will stay put during the advertisement. Newspapers devote almost two-thirds of their space to ads rather than to news, leading one English author to define a journalist as "someone who writes on the back of advertisements." Ads, especially television commercials, present images of what the audience finds pleasing about themselves. Presented in 30-second compelling symbols—"Reach Out and Touch Someone"—commercials offer viewers comfort, good looks, and amusement. They may change what we expect in other arenas, including politics. Media critic Neil Postman has charged that television's emphasis on entertaining visuals has altered how we look at our political leaders and how they present themselves: Instead of a public discussion of issues, we find a competition between reassuring visual images. In this case, the medium has changed the message of politics.

8   Most of the profits in the media industry come from advertising. Advertisers approach media with certain expectations. They want their ads to be seen by as many people as possible, they want the people seeing the ads to be potential customers, and they don't want the surrounding programs or articles to detract from the ads. As a result, advertising encourages media content—whether news or entertainment—to be conventional and inoffensive in order to keep the customer satisfied. Tobacco companies have contracts that keep their ads away from articles linking cigarette smoking to cancer. Ownership may bring "advertising" privileges. *NBC Nightly News* ran

Figure A Audiences Reached by Leading Media, 2003–2004

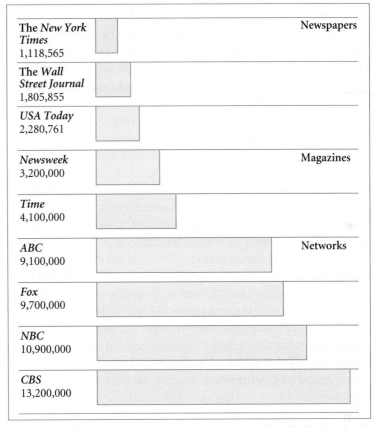

The *New York Times* 1,118,565	Newspapers
The *Wall Street Journal* 1,805,855	
USA Today 2,280,761	
Newsweek 3,200,000	Magazines
Time 4,100,000	
ABC 9,100,000	Networks
Fox 9,700,000	
NBC 10,900,000	
CBS 13,200,000	

Source: Newspapers and Magazines: *Audit Bureau of Circulations.* Networks: John Consolin, *Adweek Magazines:* Special Report, April 26, 2004.

three segments, totaling 14 minutes, about a new device to detect breast cancer without mentioning that its parent corporation, General Electric, manufactured the machine.

9   Newscasts also affect the political information available. To get the largest possible audience, television news packages itself as entertainment. This means bite-sized, action-packed news with emphasis on stimulating visuals. The credibility of the news is largely dependent on the attractiveness of likable anchors—or "talking hairdos." Television news also is divided up by commercials that may make the news seem less serious, less complex, and perhaps less worth being concerned about. One critic noted how strange it was to see a newscaster who, having just presented a report on the likelihood of nuclear war, went on to say he will be right back after this word from Burger King.

10   The framers of the Constitution believed that a free flow of information from many voices was basic to their system of government. Ideas would compete with one another without restraint in a "marketplace of ideas." Fearing that the greatest enemy of free speech was the government, the framers added the First Amendment forbidding government officials from "abridging the freedom of speech, or of the press." The phrase since has been expanded to include radio and television.

11   Media, such as television stations and newspapers, are privately owned economic assets bought and sold to make money for their owners. Profitability, not public service, has led to the increasing concentration of media ownership. The decrease in competition among newspapers mentioned earlier has been a reflection of the increase in *chains,* which are companies that combine different media in different cities under one owner. More than 80 percent of the nation's newspapers are owned by chains, and only three corporations own most of the nation's 11,000 magazines.

12   In the last ten years, market calculations left all major media outlets concentrated in a few corporate hands. In 1995, Disney purchased ABC for $19 billion, Westinghouse paid $5.4 billion for CBS, and Time Warner bought Turner Broadcasting for $7.5 billion. Earlier, NBC had been bought by General Electric. In May 2000, the combination of Viacom (which owns Paramount Pictures, Blockbuster, MTV, Nickelodeon, and Simon & Schuster, among others) with CBS created the second-largest media company in the world. But this was soon surpassed. America Online, in 2001, acquired Time Warner, the largest media corporation. The *Christian Science Monitor* concluded: "The bulk of what we see, hear, learn, sing, play, rent and consume will shortly be controlled by a dozen corporate entities."

13   In the past, federal regulators prevented such mergers, arguing that monopolies over information didn't serve the public interest.

14   Called "the fourth branch of government," the media have often rivaled the three official branches in political power. No one doubts the media's ability to shape the political agenda and public attitudes.

The Write Connection

Directions: *Write a paragraph about three things you learned or that you think are most important in the reading selection.*

Appendix A ▶ Attitude and Interest Inventory

ATTITUDE AND INTEREST INVENTORY

Complete the inventory. Then, total your points and read the suggestions for improving your reading strength next to your score. On page 528, you will find a book list. You can select the books you find most interesting from it and use them to get into better reading shape.

Name: _____ Date: _____

1. What city are you from?_____

2. What is your major?_____

3. In one week, how often do you read for more than twenty minutes at a time?
   a. Every day
   b. 2–3 times per week
   c. Maybe once a week
   d. Never

4. Do you think that reading is fun?
   a. Yes
   b. Only if I'm interested
   c. No way

5. When you were growing up, how often did you have dinner with your family?
   a. Every day
   b. Once a week
   c. 2–3 times a month
   d. 2–3 times a year
   e. Never

6. You are the _____ child in your family.
   a. Only
   b. Oldest
   c. Middle
   d. Youngest

7. When you are in a conversation, which do you like to do?
   a. I like to listen more than talk.
   b. I like to talk more than listen.

8. The last book I finished was called:

   a. _____
   b. I don't remember—too long ago

9. Check ANY of the problems below that apply to you.
   - ☐ a. If I see a word I don't know, I lose my concentration.
   - ☐ b. Unless the subject is interesting, I get bored and easily distracted.
   - ☐ c. When I read, my eyes get so red and tired that I almost fall asleep.
   - ☐ d. By the end of a passage, I realize that I don't remember many details.
   - ☐ e. I read too slowly because I have to read every single word.
   - ☐ f. Sometimes it's hard to find the next line of a paragraph.
   - ☐ g. I just hate to read.

10. Which of following subjects are interesting to you?
    - ☐ a. Murder Mysteries
    - ☐ b. Occult/Horror/Fantasy/Ghost Stories
    - ☐ c. Computers
    - ☐ d. Business
    - ☐ e. Interesting People/Real Problems/Conflicts
    - ☐ f. Spiritual, Inspirational, or Self-Help

11. Answer the following questions.

    a. My favorite thing to talk about is: _____

    _____

    b. In my spare time I like to: _____

    _____

Results of the Attitude and Interest Inventory

Look at the answers that you chose for questions 3–8. Give yourself the following points for each response (see list below). Then, add up your points and read the suggestions beside your score.

   A = 1 point

   B = 2 points

   C = 3 points

   D = 4 points

If you scored 5–10: You may read fairly often, but you don't always have confidence in your ability to understand what you read. You may read a sentence or a word many times to make sure you have understood it, even when you know you understood it on the first try. Doing this is what slows you down.

> **Solution:** Read as slowly as you want, but don't stop. Train yourself to read at a pace that allows you to see what is happening or to have a conversation with the author. Develop faith in yourself that you can understand what you read as you go. You will soon find that the next sentence confirms you were right. You will be able to read faster and more easily as you develop the confidence to trust in your ability to apply what you are learning to each new sentence.

If you scored 11–14: Reading is not the first thing you do when you have spare time. You may like to keep yourself occupied with other activities. It may not always be easy for you to focus on what others are saying. You probably prefer to be the one who is talking in a conversation. You may have some of the symptoms or problems associated with weak reading muscles, which makes it difficult to motivate yourself to read every day.

> **Solution:** You need to remember why it is important for you to be in college at this time. Without good reading skills, college courses as well as the search for a better job can be difficult. It doesn't take very long to get in shape, but it does take commitment to something that you really love or want to achieve.

Find a novel, book, magazine, or article about a subject that interests you and carry it with you at all times. Use unexpected opportunities as listed in Chapter 1 to your advantage. Read something every day. See how long you can hold in your mind the picture of what the author is saying. Try just ten minutes at a time to start with. Soon you will find that you are reading much faster and more easily. It doesn't take very long to get into shape if you have a real goal that you want to achieve.

If you scored 15–19: You have not been reading much. As a result, you probably have many of the symptoms or problems associated with weak reading muscles. Reading may actually be painful to you because it is so difficult. Reading may remind you of negative experiences in school that make you feel that you are not as smart or as capable as other students. You may even feel that there is something wrong with you and you hate the idea of having to do something that you don't believe you can do very well.

> **Solution:** Remember that you are in college for a reason. You are an adult now with real responsibilities and goals that you want to achieve. When you were a child in school, you may have felt powerless against the negative thoughts you had about yourself at that time. You probably believed them for many years. As an adult, however, you have the power to see what you need to do to change or improve your reading skills and be able to put a plan into action. You may be accustomed to hearing these negative opinions

about yourself, but do you really want to stay in that mindset for the rest of your life? Reading is the key to a more successful future. Apply *The Reading Workout* and see how fast that mindset can be put away.

Reflection

1. What was your score? _____

2. What did you learn about your reading skills? _____

   _____

   _____

   _____

3. What is one thing that you are going to do to improve your score? _____

   _____

   _____

4. When will you put your plan into action? _____

   _____

THE READING WORKOUT: BOOK LIST

Each of the books listed by subject is followed by a summary you can read to see if it is about something that might interest you. Choose the top three books that interest you and use the numbers 1, 2, and 3 to show the order of your selections.

Murder Mysteries/Thrillers

_____ *Beach Road*, by James Patterson with Peter De Jonge. A former professional basketball player tries to build his law practice and gets involved in the murder trial of the century.

_____ *The Da Vinci Code*, by Dan Brown. A murder mystery that takes the reader through 2000 years of Western history to the beginnings of an ancient secret society.

_____ *Of Love and Shadows*, by Isabel Allende. The story of two journalists who investigate a murder. Describes life under military dictatorship in Latin America.

Occult/Horror/Fantasy/Science Fiction

_____   *The Exorcist,* by William Peter Blatty. Best-selling novel about an 11-year-old girl possessed by a demon and the priests who try to save her.

_____   *Harry Potter and the Sorcerer's Stone,* by J. K Rowling. Best Seller: Harry lives with an aunt and uncle who treat him poorly. When Harry's real background is revealed, he begins a new life as a wizard.

_____   *Interview with a Vampire,* by Anne Rice. A vampire tells the story of his adventures in the world of the undead.

_____   *Watchers,* by Dean Koontz. Travis and an extraordinary dog are targets of a cold-blooded hit-man.

Computers

_____   *Designing with Web Standards,* by Jeffrey Zeldman. Learn to create faster, more compatible Web pages from the man who is called "the absolute best."

_____   *Masters of Doom: How Two Guys Created an Empire and Transformed Pop Culture,* by David Kushner. The underground story of John Carmack and John Romero, authors of such video games as *Doom, Wolfenstein 3D,* and *Quake.*

Business

_____   *The One-Minute Millionaire: The Enlightened Way to Wealth,* by Mark Victor Hanson and Robert G. Allen. This book explains how to turn dreams into a profitable result.

_____   *The Richest Man in Babylon,* by George S. Clason. Learn the mindset behind financial abundance through parables or stories written in a biblical style.

_____   *The Seven Secrets of Highly Successful People,* by Steven Covey. Best Seller: Explains easy-to-understand steps for improving behavior that is most likely to lead to success, not only in business, but in one's life.

Interesting People/Real Problems/Conflict

_____   *Hatchet,* by Gary Paulsen. A young man's struggle to survive in the Canadian wilderness.

_____   *Makes Me Wanna Holler,* by Nathan McCall. McCall's autobiography traces his life from the streets of Portsmouth, VA, to prison, to the *Washington Post.*

———— *Voices from Slavery: 100 Authentic Slave Narratives,* by Norman R. Yetman. First-hand accounts describe what it was like to be a slave in the antebellum South.

———— *Odd Girl Out,* by Rachel Simmons. Discusses the behavior of girls who try to gain control over other girls.

———— *Ordinary Resurrections,* by Jonathan Kozol. Respected educator Jonathan Kozol shares the success stories of people living in the difficult reality of urban America.

———— *Zenzele: A Letter for My Daughter,* by J. Nozipo Maraire. A mother in Zimbabwe writes to her daughter, who is in America, to remind her of their cultural heritage.

Spiritual, Inspirational, or Self-Help

———— *A Dangerous Book for Boys,* by Conn Iggulden and Hal Iggulden. This bestseller provides essential information for boys aged 9–90.

———— *Goals: How to Get Everything You Want—Faster Than You Ever Thought Possible,* by Brian Tracy. World-renowned time management expert discusses not only how to set goals but also how to organize your entire life to achieve whatever you want.

———— *The Secret of the Shadow: The Power of Owning Your Story,* by Debbie Ford. Explains how to understand the dark side of oneself to access personal power.

———— *What Mama Taught Me: The Seven Core Values of Life,* by Tony Brown. Motivational speaker and host of PBS's *Tony Brown's Journal* writes about the powerful influence of the woman who raised him to become a national success.

Questions about the Book List

1. Which book from the list seems most interesting?

————————————————————————————————

2. What interested you about the book?

————————————————————————————————

3. ———— T/F I will buy the book or check it out of the library.

4. If you answered "false" to question three, explain.

————————————————————————————————

College Reading List:

Here are some classic works that you may be assigned to read in college courses. If you are interested in a particular title, go to www.Amazon.com, where you can find a brief description of each one.

Alice in Wonderland, by Lewis Carroll

Animal Farm, by George Orwell

The Autobiography of Malcolm X, by Malcolm X and Alex Haley

The Awakening, by Kate Chopin

Brave New World, by Aldous Huxley

The Canterbury Tales (prologue and tales), by Geoffrey Chaucer

Catch-22, by Joseph Heller

The Catcher in the Rye, by J. D. Salinger

A Clockwork Orange, by Anthony Burgess

The Color Purple, by Alice Walker

Death of a Salesman, by Arthur Miller (play)

Emily Dickinson (poetry)

The Fall of the House of Usher, by Edgar Allen Poe

A Farewell to Arms, by Ernest Hemingway

Frankenstein, by Mary Shelley

The Glass Menagerie, by Tennessee Williams

A Good Man Is Hard to Find, by Flannery O'Conner

The Grapes of Wrath, by John Steinbeck

Great Expectations, by Charles Dickens

The Great Gatsby, by F. Scott Fitzgerald

Gulliver's Travels, by Jonathan Swift

Hamlet, by William Shakespeare

Heart of Darkness, by Joseph Conrad

Huckleberry Finn, by Mark Twain

The Iliad and the Odyssey, by Homer

The Invisible Man, by Ralph Ellison

The Joy Luck Club, by Amy Tan

Langston Hughes (poetry)

Letter from the Birmingham Jail, by Martin Luther King, Jr. (essay)

Lord of the Flies, by William Golding

Madame Bovary, by Gustave Flaubert

The Metamorphosis, by Franz Kafka

Moby-Dick, by Herman Melville

Native Son, by Richard Wright

One Hundred Years of Solitude, by Gabriel Garcia Marquez

Pride and Prejudice, by Jane Austen

The Prince, by Machiavelli

The Red Badge of Courage, by Stephen Crane
Republic, by Plato
Robinson Crusoe, by Daniel Defoe
The Scarlet Letter, by Nathaniel Hawthorne
Self-Reliance, by Ralph Waldo Emerson
The Stranger, by Albert Camus
Sula, by Toni Morrison
Tess of the D'Urbervilles, by Thomas Hardy
To Kill a Mockingbird, by Harper Lee
Walden, by Henry David Thoreau

Appendix B ▶ Word Parts

WORD PARTS LISTS

Prefix	Example	Root	Example
a: not	atypical	**aero:** air	aerobic
a: on	atop	**acro:** heights	acrobat
ab: away from	absent	**agora:** crowds	agoraphobia
ac: to	accept	**anim:** life force	animate
ad: to	adhere	**ann:** year	annual
af: to	affirm	**anthrop:** man	anthropology
ambi: both	ambidextrous	**aqua:** water	aquarium
an: to	annex	**arch:** rule; lead	monarchy
an: not	anarchy	**arch:** original	archeology
ante: before	antecedent	**ast:** star	astronomy
anti: against	antisocial	**aud:** hear	auditorium
as: to	ascend	**bibl:** book	bible
auto: self	autograph	**bio:** life	biology
be: make	befriend	**cap:** head	capital
bene: good	benefit	**cardio:** heart	cardiology
bi: two	bicycle	**cede, ceed:** go	proceed
by: alongside	bypass	**ceive:** get; take	receive
cent: hundred	century	**cept:** get; take	accept
circu: around	circulate	**chrom:** color	monochrome
co: together	cooperate	**chron:** time	chronological
col: with	collect	**cide:** kill	suicide
com: with	combine	**cise:** cut	scissors
con: with	conductor	**cogni:** know	recognize
contra: against	contradict	**cosm:** universe	cosmopolitan
counter: against	counteract	**cred:** believe	creditor
de: down; away	degrade	**cur:** run	current
dec: ten	decade	**cur:** care	manicure
di: two	dilemma	**dem:** people	democracy
dia: across	diameter	**derma:** skin	dermatologist
dis: not	disagree	**dict:** say	predict
dys: bad	dysfunctional	**doc:** teach	document
e: away from	evict	**duc, duct:** lead	conduct
em: in	embrace	**enn:** year	biennial
en: in	encourage	**fac:** make	manufacture
enter: among	entertain	**fic:** make	fiction
epi: upon	epidemic	**fer:** carry	transfer
equi: equal	equation	**fid:** faith	confidence

Prefix	Example	Root	Example
eu: good	euphoria	**flect:** bend	reflect
ex: out	exit	**flex:** bend	flexible
extra: beyond	extracurricular	**gam:** marriage	monogamy
giga: billion	gigabyte	**gen:** birth	generation
hemi: half	hemisphere	**geo:** earth	geology
hexa: six	hexagon	**gnos:** know	diagnose
hetero: different	heterosexual	**gram:** written	diagram
homo: same	homosexual	**graph:** write	autograph
hyper: over	hyperactive	**gress:** go	progress
hypo: under	hypodermic	**gyn:** woman	gynecology
il: not	illegal	**homo:** man	homocide
im: not	immature	**hydro:** water	dehydrate
inter: among	international	**ject:** throw	reject
intra: within	intrastate	**jud:** law	judge
intro: into, toward	introduction	**jur:** law	jury
ir: not	irregular	**jus:** law	justice
iso: equal	isosceles	**log:** speech	apology
kilo: thousand	kilobyte	**logue:** speech	monologue
macro: large	macrocosm	**man:** hand	manufacture
magni: large	magnify	**mater:** mother	maternity
mal: bad	malfunction	**mem:** mind	memory
mega: hundred, large	megabyte	**meter:** measure	thermometer
meta: change	metamorphosis	**miss:** send	mission
micro: small	microscope	**mit:** send	transmit
milli: thousand	million	**mor:** death	mortician
mis: bad	misbehave	**nat:** birth	natal
mono: one	monogamy	**onym:** name	synonym
multi: many	multicolored	**pater:** father	paternity
nano: billionth	nanosecond	**ped:** child	pediatrician
neo: new	neonatal	**ped, pod:** foot	pedestrian
non: not	nonstop	**pel:** urge, force	propel
oct: eight	octopus	**pend:** hang	pendant
olig: few	oligarchy	**phil:** love	philanthopist
omni: all	omnipresent	**phob:** fear	hydrophobia
pan: all	pandemic	**phon:** sound	telephone
para: alongside	paramedic	**photo:** light	photograph
penta: five	pentagon	**pol:** city	political
per: through	permit	**port:** carry	portable
poly: many	polygamy	**psych:** mind	psychology
post: after	postscript	**rad:** ray	radius
pre: before	prepare	**rect:** straight	erect
pro: forward	promote	**rupt:** break	interrupt
pro: favor	pro-education	**scend:** climb	ascend

Prefix	Example	Root	Example
proto: first	prototype	**sci:** know	conscience
pseudo: false	pseudonym	**scop:** see	microscope
quad: four	quadruped	**scrip:** write	prescription
quin: five	quintuplet	**sect:** cut	section
re: back, again	repeat	**soph:** wise	sophomore
retro: back	retroactive	**spect:** look; see	inspect
semi: half	semicircle	**spir:** breath	inspire
sept: seven	septet	**sta:** stand	status
sub: under	submarine	**strict:** tighten	restrict
super: beyond	supervisor	**tact:** touch	contact
syl: same, together	syllable	**tain:** hold	retain
sym: same, together	symphony	**tect:** touch	detect
syn: same, together	synonym	**ten:** hold	tenacious
tele: distant	telephone	**ten:** stretch	tension
trans: across	transmit	**term:** end	terminal
tri: three	triangle	**theo:** god	theology
ultra: beyond	ultramodern	**therm:** heat	thermometer
un: not	unusual	**tract:** pull	attract
uni: one	universe	**ver:** truth	verdict
		vers: turn	reverse
		vert: turn	divert
		voc: call	vocation
		vol: will	volunteer
		volv: roll; turn	revolve

Noun Suffixes: As you look at each of the examples below, think of the questions: "What?" "Where?" or "Who?"

Noun Suffixes	Example
-an: person who	musician
-ance: relating to	finance
-ary: place for	library
-ation: state or quality of	organization
-crat: person or people who	democrat
-cy: state or quality of	bankruptcy
-dom: state or quality of	freedom
-ee: person that	employee
-ence: relating to	violence
-ency: state or quality of	emergency
-hood: condition	adulthood
-ic: person who	critic

Noun Suffixes	Example
-ion: state or act of	condition
-ectomy: removal of	tonsillectomy
-ent: person who	president
-er: person who	teacher
-ette: small	cigarette
-ism: state or quality of	activism
-ist: person who	dentist
-itis: inflammation of	arthritis
-ity: state or quality of	reality
-let: small	starlet
-ment: state or quality of	commitment
-ness: state or quality of	happiness
-ology: study of	psychology
-or: person who	instructor
-ty: state or quality of	honesty

Adjective Suffixes: As you look at each of the examples below, think of the question: "What *kind* of person, place, or thing?"

Adjective Suffixes	Example
-able: capable of	reliable
-al: relating to	medical
-ant: tending toward	pleasant
-ary: relating to	ordinary
-ate: quality of	passionate
-en: made of	golden
-ent: tending toward	different
-er: more	smarter
-ern: direction	western
-ese: quality of	Chinese
-esque: like	picturesque
-est: most	smartest
-ful: full of	careful
-ial: relating to	commercial
-ible: capable of	audible
-ic: relating to	fantastic
-ile: quality of	mobile
-ly: every	daily
-ine: relating to	feminine
-ish: like	childish
-ive: tending toward	active

Adjective Suffixes	Example
-less: without	helpless
-oid: like	humanoid
-ous: full of	joyous
-y: having, state of	funny

Verb Suffixes: As you look at each of the examples below, think of the question: "What did he/she/it *do*?"

Verb Suffixes	Example
-ate: to make happen	activate
-ble: action repeated	tremble
-ed, d: past tense action	studied
-er: action	recover
-fy: to make happen	satisfy
-ing: continuous action	acting
-ish: action	finish
-ize: to make happen	finalize
-ure: action	endure

Adverb Suffixes: As you look at each of the examples below, think of the question: "*How* was the action completed?"

Adverb Suffixes	Example
-ily: manner of action	happily
-ly: manner of action	quickly
-wise: manner of action	clockwise

Weekly Word Parts Activities

Here is a series of word parts activities that you can complete each week to improve your vocabulary.

Word Parts Activity One

Use the word parts lists to help you complete the following sentences.

1. The noun suffix *ology* means: _____.

2. Psychology refers to the study of the _____.

3. Astrology involves the study of _____.

4. Biology refers to the study of _____.

5. Cardiology is the study of the _____.

6. Anthropology is the study of _____.

7. The root *phob* means _____.

8. Hydrophobia is the fear of _____.

9. Agoraphobia is the fear of _____.

10. Acrophobia is the fear of _____.

Word Parts Activity Two

Use the word parts lists to help you complete the following sentences.

_____ 1. If you want to build self-confidence, you will need to have
   a. money   c. time
   b. strength   d. faith

2. A nanosecond is one _____ of a second.

3. A paramedic works _____ the medical staff at a hospital.

4. Turn the word careful into an adverb. _____

5. Turn the word help into an adjective. _____

6. A person who has a morbid curiosity is interested in _____ and dying.

7. If a doctor is sued for malpractice, it means he or she did something _____.

_____ 8. When someone uses a pseudonym, it means they are using a
   a. credit card.   c. new word.
   b. false name.   d. context clue.

9. An insecticide is used to _____ bugs.

10. If you can remember the meaning of a word, it means you have the word in

   _____.

Word Parts Activity Three

Use the word parts lists to help you find the answer that has the same meaning as the word or phrase in bold.

_____ 1. Regular exercise is **good** for your heart.
   a. ambidextrous   c. beneficial
   b. democratic   d. generic

_____   2. Carmen made an appointment with **a heart specialist.**
   a. pediatrician
   b. gynecologist
   c. cardiologist
   d. podiatrist

_____   3. In some Arabic countries, men are allowed to **have many wives.**
   a. polygamy
   b. misogamy
   c. monogamy
   d. autonomy

_____   4. The United Nations was concerned about a possible **world-wide spread** of the Bird Flu.
   a. generic
   b. emetic
   c. epidemic
   d. pandemic

_____   5. George had a **fear of crowded places**.
   a. homophobia
   b. arachnophobia
   c. acrophobia
   d. agoraphobia

_____   6. I can only write with my right one hand, but Jean is **ambidextrous.**
   a. able to use one hand
   b. able to use a computer
   c. able to use a pen or pencil equally
   d. able to use both hands equally

_____   7. The **podiatrist** removed the ingrown toenail from the child's right foot.
   a. a children's health specialist
   b. a foot specialist
   c. a heart specialist
   d. a family medicine specialist

_____   8. Gina uses a **false name** when she is approached by strangers.
   a. monologue
   b. cell number
   c. pseudonym
   d. synonym

_____   9. Nancy was afraid to climb the tree because she had **acrophobia.**
   a. a sinus condition
   b. a fear of crowed places
   c. an expensive ring
   d. a fear of heights

_____   10. The sociology text presented the data regarding **monogamy** in America.
   a. having one spouse
   b. having many spouses
   c. having several marriages
   d. having one relationship

Word Parts Activity Four

Use the word parts lists to help you find the answer that has the same meaning as the phrase in bold.

_____   1. The jury members needed more evidence to **check the truth of** the man's statement.
   a. verify
   b. imply
   c. terminate
   d. politicize

_____   2. Joe's illness was **of the type that would soon end his life**.
    a. literal
    b. terminal
    c. diagnostic
    d. aquatic

_____   3. The painting **has only one color**.
    a. polychromatic
    b. monochromatic
    c. monogamy
    d. polytonal

_____   4. Dogs, cats, and horses are animals that **walk on four feet**.
    a. quadrupeds
    b. bipeds
    c. monopods
    d. pendants

_____   5. The abacus is considered to be **the first type** of computer.
    a. heliotype
    b. subtype
    c. proton
    d. prototype

_____   6. They were the proud parents of **five babies born only minutes apart**.
    a. quadruplets
    b. septuplets
    c. quintuplets
    d. triplets

_____   7. Gerilyn wanted to **climb up** the corporate ladder.
    a. intercept
    b. ascend
    c. erect
    d. inspire

_____   8. Tony was **forced out** after he showed off his new knife at school.
    a. suspended
    b. degraded
    c. interrogated
    d. expelled

_____   9. The cartoon characters are **able to move as if they are alive**.
    a. inspired
    b. ascended
    c. animated
    d. receptive

_____   10. John was **urged forward** to change his life after hearing the speech.
    a. manufactured
    b. propelled
    c. magnificent
    d. hyperactive

Word Parts Activity Five

Use the word parts lists to help you find the answer that has the same meaning as the word or phrase in bold.

_____   1. Brad is **a person who hates women**.
    a. heterosexual
    b. misogynist
    c. misanthrope
    d. autocrat

_____   2. It was the kind of needle that was **inserted under the skin**.
    a. hyperactive
    b. hypoallergenic
    c. hypodermic
    d. maternal

_____ 3. Mildred is **a person who hates people**.
   a. heterosexual
   b. misogynist
   c. misanthrope
   d. autocrat

_____ 4. Human beings are **bipeds**.
   a. animals having two cells
   b. animals having two kidneys
   c. animals having two feet
   d. animals having two glands

_____ 5. The tables were **made by hand** at a factory in Ohio.
   a. inverted
   b. terminated
   c. manufactured
   d. verified

_____ 6. A stop sign is designed in the shape of **a polygon with eight sides**.
   a. a hexagon
   b. an octagon
   c. a paragon
   d. a triangle

_____ 7. People are more likely to achieve their dreams if they are **able to hold on to them.**
   a. tenacious
   b. remorseful
   c. tactile
   d. introspective

_____ 8. Apparently this was the kind of health problem that **one is born with.**
   a. genetic
   b. regressive
   c. aquatic
   d. antibiotic

_____ 9. The committee denied Amber's request to join the club because she had **spoken in opposition of** their political views during a public interview.
   a. complemented
   b. volunteered
   c. televised
   d. contradicted

_____ 10. Grandpa said he was proud to be a **septuagenarian.**
   a. someone who has liberal views
   b. someone who has conservative views
   c. someone who believes in God
   d. someone who is in their seventies

Word Parts Activity Six

Use the word parts lists to complete the following items.

1. Write the word that means <u>not</u> typical. _____

2. Write the word that means <u>not</u> regular. _____

3. Write the word that means <u>not</u> modest. _____

4. Write the word that means <u>not</u> legal. _____

5. Write the word that means <u>not</u> violent. _____

6. Write the word that means <u>not</u> possible. _____

7. Write the word that means <u>not</u> natural. _____

8. Write the word that means <u>not</u> pleased. _____

9. Write the word that means <u>not</u> usual. _____

10. Write the word that means <u>not</u> rational. _____

Word Parts Activity Seven

Use the word parts lists to help you find the answer that has the same meaning as the word or phrase in bold.

_____ 1. She had an **inflammation of** the appendix.
   a. appendectomy   c. appendence
   b. appendicitis   d. appending

_____ 2. Maggie was the **person who owned the property.**
   a. proprietor   c. properly
   b. propriety   d. provision

_____ 3. Shelly was the **person who rented** the apartment from Maggie.
   a. lessee   c. lesion
   b. lessen   d. realtor

_____ 4. Tonya had **an operation in which her tonsils were removed.**
   a. tonsillitis   c. tonsillectomy
   b. toxic   d. tonality

_____ 5. The creature had **human-like** features.
   a. humanity   c. humanist
   b. humanism   d. humanoid

_____ 6. It was the kind of act one commits **without thinking.**
   a. thoughtfully   c. thoughtlessly
   b. memorably   d. retroactively

_____ 7. The clock was **made of wood.**
   a. woody   c. wooded
   b. woodless   d. wooden

_____ 8. He was **faster than anyone else** in the city.
   a. fastidious   c. fastest
   b. fasten   d. fasted

_____ 9. Bill is **a person who practices social equality.**
   a. democrat   c. demonize
   b. democracy   d. dominion

_____ 10. Bob is a **person who favors a restricted government role in social and economic life**.
- a. republican
- b. republicanism
- c. republish
- d. repugnancy

Word Parts Activity Eight

Use the word parts lists to help you find the answer that has the same meaning as the word of phrase in bold.

_____ 1. He was in the hospital for an append**ectomy**.
- a. a cancerous growth
- b. an inflammation of the appendix
- c. an operation to remove the appendix
- d. a catastrophic event

_____ 2. Benny and Jo broke up because they were always **contradicting** each other.
- a. stating a similar viewpoint
- b. controlling
- c. yelling
- d. stating an opposite viewpoint

_____ 3. It represents approximately **one billion** characters in computer memory.
- a. gigabyte
- b. megabyte
- c. trilobite
- d. kilobyte

_____ 4. Rory was on antibiotics for two weeks after he was diagnosed with **tonsillitis**.
- a. a cold
- b. an inflammation of the tonsils
- c. an operation to remove the tonsils
- d. a cancerous growth

_____ 5. It was a corrupt **government ruled by a few** in the nation who had selfish purposes.
- a. democracy
- b. theocracy
- c. oligarchy
- d. monarchy

_____ 6. It was a **government designed to be ruled by the majority of the people**.
- a. democracy
- b. theocracy
- c. oligarchy
- d. monarchy

_____ 7. It represents **one thousand characters in computer memory**.
- a. gigabyte
- b. megabyte
- c. trilobite
- d. kilobyte

_____ 8. Ashley is the **proprietor** of the business where Julie is working.
- a. a person who owns a business
- b. a person who rents a property
- c. a government official
- d. a realtor

_____ 9. It was a **government ruled by people who were regarded as religious leaders**.
- a. democracy
- b. theocracy
- c. oligarchy
- d. monarchy

_____ 10. It represents **one million characters in computer memory.**
a. gigabyte   c. nanosecond
b. megabyte   d. kilobyte

Word Parts Activity Nine

Use the word parts lists to help you find the answer that has the same meaning as the word or phrase in bold.

_____ 1. Mrs. Jane Pittman wrote an **autobiography.**
a. a list of source references
b. a book about someone's life
c. a book about the life of a famous person
d. a book about her own life

_____ 2. The disease turned into a **pandemic** that killed a fourth of the world's population.
a. a particular strain of bird flu   c. an outbreak of contagious disease across an area
b. the worldwide spread of a disease   d. a disease spread by cookware

_____ 3. Rory quit his job because the new boss wanted to **manage the smallest detail of every**one's work.
a. micromanage   c. mediate
b. macromanage   d. megamanage

_____ 4. The **epidemic** only spread among those who lived in one Southern Chinese village.
a. a particular strain of bird flu   c. an outbreak of contagious disease across an area
b. the worldwide spread of a disease   d. a disease spread by cookware

_____ 5. Tim was asked to do all of the copying because he was the only one who knew how to put the documents **together in proper order.**
a. collate   c. correspond
b. delineate   d. interpret

_____ 6. Sue's relationships at the office became a **smaller version of the world** she experienced in her childhood home.
a. macrocosm   c. microcosm
b. cosmopolitan   d. neonatal

_____ 7. She decided to see **a doctor who specialized in the treatment of skin conditions.**
a. cardiologist   c. democrat
b. dermatologist   d. blemish

_____ 8. The doctor told Angie to **hold off from** eating fatty foods.
   a. abstain
   b. retain
   c. maintain
   d. distain

_____ 9. Michael was asked to give **a few good words about the deceased** at the funeral.
   a. a eulogy
   b. an ecology
   c. a corollary
   d. an imagery

_____ 10. The sun **sends out** harmful ultraviolet rays.
   a. admits
   b. emits
   c. remits
   d. omits

Word Parts Activity Ten

Use the word parts lists to help you find the answer that has the same meaning as the word or phrase in bold.

_____ 1. The nine-year-old was so traumatized by the abuse that he **went back** to sucking his thumb.
   a. progressed
   b. confessed
   c. demoted
   d. regressed

_____ 2. The detective was **full of disbelief** after hearing the suspect's story.
   a. dysfunctional
   b. fortuitous
   c. incredulous
   d. empathetic

_____ 3. Molly was so smart that she was able to **go forward** ahead of her other classmates.
   a. regress
   b. progress
   c. congress
   d. enhance

_____ 4. Gayle was in a **situation where she had to choose between two possible solutions**.
   a. biennial
   b. bipartisan
   c. direction
   d. dilemma

_____ 5. It was a **story** that was **made up** by the author.
   a. non-fiction
   b. autobiography
   c. fiction
   d. interview

_____ 6. The defense lawyer looked for a witness that the jury would find to be **believable**.
   a. incredulous
   b. dysfunctional
   c. fortuitous
   d. credible

_____ 7. The sale was **stretched out until** Monday.
   a. intended
   b. distended
   c. extended
   d. suspended

_____ 8. Jim wouldn't go to the event because he was **against war**.
- a. antithesis
- b. antiwar
- c. provocative
- d. pro-war

_____ 9. In Greek mythology, he was the god of **time**.
- a. Chromos
- b. Chronos
- c. Provost
- d. Anthros

_____ 10. The nurse said, "Your new niece is in the **newborn baby** ward."
- a. maternity
- b. infirmary
- c. delivery
- d. neonatal

Photo Credits

Text Credits

Adler, Mortimer. From "How to Mark a Book." First appeared in *Saturday Review*, July 6, 1940. Reprinted by permission of the estate of Mortimer J. Adler.

Borjas, Ruber Jr., and Gill, Trish. "The Abortion Debate" by Ruber Borjas, Jr. and Trish Gill from *Letters to the Editor* Vol. 29, December 10, 1997 & Vol. 30, January 14, 1998. Copyright © 1997, 1998. Reprinted by permission of The Egalitarian.

Brandenburg, Mark. "What Does Spanking Teach Your Child?" Copyright Mark Brandenburg. Natural Family Online. Reprinted with kind permission from the author.

Brummet, Palmira, et al. "Islamic Faith" from *Civilization Past & Present 10th ed.* Copyright © 2003. Reprinted by permission of Pearson Education, Inc.

Campbell, Neil, et al. From *Biology: Concepts and Connections 5th ed.* Copyright © 2008. Reprinted by permission of Pearson Education, Inc.

Carson, Benjamin, *The Big Picture*. Taken from **The Big Picture,** by Dr. Benjamin Carson; Gregg A. Lewis. Copyright © 1999 by Benjamin Carson. Used by permission of Zondervan.

Donatelle, Rebecca J. From *Access to Health*, 10th ed.. Copyright © 2008. Reprinted with permission of Pearson Education, Inc.

Edmonds, Kenneth. From SONG FOR MAMA lyrics by Kenneth "Babyface" Edmonds Copyright 1997 Sony/ATV Music Publishing LLC, ECAF Music, Fox Film Music Corp. All rights on behalf of Sony/ATV Music Publishing LLC and ECAF Music administered by Sony/ATV Music Publishing LLC, 8 Music Square West, Nashville, TN 37203. International Copyright Secured. All rights reserved. Used by permission.

Eshleman, Ross et al. "Crowd Behavior" from *Introduction to Sociology* 3rd ed. Reprinted by permission of BVT Publishing. All rights reserved.

Gibbs, Bruce. "Seven Secrets to College Success." Copyright © 2001 – Present Article City.com

Goldberg, Natalie, "Be Specific." From *Writing Down the Bones* by Natalie Goldberg. Copyright © 1986. Reprinted by arrangement with Shambhala Publications, Inc. Boston, MA. www.shambhala.com

Grasha, A. "Power: Verbal and Nonverbal Behaviors" from *Practical Applications of Psychology*. Copyright © 1997. Reprinted by permission of Pearson Education, Inc.

Hendrick, C. and Hendrick, S. Chart adapted from "A Relationship Specific Version of the Love Attitudes Scale" by C. Hendrick and S. Hendrick, from the *Journal of Social Behavior and Personality*. Copyright © 1990. Reprinted by permission.

Hughes, Langston. "Dreams," copyright © 1994 by The Estate of Langston Hughes, from *The Collected Poems of Langston Hughes* by Langston Hughes, edited by Arnold Rampersad with David Roessel, Associate Editor. Used by permission of Alfred A. Knopf, a division of Random House, Inc.

Hughes, Langston. "Salvation" from *The Big Sea* by Langston Hughes. Copyright © 1940 by Langston Hughes. Copyright renewed 1968 by Arna Bontemps and George Houston Bass. Reprinted by permission of Hill and Wang, a division of Farrar, Straus and Giroux, LLC.

Ji-Yeoh, Yu. "Let's Tell the Story of All America's Cultures" by Yuh Ji-Yeoh from *Philadelphia Inquirer*, June 30, 1991. Copyright © 1991. Reprinted by permission.

Kells, Tina. "Liar, Liar – How Can You Tell?" by Tina Kells from About.com Teen Advise. December 26, 2007. Copyright © 2007. Reprinted with permission of The New York Times Company.

King, Martin Luther, Jr. "Where Do We Go From Here: Community or Chaos?" Reprinted by arrangement with The Heirs to the Estate of Martin Luther King Jr., c/o Writer's House as agent for the proprietor New York, NY. Copyright © 1963 Dr. Martin Luther King Jr; copyright renewed 1991 Coretta Scott King.

Laskey, Marcia, and Gibson, Paula W. From "Critical Thinking" College Study Strategies: Thinking and Learning, by Marcia Laskey and Paula W. Gibson. Copyright © 1997. Reprinted with permission of Pearson Education, Inc.

Lederer, Richard, "English Is a Crazy Language." Abridged with the permission of Atria Books. A Division of Simon & Schuster, Inc., from *Crazy English: The Ultimate Joy Ride Through Our Language*, Revised Edition by Richard Lederer. Copyright © 1989, 1990, 1998 by Richard Lederer.

Machiavelli, Niccolo. From *The Prince: A Norton Critical Edition*, Second Edition by Niccolo Machiavelli, translated by Robert M. Adams. Copyright © 1992, 1977 by W.W. Norton & Company, Inc. Used by permission of W. W. Norton & Company, Inc.

Malcolm X. From *The Autobiography of Malcolm X* by Malcolm X and Alex Haley, copyright © 1964 by Alex Haley and Malcolm X. copyright © 1965 by Alex Haley and Betty Shabazz. Used by permission of Random House Inc.

Mayo, Louise A., et al. *American Dreams and Reality: A Retelling of the American Way, Vol. I* 5th ed. Wheaton, IL: Abigail Press Inc., 2005.

Re, Judith, "Conversations with Ease." Adapted from *Social Savvy: A Handbook for Teens Who Want to Know What to Say, What to Do and How to Feel Confident in Any Situation* by Judith Re. Copyright © 1991 by Judith Re published by Fireside Publishing/Simon & Schuster. Reprinted with permission of the Carol Mann Agency.

Ruffin, Roy J. From Ruffin/Gregory, *Principles of Economics.* Excerpted from pp. 4, 5, 24, 232, 268, 310, 286, 488 © 2001 Pearson Education, Inc. Reprinted with permission of Pearson Education, Inc. All rights reserved.

Sandburg, Carl. "Fog" from *Chicago Poems* by Carl Sandburg, copyright 1916 by Holt, Rinehart and Winston and renewed 1944 by Carl Sandburg, reprinted by permission of Houghton Mifflin Harcourt Publishing Company.

Schwarzenegger, Arnold. From "The Education of an American" by Arnold Schwarzenegger from Perspectives 2001 Conference, Sacramento, CA, September 21, 2001. Copyright © 2001 by Arnold Schwarzenegger. Reprinted by permission of Oak Productions, Inc.

Sherry, Mary. "In Praise of the 'F' Word" by Mary Sherry from "My Turn" column. *Newsweek,* May 6, 1991. Copyright © 1991. Reprinted with permission from the author.

Sledge, Martha. From *The Longman Textbook Reader,* 5th ed compiled by Martha Sledge. Copyright © 2003 Longman. Reprinted by permission of Pearson Education, Inc.

Soto, Gary. "Fear" from *Living Up the Street: Narrative Recollections* by Gary Soto. Copyright © 1985 by Gary Soto. Bantam Doubleday Dell Publishing Group. Reprinted with permission from the author.

Stewart, D. L. "Hungry Hounds Eat Up Attention" from *Dayton Daily News*, October 7, 2005. Copyright © 2005. Reprinted with permission of the author.

Taflinger, Richard F. Adapted from "Sitcom: What It Is, How It Works" by Richard F. Taflinger, PhD. Copyright © 1996 by Richard F. Taflinger. Reprinted with permission of the author.

Trump, Donald, from "Money: How to Be a Good Investor." From *Trump: Think Like a Billionaire* by Donald J. Trump and Meredith Melver, copyright © 2004 by Donald J. Trump. Used by permission of Random House.

Underwood, Corinna. Adapted from *Urban Legends: A Modern Day Mythology*, by Corrina Underwood. *After Dark Newsletter*. August 2004, Vol. 2 No. 8. Reprinted with permission from Premiere Radio Networks.

Uno, Gordon E., et al. *Biological Science: An Ecological Approach* 4th ed. Rand McNally & Company, 1978.

Verderber, R. Adapted from "Understanding Active Listening." From R. Verderber, *The Challenge of Effective Speaking* 10E. © 1997 Wadsworth, a part of Cengage Learning, Inc. Reproduced by permission. www.cengage.com/permissions.

Wasserman, Gary. Adapted from *The Basics of American Politics*, 12th ed. Copyright © 2006. Reprinted by permission of Pearson Education, Inc.

Wilson, R. Jackson; Gilbert, James; Kupperman, Karen Ordahl; Nissenbaum, Stephen; Scott, Donald M., *The Pursuit of Liberty, Volume 1*, 3rd edition. © 1996. Reprinted by permission of Pearson Education, Inc., Upper Saddle River, NJ.

Index